Blackness

and Race Mixture

The Dynamics
of Racial Identity
in Colombia

Peter Wade

The Johns Hopkins University Press

Baltimore and London

Johns Hopkins Paperbacks edition, 1995
04 03 02 01 00 99 98 97 96 95   5 4 3 2 1

The Johns Hopkins University Press
2715 North Charles Street
Baltimore, Maryland 21218-4319
The Johns Hopkins Press Ltd., London

Library of Congress Cataloging-in-Publication Data

Wade, Peter, 1957–
    Blackness and race mixture : the dynamics of racial identity in Colombia /
Peter Wade.
        p.   cm. — (The Johns Hopkins Studies in Atlantic history and culture.)
    Includes bibliographical references and index.
    ISBN 0-8018-4458-4 — ISBN 0-8018-5251-X (pbk.)
        1. Blacks—Colombia—Race identity.   2. Colombia—Race relations.   3. Colom-
bia—Social conditions.   4. Miscegenation—Colombia—History.   I. Title.
II. Series.
F2299.B55W3   1993
305.896´0861—dc20   92-15581

A catalog record for this book is available from the British Library.

To the people of Colombia,
particularly the people of the Chocó,
and to my parents, for their
constant support

Contents

Contents

IV
Blackness and Mixedness

Illustrations

Maps

Preface and Acknowledgments

My connection with Colombia started in the Caribbean coastal city of Cartagena, the slave-trading center of colonial New Granada. I lived and worked there for ten months as a tourist and English teacher and gained a certain "tropical" perspective on Colombian society. My travels had brought me down the Caribbean coast of Central America, and all along that littoral, blacks and black culture were a vibrant presence. Cartagena, too, shared that feeling and that history, making it rather distinct from the interior of the country, which was much more Andean in feel, lighter skinned, cooler, temperate, mountainous. In Cartagena, it was obvious enough that black people generally occupied an inferior position in society. It was also apparent that their own particular culture contained a certain element of resistance to the white world, laughing at it even as it disparaged them.

When I returned to do fieldwork for a Ph.D. in social anthropology, I was concerned largely to help undermine the myth of racial democracy which still holds considerable sway in Colombia, and to counteract what one prominent Colombian researcher has identified as the "invisibility" of blacks on the national academic scene, despite her own efforts and those of a few dedicated researchers, Colombian and foreign (Friedemann 1984a). Although "blacks" are perhaps 10 percent of the population, the great majority of ethnohistorical and anthropological work in Colombia concentrates on the indigenous population.

The thesis fulfilled this aim, although perhaps not as thoroughly as I would have wished, but it also went beyond the simple existence of discrimination. By the time I undertook postdoctoral research, although accumulating hard evidence of discrimination was still a relevant task, I was more concerned with the necessity of placing Colombian blacks in the context of the overall racial order of the society and its political economy. There was undoubtedly discrimination, but there was also the undeniable fact that Colombia was largely a mestizo (mixed-blood) nation and had been so for several centuries. The problem then was to reconcile these two factors. As will become apparent, this involved addressing issues of race and class, of the roles of miscegenation and black consciousness in creating a true "racial democracy," of emerging Colombian nationhood, and of the significance of the spatial constitution of society. The last issue was an unusual one for me, but it was needed in order to conceptualize the importance of Colombia's obvious and extreme regional differences. These, then, are the issues that this book addresses in seeking to understand the nature of blackness in Colombia, the nature of the country's racial order, and the racial and ethnic identities that persist and change within it.

In a broader context, I am also concerned with the way "race" in Latin America has been presented academically, especially in relation to black populations. The ambiguity and relativity of racial identifications have been widely noted, and this is frequently connected to the comparative insignificance of "race" in the region, in contrast with, say, the attitude in the United States. Acknowledging that important differences do exist, I also question such conclusions in two ways. First, in Colombia at least, racial identifications are not always so ambiguous. This is where the Pacific coast region of the country—the home territory of the people who form the focus of the book—is important, since it is an unequivocally "black" region. Second, the equation of ambiguity with insignificance is itself questionable. The assumption that only when racial identifications are relatively clearcut and are allied to explicit and systematic discriminations can "race" be socially significant tends to ignore the real importance of racial identifications in Latin America. Such oppositions can also tend to suggest that racial identifications in Latin America are not a real issue because "race" in its "real" or pure form is not present: it is offset by class, it is based on mere "appearance." The corollary of such an argument is that in the United States race is present in its "real" form, based on "ancestry," and this reveals a clear tendency to reify "race," and even reconstruct it as a naturally problematic and unyielding category.

My aim in writing is more than the presentation of data and attempts at explanation. The official image of Colombia is that of a racial democracy, and even, in the new Constitution of 1991, of an ethnically plural society, but beneath or rather parallel to and integrated with this image is a pervasive, apparently self-evident social order in which Colombia is a mestizo, or mixed-blood, nation that is gradually erasing blackness (and indianness) from its panorama. It is this seemingly "natural order" of Colombian society (cf. Taussig 1987, xiv) which I want to disrupt. I want to evoke a sense of Colombia that *includes* its blackness as a persistent, live, adaptable, and resistant element, an element that is, in fact, an integral part of Colombian people's sense of their country, albeit a part often undervalued and distorted by nonblacks. I do not think that this aim vitiates my analysis. As Weber pointed out, all investigation is value laden to the extent that values define what are conceived of as problems and areas of interest. This, however, does not negate the possibility of assessment and validation in a process of discarding inappropriate interpretations. Discarding is not accomplished by reference to some absolute standard of validity, but according to the canons operative and themselves contested within the academic community: some interpretations do not fit the "facts," however these may be established; some are too general, some too particular, and others are based unselfconsciously on taken-for-granted categories that shape the analysis. From this last problem derives perhaps one of the most powerful stances for social science: to produce critical interpretations that show up internal contradictions and implicit assumptions, and in doing so suggest alternative ways of narrating the same material. Such approaches cannot progress towards unvarnished truth, because they ultimately feed back into social contexts in which people are concerned with the same realms of social action which generated the critiques, and this reflexive relation creates an ever-changing field of analysis.

Thus, I cannot scientifically prove that racial prejudice is "wrong," because science in this sense cannot adjudicate on moral values, nor can I finally prove that my interpretations of Colombia are in some sense the best. I can point out the contradictions between the official vision of racial democracy and experiences and patterns of social relations which undermine that image. I can show how an insistence that racial democracy already exists may actually make it more difficult, even impossible, to achieve. I can show that the very image of racial democracy as it has emerged in Colombia encompasses notions that belie its claims. And I can destabilize the images, categories, and meanings that underlie the official picture and the "natural order" that parallels it; doing this questions not only racial categories in Colombia but also racial categories in general. In a country such as Colombia, torn by a "dirty war" over human rights and social justice, and over the traffic in drugs, but also struggling for a more democratic society, my concern with issues of "race" may seem unimportant. But as I hope this book will show, "race" is not unimportant in Colombia, and of course is itself intimately intertwined with issues of social justice.

I am indebted to many people in Unguía who helped and befriended me: Elean Castro, Cristina and Rosa, Nacho and Eucaris, the García family, Victor and Angela, Migdalia and Marilexis were all special friends. In Medellín many people at the Universidad de Antioquia and the Universidad Nacional offered me their help, particularly Pedro Morán, Victor Alvarez, and Edgar Arroyo. The people working in the city's institutions were almost unfailingly helpful, and I appreciate the help and friendship of the staff of Desarrollo Comunitario— Fernando, Germán, Beatriz, and Blanca Nohelia in particular. I made many friends in Medellín and cannot mention them all, but I must give an *abrazo fuerte* to Rosario, my constant companion, and to Carlos and Noris, with whom I lived for many months. Jorge, Adriana, and Nelly were also good friends. In La Iguaná, I thank Octavio Palacios and País for their help. Thanks are also due to Rosa and her family in Quibdó and other towns of the Chocó for their unfailing hospitality (and for seeing me through typhoid). In Bogotá, I thank the staff of the Department of Anthropology at the Universidad de los Andes, particularly Carlos Alberto Uribe. I am also grateful to the Instituto Colombiano de Antropología, especially Alexander Cifuentes. Special thanks go to Clemencia and Jaime for their generous hospitality and friendship.

I am grateful to all those people and institutions that supported me in material or more intangible ways during research: John Green has been a constant source of encouragement. I give special thanks to those who, anonymously or otherwise, read and commented on the manuscript: Norman Whitten was particularly helpful. Thanks for the maps and figures go to Paul and Sandra at the Department of Geography of the University of Liverpool, where I currently work. My Ph.D. research was financed by a studentship from the Economic and Social Research Council (1981–84), and postdoctoral research was carried out during the tenure of a research fellowship at Queens' College, Cambridge (1985–88), with fieldwork made possible by grants from the Social Science Research Council of the United States of America and the British Academy (1986–87). Thanks are due to the Compañía Colombiana de Discos (Codiscos) of Medellín for permission to reproduce song lyrics in chapters 7 and 14. Thanks are also due to Miguel A. Caicedo for permission to use the poem given in chapter 7.

Colombia

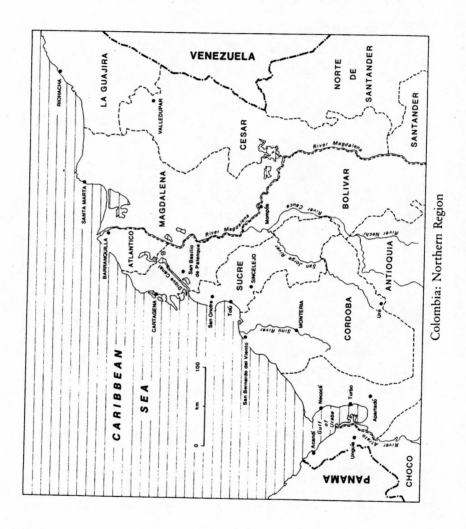

Colombia: Northern Region

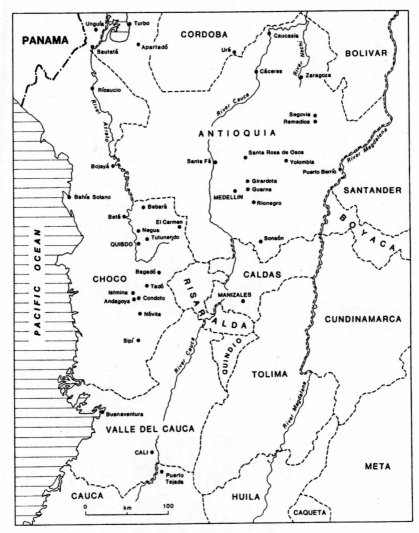

Colombia: Northwestern Region

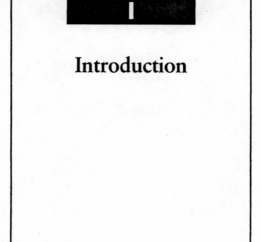

Introduction

1

The Racial Order
and National Identity

The study of blacks in Colombia, despite the seminal efforts of a few dedicated researchers, is neglected relative to the ethnohistorical and anthropological study of the indian populations. The idea of a "racial democracy" in Colombia is still pervasive, and despite refutations of this myth from academic and popular circles alike, some people of all colors and classes can still be heard to avow the insignificance of race as an issue, especially as far as blacks are concerned.

The reasons for this have, in my view, to do with the complex interweaving of patterns of both discrimination and tolerance, of both blackness or indianness and *mestizaje,* or race mixture. This interweaving takes place within a project, managed mainly by elites, of nationhood and national identity which holds up an image of Colombia as essentially a mestizo or mixed nation. Blacks and indians can, therefore, although in different ways, be both excluded as nonmestizo and included as potential recruits to mixedness. Such a racial order, I believe, is not characteristic of Colombia alone, but has echoes in many regions of Latin America. In this book, I examine the coexisting and interdependent dynamics of *mestizaje* and discrimination in a variety of contexts, at different levels of resolution and in distinct realms of social action.

To talk about "blacks," "indians," and "race" in Latin America, or indeed anywhere else, is in itself problematic. It is generally accepted that "races" are social constructions, categorical identifications based on a discourse about physical appearance or ancestry. This is not a universalizing definition good for all places and times because what is to count as relevant "physical difference" or relevant "ancestry" is far from self-evident. There is apparently the "natural fact"

3

of phenotypical variation from which culture constructs categorical identifications according to social determinations, but positing a nature/culture relation mediated by this "productionist logic" (Haraway 1989, 13) obscures the fact that there is no prediscursive, universal encounter with "nature" or therefore with phenotypical variation. These have always been perceived and understood historically in different ways, through certain lenses, especially those ground in the colonial encounters that have privileged the phenotypical differences characteristic of continental space, rather than those characteristic of, say, "short" and "tall" people. As such, racial categories are processual in two ways: first, as a result of the changing perceptions of the nature/culture divide that they themselves mediate; second, as a result of the interplay of both claims to and ascriptions of identity, usually made in the context of unequal power relations. The second process is of particular significance in the Latin American context because one feature of a racial order based on race mixture is ambiguity about who is and who is not "black" or "indian." In the United States, South Africa, and many European countries, although ambiguities do exist, there is more general agreement between claims and ascriptions, and thus more clearly defined categorical boundaries to races, than in Latin American countries such as Colombia. There, the boundaries of the category "black" or "indian" are much disputed and ambiguous, even while clear images of a "typical" black or indian person exist for everyone, including "blacks" and "indians." In this book, although I will not always enclose the terms "black," "indian," or "race" in quotation marks, it should be understood that if by their very nature they are not self-evident categories, this is especially so in the Latin American context.

Ambiguity about blackness or indianness does not, however, mean the insignificance of blacks or indians, or more exactly, of people for whom blackness and indianness is an important aspect of personal and social identity. In this book, my concern is with blackness, and I focus on a region of Colombia, the Chocó province of the lowland Pacific littoral, where this is particularly evident. There, blacks form about 80 or 90 percent of the population, and blackness has been and still is a critical feature of regional history and identity. I look at the region's inhabitants, the Chocoanos, in the heart of this province and also in the two sites of my fieldwork: one right in the north of the Chocó, in an area heavily influenced by nonblacks; the other, beyond the Chocó, in the city of Medellín. My aim is to examine the coexistence and codependence of blackness and nonblackness, of discrimination and race mixture in these regional contexts. My contention is that the Chocoano material illuminates the more general nature of the Colombian racial order and Colombian national identity. By the same token, the Colombian material sheds light on other Latin American nations in which discrimination and *mestizaje* also coexist and in which projects of national identity have also had to deal, albeit in different ways, with a past and a present of racial heterogeneity.

Blacks are present and blackness is an issue in other areas of Colombia besides the Chocó: the whole southern Pacific littoral is, if anything, blacker than the Chocó; the areas around Cali and Cartago have significant black populations; the Caribbean coastal region has concentrations of blacks in various areas, and more generally has a heavily negroid population; there are pockets of blacks, often migrants, in most cities, including Bogotá. I do not pretend to cover all these different contexts, some of which have already been studied (see, for example, the works by Whitten, Friedemann, and Taussig listed in the References), but I do introduce two other Colombian regions into the picture, although neither is my principal focus. One is Antioquia, the other the Caribbean coastal region, both neighbors of the Chocó. Their presence in the book has two purposes. One is mainly pragmatic. My first field site was a frontier area colonized by people from the central Chocó, Antioquia, and the Caribbean region; my second was in Medellín, provincial capital of Antioquia. Some knowledge of these other two regions is thus clearly indispensable in order to comprehend the ethnic interaction between their people and the Chocoanos. The second purpose is more strategic. My aim in this book is to examine the interplay of discrimination and *mestizaje*. My main focus is on the Chocoanos. But this interplay had very different outcomes in different regions, according to local conjunctures of political economy and demography, and Antioquia and the Caribbean coast form perfect counterpoints to the Chocó in this respect, with the Caribbean coast intermediate between the evidently black Chocó and heavily "whitened" Antioquia. In short, if the national racial order of Colombia is based on the contradictory but interdependent coexistence of blackness, indianness, mixedness, and whiteness, then it makes sense to examine other regions where these elements and conceptual categories worked themselves out in different ways. The first chapters therefore explore these two regions before turning to concentrate on the Chocó itself. In the rest of this introduction, I elaborate the themes of blackness, indianness, race, and the nation.

Black Adaptation and Black Resistance

Blacks from the Chocó, and I would argue in Colombia and more generally Latin America, have participated in two overall processes.

On the one hand, they have culturally adapted to values and norms the basic orientation and tone of which have been set by a dominant majority, directed essentially by elites, whether colonial or republican. These blacks have in the process begun to participate more fully in national hierarchies of prestige and status. Phrasing it in ethnic terms, they have left behind a culture associated by them and by others with *los negros* (the blacks), and adopted a culture that, while it may be called mestizo (mixed-blood) rather than white, is certainly seen as nonblack. On a physical level, the cognate process to cultural adaptation has been the scattering of blacks and also *mestizaje,* or race mixture. Thus, cultural adaptation, demographic dispersal, and race mixture have been and still are processes that are linked, not by necessity, but by the historical structures of the Colombian racial order.

On the other hand, in the Chocó and in other Colombian contexts, blacks have nucleated and congregated together, partly through choice and partly through the actions of the nonblack world, and in these situations they have created and maintained cultural forms that are identified as black culture, whether or not this has some traceable African derivation. In Colombia, even in the Chocó, black culture is generally more Iberian in derivation than in, say, Brazil or Cuba. Nevertheless, it has specific traits that are recognized by blacks and nonblacks alike. This black culture, while not divorced from national scales of prestige and status, tends to emphasize the essential human equality of black people in a community. They are, as it were, all black together. On a physical level, the cognate process has been a relative absence of race mixture. Thus, the continuity of black cultural identity, demographic nucleation, and the absence of race mixture have historically made up a triad of interlinked processes.

Behind these two interwoven dynamics lies racism, often subtle, not systematic or thoroughgoing, but pervasive and occasionally blatant. To avoid the stigma to which blackness and black culture, especially as they are manifest in the Pacific region, are subject by the dominant nonblack world of whites and mestizos, black people may adopt the mores of that world. Alternatively, they may retrench for protection or due to rejection by the nonblack world. This is not simply a matter of choice about ethnic identity: the possibilities for either alternative are heavily structured, mainly by economic and political processes that circumscribe and indeed constitute the parameters of choice. It is well known, for instance, that upward mobility for black people is often accompanied by cultural adaptation and, in many cases, marriage to a lighter-skinned person. This is because upward mobility generally brings a black person into greater contact with the nonblack world. In this sense, black adaptation is structured by the chances of economic advancement. However, the structuring of choice about race and ethnicity goes deeper still and takes place on a collective as well as a personal level. Thus, for the blacks who, through a series of economic and political processes, have been isolated in the Pacific coast region of the country, an area with few connections to the nonblack world, the option of cultural adaptation and race mixture is a distant one. In this situation, a relatively coherent black identity evolves, and for them, leaving the area, adapting to other modes of behavior, and ultimately marrying a nonblack person may be seen as a betrayal of the ethic of equality and of black community. On the other hand, for blacks who, for different historical reasons, were integrated early on into the region of Antioquia, an area with a substantial nonblack presence, cultural adaptation and race mixture became the dominant trend. National hierarchies of prestige and status are dominant, and the existence of a black identity that might allege betrayal is absent.

Nonblack racism is only half the story. Just as blacks may either adapt and mix, or nucleate, resist, and not mix, so there is a dual aspect to the nonblack world. Blacks may be considered inferior and discriminated against, but they may also be accepted. This does not mean that their color is forgotten, but simply that blacks as a category are not repressed in a systematic way. In Fernandes's (1969) terminology they are "accommodated." Their acceptance, however, is limited and individualistic, conditional on (a) not constituting a demand for acceptance en masse of blacks as a category, that is, not constituting a perceived threat as far as the nonblacks are concerned, and (b) adapting culturally, a process consolidated, more for their offspring than themselves, by embarking on a pathway of *mestizaje*. This does not mean that mulatto offspring will necessarily avoid discrimination, but depending on their appearance, they may be less affected by it, and if they again "marry lighter," their offspring have an even greater chance of avoiding discrimination directed at blacks and mulattoes. In short, then, the double dynamic of black adaptation and autonomy works in tandem with a double dynamic of nonblack conditional acceptance and racism. As before, the alternatives of conditional acceptance and racism are not simply choices made by nonblacks: their occurrence and distribution are structured in the same way as the pressures and options affecting the black world. Thus in the Chocó region of colonial Colombia, a small white elite confronted a large majority of blacks, many of them slaves: for mainly political reasons, social acceptance of blacks was restricted and race mixture confined mainly to semicovert relations between elite men and lower-class and slave black women. In Antioquia, white elitism was less pronounced, there were more lower-class whites, and blacks, including slaves, were a less crucial part of the labor force and were more widely dispersed. Both areas displayed marked racism but in different forms. In the Chocó, it manifested itself as oppression of the blacks by a white elite. In Antioquia, it was evident as a denial of blackness, an effort to purge it ideologically from regional identity, just as it was being purged physically from the ranks by being absorbed to the point of invisibility. The point, then, is that political and economic forces were behind the different ways in which the processes of black adaptation/ black nucleation and nonblack acceptance/nonblack racism evolved in these two regions.

Mestizaje, Blanqueamiento, and Colombian Nationhood

The basic theme of this book as outlined above has a simple opposi-tional quality to it: black versus nonblack. But it is important to see this in its overall context: the Colombian nation and its historical development. New Granada, as the colonial region roughly corre-sponding to Colombia was known, gained independence with a highly mixed society. The indian population, although with important seden-tary groups reaching up to one-third of local totals in some areas, had been severely reduced, while many indians had mixed into the mestizo majority; by 1778, indians formed about 16 percent of the New Gra-nadian population. Slavery, crucial in some areas, had never reached the proportions of Brazil or the Caribbean and arguably had only existed in the context of a fully fledged "slave society" with all the "web of dependencies, habits, feelings, exchanges, etc." in Cartagena and in the Cauca Valley (Jaramillo Uribe 1989, 70; Colmenares 1979). Blacks, unevenly distributed like the indian population, were also an overall minority in a society composed mainly of people of mixed ancestry.

Despite high degrees of racial and cultural mixture, social stratifi-cation in which racial characteristics played an important part was strongly marked, forming the so-called *sociedad de castas* (society of castes, breeds, or races), in which different social strata were recog-nized and named, their positions supposedly determined primarily by degrees of racial mixture (Mörner 1967). At the bottom of this hierar-chy, status was still defined institutionally for some. Tributary indian labor in the form of the encomienda persisted in some regions until the late colonial period, while slavery existed as a legal category and as a real status for blacks until 1851. At the top, the political and economic elite prided itself on its *limpieza de sangre,* clean blood, supposedly free from the "taint" of black or indian (or Jewish or

8

Moorish) blood. The ranks of the mixed themselves were also strongly heterogeneous, with supposed ancestry and physical appearance powerful signs of status and position. Although by the late eighteenth century the *sociedad de castas* was cracking up as a result of the continuing miscegenation that it tried to control, Jaramillo Uribe contends that there was also a period of retrenchment as the white elite, American creole and Spanish, tried to defend its position against encroachments by the mestizos. He gives accounts of long litigations in late eighteenth-century New Granadian society about alleged acts of defamation of honor in which slurs were cast on a person's racial heritage or social position by attributing to them a racial status below that which they claimed as their right (1968, 181–86). Juan and Ulloa observed in late eighteenth-century Cartagena that "every person is so jealous of their tribe or caste, that if, through inadvertence, you call them by a lower degree than what they actually are, they are highly offended, never suffering themselves to be deprived of so valuable a gift of fortune" (1772, 1:30). In the obsessive concern with color and status which characterized this *sociedad de castas,* only one thing was certain: to be black or indian was bad, to be white was good. To be rich alone was useful but inadequate: to enter universities, the church, or the administration required proof of *limpieza de sangre,* clean blood, and any doubtful heritage was a major obstacle. True, after 1783 the crown could by decree dispense a *cédula de gracias al sacar,* a royal cleansing, a certificate of whiteness, and from 1795 this license could be bought for about twice the price of a prime slave. But universities or the Church often found it hard to swallow this sidestepping tactic, and long litigation sometimes dogged the attempts of royally cleansed individuals to act on their new status (Rout 1976, 157; Mörner 1967, 45).

After independence there was both continuity and change. The low status of blackness and indianness was still marked. As one of the many European travelers of this period, Gaspar Mollien traveled through Colombia in 1822. Passing along the Cauca Valley, he noted: "The muleteers, proud of being white, are ashamed to go on foot, so it is difficult to distinguish the rich from the poor." He also observed: "The pride inspired by color is no less great in the valley of Cauca than in the colonies of the Antilles" (1824, 282, 285). Now, however, new problems had to be faced by the political and intellectual elites who saw it as their task to create and define a nation that could compete on the world scene, a nation that could be modern and progressive according to the tenets of liberal thought which pervaded Latin America especially from England, France, and also North America (Zea 1963; Jaramillo Uribe 1964). Initial battles were simply for internal political consolidation as federalist and centralist interests by turns held sway, not only in Colombia but elsewhere in Latin America as well. Between 1850 and 1880, however, most Latin American nations had begun to resolve this issue, as communications improved and national bourgeoisies consolidated themselves (Oddone 1986, 220). Throughout this period, there was also concern for how to characterize national identities: Latin American elites struggled with the problem of how to understand and represent their emerging nations. As Anderson (1983, 50) argues, the emergence of nationalism in Latin America did not involve a European-style political baptism of the lower classes, but was mediated by creole elites who had been excluded from political control during the colonial period by virtue of their American birth. It was they who defined national identity, and in so doing, argues Anderson, they consciously redefined the subordinate masses as "fellow-nationals" (1983, 52). But the matter was not quite so simple.

On the one hand, nationalism was about being distinctive in a global context of other nation-states for which nationalism was already an important force. On the other hand, European political philosophies, especially late nineteenth-century positivism, had achieved common-sense status among intellectual and political elites in much of Latin America. There were arguments about detail, but the worth of essential concepts such as freedom, liberty, progress, industry, science, reason, and education was accepted as self-evident. But modernity and progress were being achieved by European nations that had negligible or no populations of blacks and indians, or in the United States where strict barriers separated whites from blacks and indians. In Colombia, as in other Latin American nations, the vast majority of the population was nonwhite. Could they emulate Anglo-Saxon progress? Should they emulate it unquestioningly? Were they cursed by the Spanish legacy of conquest and seigneurial society, anathema to liberal ideas of freedom, and by the mixed blood of their populations? Or was creoleness something original and different which they could bank on, at least for a sense of national or even pan-national pride, if not for progress and modernity?

These debates raged throughout Latin America, and race was very often a crucial dimension in them (Zea 1963, 187–98; Jaramillo Uribe 1989, 168–72; Graham 1990; Wright 1990; Skidmore 1974). The outcomes varied in different countries, but a central feature was the attempt to compromise between the conflicting aspects of the dilemma, the clearly mixed nature of the populations versus the clearly white connotations of progress and modernity. The compromise consisted of asserting that, on the one hand, the heart of Latin American identity lay precisely in its mixed, or even its indian or black, populations. Herein lay both the celebration of the mestizo and the roots of *indigenismo,* that is, the celebration of an indian origin. The glorification of blackness was generally more muted, receiving, for example, an ambivalent airing in Gilberto Freyre's work. On the other hand, however, mixedness, and even more so blackness and indianness, were treated in a certain light. Models of modernity and progress were not abandoned; rather, racial mixture and black and indian populations were harnessed to them, to provide a distinctly Latin American response to the dilemma. Blacks and especially indians were romanticized as part of a more or less glorious past, but the future held for them paternalistic guidance towards integration, which also ideally meant more race mixture and perhaps the eventual erasure of blackness and indianness from the nation. The mestizo was idealized as of bi-ethnic or tri-ethnic origin, but the image held up was always at the lighter end of the mestizo spectrum. The future would bring, almost magically, a whitening of the population through race mixture, and this could be helped along more realistically by immigration policies attracting European immigrants and keeping out blacks (Skidmore 1974; Wright 1990; Helg 1990). This is the ideology of *blanqueamiento,* or whitening, seen in a nationalist context. Here, then, we see one aspect of the coexistence of *mestizaje* and discrimination. Compromise resulted in the coexistence of two variants on the nationalist theme: on the one hand, the democratic, inclusive ideology of *todos somos mestizos*—everyone is mestizo, and herein lies the particularity of Latin American identity; on the other hand, the discriminatory ideology that points out that some are lighter mestizos than others, prefers the whiter to the darker, and sees the consolidation of nationality in a process of whitening. In both variants, actual blacks and indians are disadvantaged, but less so in the more democratic variant that tries to be inclusive. The problem lies in the coexistence of the two variants and the possibility of slipping from one into the other.

This process of compromise can be seen in the Latin American reaction to biologically determinist theories of race. Positivism presented a serious challenge insofar as the European theories of race associated with it and which were current at the turn of the century tended to class indians and especially blacks as biologically inferior. Hybrids would be deleteriously affected by these races. Latin American elites often espoused these theories but also tended to elude their negative implications by playing down biological determinism, emphasizing environment and the impact of education, and reevaluating the hybrid, while at the same time agreeing on the inferiority of blacks and indians and consigning them to the past and to backwardness (Skidmore 1974; Wright 1990; Graham 1990).

Different countries played different variations on the theme of compromise. In Peru and Mexico, with their large indian populations, *indigenismo* was a powerful force. As Knight argues for Mexico, *indigenismo* at least in its official form, allied to the Revolution and to processes of defining Mexican nationality, was actually as much about mestizos as indians. José Vasconcelos, although not exactly an *indigenista,* set the tone, coining the term *raza cósmica* for the mestizo "race" and arguing for the superiority of the hybrid. Commenting on Manuel Gamio, early Mexican anthropologist and ideologue of official *indigenismo,* Knight continues, "It was with the Revolution that the mestizo cult blossomed. 'In the great forge of America,' wrote Manuel Gamio, 'on the giant anvil of the Andes, virile races of bronze and iron have struggled for centuries.' From this struggle emerged the mestizo, the 'national race' of Mexico, the carrier of 'the national culture of the future'" (1990, 85). As Knight recognizes, different positions could be taken within *indigenismo* from incorporationist to indianist (cf. Hewitt de Alcántara 1984). The central point is that European superiority was challenged, while an image of national identity was projected that highlighted the originality of Mexican—or Latin American—indian-based identity and simultaneously consigned indianness to a backward past.

In contrast, Argentinian and Uruguayan leaders managed to attract large numbers of Europeans and whitewash their small black and indian populations. Many saw in this a sensible solution to the problem. Jorge Díez, an Ecuadorian, traveling through the tropics, thought that the South American mestizo was a poor basis for a true *raza cósmica:* "The elements currently available are not enough"; it was a matter of "enriching the blood and stimulating the vitality [of the mestizo] with the collaboration of new and valuable factors." When he says that "Argentina and Uruguay have known how to grasp the essence of the problem," it is clear that he refers to white immigration (1944, 193). Not everyone was so lucky, however, and Wright (1990) documents how, despite a desire to emulate Argentina in this respect, Venezuela failed to attract many European migrants, at least until quite recently.

In Colombia, the numerical preponderance of people classed as mixed gave a good basis on which to build ideas about a whitened mestizo nation, helped along perhaps by European immigration. At an official level, no bones were made about the desirability of whitening the population at large. In 1824, the British consul reported that "the preponderance of African blood along this very extensive line of coast [the Atlantic littoral], in agitated times like the present, cannot fail to excite serious reflections in this country. Those in power . . . feel the full importance of the expediency of inviting Europeans to find homes in Colombia . . . where their descendants must improve the moral and physical properties of the Colombians" (Humphreys 1940, 267). Bushnell (1954, 144) also observes that new liberal immigration laws promulgated in 1823 were designed to encourage white immigration in order to outnumber colored people and defuse the threat of "race warfare." Race warfare was only a concern during the "agitated times" of the newly formed republic of Gran Colombia (1819–30). A more deep-seated concern was with progress. In the early 1850s, the Comisión Corográfica set forth to map and examine the new republic and assess its possibilities for development (Restrepo 1984). Its results were important both for their wide diffusion and for their contribution to the consolidation of the emerging nation. Blacks were not seen as good material for the developing nation, and Agustín Codazzi, a geographer, commented tersely on the blacks of the Chocó province that "a race almost all of which passes its days in such indolence is not that which is called to make the country progress" (Comisión Corográfica 1958, 324). Another commission member, Santiago Pérez, in a more personal account of his travels, published in newspaper articles, was more explicit about the Chocoanos, noting the "savage stupidity of the black race, its *bozal* insolence, its appalling laziness and its scandalous shamelessness" (quoted in Restrepo 1984, 153; *bozal*, literally "raw" or "untamed," was the colonial term for an African-born slave). Others of the political and intellectual elite expressed themselves in similar terms. José María Samper, a parliamentarian of nineteenth-century Colombia, wrote in 1868 on the blacks of the Caribbean coastal region, the *bogas* who poled huge rafts up and down the Magdalena from the coast to Bogotá:

> There [i.e., in the coastal region] the primitive man, coarse, brutish, indolent, semi-savage and burnt by the tropical sun, that is, the Colombian *boga,* in all his insolence, his stupid bigotry, his cowardly self-satisfaction, his incredible indolence and his shameless speech, the child of ignorance rather than corruption; and here [i.e., in the highlands] the European, active, intelligent, white and elegant, often blond, with his poetic and penetrating glance, his ringing and rapid speech, his elevated spirit, his ever distinguished manners [. . .] the *boga,* descendant of Africa and child of the crossbreeding of races debased by tyranny, possesses of what is human virtually nothing except the outer form and the primitive needs and powers. . . . The *boga* of the Magdalena is nothing more than a brute who speaks a dreadful language,

always lewd, carnal, insolent, a thief and a coward. (quoted in Peñas 1988, 59)

Laziness and indolence were crucial elements in the perception of black people, and these were critical failings in the new national order. Marco Fidel Suárez, president and influential essayist, wrote in 1882 an essay entitled "Progress" which is a perfect example of the new liberal morality that penetrated Colombia from Europe.

> Work being the indispensable condition of progress, this does not exist among the savages, who like beasts, harvest without having planted, and by this token are slaves like the beasts; since it is a law that truth, good and freedom can only be achieved by means of continuous effort: *work* signifies effort, and in effect, work is the path towards civilization, it is the law of activity as it is realized in man, it is progress itself: idleness in contrast, is the negation of this law and the cause of all ruin; it is a stream which when blocked becomes a lake of impure waters. (1958, 1:1267)

If blacks were incorrigibly lazy, then what hope for them in this vision of the world? Not everyone saw blacks as incorrigibly or biologically lazy or inferior: such a belief would have dangerous implications for ideas about the mestizo as a basis for national identity. But these implications would, of course, recede the whiter the mestizo became, and some writers clearly saw a whiter future as the only real solution. José Eusebio Caro, in many ways a representative thinker of the late nineteenth century in Colombia, had a dream (admittedly utopian) of an Anglo-Saxon future in which "the diversity of races will end, because the white race will absorb and destroy the indian, the black, the yellow, etc." (quoted in Jaramillo Uribe 1964, 198). José María Samper, writing in 1887, also held that the "pure indian" was only assimilable through education and other social influences "to an insignificant extent." In his view, "there is no alternative but that of absorption, by means of crossing, and that [is only effective] after the third or fourth generation [of crossing]." The crossing, of course, would have to be with a "superior race" such as the Spanish (quoted in Pineda Camacho 1984, 205).

In the twentieth century, some writers continued to hold these views. Laureano Gómez, president between 1949 and 1953, supporter of Franco and archconservative, spoke pessimistically in 1928 on the theme of Colombia's progress as a nation. Territory and race were the two fundaments of nationality, and Colombia was badly endowed on both fronts. Its broken territory was cursed with an abundance of tropical jungle, refractory to development. Racially it had an uninspiring heritage. "Our race comes from the mixture of Spaniards, indians and blacks. The latter two flows of heritage are marks of complete inferiority. It is in whatever we have been able to inherit from the Spanish spirit that we must look for the guiding lines of the contemporary Colombian character." Blacks he saw as living in a state of "perpetual infantility," with a "rudimentary and unformed" spirit and wrapped up in "the fog of an eternal illusion." The other "savage race," the indians, was a "barbarous element," resigned to "misery and insignificance." And even the Spanish were ecstatic, ignorant, and fanatical (1970, 44–47).

Critics of this speech attacked his pessimism, his environmental determinism, and his representation of the Spanish and indian heritage. In a second speech, he defended himself by citing the Frenchmen Vidal de la Blache and Lucien Febvre as his geographic muses (both critics of environmental determinism) and by lauding some features of Spanish and of Aztec and Inca cultures. Colombia was not doomed, he said, but simply in need of a firm hand to guide it out of the dire straits in which it found itself (1970, 67–140). Apparently, no one attacked his views on blacks, since he saw no need to defend himself on that score.

In 1920, a student association in Bogotá invited a series of speakers to address the topic "The Problems of Race in Colombia" (Jiménez López et al. 1920). The first speaker, Jiménez López, a psychiatrist, held that "the race" in Colombia was in a process of physical and moral degeneration. This biologism referred to the natural processes of any "social organism" (1920, 33), but it was intimately interwoven with an environmental determinism that held that the tropics gave rise to stable, well-adapted populations of indians and blacks who were nevertheless "incapable of producing, or even assimilating, high forms of human culture" (1920, 47). These high forms, apart from being threatened by natural degeneration when deprived of "new blood," were also undermined in the tropics both by the environment and by intermixture (1920, 33). The only fundamental solution was white immigration: "A current of European immigration of sufficient numbers would gradually drown the aboriginal blood and the black blood which, in the opinion of the sociologists who have studied us, are a permanent element of backwardness and regression in our continent" (1920, 75).

Opposition to this pessimistic view of the Colombian nation was widespread (Jiménez López et al. 1920, 333–35). Such biologism had overly negative consequences for an attempt to delineate national identity in a favorable light. Every speaker after Jiménez López contested his view of the Colombian "race" as degenerate. They disagreed that degeneration was inevitable, and some put greater emphasis on historical factors such as the conquest, or on social conditions such as an inadequate educational system. But, while some saw the indians' current position partly in terms of their history, there was no defense of the blacks, and the hygienist Jorge Bejarano noted how the blacks, "favored by their savage customs and their slight intellectuality and morality, reproduced themselves prodigiously" at the expense of the "European race, superior morally and intellectually" (Bejarano, in Jiménez López et al. 1920, 192). Thus the degeneration thesis was rejected in favor of reclaiming a Colombian national identity in which blackness and indianness still tended to be seen as elements to be superseded.

The disagreement among these speakers, however, is indicative of a variety of emphases regarding the "racial problem." Not everyone saw it as an overriding factor in the national panorama; blacks and indians were not seen as the sole cause of the deficiencies of the Colombian "race" or nation. Luis López de Mesa, psychologist, philosopher, and intellectual, writing in 1934 on the formation of the Colombian nation, assumes the "racial" nature of regional population traits, to which he assigns greater or lesser indian or black heritage. But while blacks and mulattoes have the traits of "fantasy, sensuality and laziness" (1970, 97), López de Mesa is equally critical of the endogamic white elite of Popayán, and he has both good and bad things to say of the mestizo of Boyacó and the mulatto of the Atlantic coast. White immigration would tend to "enrich the qualities of [Colombia's] racial fusion," but the emphasis is as much on the social input of skills and habits as on the "enrichment of [Colombia's] good stock" (1970, 122–23). In this vision, then, while blacks and indians are not seen as an ideal heritage, transmitting certain traits of laziness (1970, 19), neither are they roundly castigated for contaminating the Colombian nation: "Creole laziness is conditioned by elements which can be dominated," such as ill health and undisciplined habits (1970, 20–21). Instead, there is a powerful emphasis on mixedness and lack of social distinction: "We are Africa, America, Asia and Europe all at once, without grave spiritual perturbation"; and this becomes not "the old democracy of equality of citizenship only for the conquering minority, but an integral [democracy] without distinctions of class or breed" (1970, 14, 13). This affirmation of democratic mixedness, while it also marginalizes blacks and indians, diverges from the outspoken condemnation of them characteristic of other perspectives. Rather, the emphasis is on mixed populations, and blacks and indians as such tend to vanish into peripherality, appearing occasionally, like the Cauca Valley blacks who are "constantly lazy, almost vegetative" (1970, 108). Here we see precisely the business of compromise in defining national identity: blackness and indianness become marginal and inferior, while too great an emphasis on "contamination" or "degeneration" is avoided since this would lead to an overly negative view of Colombian nationality and its future.

Surprisingly, the simple condemnation of blackness similar to that expressed in earlier times is still evident in quite recent publications. In a 1953 book on the geography of the Cauca region, Miguel Antonio Arroyo writes that "the black has not been able to free himself of the moral deficiency of improvidence," and since the indian is introverted and indifferent, it is vital to engineer "a better direction for the mixtures, starting centrally from white towards red and from white towards black . . . so that the descendants remain influenced by the dominant characteristics of the European stock" (1953, 104, 110). Eugenic policies should aim for a morphological type similar to that of "the ancient Mediterranean civilizations," while indian-black unions should be avoided since they produce "tenacious or insoluble subtypes which retard racial uniformity" and are refractory to "the dominant capacity of the white race" (1953, 110–12). Miguel Camacho Perea, writing on the department of Valle del Cauca, a little farther north, also envisages the eventual creation of a "cosmic race": he notes that the black is well adapted to tropical climates and arduous labor, but "without stimulus he gives himself over to laziness." The black who lives in the river valley itself is described (in López de Mesa's exact words) as of a melancholy type with "a disposition to music and indolence. He submitted to the apathetic nature of his spirit and was constantly lazy, almost vegetative. He contents himself with the easy sustenance of fish and plantains along the banks of the Cauca and its affluents" (1962, 82, 88). Gustavo González Ochoa, an Antioqueño, remarks more dogmatically that the importation of blacks was "one of the greatest errors committed by any statesman or sociologist of all time," since they are "an inferior race" that, luckily, was controlled and punished to a degree that "prevented the black race, prolific like no other, from taking over the continent" (1942, 129).

Remarks of this type cannot be taken unproblematically as representative of some official ideology about blacks in post-1940s Colombia. They are typical of widespread ideas about blacks as lazy, unprogressive, and marginal to the main currents of national progress; but in a fashion characteristic of the coexistence of *mestizaje* and discrimination, it is more common to encounter the celebration of mixedness alongside silence about blacks than to find explicit derogation of them. This follows the trend illustrated in earlier times by Luis López de Mesa. For example, in a recent book that tries to delineate features of a Colombian social psychology, Rubén Ardila considers the concept of "race" and rejects it as having no basis in biology. He then slips almost unawares into rejecting its social significance on the same grounds, reinforcing this with the idea that Latin America is a mestizo continent "for which race has practically lost all meaning." Colombia is "definitively a mestizo country," although in some regions "certain homogeneous groups can be distinguished" (1986, 59–62). Equally, in a UNESCO publication on cultural policy in Colombia, Jorge Eliécer Ruiz of the Colombian Institute of Culture devotes several pages to pre-Hispanic culture and recognizes the sociocultural diversity of the country which requires policies allowing for "plurality in feeling and form" (Ruiz 1977, 60). Blacks are barely mentioned as slaves and as an influence in popular music (1977, 12, 19).

This silence about blacks is not simply—or even at all—an unwillingness to express racist views in public. Derogation of blackness coexists with ideas about *mestizaje* as a unifying theme in Colombianness. But while regional variety is acknowledged and seen as a rich cultural tapestry, these visions of unity are constructed to the detriment of existing ethnic and racial minorities. Otto Morales, the Colombian writer and politician, in his *Memorias del mestizaje* (1984) asks, "When did the mestizo emerge? I have no doubt that this historical moment is the same as the instant at which people born here after the Discovery became conscious that these lands belonged to them" (1984, 32–33). He continues, characterizing "our artisans and modest carvers" under the dominion of the Spanish rulers, "There they were, with their rough faces, of irregular shape, sometimes with slanting eyes, some with black layers in their skin, and with some white coloring, listening to orders. And no one was to challenge [those orders]. . . . This insolence would not be tolerated" (1984, 34). Here racial differences are only hinted at and are in any case submerged in a common destiny of liberation from Spanish domination. The issue of usurpation of indian land by nonindians and of black slaves listening to orders from white masters is casually transformed into the issue of American mestizo subjugation to Spanish rule. This type of discourse is populist and democratic, and it glosses over racial minorities in visions of mestizo identity. But the heritage of compromising between the originality of Latin American mestizo identity and the ideologies of progress allied to whiteness means that behind this democratic discourse of mestizo-ness, which submerges difference, lies the hierarchical discourse of *blanqueamiento*, which points up racial and cultural difference, valorizing whiteness and disparaging blackness and indianness. There are thus two faces that ideas about nationality and race mixture can present. One, democratic, glosses over difference, pretending it does not exist. The other, hierarchical, highlights difference by privileging whiteness.

It is immediately apparent that these ideologies about race mixture involve highly contradictory elements. On the one hand, the glorification of the mestizo draws its meaning and force from the history of *mestizaje* and the emergence of a large set of mixed people in the country. It lauds this process and sees in it the essence of Colombian development and progress. It thus tricks itself out with a democratic populist rhetoric of *mestizaje* understood as a morally neutral convergence of three races onto a nonhierarchized middle ground. On the other hand, *blanqueamiento,* by envisaging a future in which blackness and indianness are not only absorbed but also *erased* from the national panorama, giving rise to a *whitened* mestizo nation, smuggles in discrimination and turns the vision into an impossible utopia. Because, by definition, every whitening must also be a darkening, and if darkening is avoided by lighter people discriminating against the darker, then no ultimate progress towards a totally mestizo nation, let alone a whitened mestizo nation, is possible. This possibility of seeing in nationalist discourse about race mixture both a celebration of mixture and a discrimination against blacks and indians is a characteristic of the contradictory coexistence of *mestizaje* and discrimination in Colombian society.

The Colombian Racial Order

Until now I have talked mainly in terms of ideologies about race and nation which are managed and propagated by a political and intellectual elite. This is partly because these elites have expressed their beliefs in textual form. It is crucial to realize, however, that these ideologies are not simply constructions limited to that elite or foisted by them onto other classes. They derive from the elite's encounter with the world as they experience it and from their interest in shaping that world, and they resonate strongly with other people's perception and experience of the world. These ideologies have hegemonic—which is not to say uncontested—status. I am concerned in this book not simply with elite ideologies (cf. Skidmore 1974; Graham 1990; Wright 1990), but also with social practices that are guided by and themselves reproduce those sets of ideas and values. Thus *mestizaje* and *blanqueamiento* are not just concepts in different variants of nationalist thought; they are sets of practices which are imbued with meaning by, and also reconstitute, the hierarchies and social interactions expressed in ideologies of *blanqueamiento* and *mestizaje*. I have given the preceding account of elite ideology because practices have to be understood in the context of elite ideas about race and nation, ideas that by their resonance with real social hierarchies and real experience have the power to constitute, in Foucault's terms, not error, illusion, or alienated consciousness, but truth itself (Foucault 1980, 133)—although that "truth" can be contested.

We are now in a position to characterize the structure of the Colombian racial order in broad terms. It can be visualized as a triangle whose uppermost point is white and whose bottom corners are black and indian (Whitten 1985, 43, develops this idea in an Ecuadorian context; see also Córdoba 1983). The white apex is associated with power, wealth, civilization, the creation and government of Colombian nationhood, and high positions on the scales of urbanity, education, and *cultura* (culturedness or cultivation). The lifestyle, material standard of living, education, manners, speech, and family structure of whites are recognized as having high status in the national hierarchies of prestige and status. The bottom two corners are seen from above as primitive, dependent, uneducated, rural, and inferior. More specifically, blacks are stereotyped as lazy and unprogressive, uneducated, and having a rough, rural mode of speech. Further images are constructed around the ideas of an "abnormal" family structure with an "irresponsible" father and around the blacks' supposed love of music, dancing, and celebration. Indian culture is seen as still more foreign and distinct than black culture, especially in lifestyle and language. The indians, too, are seen as refractory to progress and development. These images are a consequence of the fact that the triangular racial order presented here overlaps strongly with a basic class order that, beginning with colonialism, slavery, and the exploitation of indian labor, has structured race in this hierarchical fashion. Class and race hierarchies are not coterminous, since there are lower-class whites as well as some middle-class blacks, but their historical coincidence has been enough to create the basic hierarchy of the racial order.

Although those people who classify themselves as *negro* or *indio* (or *indígena*) may resist specific characterizations of themselves as primitive or inferior, and in specific cases overtly contradict the epithets of rural or uneducated, they will admit that the majority of those who classify themselves as black or indian (and even the majority of those classified as such from above, which is a larger category) are mainly rural, relatively uneducated, and situated in the lowest strata of Colombian society. I found that some blacks accepted the general idea that blacks as a category were unprogressive, even while they rejected the idea that they personally were lazy and also pointed out that blacks performed hard, heavy labor. That is, while the moral

20

connotations of the hierarchy may be contested, some fundamental aspects of the hierarchy itself have the status of self-evident truth. However, the black dynamic of nucleation, resistance, and autonomy represents a countervailing force here which I examine in depth in later chapters.

The essential process connecting the three points is *mestizaje,* both physical and cultural. It is crucial that the white category is at the top. Hierarchy is fundamental not only to the respective ordering of these three categories but also to the process of *mestizaje* itself. Objectively, this is as much a process of darkening as of lightening, but the very hierarchy that it mediates means that moves upwards, away from indian or black and towards white, are more valuable. *Mestizaje* takes on powerful moral connotations: it is not just neutral mixture but hierarchical movement, and the movement that potentially has greatest value is upward movement—*blanqueamiento* or whitening, understood in physical and cultural terms. On a cultural level, a similar situation pertains. It is commonplace to say that the cultural middle ground in Colombia is a syncretic culture in which elements traceable to pre-Colombian America, Africa, and Europe can all be found. What such an observation misses, however, is that there are different positions within this syncretic hierarchy. The nearer to "black" or "indian" culture something is thought to be, the lower down the hierarchy it is located. In contrast, cultural forms taken to be derived from the white world are accorded greater value. As before, in specific cases, some blacks or indians may reject *blanqueamiento*— that is, adopting nonblack/nonindian cultural ways, or marrying a nonblack/nonindian. It may seem like a betrayal of their origins. Many, however, do not take this attitude. More generally, everyone accepts that whites are on top and that blackness or indianness can be an obstacle to social advancement; in this sense, the potential value of *blanqueamiento* has the status of self-evidence.

The Dynamics of Mestizaje. The structure of the racial and national order of Colombia outlined thus far indicates that transformations of identity and culture can occur through movements up and down the hierarchy. The nationalist vision is of a collective transformation towards a (whitened) mestizo-ness. When looked at more closely, the actual dynamics of mixture are much more complex than this simple utopian vision suggests. In terms of socioracial classifications, *mestizaje* gives rise to a great potential for negotiation and manipulation in the claiming and ascribing of racial identities such as *negro, indio, blanco,* mestizo, and so on. In schematic terms, at the physical level, black mixes with white to produce *mulato,* indian mixes with white

21

to produce mestizo, and black mixes with indian to produce *zambo*. In reality there is an infinite range of both phenotype and social categorization: this is reflected in the multiple terminology that exists for classifying people by their phenotypical appearance (Harris 1970). This terminology reflects the institutionalization of race mixture in Latin America, but this does not detract from the fact that the three polar categories retain their integrity and their meaning (Sanjek 1971). Whatever the ambiguities of the middle ground, *negro, indio,* and *blanco* remain powerful symbols and identities that are ascribed to and claimed by real people. *Mestizaje* is not seen as a generalized, random mix-up, but is seen as the mixture of three *razas* that are separate from each other but connected via processes of race mixture. The categorization of people as black, indian, white, or mixed is, like any ethnic categorization, subject to variation according to circumstance and interest: in the Colombian context, the institutionalization of race mixture has increased the manipulability inherent in the process of classification and made categories such as "black" or "indian" much more problematic than in, say, North America. Nevertheless, the basic hierarchy of white, black, and indian structures this ambiguity.

In terms of cultural syncretism, the position is even more complex, as different cultural forms interpenetrate, mix, and are socially reconstructed and redefined over time in the context of interactions between black, white, and mestizo people which take place in the setting of a hierarchical racial and cultural order. A great deal of "black culture" is, in fact, of European origin, or in some cases of indian origin. Blacks have appropriated different aspects of European and indian culture and imprinted them with a particular stamp, sometimes derived from an African mold. As such, the new synthesis remains classified as "black" culture if it is practiced in a predominantly black context. Thus Catholicism as practiced in the Pacific region has particular features (Price 1955; Friedemann and Arocha 1986; Bastide 1978); and European dances and musical genres introduced into black regions by Spanish slave owners evolved a form peculiar to the region. This reclassification also occurs in the cultural middle ground. Black and indian forms penetrate into this world as black and indian people also penetrate it, altering their social identity in the process, and these cultural elements are gradually redefined as mestizo forms, losing their previous identification and adapting their actual form. In short, cultural forms move, adapt, and are redefined more freely than racial types in the context of ethnic interaction with its shifting ground of claims and ascriptions. This adds another element of fluidity to the already manipulable racial identifications noted earlier. If this fluidity stems partly from ambiguity about who is classed as or identifies him- or herself as *negro, indio, blanco,* mestizo, and so on, then it also derives from ambiguity about whether the behavior of someone or a set of people is classifiable as black culture or is given some other category of cultural affiliation.

One of the means by which black forms become part of a more generalized mestizo culture is via the process of black adaptation. Blacks take on the cultural mores of the nonblack world, but some- times part of that adaptation involves the penetration of black cultural forms into the nonblack world, their adaptation and their redefinition as forms proper to the mixed, nonblack world, although not necessar- ily appropriate to the white elite world. There is, however, another related process at work, and this is based on a more covert perception of black culture by the nonblack world. The argument here derives from Taussig's (1987) analysis of the powers of lowland indian (and black) sorcery, magic, and healing techniques, and I think the same type of approach can be extended to the black music, dance, fiesta, and also black sexuality. Baldly stated, blacks are seen as primitive but also therefore as possessed of some special powers, especially magical, sexual, musical, and rhythmic ones—powers traditionally defined by the Catholic church as corrupt but which still (perhaps as a result) hold a certain fascination. The blacks and the indians, while they bear on their shoulders the load of white and mestizo discrimina- tion, also have powers not granted their masters, powers that stem, in indecipherable proportions, from their own original cultures (indian hallucinogens and shamanism, African dance and music), from image making about the mysterious forces of indians and blacks, and from indian and black reaffirmations of themselves and their cultures in the light of such images. The nonblack world turns to these cultures to tap their powers for certain specific purposes: for healing and sorcery, sexual gratification, entertainment, or catharsis. Of course, the force of these powers varies with the "purity" of the culture from which they derive: ideally, the most powerful is the most "original," the closest to the "roots" of the culture (or what are thought to be its roots). Thus it is blacks, or black regions, which historically or cur- rently appear to be the most far removed from nonblack culture and territory, which also appear to have the greatest power. But ironically, the more the nonblack world attempts to avail itself of these powers, the more distant they become. Elements of the original form become incorporated into new configurations, retaining, albeit in diluted form, some of the powers of the antecedent. The new configurations become adapted for use by the nonblack world and may even lose their initial significance altogether. Hence, again, black forms pene-

23

trate, are adapted, and redefined. Classic examples outside the Colombian context are the evolution of rock and roll in the United States (see, for example, Lipsitz 1981), the evolution of public processions and carnivals from old black associations and cults in Brazil (see Marks 1974), or the growth and spread of Umbanda in that country (see Brown 1986).

The Colombian nation feeds on the different powers attributed to and claimed by each racial realm: the blacks and indians can try to feed on the wealth and political power of the whites, their education, and "civilization," and indeed on their very whiteness, as they escape the lowest rungs of the hierarchy by whitening themselves through *mestizaje;* the whites and mestizos can try to feed on the labor and what they see as the healing powers and the musical and sexual talents of the blacks and the indians.

The Structuring of the Racial Order

The foregoing gives a sketch of the basic structure and dynamics of the Colombian racial order. It is vital to see that the racial order I have outlined is not autonomous and self-regulating. Seen both as a structure of racial patterns and as choices made about racial and ethnic identity by individuals, the racial order emerged and is structured in its operation by underlying forces of the political economy. *Mestizaje* and mestizos arose in their particular Latin American form due to the basic political economic structure of Latin American society. They did not arise as a simple result of the Iberian legal tradition as Tannenbaum (1948) first suggested, nor as a corollary of the role of Catholic religious institutions in "integrating" slaves, blacks, and indians into the lower orders of colonial society, as others have suggested (see Solaún and Kronus 1973 and Klein 1967 and 1969 for a discussion), although these influences are not to be denied (see Wade 1986, for example). Rather, they arose out of the demographic, political, and economic conditions of colonization. Relevant here are the connections made by Mintz (1969) and by Elkins (1969), among others, between capitalism and slavery, which suggested that the repressiveness of the slavery regime varied with the dynamism of capitalism and the degree of integration into the world market. Elkins (1969), comparing capitalist and noncapitalist colonial regimes, remarked on how the "dynamic and unencumbered origins" of capitalism in the North American slave states "stamped the status of slave upon the black with [profound] clarity." In contrast, the less dynamic and more regally controlled Latin American colonial economies did not enforce this equation between slave and black with such rigor (although El-

24

kins also gives a good deal of weight to legal and religious institutions). Harris (1974) argues that the Brazilian planters' need for nonslave labor gave rise to the social recognition of the mixed offspring of black-white unions as a distinct free, mixed social class, whereas in North America such a recognition was suppressed by competitive relations between the blacks and a large mass of poor whites who allied themselves to the planters' racist ideologies. Mulattoes were thus generally classed as "blacks," and most blacks were slaves. Jordan (1969) draws attention to the relative proportions of whites and blacks in the colonial population and to male/female ratios in explaining rates of race mixture and the social recognition of an intermediate category. In his view, large proportions of blacks and a shortage of white women were conducive to miscegenation and its social acceptance. Hoetink (1969) points to the significance of white family organization in affecting these factors (see also Hoetink 1973).

My view is that in Latin America a small, mainly male conquistador nucleus, often with little family organization in place, grafted onto a larger subservient population. The relative proportions of the three racial categories and the sex ratios among the whites encouraged miscegenation between the white men and women of the subordinate categories. Social recognition of an intermediate racial category occurred in most areas of the New World, except, broadly speaking, in the North American slave states, and it seems that only under the specific circumstances pertaining there was this recognition suppressed. Equally, in all the American colonies, the pressures emanating from below, from the blacks and indians wanting to escape their subordinate legal and racial status, had to be actively repressed and severely controlled if they were not to result in the emergence of a free class and an intermediate category. In Latin America, the white population was generally unable to exercise this type of repression in a systematic way and, indeed, often had no overriding reason to do so, had they in fact been capable. Although the Spanish and Portuguese colonists might have ideally preferred to keep all blacks as slaves, and indians as tributary (or even slave) labor, the apparatus needed to do so was ultimately beyond their reach. In addition, they were dealing in several areas with a very large, dense, sedentary, and well-organized indian population. Contrast North American slave states where a very different colonizing society effected precisely such a repression on the blacks and their mixed offspring, and an even harsher repression on the sparser indian population. In Latin America, the resulting free population, made up of freed blacks and mulattoes and of indian-white mixtures and acculturated indians, might in certain circumstances also serve as a labor force that was more adaptable and easier to use than slave or tributary labor—although I diverge from Harris's (1974) argument that this was why such a population emerged (Wade 1986). Further still, this free population was not a *fundamental* threat to the Iberian and Creole whites' status, although the elite did feel the need to control and restrict the movement and liberty of this free class (Cohen and Greene 1972). Contrast again the slave states of North America where large numbers of poor whites were at the same social level as, and thus felt threatened by, the blacks. I would argue that legal tradition, religious institutions, and cultural attitudes were grist to this mill of economic, political, and demographic forces—which is not to deny the former their autonomous causality. The point is simply that the whole emergence of the Latin American, or in this case Colombian, racial order with its twin processes of *mestizaje* and discrimination was largely created over the long term by political, economic, and demographic factors. Similarly, today, the interweaving of these processes and of the dynamics that affect the black population is structured by such forces.

This implies a certain position with respect to the conceptual relation between race and class, and, given the hotly debated nature of this question in much of the literature about race, I feel it is necessary to briefly outline my own position. As I state above, I regard "material factors"—economic and political relations with their associated labor systems and population ratios—as predominant factors in the long run. It is basically these that have given rise to the contrasts between North American, Caribbean, and Latin American socioracial systems. These factors structure the racial order in Colombia and its twin processes of *mestizaje* and discrimination. This does *not* mean that I regard race as "reducible" to class, that is, to some aspect of the class struggle. Material factors are themselves subject to cultural perception and construction (Sahlins 1976), so that, for example, the Iberian conception of "black" or "slave"—different from the Anglo-Saxon one—may have affected the structures of social relations between Iberians and blacks or slaves. This introduces a two-way relation between material factors and cultural constructions, but the point is that concerns of power, subsistence, and wealth have a greater capability of restructuring these social relations (and hence these conceptions) than do the conceptions themselves.

Race may not be reducible to class, but this does not clarify its actual status. To say race is "symbolic" sets up an unrealistic distinction between the "symbolic" and the "real," consigning the former to insignificance, but the conceptual difference between race, power, and class (for want of a better term) must be recognized. Power inheres in the organization and mobilization of people and of force. Subsistence and wealth inhere in the organization and exploitation of things that are made productive (e.g., land, labor). These two dimensions obviously overlap. Race can be an axis around which to organize these two realms of activity, but they cannot be inherent in it. In this sense, all "race relations" are simply types of social relations— economic and political, but also cultural and psychological—which pertain between categories or individuals who classify one another in terms of racial identifications (Banton 1983, 405). But precisely the use of these identifications means that social relations emerge in specific racialized ways (*racial* discrimination, *race* mixture) which constitute structures of race relations. These often appear as autonomous (hence people apparently discriminate or miscegenate "by choice"), but these relations are structured by the politics and economics in the orchestration of which they are themselves involved. But the totality of race relations is not completely determined in this way. There are cultural dimensions that are relatively autonomous: there are struggles over cultural authority, or over "symbolic capital" (Bourdieu 1977); there is, for example, *blanqueamiento*, which involves a quest for whiteness, connected but not reducible to power and wealth. In sum, since race is a mode of organization of various social relations, race relations must be heavily structured by the political economy that they partly orchestrate, without, however, being determined in their entirety by the latter. This gives race some "relative autonomy" (Hall 1980; Solomos 1986) and admits of a Weberian emphasis that can envisage social closure around principles of race (Parkin 1979; Rex 1986a; Whitten 1965).

This analysis of the relation between racial structures and the political economy is distinct from the analysis of the relation between social structure in general and human agency. Here I envisage a recursive relation in which larger structures of race, class, and power are in one sense themselves the outcome of the repetition and interconnectedness of individual actions, but are also the medium for those actions, being the generative context in which choice, interest, and perception arise (Bourdieu 1977; Giddens 1984). The recursive relation between agency and structure is a symmetrical one, whereas that between race and the political economy is a hierarchical one in which politics and economics have a more directional role in the long term. The agency/ structure and race/political economy relations are crosscutting, not parallel. When, for example, I talk of the racial order being structured by economic factors, I mean that economic factors structure both people's individual choices about race and ethnicity and the patterns of race and ethnicity that emerge out of those choices, but which simultaneously constitute the context within which those choices were generated. This is not a simple determination, both because social action in general is not the mere precipitate of structural dictates and because racial structures and actions are not entirely contained by the political economy that partly determines them.

2

The Study of Indians

and Blacks

in the Racial Order

In sketching out the racial order of Colombia, I have presented both blacks and indians as located at the bottom corners of the "triangle," with the implication that their positions are analogous. In many senses this is true, as both are seen in the nationalist project as inputs into the future and into mestizo-ness and modernity, things that are not seen as inhering in blacks and indians in their own right. But there are also very significant differences between the two categories which are reflected both at the level of ideological constructions of nationality and at the level of social practice, especially regarding state policy and academic study. In simple terms, blacks have not been regarded as legitimate objects of state or intellectual concern, and in this chapter I look at why this is so.

From the beginning of the conquest, indians and the New World took on in the minds of Europeans an aspect very distinct from that of blacks and Africa. Perhaps the clearest indication of this was the different legal and moral status accorded to indian and black slavery. Laws did not, of course, dictate social reality, but the fact that indians and blacks had very different legal positions is indicative of a difference in their places in the racial order.

Roman and canon law agreed that slavery was contrary to natural law (Davis 1970, 113), but it was also permitted by both legal traditions (not to mention the Bible and Aristotelian philosophy) under certain conditions, such as for the captives of a just war or as a punishment for criminal acts. When the Spanish encountered American indians, the initial tendency was to class them as "barbarians" (i.e., non-Christian and uncivilized) and also to some degree as "natural slaves" (an Aristotelian category of people naturally destined for

29

slavery) (Pagden 1982, 29–30). But early on, this was a major bone of contention, and the clergy, in view of the drastic demise of the indians and the evident brutality of the colonists, began to protest— not so much against slavery as an institution as against its justice in this case. Beginning with the famous 1511 Antonio de Montesinos sermon against colonist brutality on Hispaniola, and spurred by the Las Casas–Sepúlveda debates of 1550–51 on the legitimacy of indian slavery, there emerged a body of legislation designed to protect the indian, albeit in a principally paternalist fashion (Hanke 1959, 1969). Thus indian slavery was legally prohibited from 1542 in Spanish America and from 1570 in Brazil. Reality was, of course, rather different, and indian slavery persisted in many fringe areas and especially in Brazil (Lockhart and Schwartz 1983; 71–72; Hemming 1987). In addition, colonist respect for protective indian legislation was scant in many areas.

For blacks, however, the situation was quite distinct. Despite a few clerical critics (Davis 1970, 210–20), slavery was never seriously questioned as a legitimate status for blacks. Manumission from slavery was enshrined both in law derived from the thirteenth-century Seite Partidas and constituted in the colonies by piecemeal legislation, and in slave owners' practice. But whatever the arguments about the leniency and moral benevolence of Latin American slave systems (see Foner and Genovese 1969, Russell-Wood 1982), the idea of black slavery was legally and socially accepted. Thus Davis identifies a clear "double standard in judging Negroes and Indians" (1970, 24; cf. Hanke 1959, 9). Jaramillo Uribe also observes that "while in three centuries of conquest and colonization a voluminous and complete legislation protecting indians emerged, the laws of the Indies referring to blacks barely contain one or another humanitarian norm, and are composed almost entirely of penal dispositions, characterized by their particular severity" (1968, 31).

The reasons for this difference are several. In practical terms, indians were tied into their own local communities and thus harder to enslave effectively. In contrast, blacks had been uprooted from their homeland and were more easily exploitable (Lockhart and Schwartz 1983, 72). The crown was also worried by the lack of control over the colonists and their use of labor that indian slavery would have implied: black slavery was much more controllable (Harris 1974). In moral terms, indians occupied an ambivalent position. Classed on the one hand as "natural slaves" and "barbarians," they were also seen as uncorrupted natural beings. They were not Christian, but neither had they rejected Christianity: the justness of the wars against them (and hence their enslavement) was therefore questionable (Pagden

1982). Their society and culture was palpably under threat: demographic collapse, colonist abuse, and its consequences were openly visible, provoking outrage amongst some observers. Finally, the act of enslavement had to be carried out by the colonists themselves, raising questions about its justice in specific cases. In contrast, Africa had no connotation of an earthly paradise and was classified as infidel territory under Islamic influence: the justice of wars against the region had received frequent papal backing. Indeed, a common justification for slavery was its positive consequences for the inhabitants of an infidel and barbarous region (Saunders 1982, 38–40). African societies did not suffer the evident collapse that Amerindian ones did, and in any case, mostly mercantile and coastal relations meant negative impacts were less visible and less obviously linked to European influence. The act of enslavement was also carried out by Africans themselves or a small body of traders and thus its justice could be conveniently set aside. Finally, African slavery was already well established in Europe at the time of the conquest of the Americas (see Davis 1970, 187–210; Friede and Keene 1971, 417, 239–41).

Indianness and blackness thus had very different statuses from the beginning of colonial society. Such differences were also reflected in other domains. For example, in 1514, the marriage of Spaniards and indians was permitted (although rarely encouraged), whereas black-white intermarriage was frowned upon more heavily. Regulations decreed in 1778 obliged whites under 25 years of age to seek parental permission for marriage, the aim being to limit mixed marriages. But the Council of the Indies agreed that white intermarriage with indians should not be opposed "as their origin is not vile like that of the other *castas*." By 1805, viceregal (or in Cuba provincial authority) permission was needed for whites of any age with *limpieza de sangre* to marry persons of black or mulatto origin (Mörner 1967, 37–39; Martínez-Alier 1974). Not only were indians and blacks in different positions in colonial society, but so too were their mixed descendants. The Audiencia of Mexico, clarifying the 1778 regulations, observed that mestizos and *castizos* (of putative indian-white descent) "deserved to be set apart from the other *castas* as was already done in some respects both in law and public esteem" (Mörner 1967, 39). "Other *castas*" here would refer to people of putative white-black and indian-black descent. Such people were also liable to pay tribute, from which mestizos were generally exempt (Bowser 1972, 38; Mörner 1967, 44). Although in practice, differentiating between mestizos and other mixed-bloods would prove increasingly impossible, both the law and social attitudes in Latin America viewed indian descent as preferable to black descent (Mörner 1967, 35–52).

31

With independence, the racial order of Latin American societies began to lose at least its legal basis in many respects. Legal, though not actual, discrimination against mixed-bloods was generally, albeit sometimes slowly, dismantled. Slavery was abolished in most countries by the 1850s, persisting only in Cuba and Brazil until the late 1880s. Equally, measures were taken against indian status. In the liberalizing atmosphere of nineteenth-century Latin American nations struggling to define their identities, the idea of communal land ownership and a separate ethnic category was inimical. Indian tribute was generally abolished (although it was reimposed in Peru between 1885 and 1895), and legislation was promulgated to undermine the legal basis of the indian community, although in practice this was frequently ineffective in the absence of actual territorial and economic integration, or in the face of concerted indian resistance (Halperín Donghi 1987). Thus the Lerdo Law (1856) and the 1857 Constitution in Mexico attacked communal land ownership, while in Colombia 1861 legislation continued to undermine indian *resguardos* (reserves) which had been under attack since the colonial Bourbon regime (Bauer 1984, 169; Kalmanovitz 1984, 221–24; García 1978).

Changing legislation did not, of course, mean the de facto disappearance either of indians and blacks or of discrimination against both them and mixed-bloods. If anything, indians in many areas were even more brutally repressed and murdered (Klein 1984, 559; Dean 1989, 234). But as during the colonial period, indians as a category had a different position from that of blacks. They not only remained as members of distinguishable communities and cultures (which blacks also did to varying degrees), but they often later gained some legal recognition of their status as well, and they became positive targets of both state policy and intellectual discourse.

Thus, as early as the 1860s, there was some recognition of the negative results of the legal attacks on indian communities (Safford 1987, 89). In Peru, the *comunidad indígena* was recognized as a juridical category in the 1920 Constitution under the Leguía administration, which also created a department for indigenous affairs and the national *Día del Indio*. In Mexico, a Departamento de Asuntos Indígenas was created in 1936, an Instituto Indígena Interamericano in 1940, and an Instituto Indígena Nacional in 1948. In Peru and to an even greater extent in Mexico, indians also became a positive element in a discourse about nationality. *Indigenismo* had, and has, different variants—for example, incorporationist and anti-incorporationist (Hewitt de Alcántara 1984)—and a single exponent such as Manuel Gamio, director of the Instituto Indígena Interamericano, could mix romantic glorification of indian culture with more positivist notions of education and incorporation into a single mestizo nation (Brading 1988). While "official *indigenismo*" was ultimately strongly incorporationist and relied on ideas about indian backwardness and a future of mestizo homogeneity, the point is that indians were also given a symbolic role as emblems of national identity, or perhaps the roots of national identity, even while they were exploited and disparaged in practice. A glorious indian past could be useful as a badge of Latin American originality.

All this may not be surprising in societies with large indian populations. In Colombia, too, with under half a million "indians" at current estimates, a similar situation exists. There, legislation passed in 1890 braked slightly the movement to divide up indian *resguardos* and also legalized indian councils. This was with the express intention of "governing" and "civilizing" the indians. Although much subsequent legislation continued to undermine indian land rights, *resguardos* still exist today under the terms of the 1890 decree (García 1978; Valencia y Valencia 1972). In the 1920s and 1930s, the radical thought of José Mariátegui and Víctor Raúl Haya de la Torre in Peru and the work of Moises Saénz and Manuel Gamio in Mexico impinged upon an intellectual minority—people such as Gregorio Hernández de Alba, Antonio García, Juan Friede—which in 1942 created the Instituto Indígena de Colombia as an unofficial entity. These beginnings were to define the scope of Colombian anthropology (and ethnohistory) from then on. Seminal writers such as Hernández de Alba, Gerardo Reichel-Dolmatoff, Luis Duque Gómez, Roberto Pineda Giraldo, Milciades Chaves, Edith Jiménez de Muñoz, Blanca Ochoa de Molina and Eliécer Silva Celis all concentrated overwhelmingly on indian themes. Only three early anthropologists focused on blacks—Velásquez, Escalante, and Arboleda (see next section)—while a few, notably Virginia Gutiérrez de Pineda, included rural and urban mestizos in their studies (Friedemann and Arocha 1979). This bias transmitted itself to the departments of anthropology set up in the 1960s and 1970s, often under the direct aegis of these researchers, and these again designed their curricula principally around the study of indians (Friedemann 1984a; Pineda Camacho 1984).

The state was also concerned with the "indian problem," and, although it devolved a good deal of control to the Catholic church (and from 1962 to the Summer Institute of Linguistics, a North American evangelical organization), it also founded in 1941 the Instituto Etnológico Nacional, to become the current Instituto Colombiano de Antropología in 1961. Under the directorship of Paul Rivet, the IEN became a purely academic body, devoted principally to the study of indigenous societies. As such it lived in tension with the Instituto

Indígena de Colombia and its more politically committed and applied anthropological orientation (Pineda Camacho 1984; Friedemann 1975). In 1960, the state created a División de Asuntos Indígenas, headed originally by Hernández de Alba, which effectively became a monopoly on all development initiatives that affected indians. Despite its lip service paid to respect for cultural autonomy (Valencia y Valencia 1972), many see the state's policy as essentially integrationist in design, and verging in practice on the ethnocidal by virtue of negligence and inactivity (García 1978; Friedemann 1975; Pineda Giraldo 1987). In the 1980s, there have arguably been some positive changes in government policy towards indian land rights and political organization, partly as a response to a resurgence since 1970 of traditions of indian resistance and protest and the state's need to negotiate with and perhaps co-opt these forces. These changes, however, are located alongside traditional vested interests, also sponsored by the state, in colonizing indian land and exploiting indian labor (Gros 1988; Pineda Giraldo 1987).

Indians in Colombia, then, as in other Latin American countries, have been a category of special interest for intellectuals and the state—which is not to say that their objective conditions of livelihood have therefore been improving. Although indianness as a symbol of national identity does not have the same power as in Mexico or Peru, the concern with indians among the intellectual elite gives them some of this status (and in any case the mestizo is always an image of mixedness which is preferable to that of the mulatto in Colombian nationalist discourse).

Blacks, while sharing in many respects the contempt heaped upon indians in daily life, take a rather different place in Latin American racial orders. Simply put, blacks have been of much less interest to the states, intellectual elites, and the mestizo populations of Latin America. In literary circles, especially from the 1930s, and particularly in Cuba, there did emerge important currents of prose and poetry which unearthed themes related to blackness and addressed them directly (Mullen 1988; Jackson 1976; see also Friedemann 1984a; 520–38), but this did not generally manage to cast blacks in the same mold as indians. In Brazil, with its very large black population and clearly differentiated traits of black culture, there has been a tendency to do for blacks what other countries had done for indians. There in the 1930s, writers such as Arthur Ramos, and especially Gilberto Freyre and Edison Carneiro, attempted to recast the negative evaluations cast on blackness and African heritage, reassessing their role in the definition of Brazilian national identity. Parallel to some currents of *indigenismo*, the perspective was essentially integrationist (Skidmore

1974, 184–92). More recently, blackness has become increasingly politicized (Fontaine 1985), and at the national government level there is now an Assessoria para Asuntos Afro-Brasileiros, attached to the Ministry of Culture.

In Cuba, too, with a large black population and little chance of appealing to indian origins, attempts to valorize blackness and Africanness had some basis. Writers such as Fernando Ortiz and Alejo Carpentier were important here (although the early work of the former is overtly racist and recommends erasing black culture from Cuban society), and the whole notion of *afro-cubanismo* was strong for a period, although it also had to fight against the powerful repression of blackness as a defining element of Cuban nationality. After the 1959 Revolution, while racial discrimination was soon officially deemed to have been superseded, Castro gave some recognition to the idea of Cuba as a Latin-African state, especially as a justification for making links with African nations. This view, however, gave little space to black identity within the country, and more to the African ancestry of Cubans in general (Helg 1990; Taylor 1988; Benítez Rojo 1984). Venezuelans, on the other hand, "showed no inclination to idealize the African contribution to their culture" (Wright 1990, 113). In the forties, several authors did address the theme of blackness and black culture in a positive fashion, although generally from an assimilationist standpoint—Miguel Acosta Saignes being a significant exception (Wright 1990, 119). But these writers formed a minority voice.

In Colombia, very few people among the political and intellectual classes have had much interest in romanticizing or glorifying the African or black heritage of the nation's culture; very few were concerned with black communities, past or present, with most work being concentrated on the institution of slavery rather than on blacks as such (e.g., Colmenares 1979; Jaramillo Uribe 1968; 7–84); no institutes were set up—except recently by the blacks themselves—to study blacks, and certainly not by the state, which only in 1986 helped to finance a congress on blacks (Cifuentes 1986). Friedemann calculates that between 1936 and 1978, 271 people became professional anthropologists; only 5 have focused on blacks. Literary concerns with blackness have been important in their own right, but again limited in impact. In short, in Friedemann's terms, blacks have been "invisible" in the national arena (1984a).

The reasons for this different emphasis given to blackness and indianness in the national racial order as it is conceived and represented by elites are rooted in the colonial period and hark back to the issue of indian and black slavery, discussed above. They also relate to ideas about mixedness and national identity. Ideologies of *mestizaje* and even more of *blanqueamiento* tend to envision blacks and indians as retrograde inputs to a modernizing future of mixedness, or increasing whiteness, but *mestizaje* at least also simply attempts to gloss over ethnic difference entirely in assertions about Colombian mixedness. And blacks are much more likely to be included in such claims as "ordinary citizens" than are indians. Indians appear in this sense to stand culturally outside the national racial order—part of their identity as indians, ascribed or claimed, is to have distinct cultures and languages. Their pre-Colombian history can also be invoked as an artistically complex and rich heritage, which reinforces an image of difference and separateness. They can therefore easily constitute the typical "exotic" anthropological "other." In contrast, blacks, lacking the clear distinctiveness of Cuban or Brazilian black culture, and with a history apparently "lost" in Africa and fragmented by slavery, tend to be seen more easily as Colombian citizens, albeit not typical ones nor ones that would be used to represent Colombia in most discourse about national identity. Hence the remark reported by Friedemann from an anthropological colleague to the effect that the study of blacks was not "anthropology" (1984a, 509).

Caution is therefore needed with arguments in which blacks, like indians, are classed as "non-nationals" (Whitten 1985, 42). For Colombia, too, it is common in academic and planning circles to hear black regions such as the Pacific coast or indian communities contrasted with so-called "national society," referring to the mestizo and white majority of the more central, more developed regions of the country. But while this highlights the similarities between the categories black and indian in the national racial order, it also obscures the differences. Indians, of course, may emphasize their status as citizens as part of a struggle for civil rights, but for blacks the status of national citizen is much more taken for granted (which does not mean it is necessarily respected). More precisely, it is the slippage between including blacks as ordinary citizens and excluding them from the heart of nationhood which characterizes the position of blacks in the Colombian racial order.

Even more caution is needed with the approach taken by Stutzman (1981), who, following a concept of ethnicity outlined by Aronson (1976), has suggested that black ethnicity is a conscious volitional idiom of disengagement from national culture and values. Specifically, by turning in on their own black collectivity and maintaining a degree of cultural and ethnic integrity, blacks are making a positive statement of dissent from the whole ideology of *blanqueamiento* and the particular concept of nationhood which accompanies it. There are a number of problems with this approach. First, it has to be recognized that a significant factor in "disengagement" by blacks is their rejection at the hands of the majority. In this sense, ethnicity is not simply volitional, but may instead be seen partly as making a virtue from a necessity. Second, and as a result of the first point, not all blacks who supposedly "disengage" in Stutzman's sense actually reject the value of *blanqueamiento*. Third, while some blacks do implicitly or explicitly reject the idea that blackness is inferior and thus contest the idea of *mestizaje* understood as a progressive lightening and erasing of blackness from the national panorama, it would be wrong to envisage this as a "disengagement" from the Colombian nation as a whole. To suggest to any black person that she or he was other than Colombian and, excepting a handful of Protestant converts, other than Catholic would be nothing less than an affront. Other nonblack people may regard some blacks as not fully representative of the Colombian nation, but it would be wrong to suppose that blacks themselves withdraw from Colombian culture and nationhood. Rather, they pose a challenge to the way these are conceived by the nonblack majority.

In sum, then, while there are significant similarities in the positions of blacks and indians in the national racial order, there are also differences. Indians may be seen as very different from the rest of society and therefore either to be protected and studied or to be treated like animals. Blacks are likely to be caught between, on the one hand, ideologies of *blanqueamiento* which privilege whiteness (or light-skinned mixedness) and discriminate against blackness and, on the other, ideas of national homogeneity which rhetorically include blacks as equals but by the same token deny them specific status (e.g., as targets of racial discrimination). Discrimination against blacks, and indeed blacks themselves, thus recede into the background.

Black Studies in Latin America

During the early decades of the twentieth century, the investigation of blacks in Latin America tended to be folkloric and also "steeped in the evolutionism of Comte and Spencer, and the phrenological studies of the Italian medical specialist Lombroso" (Brown 1986, 4). Brown picks out Raymundo Nina Rodrigues for Brazil as typical of this trend. In Cuba, the early works of Fernando Ortiz also fit into this mold. Ortiz, for example, embarked on a major study of Afro-Cuban criminality, *Hampa afro-cubana,* of which the main results were: *Los negros brujos* (1906), "Los negros esclavos" (1916), and "Los negros curros" (1926–28); Lombroso contributed a dedication to the first volume. Ortiz also wrote on historical aspects of black social organization, for example, in his famous essays on colonial associations of slaves and free blacks, "La fiesta afro-cubana del Día de Reyes" (1920) and "Los cabildos afro-cubanos" (1921), which have since been widely cited in subsequent references to these organizations (e.g., Bastide 1971; Friedemann and Arocha 1986). The evident racism of much of Ortiz's early work—with frequent references to the "infantile" mentality of the blacks—was superseded in later investigations into black music and dance (1965, 1951, 1952). At this early stage in Brazilian and Cuban writings, however, blacks were explicitly seen as backward, primitive, and savage, and these studies were dedicated to the problem of how to overcome the crime, degradation, corruption, and cultural backwardness with which these populations threatened Brazilian or Cuban national development.

These authors often looked for African survivals, and one tradition of Afro-American studies continued in this vein, although largely stripped of the overtly racist ideologies that characterized the early material of Nina Rodrigues or Ortiz. This was the work of Melville Herskovits, who from the 1930s onwards produced a great deal of material on black culture in the Americas (see, for example, Herskovits 1966), although the search for African survivals is now less fashionable. More recently, a basic concern with black culture has been prominent in such works as Bastide (1971, 1978), Whitten (1974), and Whitten and Szwed (1970) and in a host of studies on Afro-Brazilian religion (see Brown 1986). There are many others who investigated black history and culture in their respective countries—Gonzalo Aguirre Beltrán in Mexico, Miguel Acosta Saignes in Venezuela, Ildefonso Pereda Valdés in Uruguay, to name but a few of the older generation—but they are too numerous to detail here (see Rout 1976 for references).

Meanwhile, there developed in Brazil during the 1940s a more sociological tradition, beginning with Gilberto Freyre, which introduced the concept of "racial democracy" and held that "with respect to race relations, the Brazilian situation is probably the nearest approach to paradise to be found anywhere in the world" (Freyre, quoted in Fontaine 1980, 122). Pierson's seminal study of blacks in the northeast of Brazil admitted race prejudice but also immediately denied it any real status: "Prejudice exists in Brazil, but it is *class* rather than *race* prejudice" (1942, 349). He saw Brazil as an example of a racial democracy in which there was no racial consciousness—even though color was a sign of status—because economic criteria were dominant and could offset racial markers (see Bastide 1957).

In the 1950s, the director of social sciences in UNESCO, the Brazilian Arthur Ramos, an Afro-Brazilian specialist, initiated a UNESCO-sponsored investigation of race relations in Brazil, intended originally to reveal how a racial democracy had emerged and to put this forward as a model for the rest of the world (Fontaine 1980; Graham 1970; Bastide 1957). This effort produced a mass of investigative work, unparalleled elsewhere in Latin America, although various scholars in other areas were at work on Afro-Latin themes at the time (see Rout 1976). There was no single perspective to this body of work, but it concentrated on tracing the transformation of a slave society into a class society and on the position of blacks in contemporary Brazilian society. The concept of racial democracy was generally not sustained (Dzidzienyo 1979), but there were different views on the relation of race to class and on how Brazilian society might evolve. Fernandes (1969) saw prejudice as an anachronistic hangover that would dissolve as the "competitive social order" of a class society expanded and became dominant, although white indifference to black and mulatto problems would have to be specifically challenged and changed. Cardoso (1962), Ianni (1966), Bastide (1965), and also van den Berghe (1967) tended to emphasize how racism did not disappear but adapted to changing circumstances as industrial capitalism expanded in southern Brazil, bringing greater competition and the dissolution of traditional white-black paternalism. Marvin Harris, who had participated in the UNESCO study and had laid some emphasis on prejudice and the possibility of increasing racial conflict in the town he studied (1952), later produced much more programmatic statements to the effect that "the issue of racial discrimination is scarcely a vital one" (1974, 63), due to the "structural inconsequence of racial factors" (1968, 264), which meant that "as far as behavior is concerned, 'races' do not exist for the Brazilians" (1974, 64). In his view, class was the major factor in Brazilian society.

The relations of race and class were thus unclear: race was seen variously as an anachronism, an integral part of capitalist society in Brazil, or as an almost insignificant epiphenomenon. The scenario for the future of race in Brazil was likewise unclear: the disappearance of race or its perpetuation? The status of *mestizaje,* too, remained uncertain. Whereas it was once hailed as the evidence of racial democracy and as a means for promoting it, the racism underlying it now received more attention (Skidmore 1974; Jackson 1976). Banton in an early review of the Brazilian literature noted that "to be mobile in this way [i.e., marrying a whiter person] blacks have to accept the valuations which put them at an initial disadvantage" (1967, 280). Nevertheless, other authors still emphasized the integrative effect of miscegenation. Solaún and Kronus (1973) held that in Cartagena, Colombia, the "miscegenation-tolerance syndrome" was a powerful force of integration and, they optimistically predicted, would expand as the economy expanded, ultimately demolishing discrimination. For Brazil, Harris laid emphasis on the "maximization of ambiguity" in racial identifications (1970; cf. Sanjek 1971) and the impact of this on undermining a thoroughgoing minority system (1974, 54). Degler (1971) held that miscegenation was no solution since by blurring boundaries it had robbed blacks of the potential for political solidarity that they would need to improve their position, as North American blacks had done. Banton in a later book thinks that "group" strategies of political protest are helpful only in the short term for people who already constitute a group (which he says blacks in Brazil do not), but that "in the long term" miscegenation may offer a solution (1983, 71). How long such a term might be Banton does not specify, but Degler notes the "glacial pace" of homogenization (1971, 193). Both Degler, in the 1986 preface to the second edition of his book, and Toplin (1981) think they detect a convergence between the United States and Brazil in terms of a decreasing boundedness and homogeneity of blacks in the former and an increasing black consciousness in the latter.

A more recent collection (Fontaine 1985) tends to side with Toplin and Degler: several authors document "increasing racial identity" and "black political mobilization" (Fontaine 1985, editor's introduction). One author, Silva, also criticizes Degler's idea that mulattoes receive better treatment than blacks and can thus escape through the "mulatto escape hatch." Degler thought that this hatch was the crucial difference between race relations in the Unites States and those in Brazil and accounted for its emergence mainly in terms of demographic ratios, and Portuguese machismo and family organization. Silva claims to show that mulattoes and blacks suffer almost equal discrimination and are better thought of as a single group (Silva 1985; see also Hasenbalg 1985).

All this, then, forms a general background to the present work, even though much of the debate has taken place in Brazil. In Colombia, the same controversy has not been apparent. As Friedemann shows in a comprehensive review of the literature (1984a), the main problem has been to get past the apparent "invisibility" of blacks on the academic scene. José Rafael Arboleda Llorente (1950, 1952) and Aquiles Escalante (1954, 1964), both students of Herskovits, set the basis for the study of blacks in Colombia with an ethnohistorical and cultural orientation (Friedemann 1984a, 542). Manuel Zapata Olivella has produced copious material on customs, songs, dances, myths, religion, and so on (see, for example, 1960–62, 1967). He has also been a powerful influence in bringing attention to the country's black population, being instrumental in realizing the First Congress of Black Culture in the Americas (see FCIF 1988) and in producing novels such as *Chambacú: Corral de negros* (1962) and *Changó, el gran putas* (1983). Rogerio Velásquez has published much "folkloric" and historical data for the northern Pacific region (e.g., 1959, 1961b). West (1957) wrote an invaluable historical geography of the Pacific region, and Price (1955) examined religious syncretism in both coastal regions. More recently, Nina de Friedemann has produced a steady stream of excellent and pioneering work (see Friedemann and Arocha 1986 for an account of much of this; see also Friedemann 1984a). Michael Taussig has also contributed some notable pieces (1978, chap. 3; 1980a; 1980b; 1987). Norman Whitten has written extensively on the Pacific lowlands cultural area of Ecuador and Colombia (1965, 1974; Whitten and Friedemann 1974).

Friedemann, Whitten, and Taussig have been important influences in the Colombian sphere as far as the present volume is concerned. Both Friedemann and Whitten tackled their theme from the perspective of adaptation, which gave a more solid anthropological basis for the study of black culture and social organization than the Herskovitsian and descriptive perspectives that had previously been dominant. It meant looking at black social and cultural forms in historical relation to ecological, economic, political, and social contexts, including the dominant nonblack society and, in Whitten's case, the international market (1974, 7). It meant looking at the social, economic, and political realities of black communities and at questions of racism and "black disenfranchisement" (Whitten 1974, 183). Whitten, for example, basing his 1965 study on San Lorenzo on the Pacific coast of Ecuador and including the whole "wet littoral" in a later book (1974), linked the history of the area to a boom-bust cycle based on international demand for local resources. This cycle dictated the changing ethnic mix of the region over time and hence influenced economic opportunities for blacks, ethnic relations, and concepts of blackness held by nonblacks. Friedemann also looked at black people's loss of land (1976) and at kinship organization in the Pacific region (1966–69), ethnic relations there (1977b), and social organization in a black village in the Caribbean region (1980). The perspective adopted by Whitten and Friedemann also entailed looking at the whole system of miscegenation and ideologies of *blanqueamiento* and unmasking the racism on which they are founded. Friedemann, especially, has been particularly concerned with correcting the "invisibility" of blacks in Colombia's accepted history and anthropology, uncovering the African contribution to Colombian society, and analyzing the development of black culture and its resistance to white domination. She uses this as a basis for encouraging the *reivindicación* (reclaiming) of black culture and the promotion of black consciousness as part of a more general claim for human rights and equality (1984a, 555).

Taussig's work on blacks has been rather different, generally part of larger and more complex arguments about the "fetishization of evil, in the image of the devil . . . an image which mediates the conflict between precapitalist and capitalist modes of objectifying the human condition" (1980a, xii); or about how "capitalist development of the Third World has added to the power of its sorcerers and magicians" (1980b, 217; see also 1987); or about the development of capitalist agriculture (1978, chap. 1). In the process, he elaborates a number of themes about black culture and society: the idea of black resistance to white domination, by means of constructing religious images and by means of constructing autonomous lifestyles; the myths of power constructed around subordinate peoples; the idea of a "moral topography" (1987, 253), of a geography of meaning.

My debt to these three authors, among others, will become clear in the following pages. I, too, look at a black region in an overall context, focusing on miscegenation, *blanqueamiento,* and national ideologies; on the development of black culture within a system of *mestizaje* and syncretism; on the idea of black resistance; on the powers constructed around the idea of blackness (a construction participated in, on unequal terms and for different motives, by blacks and non-blacks); and on the idea of landscape and topography. Friedemann identifies a dual process of black *resistencia* and *despersonalización* (1984a, 529), that is, resistance and depersonalization, or loss of identity, which she sees as characteristic of black behavior. Carrera Damas (1977) also refers to processes of flight from blackness and confrontation with the white world. These are clearly connected to the processes I outlined in the previous chapter.

In this book I develop these themes. The emphasis is on the black inhabitants of the Chocó, but the contradictory coexistence of discrimination and *mestizaje* forms the overarching framework for the book. The reason for this is that it is impossible to understand regional blackness in Colombia without consideration of the overall racial order in which it is located. While previous characterizations of *huida* and *enfrentamiento* have been pitched at a very general level, I seek to analyze the contradictory and complex relationships of discrimination and *mestizaje* in a much more detailed and concrete fashion, as they are embedded in local contexts of social relations. I examine *mestizaje* and *blanqueamiento* not just as ideologies, but as social practices, and, with the focus principally on the Chocó, I use detailed ethnographic material to analyze how these practices operate at a variety of different levels—regional, local, and personal—and in different domains—politics, marriage, housing, music. The moves between levels and domains of social practice reveal for the Chocoanos common dynamics in apparently very different circumstances, and this analysis helps reveal how the racial order of Colombia is constituted and reproduced through its twin processes of *mestizaje* and discrimination. The discovery of similarity underlying difference is not, however, an attempt to reduce all situations to a single principle. On the contrary, I emphasize the embeddedness of racial dynamics in contexts of social relations and look at sets of circumstances in which the racial order is structured in different ways by local conditions. This opens the way to seeing why Chocoanos sometimes "flee" and sometimes "confront," or more generally, how miscegenation and discrimination balance out in the overall system. It is not just a matter of race or of choice about race: the recursive relations between racial patterns and racial choices are structured, principally by economic factors, and some choices are more likely than others under certain conjunctures of circumstances.

The regionality of blackness in the Pacific coast region and the significance of local conjuncture draw attention to the importance of a spatial dimension. I suggest that the racial order is broken up by conjunctures of circumstances into regions or locales that appear very different from one another, but which are outcomes of the same processes. Colombia has long been seen as a country of regions: here, by examining the Chocó, but also Antioquia and the Caribbean coastal region, I look behind this common observation to reveal how region has become a powerful language of cultural and racial differentiation and how the country's racial order and its images of emerging nationhood are intimately bound up with a geography of culture. I look at space as a landscape of meaning, a "moral topography," exploring it as a metaphor for race and culture, but I also look at it as a means through which social relations constitute themselves in a concrete form. I argue that race has been regionalized in Colombia and that in certain contexts this is fundamental because the processes of frontier expansion operating in the first field site, and the processes of migration to the interior operating in the second field site then constitute contexts of social relations in which racial identities are a major factor. For the Pacific coast region, spatial relations involve racial relations because race and region overlap. This also helps to explain why I maintain a distinction between blacks and nonblacks, despite the nonwhite/white categorization that both Silva (1985) and Hasenbalg (1985) suggest. Blacks in Colombia are a smaller category and are much more regionally concentrated; the mixed population is just as much mestizo as mulatto due to the greater indian heritage. Therefore, while a white/nonwhite distinction may make more sense in Brazil, for Colombia I argue that a black/nonblack distinction is more appropriate in some contexts: it is one aspect of the way race relations are spatially structured (see also Whitten 1974, 199).

Finally, in understanding *mestizaje,* especially of a cultural but also of a physical nature, I contend that Taussig's idea of mythical images of "natural" black gifts and powers must be drawn into the analysis. This is an area that has barely been touched in this context. White fascination with blacks has been noted before (e.g., Levine 1977), especially with respect to the eroticization of black women (Bastide 1961; Venture Young 1977; Jackson 1976; Prescott 1985), but this has generally been viewed simply as an aspect of white prejudice. Here I link it into the overall dynamic of *mestizaje,* for some of the sexual union between blacks and nonblacks, and some of the cultural syncretism of music and dance in Colombia, are stimulated by nonblack ideas about the erotic, sensuous, physical nature they attribute to people they otherwise tend to disparage. These ideas are not simply created unilaterally by nonblacks, but are formed in the process of blacks looking at whites looking at blacks.

A Brief Outline

Part 2 examines the cultural topography of Colombia, focusing on the place of blackness. Colombia is a country of regions, and the most fundamental contrasts in the Colombian sense of place are between the Andean interior, the tropical coasts, and the Amazon jungle. Chapter 3 explores these basic contrasts in the cultural landscape of Colombia. The following two chapters have a dual purpose. They present Antioquia, a white-mestizo region, and the Caribbean coastal region, a mixed area but with strong black associations: these two areas crop up later in the text in relation to the Chocó and some familiarity with them is needed. Also however, I use these two regions to examine the historical process of *mestizaje* and discrimination, and the related processes of black community and adaptation to the nonblack world in each area, showing how they were structured in very different ways by local conjunctures of economic, political, and demographic forces. Apparently diametrically opposed outcomes have a common process underlying them.

Chapters 6 to 8 bring the black Chocó province of the Pacific coast region into focus, a region whose people provide the dynamic and substance for the rest of the book. I start with images of the area from the outsider perspective of nineteenth-century travelers' accounts, images that are still current today among Colombians from outside the region. The basic history of the province and *mestizaje* there are outlined as a complement to the processes that occurred in Antioquia and the Atlantic coast region. The Chocó is an example of a region where discrimination and black community were predominant forces, although they were never divorced from processes of adaptation and acceptance. The following chapter illustrates this by looking at Quibdó, the provincial capital, in the first half of the twentieth century. The biography of a famous Chocoano is used to show how, in the life of a single person, cultural adaptation and upward mobility, encouraged by white acceptance, finally came to grief against the barrier of white discrimination. This outcome was influenced by the specific circumstances of rather polarized and very hierarchical black-white relations in Quibdó at the time, but it also prefigured a transformation of some aspects of those relations. In effect, the blacks ousted the whites from political control of the region. Even here, however, *mestizaje* and *blanqueamiento* were important forces, with miscegenation and upward mobility interlocking to create a mulatto "elite."

The Chocoanos are poor, and yet their region is rich in certain resources. This contradiction is fundamental to the way the forces of miscegenation and discrimination have been and still are structured for them (e.g., via colonization and migration). In chapter 8, I turn to the economy of the Chocó, exploring this contradiction and highlighting the way the region's resources have been extracted and its population exploited for their labor power, while opportunities of economic progress for Chocoanos remain few. The economic position of the Chocó today is an extension of its colonial role, and it is this nexus of relations of regional inequality which is an integral aspect of race in the Chocó.

In part 3, I turn to the specific sites of fieldwork, focusing on the Chocoanos in a frontier and an urban context. The village of Unguía in the northern Chocó, an area as much within the Caribbean as the Pacific sphere of influence, is a context of colonization, a frontier zone in which capitalists, peasants, and merchants from the interior of the country are penetrating a peripheral region occupied previously by blacks (and some indians). A channel is opened up for *mestizaje,* economic activity, and, perhaps, advancement. Blacks try to take advantage of these economic opportunities, there is some cultural change, and some blacks find white or mestizo partners, with or without a conscious motive of *blanqueamiento*. But discrimination limits these forces of *mestizaje*. The situation is complex because Caribbean coastal people are present as well as Chocoanos and Antioqueños, but

45

overall the racial hierarchy is perpetuated and ethnic distinctiveness is maintained despite blurring of boundaries by interaction in work, friendship, and conjugal relations.

From colonization, I move to migration and the site of my second fieldwork: Medellín, capital of Antioquia. Here Chocoanos form a small and easily distinguishable black minority. Forces of dispersal, cultural adaptation, and physical race mixture are even stronger here than in the first site, but again black nucleation and congregation still exist as a means of coping with the city and with discrimination. I look first at the the history of the Chocoano presence in the city, before examining the urban economy, the work that Chocoanos do, and their role in the local political economy: discrimination and the chances of upward mobility are the main focus. I then turn to the Chocoanos' relation to the city's spatial structure and housing processes, focusing on two neighborhoods where there were concentrations of Chocoanos and ethnic conflicts and examining discrimination in the housing market. Processes of nucleation and dispersal are a central concern.

In part 4 I turn to the relationship of Chocoano blacks to their own culture and community and to nonblack culture, in this case the Antioqueño culture of Medellín and Unguía. In chapters 13 and 14 I look at nonblack images of blackness and black images of the nonblack worlds, tracing again the interplay of accommodation and discrimination, assimilation and resistance at an experiential level, using students' written essays on these themes and also interview material. Here I also bring out the nonblack fascination with supposed powers of blackness. In chapter 15, I pick up this theme again, examining processes of black congregation and cultural resistance, historically and more recently, using music as a focus. Here I trace the complex syncretism that occurs through the cultural hierarchy as white forms become black and return to the white world again: this pattern can be observed in Medellín itself. Throughout, a recurrent feature is the fascination of the nonblack world with black music, which becomes popular there in an adapted form. In chapter 16, I look at processes of *blanqueamiento,* in Unguía and in Medellín, analyzing the factors that structure its practice. I also reexamine Degler's (1971) idea of a mulatto escape hatch and Silva's (1985) criticisms of it, assessing their relevance to my material.

In the penultimate chapter, forces of black nucleation versus assimilation are examined in their relation to black identity and political solidarity at a regional and collective level, starting with ideas about equality and hierarchy suggested by Taussig (1980a). I suggest that within black communities of the Chocó there is an ethic of essential human equality signaled by blackness, but it is in tension with national hierarchies of prestige and status which are entailed in the process of *blanqueamiento* and which penetrate into the black community itself. This tension is manifest in accusations of egotism and envy, as people try to both police equality and compete for prestige. The resulting infighting undermines solidarity, and this is seen as a direct result of the nature of Colombia's racial order. Finally, in the conclusion, I look at broader issues about race, class, and the nature of racial categories, drawing from the Colombian material some important general considerations. I end by raising the issue of continuity and change and the role of black consciousness and protest as a political force for the future.

II

Cultural

Topography

3

A Sense of Place:

The Geography of Culture

in Colombia

Hacer patria es matar costeños, entonces haga patria.

A whole history remains to be written of *spaces*—which would at the same time be the history of *powers* (both these terms in the plural)—from the great strategies of geopolitics to the little tactics of the habitat.

To make sense of Colombia, the visitor, or the reader, must acquire a sense of place, not just in the physical sense of mountains, valleys, savannas, and jungles, but in the other meaning aptly captured by the phrase "a sense of place," as in "to know one's place." It is not simply a matter of knowing where you are going—up, down, backwards, forwards—on the official map but also of sensing your way across the almost tactile, palpable terrain of the coastal smell of dried fish or the Andean smell of pine trees, the feel of tropical heat or rarified mountain air, the brash sound of Caribbean salsa or the gentle guitar melodies of the interior of the country, the sight of African black or Spanish swarthy white. It means being able to see the old roots embedded in the lines, colors, and contours, roots still flowing with colonial sap despite the burgeoning of gaudy modernity. In Taussig's recent phrase, it means getting to know the "moral topography" (1987, 253), the terrain of reputation. In his words, "geography is also a map of social history and a cosmological charter represented in to-

51

pography . . . physical space . . . is also semantic space" (1980b, 220). This cultural geography is not a neutral cultural construction but derives from dominant ideologies and discourses that have a hegemonic status since they are propagated by the most powerful classes and regions of the country. The moral topography is not just a mental map but "a mosaic of articulated differences in which heaven and hell, virtue and corruption, caste and class distinctions and the mnemonic function of landscape in sustaining collective memory" are inscribed (Taussig 1980b, 220). The black tropical coasts are looked down on by the temperate Andean white and mestizo interior, which speaks with a shudder of the Pacific coast's snakes, humidity, malaria, and blackness.

Space and Society

Regions and the geography of culture are important aspects of writing about race and nation in Colombia. But before I explain why this is so in specific terms, I want to examine the idea of spatiality, because in a sense race in Colombia is not simply "reflected" in spatial categories, it is constituted by spatial structures.

Anthropology and sociology have tended in the past to ignore space as an analytically significant dimension (in contrast to the importance attached to time and to history). Equally, geography during some of its lifetime tended to divorce itself from social theory and attempted to constitute a "spatial science" in which spatial patterns were explained by spatial processes. More recently, the extensive criticism of positivism in geography has reinstated the more explicit consideration of social processes, and thus of social theory (see Gregory and Urry 1985). For many social theorists—or sociologists and anthropologists engaged in the analysis of social phenomena—space continues to be a dimension that is either taken for granted or seen as a mirror or symbolic expression of certain social structures or concepts. Thus, for example, the spatial ordering of a lowland indian *malocca* expresses certain aspects of social structure, just as the arrangement in space of a city's various parts "says something" about the society that created the urban environment. Perhaps an exception to this tendency was the Chicago school, which, with its interest in human ecology, made spatial structures an integral part of their theories, seeing communities engaged at some level in a biotic struggle for an urban niche. More recently, Giddens has opened up the field with his concepts of time-space routinization and distanciation (see Giddens 1984). In human geography, too, there has been debate about social relations and spatial structures.

The view that in broad terms seems to represent a consensus among those currently engaged in the debate rejects the possibility that space has its own inherent nature; instead, "the significance of spatial relations depends upon the particular character of the social objects in question" (Urry 1981, 458, quoted in Saunders 1986, 276). "Thus space is a set of *relations* between entities and is not a substance. As a result, therefore, there is liable to be a category mistake involved if we talk of 'society' and 'space' as interacting" (Urry 1985, 25). Instead, space and society are inseparable: Soja contends that "spatiality *is* society . . . its concretization, its formative constitution" (Soja 1985, 95); or, as Gregory says, "spatial structure is not merely the arena within which class conflicts express themselves, but also the domain within which—and, in part, through which—class relations are constituted" (1978, 120). Paraphrasing Giddens on the concept of social structure, Soja states that space is "both the *medium* and the *outcome* of social action and relationship" (Soja 1985, 94). In concrete analysis this seems to mean that society produces spatial structures (through the process of being constituted as a concrete society) but that these spatial arrangements act as a constraint on, and a set of resources for, further developments of society. Once social relations have a given spatial form, this affects the way those relations can change and develop (Harvey 1982; Massey 1984; see also Gregory 1989).

Part of this more recent approach to space and society is the breaking up of holistic concepts of society into what Giddens (1984, 118) calls "locales" or more generally into regions, although these are always seen in the context of their relationships of interdependence (Massey 1984, 118; Gregory 1989, 84). For if society is constituted spatially (as well as temporally), this tends to occur by means of creating "pockets of local order" (Hägerstrand, cited in Gregory 1989, 84), which are concentrations of certain social interactions—in Giddens' phraseology, "the zoning of time-space in relation to routinized social practices" (1984, 119). The local regions are, however, interdependent and connected, and their interconnectedness is part of the spatial constitution of society: "The uniqueness of place and the constantly evolving and shifting systems of interdependence are two sides of the same coin" (Massey 1984, 120). An examination of the relation between space and society thus leads to a consideration of how society must constitute itself in a spatially differentiated or regional way.

This provides a background for a consideration of space and race in Colombia. Colombia is a highly regionalized country, and for historical reasons race also has a regional dimension. There are oppositions between the "black" coasts, the "white-mestizo" interior, and the "indian" Amazon lowlands, and these broad and inclusive categories are used at a very general level: race is often spoken of in a locative voice, as it were, and this is because racial identities are broadly regionalized. More pertinent, in some contexts, such as that of the Pacific coast, social relations that involve racial identities operate through regional structures, and in this sense race relations are regional relations. Spatial structures can be seen as the outcome of and the medium for social relations that have a discourse of race.

The Regionalization of Race in Colombia

The operation of *mestizaje* has not occurred uniformly over the different regions of Colombia. Different economic, political, and demographic factors have brought about a number of distinct regional patterns that correspond in the broadest sense to the major differences in the country's topography. Keeping things simple for the moment, we can distinguish the Andean highland ranges, the two coastal regions—Pacific to the west and Atlantic or Caribbean to the north—and the rolling plains and jungles of the Amazon and Orinoco basins to the east. Harris (1974) has argued for Latin America generally that the Andean highlands tended to have large, dense, settled indian populations with fairly advanced political differentiation; the main examples are the Inca and Aztec empires. This facilitated the exploitation of indian labor, partly because political channels already existed to organize the work force. The lowland regions, in contrast, had sparser, less settled indian populations with a lower degree of political specialization: they tended to be more refractory to domination and often more hostile. He then goes on to argue that in the lowlands the indian labor force tended to disintegrate quite soon under the colonial regime and was replaced by slaves, while in the highlands the Spanish could continue to exploit indian labor with relative ease. The main contrast then is between Brazil and the Hispanic American regimes in Meso-America and the Andes. In the former zone, slaves were numerous, and a free class, mostly mixed, soon emerged, outnumbering the whites, blacks, and indians. In the latter, the indians remained a major component, and the free mixed group was smaller. Overall, Colombia fits into the Brazilian side of Harris's contrast. By 1770, the Audiencia of Santa Fe de Bogotá (roughly Colombia minus some of the southern area) had less than 20 percent indians and nearly 50 percent *libres* (free people of all colors, except the *blancos*). The Audiencia of Quito (roughly Ecuador and some of southern Colombia) had 50 percent indians and only 10 percent *libres*.

Within Colombia, however, the situation was more complex. At this level, there was also a highland/lowland contrast in that the Andean highlands held the relatively large and densely settled Chibcha chiefdoms, while the lowlands generally had sparser and less specialized cultural groups. Under the colonial regime, the indian population as a whole disintegrated both through mortality and through the cultural assimilation of indians into the ranks of the *libres*. By 1778, almost half of those who remained within the census classification of *indio* were in the eastern highland provinces of Santa Fe de Bogotá and Tunja, although these nearly seventy thousand individuals formed less than 20 percent of the local population, compared with 40 percent of *libres* and 37 percent of *blancos* (Pérez Ayala 1951). Although the highlands held the largest concentration of indians, significant communities of this ethnic category were censused elsewhere, notably in the lowland Caribbean region, in the plains of the Amazon basin, and in the Pacific littoral (see table 1 in appendix A).

Slaves were concentrated in regions where indian labor was problematic. Difficulties stemmed from the scarcity or hostility or isolation of the indian population or because the main labor requirement was in the gold mines, where indians were generally considered less productive than African slaves and less resistant to the rigors of the work. Such was their mortality in the mines that in 1729 a royal edict outlawed their use for this purpose (King 1945, 299). Slaves were concentrated primarily in the gold mines of the Pacific coast region, where they formed a majority until outnumbered by *libres* in the late eighteenth or early nineteenth century. In the more southerly part of this littoral, the mines were generally owned by Spaniards or Creole whites living in Popayán, and their slaves also worked the gold placers and haciendas in the southern Cauca Valley (Taussig 1980a, 46). There were also large numbers of slaves in the gold placers of Antioquia, although they were more dispersed here, and the Caribbean coastal region had a significant concentration of slaves, about a third of which clustered in the slave port of Cartagena and its environs.

The Spanish presence began, naturally enough, on the Atlantic coast, and permanent ports were established at Cartagena and Santa Marta. But the English pirates harassed these towns, the climate was fierce, malarial, and with abundant mosquitoes, the soil would yield only one crop a year, and there were still hostile indian groups in the hinterlands. In the Andean interior, specifically in the eastern cordillera, the conquistadors found the Chibchas, a more favorable climate, and easier agricultural production. Eventually, the Andean region became a kind of "corridor" running from north to south, as Francisco Silvestre described it in 1789, where most of the power and wealth of colonial New Granada was concentrated (1950, 81). Whites settled overwhelmingly in the eastern highland provinces of Tunja and Santa Fe de Bogotá. Here in 1778, some 128,000 whites were counted, out of a total of slightly more than 188,000 for the Audiencia of Santa Fe as a whole. Apart from this area, whites were found in large numbers in the city of Cartagena and in the provinces of Antioquia and Mariquita (a small province in the Magdalena River valley, just west of Bogotá). Outside the Audiencia, but still within contemporary Colombia's borders, the province of Popayán had a large white population, centered principally in the city of Popayán itself. In fact, by 1778, within the area now called Colombia, the provinces of Bogotá, Tunja, Cartagena, and Popayán held two-thirds of the total population, not just the whites.

Different regions thus emerged with varying proportions of each racial group. In general terms, the Andean highlands held the majority of whites and indians, the Amazon plains and jungles were dominated by indians, and the coasts had a strong black element with not inconsiderable numbers of indians (see table 1 in appendix A; see also Smith 1966 for a contemporary survey). In most areas, *libres* were a majority, but the racial mix of this category varied greatly.

The proportions of Spaniards, blacks, and indians present were only one factor in the racial mix of each region. Processes of *mestizaje* also differed regionally, according to the local economic and social context. Thus, for example, the large numbers of black slaves in Antioquia mixed to such an extent that the region's black heritage is today obvious only in certain lowland mining districts. The slave component of the Caribbean coastal region, proportionally less of the total than in Antioquia, has engendered a much more apparent contemporary black presence, although it is most obvious in a quite narrow belt along the littoral itself and along the lower Magdalena River. Again, in the Pacific coastal region, black-indian mixture has been limited compared with the Caribbean coastal region where colonial policy encouraged it.

The location of indian or black labor and the concentration of Spanish settlement in the highlands created a pattern of regionalization which was reinforced by other factors. The country's exceptionally rugged terrain and the communication difficulties it imposed combined to "fragment the economy into an agglomeration of loosely integrated and largely autonomous regional economies" (McFarlane 1977, 23). The regions were under one viceroyalty administration and had an interregional trade, but they were by no means well integrated, and transport was a major problem. For the colonial era, Twinam tells us that the journey from Cartagena to Medellín took fifty-two days, while the round trip to Honda, the port on the Magdalena for access to Bogotá, took twenty-six days (1982, 83–84). Marzahl (1978, 7–8) notes that the trip from Popayán to Cartagena took three months, while Honda-Cartagena could take thirty to sixty days (Gilmore and Harrison 1948, 336). Each region had to channel its links to Europe through Cartagena, often via Honda, and it was in many ways as strongly linked to Spain as it was to the other regions of New Granada. The whole economy of the viceroyalty depended fundamentally on the exportation of precious metals and some animal skins, in return for which luxury goods were imported from Europe. Agriculture was limited and provided for regional demands and a certain amount of interregional trade.

Independence did not initially alter this situation—in fact, rather the reverse. Greater trade with other European countries, especially England, integrated select areas even more closely into an external economy, "leaving the vast remainder of the country a mosaic of autarchic units" (Taussig 1987, 296). Transportation improved only slowly. The British consul reported in 1889 on the "terrible condition of the chief roads," noting that Bogotá's road link to Honda on the Magdalena, and thus to the outside world, was almost impassable and that the time taken "transporting goods over that short distance ha[d] been greater than that taken from Europe to Honda" (quoted in McGreevey 1971, 245–46). As late as 1913, Phanor Eder could still write: "In the matter of transportation Colombia is still in the middle ages." In 1919 Colombians and Germans together founded the first airline in the Americas, which in 1940 became AVIANCA, the present national Colombian airline, but Parsons wrote in 1949: "Despite the penetration of railroads, trucks and aircraft, the pack mule and the pack ox remain indispensable to the mountain-bound Antioqueño economy. Loaded pack trains still tread the streets of Medellín every morning" (1968, 160). Meanwhile, regional oligarchies ruled "at a time when nationality had not been constituted and [they were] faced with the absence of a homogeneous class which had a national sphere of domination" (Tirado Mejía 1984, 347). Power shifts "led from centralism to provincial fragmentation, then to federalism through the consolidation of provinces to form states, and finally in 1861 to the creation of sovereign states," sanctioned by the Liberal constitution of 1863 as the United States of Colombia, a situation that prevailed until 1886 when Rafael Núñez imposed a strongly centralist regime once more (Park 1985, 15).

What this amounts to is that in the process of Colombian society constituting itself spatially, or becoming concrete in space, regions were created and these had very different racial mixes. In short, at a very general level, race became regionalized. The Andean highlands emerged as a white-mestizo region with indian-white mixtures being common. The Pacific coast became a mainly black region. The Caribbean coast developed a tri-ethnic mix with strong black and indian heritage in the lower classes and some purer black and indian enclaves. And the Amazon region remained predominantly indian. There is a distinctive spatial pattern to the overall structure of Colombian nationhood and its racial order.

Given this spatial differentiation, contexts can arise where blacks (and/or indians) form a majority of the population and have a relatively definite identity as blacks vis-à-vis others who are classified, and classify themselves, as belonging to a nonblack world in terms of their socioracial categorization and their cultural behavior. These contexts are naturally varied. In some cases, notably that of the Pacific coast, whole regions, easily identifiable ecologically and geographically, are "black": relations of race and region overlap heavily (Friedemann 1966–69, 1974; Friedemann and Arocha 1986; Whitten 1974; Whitten and Friedemann 1974; West 1957; Villa 1985; Córdoba 1983; Zuluaga 1986). Other contexts are much more localized and community oriented. In the Caribbean coastal region, there are contexts ranging from some coastal villages (e.g., Berrugas, La Boquilla, Barú, San Bernardo del Viento) to some more inland villages (e.g., San Onofre, Palenque de San Basilio), to rural areas along the coastline, to the elite neighborhoods of Cartagena where blacks form a servant class, and to the low-income shanties of the same city (see Fals Borda 1976, 1979, 1981, 1984, 1986; Friedemann 1978, 1980; Friedemann and Patiño Rosselli 1983; Escalante 1954; Price 1955; Partridge 1974; Uribe and Uribe 1975). A further example is the Cauca Valley, both north and south of the dividing line between the two departments of Cauca and Valle del Cauca. Here black peasants descended from the slaves and free blacks that worked on or lived near the large haciendas and placer mines around Puerto Tejada and Santander form a population that has its own black identity (Friedemann 1976; Taussig 1980a, Atencio Babilonia and Castellanos Córdova 1982; Friedemann and Arocha 1986). In all these situations, circumstances have combined to create identifiable black communities with a certain cohesive identity as blacks in their relations with nonblacks.

For the Pacific coast, the fact that social relations of race have developed a regionalized form means that the study of those relations and their change over time is embedded in a series of regional relations. In this sense "space is both the medium and the outcome of social action and relationship." Significant nexuses of race-region relations are constituted by two important processes that are part of

Colombia's economic and social development: the expansion of the frontier and migration from poorer to richer regions. In each case, these processes can become means by which the typical Latin American ambiguities surrounding the definition of blackness and nonblackness become reduced, there is more agreement in claims and ascriptions of racial identities, and black/nonblack oppositions can occur, forming important exceptions to the so-called "maximization of ambiguity" (Harris 1970). In each case, too, hegemonic notions of *blanqueamiento* are brought to bear. For while the dominant notion of national identity associates progress with whitening, progress is also connected to territorial integration through colonization and migration. In this vision, as the nation becomes one territorially, it also becomes one racially and culturally.

The Frontier and the Incorporation of Black Enclaves

The black regions, localities, and enclaves are often peripheral, but they are not isolated. Places such as Puerto Tejada (near Cali) or La Boquilla (near Cartagena) are much more closely connected to major national centers than, say, a riverine settlement in the Pacific coast region, but all have links of some kind. These regions and communities are thus to a greater or lesser extent involved in the forces and pressures that I outlined in the first chapter. In some cases, the links of black communities with the nonblack world are created and intensified by their location in the expanding frontier zone of the national political economy, which tends to increasingly incorporate areas such as the Pacific coastal region into its compass.

Viewed from a long-term perspective, much of the history of Colombia has been one of expansion from the main colonial centers of population around Bogotá and Tunja in the east, Popayán in the southwest, and Cartagena in the north. After about 1850, an export agricultural economy expanded in Colombia, based on short-lived booms in tobacco, cotton, and cinchona bark (from which quinine is extracted) and on more stable exports in coffee and bananas (and more recently marijuana and cocaine). Both small peasant colonists (*colonos*) and entrepreneurs began to exploit forest resources and, more important, land in the temperate and subtropical middle and lower elevations of western and northern Colombia, until then relatively sparsely occupied and unexploited (LeGrand 1986). Generally, *colonos* went first, often as much pushed out of the older regions of settlement by *minifundismo,* growing polarization of landholding and political conflict, as drawn into the frontier areas by the new opportunities of the export agricultural economy. They were accompanied in some cases and more often succeeded by larger entrepreneurs, land-owners, and speculators who took the lion's share of what had been *baldíos*, public land, by fair means or foul, often pushing the smaller *colonos* aside in the process (LeGrand 1986; Fals Borda 1979; Havens and Flinn 1970; Parsons 1952, 1968). The "frontier," then, has a long history during which ever-greater areas of Colombia have been incorporated into the national political economy. The driving force has been that of capital accumulation, responding to both international and national factors (Foweraker 1981).

The frontier, however, is not a single homogeneous event. The Pacific coast, for example, has been a frontier zone since early colonial times. The original indigenous population has witnessed colonization first by Spanish miners and their slave gangs, then by free or refugee black *colonos*. Republican elites maintained some mining and commercial interests there, while rubber tappers and others exploited some forest resources at certain times (Brisson 1895; Parsons 1967). The allocation of public lands to entrepreneurs, or their usurpation of them, also affected the area (LeGrand 1986, 52–53). In this century, international mining enterprises established large-scale operations in certain areas, while more recently entrepreneurs from the interior of the country have invested in mining activities. Timber extraction oriented to both national and international markets has developed considerably. Where good land for ranching exists, a process of colonization by small *colonos* and larger entrepreneurs has occurred (Parsons 1967; Wade 1984; see also Whitten 1965). Alternatively, development projects have sought to increase black peasant productivity. In addition, while one effect of all these activities has been to incorporate the region more into the national economy and bureaucracy, its continued relative isolation has attracted the cultivation of coca leaf and marijuana in particular areas. The Pacific coast, then, has long been at the frontier of the national, and through this the international, economy, never isolated from it but never fully incorporated into it. Recently, however, the kind of post-1850s expansion which pushed the national economy beyond the old colonial population centers—an expansion carried out by mainly mestizo and white colonists and entrepreneurs—has penetrated more definitively into the area, not necessarily through the colonization of land, but also through mining, commerce, and timber extraction. (Cf. Whitten 1974, 7–9, 74–80. He sees the "social demography" of the Pacific region as hinging on "the demand by world markets for natural resources in the wet littoral.")

The expanding frontier is not simply an economically motivated penetration but is also seen from the perspective of the center as an expansion of progress and civilization into previously benighted areas. It is a consolidation of the Colombian nation by an extension of the cultural mores of the center to the boundaries of the national territory, drawing the periphery into the process of *mestizaje*, understood as *blanqueamiento* (Stutzman 1981; Whitten 1985, 45). This puts pressure on local instances of black culture by counterposing them more sharply to variants of national nonblack culture. It brings into focus the opposition between the black and white nodes of the Colombian racial and cultural order (and often the indian node as well), an opposition that is usually blurred by a great range of intermediate mixed types. Here, however, the locals are generally identified, and identify themselves as blacks, while the outsiders are commonly categorized, and categorize themselves, in a way that opposes both mestizo and *blanco* together to the local black community (cf. Schubert 1981, Whitten 1974, 199). The immigrant representatives of the culture of the interior of the country are generally in control of the economic structures that become established in these frontier zones. The basic hierarchy of culture, power, and race is thus reestablished in the local context but now in a more acute form, since the lowly status of black culture is constantly reiterated by the success of the nonblack immigrants and by their often deprecatory attitudes towards blacks and black culture. There is pressure on the blacks to adapt culturally, and such adaptation may bring economic benefits as well in terms of increased access both to local bureaucratic institutions that form part of the encroaching political economy and to the economic opportunities controlled by the immigrant whites and mestizos. Not all the blacks adapt in this way, however. This is partly because not all of them can hope to gain access to the local opportunities created by the expanding frontier: on the contrary, a minority do so. Therefore they rely on the networks and resources of the black world and reconstitute themselves as communities with their own strategies of survival and advancement (Whitten 1974; Whitten and Friedemann 1974). An integral aspect of this is the exclusive tendencies of the immigrants, manifested in racist attitudes, who retain control of economic opportunities within their group and deny the blacks access to these. By adopting cultural behavior that the immigrants see as more appropriate, blacks may overcome their exclusivity to some extent, but unless the black person abstracts him- or herself entirely from the black social and cultural matrix—and sometimes even then—residual exclusivity and racism remain. Furthermore, as I noted earlier, acceptance of blacks is conditional not only on their adopting nonblack mores, but also on the individualistic nature of their adaptation. If blacks as a category threaten to become competitive, racism tends to harden and ethnic boundaries are more tightly drawn (cf. Whitten 1974, 187; see also van den Berghe 1967; Harris 1952, 80; Bastide 1965, 21 for comments on this process in Brazil).

Black Migration to the Cities

The increasing incorporation of frontier zones is one major nexus of black/nonblack relations in Colombia. The very nature of the frontier zone gives rise to the opposite process: the migration of blacks out of their black regions and communities to the more economically active areas in search of work, to simply survive, or with hopes of advancement. Black migration is a varied phenomenon. Blacks from the Caribbean coastal region tend to converge on Cartagena and Barranquilla but also go further afield to Medellín and Bogotá. Blacks from the southern Cauca Valley generally go to Cali but may also go as far as Ecuador (West 1957, 107; Schubert 1981). Migration out of the Pacific region has been multidirectional, destinations including Ecuador, Panama, the Caribbean coastal region, and the interior of the country (West 1957, 107). The extent to which emigration gives rise to a context in which black and nonblack identities lose the ambiguity of their definition and become fairly clear and oppositional depends on the nature of the destination. Migrants from the Pacific coast region to Cartagena and Barranquilla, for example, while they may be distinguished culturally by local blacks (and even held to be inferior: the "real" blacks), will not create such an opposition in their own right, but rather slot into structures that already exist. In Cartagena, for example, oppositions occur in certain contexts, such as the black servant class in the nonblack elite suburbs, and there is also a generalized correspondence of race and class. Overall, however, *mestizaje* has had too long a history there to create the kind of black/nonblack opposition found within the Pacific region. The same is true of Cali, although again in certain contexts black communities can be identified within the city (e.g., Ashton 1970).

The situation is altogether different when blacks migrate to Medellín or Bogotá, where the indigenous black population is practically invisible. Here black migrants form a very distinct minority. As is generally the case, migration obeys primarily economic motives, as does the increasing incorporation of the Pacific frontier zones, but again issues of race, cultural and physical *mestizaje, blanqueamiento,* and nationhood become apparent. In the city, the pressures affecting blacks and black culture are even more powerful than in the Pacific region. First, the blacks are very much in the minority, a fact that in one sense encourages their acceptance on an individualistic basis and which also multiplies the pressures inducing the adaptation that such an acceptance requires. Second, the migrants are on foreign territory: they are the strangers, and there is little chance of retrenching into an already established black culture. Third, cities such as Medellín and Bogotá are acknowledged centers of wealth, progress, political power, and whiteness.

The weak position of the blacks as strangers is therefore compounded by the forceful presence of white-mestizo culture encapsulated in its quintessential urban form. Blacks generally come into this confrontation as poor, uneducated, rural people who mostly enter the lowest strata of city society, and this hampers still further the possibility of taking an assertive stance with respect to black culture. A sharp contrast emerges between the city and its nonblack culture and the black migrants whose ways are seen as typically rustic, untutored, and black. Nonblack rural migrants may also suffer from association with the "country bumpkin" image, but black culture is seen as even further down the hierarchy of civilization and urbanity. Blacks have left areas classified from the center's perspective as primitive and peripheral and have penetrated into the nation's territorial and cultural heartland. To conform to this environment is seen by the center as a logical choice in favor of progress, modernity, and national unity, and blacks too feel the force of this logic.

Whatever the pressures persuading blacks to adopt different cultural forms and perhaps find lighter-skinned partners, the opposite process also operates. Blacks use a black ethnic network to cope with housing and employment in the city; they experience discrimination, both in these spheres and on the street; there is a loyalty to certain aspects of their own culture and, for some, a conscious assertion of their desire for black people and black culture to be respected as such. These factors create positive resistance to the wholesale adoption of forms identified with local city culture, and, to some extent, there is a spatial component in their manifestation. Black nuclei, temporary and permanent, form in certain neighborhoods and become points of congregation. Resistance to cultural assimilation, however, does not mean the simple "survival" of black rural forms in the city. These too change and adapt without necessarily losing their identity as black culture. In effect, new urban forms of black culture are being elaborated.

In any case, the option of whether to adapt or resist is not just a question of free will. Choice is structured by urban processes of economic consolidation and housing, which involve factors of time and family cycle and which affect the spatial distribution of blacks in the city.

Colombian nationhood is a relational totality in the sense that any region, albeit ambiguously and contestably bounded, exists in relation to others, and the meanings attached to each derive in part from relations of difference. Thus, for example, the Atlantic coastal region is "black" in relation to the Andean interior, but "not so black" in relation to the Pacific coast. The terms *costeño* (coastal dweller of Atlantic or Pacific coastal region) and *cachaco* (literally, "dandy," a typical term for someone "from" the interior) may thus be in relational opposition, dividing both coasts from the interior and implying an equally relational opposition between blacker and whiter. But there is also opposition between the Atlantic and the Pacific coast, the former not so black, poor, or peripheral as the latter. Depending on the context in which relational oppositions are being established, *costeño* can then be used both as a general synonym for *negro* and as a way of distinguishing lighter-skinned Atlantic Costeños from their blacker co-regionals, implicitly categorized as *negros*. In the first case the whiter interior contrasts with the blacker coasts, considered together; in the second, the not-so-black elements of the Atlantic coast contrast with the local "blacks," who are by implication thrown together with those in the Pacific coast region.

These relations of difference, however, are far from democratic, and the people of the interior tend to arrogate to themselves the privilege of original presence, consigning the peripheries to a derivative status defined in terms of absences—of wealth, progress, and whiteness. In fact, of course, it is a poor black periphery that makes possible the affirmation of a central wealthy nonblackness, which is always in fact relative and contingent. The inscription of difference in landscape is fundamentally important not only because this constitutes certain social relations (involved in migration, colonization) in racialized ways, but also because difference is experienced in a spatially embodied fashion. One travels bodily from hot to cool, from black to white, when moving from the Pacific coast to Bogotá: it is in this sense that landscape has such a mnemonic function in "sustaining collective memory" (Taussig 1980b, 220).

The regionalization of race gives an added dimension to the constitution of Colombian nationhood, with territorial, moral, and racial integration mirroring one another, and it also presents a framework for understanding the specific contexts of my fieldwork: the frontier (Unguía) and the city (Medellín). For it is in the relations of the Chocoanos with people from neighboring regions who are also present in these contexts that the meat of the analysis lies. Unguía, located in the Chocó but near the Panamanian border, is an area traditionally associated as much with Caribbean Costeños as with Chocoanos; more recently, whites and mestizos from the temperate Andean highlands of Antioquia have also penetrated heavily. In the city context, the Chocoanos confront a majority of Antioqueños, since Medellín is the provincial capital of Antioquia. Both the fact that differences and similarities are relationally constituted and that this occurs in a hierarchical frame of meaning and power are important features of what happens to Chocoanos in the frontier context, where Costeños and Antioqueños are present, and in the city context, where Antioqueños rule the roost. Accordingly, in the next two chapters I look at Antioquia and the Atlantic coast in order to see how both their realities and their reputations have emerged, and how *mestizaje* and discrimination have been structured by regional conjunctures of economy and demography to give rise to very different outcomes. This will help to illuminate what happens in Unguía and in Medellín.

4

Antioquia

There is a myth of *la raza antioqueña* which eclectically blends regional history, literature, geography, anthropology, folk legend, sociology, economics, and psychology to argue that Antioqueños form a specific race, a distinct culture and a probably superior people in Colombia.

The Antioqueños, or *paisas* as they are commonly known by themselves and others, are crucial figures in this book in several ways. First, the Antioqueños have a particularly strong sense of regional ethnic identity which is a result of specific local economic and political processes. Their identity is also an important factor in organizing and justifying in an informal way their colonization of other, poorer parts of the country, such as the Chocó. Second, part of *paisa* ethnic identity is a myth of racial purity and lack of black and indian heritage. Many Antioqueños, even in the poorer classes, are light skinned and Caucasian looking. In fact, the reputed absence of black presence and heritage is quite false, but the myth does inadvertently reveal a history of powerful processes of race mixture which to some extent bleached out the blackness that had been prominent in the colonial population. Antioquia is therefore a prime example of a region where economic, demographic, and political processes structured *mestizaje* in such a way as to encourage the dispersal of blackness. The mythical celebration of whiteness is a symptom of this process but also a cause insofar as it expresses the overall ideology of *blanqueamiento* which spurs the dispersal of blackness.

Epigraph: Ann Twinam (1982, 8).

Third, as one of the richest regions in the country, Antioquia is the source of many merchants and capitalists who colonize the Chocó and the Atlantic coast region. It is not only capitalists who venture forth, however, since Antioquia, although relatively wealthy as a region, still suffers from great inequality of income and land distribution, prompting emigration of peasants and traders in search of betterment. As a rich region, Antioquia is also the destination of many Chocoano (and Costeño) migrants, who engage mainly in menial labor. Last, as such, the Antioqueños form a major counterpoint of nonblackness to which the black Chocoanos and, to a lesser extent, the Costeños relate. Relations between Antioquia and the Chocó form the main nexus of the regional and race relations examined in this book.

Paisa Identity

Seen on the map of Colombia, our region resembles a rapacious giant who looks and sets out towards the sea, where hope springs green in the jungle. To the east it has its geographic profile caressed by the river of the motherland: the Magdalena. It raises its head in pursuit of the Caribbean Sea and settles its talons on the limits with Old Caldas, from which it was separated in 1905, and pours its inexhaustible treasures into the veins of the Cauca, the Porce and the Nechí rivers.

A portrait of authentic Antioqueñeity. The Antioqueño: emotive, impressionable, ingenuous, brusque, noble, strong, spiritual and loyal; jocular, demonstrative, lively, protective of his property, his love and his family's daily bread. The *paisa* is a rover and an adventurer and is to be found far and wide; he is captivated by travel and he is gone. The Antioqueño is the piper of Giradota, the *trovador* of Concordia, the balladeer of Titiribí or Angelópolis; he is the muleteer of the paths of Urrao or Angostura, the gold-panner of the Porce river, a horse-breaker in Salgar, shaft-miner in Zaragoza, he sings of all places, of women, of flowers and of the landscape in polished verse in which is also revealed the thinker, the scholar or the philosopher. He is everything, because of everything he has a part: peasant, businessman, industrialist, enamored of work, inventor, drinker of *aguardiente,* and he puts himself in the hands of the Virgen of Carmen.

That is Antioquia. And God keeps his proven virtues in the Faith of the elders; let it not lose sight of the image of its race and the dictates of its history; let it glorify its heritage, ever singing the verses of Epifanio. . . . Let it carry the plough in its hands . . . let it free itself from the centralist yoke . . . let Antioquia sing with Gregorio Gutiérrez his poem to the maize plant, his song to Aures and the dreams of the little hut with the great Suárez.

(Glossary: Old Caldas is now Risaralda, Quindío, and Caldas. The place names [Giradota, etc.] are all municipalities of Antioquia. Epifanio Mejía is an Antioqueño poet, as is Gregorio Gutiérrez; the latter was born in a little hut [*choza*] which is still preserved intact as a monument; he wrote a famous poem eulogizing maize, a staple of the Antioqueño diet. Marco Fidel Suárez was an Antioqueño, son of a washerwoman, who rose to be president of the republic.)

This emotive, flowery, and assertive celebration of *paisa* identity, taken from the pamphlet *Agenda de Antioquia* (Antonio González 1982), is unashamedly brazen in its claims. But it is not alone in this kind of attitude. I encountered a more grass-roots version of *paisa* identity at the Festival de la Trova, which occurs every year in Medellín, *capital de la montaña*, mountain capital of Antioquia. My interest was in black Chocoano migrants to the city, and I didn't expect to meet many of them at the festival, a hearty and vociferous celebration of Antioqueño identity and culture. In fact, I ran into a Chocoano friend in the foyer, and she guided me to her table. Inside the place was packed. On stage, *trovadores* battled it out for the title of the King of the Trova.

The *trova* is a short, spontaneously invented verse, composed according to well-defined rules of meter and rhyme, generally sung to guitar accompaniment, using a little-varying melody to carry the verse. It is a satirical, humorous form of poetry, although sometimes also serious, in which two *trovadores* compete, producing alternate verses, attempting to invent the most felicitous *trova* on a given theme, which they can change and develop as they go along—part of the aim being to steer the subject into areas where one's rival feels least at ease. In other cases, two *trovadores* may collaborate, picking on nearby individuals as fuel for their inventiveness, or using a mutually acceptable theme. Off the stage, the verse frequently becomes risqué in its allusions. In Colombia, the *trova* is particularly popular in Antioquia and is considered to be part of the regional culture. Local competitions are held, sponsored by commercial interests, and there is also a yearly festival; in addition, there are occasional "King of Kings" competitions. *Trovadores* are amateurs, and many ordinary individuals are able to *trovar:* in this sense it is part of popular culture. In competition, a panel of judges evaluates the skill of each *trovador,* and, of course, the audience expresses its own opinion with each verse produced. Here are a couple of innocuous examples.

Trove, trove compañero	Sing, sing companion
No se me quede parao	Don't just stand there
Que dirá la gente	For people will say
Que lo tengo agallinao	That I've got you scared

Que me tiene agallinao	That you've got me scared
No puede decir la gente	The people cannot say
Soy un macho muy sobao	I'm a worldly man
Bebedor de aguardiente	A real drinker of *aguardiente*

All the *trovadores* had the traditional symbols of Antioqueño garb: the *carriel* (a shoulder bag of a particular design), a poncho of light cotton (also called a *mulera,* since it is used to blinker mules while loading them), a *sombrero aguadeño* (a straw hat, approximating a trilby in shape), and in some cases *alpargatas* (rope-soled sandals). These are the classic accoutrements of the Antioqueño peasant and national symbols of *paisa* identity.

The *trovas* being produced on stage, amplified into the large hall, were somewhat beyond my linguistic reach, but it was clear enough that between ribaldry and funny verses based on any topic, glorification of the *paisas* was a favorite theme: the *carriel,* the *sombrero aguadeño,* the local football teams, the simple fact of being Antioqueño. In the audience, people cheered and clapped a good *trova,* and occasionally one would see two men in the audience engaged in a brief duel of *trovas* in which those in earshot were the judges. In the men's toilets, in the queues that stretched from the urinals back into the corridors, a more ribald form of the *trova* was in full flow, with the frequent use of rhymes such as *disimúlo-culo* (dissimulation-arsehole). The striking thing was the democratic and participatory aspect of the poetry: every other man (not, apparently, women—not even, as I was careful to enquire, in the toilets) seemed to have the gift of poetic improvisation.

These sketches give some idea of the nature of Antioqueño identity as voiced by partisans. More scholarly treatments have also found in the Antioqueños a distinctive element. They have attracted attention by virtue of a powerful process of agricultural colonization in the nineteenth century, their control of coffee cultivation, and the precocious process of locally financed industrialization, based mainly on textiles, that began early this century. There has been much debate about the origins and nature of these occurrences and of the famous Antioqueño entrepreneurial spirit. Antioqueños have a reputation as roving traders who will range far and wide in search of profit and as shrewd businessmen and entrepreneurs. Gutiérrez de Pineda (1975), for example, has an extended discussion of the importance of material values in the *paisa* regional culture and how this is reconciled with the devout Catholicism of a region that in 1960 supplied half the country's bishops (Pérez Ramírez 1961, 100). Another Colombian scholar also notes the coexistence of religious piety and a mercantile mentality, examining the so-called "Protestant ethic" in Antioqueño Catholicism (Fajardo 1966). Parsons, on the other hand, simply labels the Antioqueños the "self-styled Yankees of South America" (1968, 1).

More recently, attention has focused on the entrepreneurship of some Antioqueños in drug trafficking, principally on the kingpins of the Medellín cartel such as Pablo Escobar, Gonzalo Rodríguez Gacha, and the Ochoa family, although Antioqueños are also active in organizing the drug trade in Miami and other North American cities. The single-minded concentration of media and government on the Medellín cartel distorts the focus away from the more widespread nature of drug trafficking (Arango Jaramillo 1988; Castillo 1987), but it is perhaps no accident that a handful of Antioqueños should have such a prominent place in the traffic, and in public awareness of the traffic.

Antioqueño identity and Antioqueño economic success are both part of the same process of regional historical development. The economy of Antioquia was the basis for the Antioqueños' achievements of colonization and entrepreneurship, and it was objectively an unusual formation. The indian population suffered a particularly drastic decline, despite dense precolonial settlement; by 1778 indians were less than 5 percent of the province's population, compared with nearly 19 percent for the Audiencia of Santa Fe de Bogotá as a whole (see table 1 in appendix A). Thus a large indian bonded labor force was not available. African slaves became predominant early on in the mines, which were Antioquia's economic mainstay. Mining in Antioquia had two main phases. In the sixteenth century, indians and then large *cuadrillas* (slave gangs) were used principally in intensive placer deposit mining in the northeast lowlands of the region around the lower Cauca and Nechí rivers: Zaragoza was a major mining center with a reported three thousand to four thousand slaves and three hundred white miners in 1617 (West 1952). By 1700, the mining in this area had more or less collapsed after a period of decline lasting several decades (West 1952; Parsons 1968, 41; Brew 1977, 44), and the "creole placer" era took over (Twinam 1982, 31), centered on the highland placers of Rionegro and Santa Rosa. Slaves were also used here (Patiño 1985, 51ff.), but "*cuadrillas* were a thing of the past" (Parsons 1968, 52); the slaves were distributed in a more dispersed fashion, and the production of the *mazamorreros,* free independent gold panners, was two or three times that of the white miners with their slave gangs (Twinam 1982, 32). During the eighteenth century, mining, although a principal feature of the economy, did not produce a great deal of capital accumulation for the elite. A good Antioqueño mine might produce two thousand gold pesos annually, compared with Chocoano mines, which produced between two thousand and thirty thousand (Twinam 1982, 33; Sharp 1976, 205).

The move to the highlands was prompted by a need for agricultural production to feed the slaves (Alvarez 1985, 13; Tovar Pinzón 1987, 372, 417). More generally, agricultural development was limited for the elite by the absence of indian labor and the free population's independent exploitation of the gold-bearing streams, which freed them largely from dependence on the elite's land: labor was therefore somewhat scarce. Commerce, although also important, was restricted by the region's extremely rugged topography, yielding profits modest in comparison with those of Popayán's or Cartagena's merchants, and this also hindered the development of an export-based regional agriculture. Thus neither "human nor natural resources allowed the development of an interprovincial export agriculture or of a peonage-based hacienda system" (Twinam 1982, 94). The elite invested eclectically in mining, land, and commerce, with none of these becoming the dominant partner.

At the end of the eighteenth century, there was a crisis in the central highland valley area around Medellín: soil was overused and the population was growing. At this time, a colonial inspector, the Oidor Juan Antonio Mon y Velarde, appalled by the deplorable state of agriculture and the region's general idleness, vagrancy, and backwardness, instituted reforms establishing new agricultural settlements, appropriating unused elite land and introducing silver coin instead of gold dust (Parsons 1968, 5; Twinam 1982, 41, 91, 106). This was the beginning of the famous Antioqueño colonization towards the south, bringing what are now called Risaralda, Quindío, and Caldas into the *paisa* dominion and entering the northern Valle del Cauca and northern Tolima. It was carried out mainly by the humble rural classes, keeping to the healthy, temperate valley slopes, in search of land and also gold, establishing new towns, winning land battles against, or even encouraged by, the elite, and backed by legislation restricting the concentration of landholding (see Twinam 1982, 106; Brew 1977, 164, 178; Parsons 1968, 69, 72). The result in Parsons' view was "this anomaly of a democratic society of smallholders on a continent dominated by traditional Latin latifundism" (Parsons 1968, 101). Parsons' influential view of Antioquia as a "democratic" society has since been challenged (Christie 1978), and it is clear from several studies that inequality of landholding and wealth was marked (Christie 1978; Tovar Pinzón 1987; Twinam 1982). However, even while the position of the large landowners must be recognized, it seems that the reforms of Mon y Velarde were instrumental in giving the poorer rural classes access to land (Tovar Pinzón 1987, 387–409). Twinam (1982) also maintains that domination of landholding was not the elite's principal concern.

To this basis were added technological innovations in mining (Brew 1977, chap. 3), an increase in trade, regional, intraregional and international, which made commerce the principal basis of the elite's wealth (Brew 1977, 89), and finally, in the 1860s, the advent of coffee, experimented with by the elite and later adopted on a wide scale by the peasantry as a good cash crop, increasing rural incomes. Elite capital and peasant cash flow increased simultaneously, and the elite, with their mining experience and economic eclecticism, ventured into industry (mainly textiles) in the early 1900s, expanding to employ one-third of all Colombia's industrial work force by 1965, while the region produced 70 percent of all Colombia's coffee in 1968 (Parsons 1968, 144, 181; Brew 1977, 407–8). There is debate about the precise causes behind these later developments. One view emphasizes the crucial impact of Mon y Velarde's reforms (e.g., Parsons 1968; Tovar Pinzón 1987), while another focuses on miners, wealth, and mining experience as the basis for development (e.g., Brew 1977, 133). Twinam argues for the role of the elite's economic eclecticism, adaptability, and flexibility (1982, 149).

Antioqueño development has some unusual features—dynamic colonization, a commercial and entrepreneurial elite, and, despite inequality, a noticeable history of economic growth that has benefited both the rich and, to a lesser extent, the poor. These features correspond quite neatly to critical aspects of *paisa* identity—the independent rover, the adventurer who makes good, the shrewd merchant or businessman. Today, colonization continues with peasants and capitalists, farmers, shopkeepers, and big businessmen moving into the Atlantic coast region, the Urabá region, and the Chocó. These colonists tend to maintain a strong *paisa* identity, to cooperate among themselves, and, especially in the Chocó, to form ethnic enclaves—clearly colonization and identity go hand in hand. Twinam argues (1980) that the Antioqueños' very "deviance," which came into the public eye with the great southward colonization and was thrown into sharper relief with commerce, coffee, and industry, provoked accusations of ethnic alienness in the form of imputations of Jewish origin, in those days a racial slur and still a popular belief, although discredited by both Twinam and Parsons. The Antioqueños then constructed countermyths of ethnic and racial distinctiveness and "gave birth to an ongoing mythology which continues to promote a positive, aggressive regional self-image" (Twinam 1980, 103).

This explanation tends to emphasize the conscious counterconstruction of identity by Antioqueño scholars and the eulogies dedicated to *paisa* identity in an official literate discourse. But it must be the case that a great part of *paisa* identity developed in a plebian milieu: in the intimacy of the colonists' rural households; through the fireside Catholicism, where kneeling children were slapped if they dozed while saying their rosary as they knelt in front of the hearth; around those Antioqueño women who mothered twenty or thirty children (contributing to a population growth rate higher than that of most other Latin American groups; Parsons 1968, chap. 8); around the muleteers who coaxed their beasts into the rugged terrain's every nook and cranny, who fed the region's capital and local markets, and who pushed southward with the colonists themselves; around the maize with which they made their *arepas* (corn cakes) and *mazamorra* (a maize drink). In short, it developed around the daily business of life, but a communal life that was felt to be dynamic, pushing forward, expanding, fertile, strong, which was in typical Antioqueño parlance *verraco,* a word literally denoting a wild boar, implying dynamism, toughness, and energy and now a standard Antioqueño, and indeed Colombian, idiom: *"Qué verraquera!"* (That's tremendous, fantastic!); *"es un verraco ese tipo"* (he's amazing, that guy); *"es un trabajo muy verraco"* (it's a really tough job). *Paisa* identity was formed in a pushing forward, an expansion, a laborious colonization of new lands, a growing economic power—all of which took place amid accusations of alienness and racial peculiarity.

Racial Identity and Race Mixture

Paisa identity did not form simply around *arepas* and *carrieles:* there also arose the concept of *la raza antioqueña,* a synthetic concept of ethnic and racial particularity, or more accurately, purity. Describing the people of Sonsón, a municipality founded early on in the colonization process, Juan Botero Restrepo says that they are "typical Antioqueños" and that they "are descended from the tough Antioqueño vein, kept ethnically pure, with no mixture of indians or blacks" (1978, 224). Gustavo González Ochoa, writing in *La raza antioqueña,* says, "There is little, if indeed any, African contribution, and in any case never to the extent supposed by some"; in fact, he continues, "our man of today is the result of the perfect acclimatization of the white race." He admits that within Antioquia's boundaries there are blacks, but only in the regions from which "the white man fled, fearful of the very conditions [climatic, etc.] which suited his inferior" (1942, 129, 132): he refers here to the northeastern lowland mining districts where the sixteenth-century gold boom took place. Some Antioqueños would shudder or simply laugh at this kind of blatant racism. However, it was published in 1942, and again in 1960, in a tome edited by the University of Antioquia, and it reflects, albeit in an exaggerated form, a widely held contempt for blackness which is part of Colombian society in general, and in particular of Antioqueño regional identity insofar as this is constructed on the basis of a supposed whiteness. Even when Clemente López Lozano, narrating the history of the municipality of Rionegro, more realistically admits the existence of "the great Rionegro race mixture," he stresses that it is a tri-ethnic synthesis "perfected" by the Spanish (1967, 20). A superficial look at the highland Antioqueño population reinforces this ideology. There are few blacks, and the mulattoes are generally heavily mixed. Bell's handbook for Colombia, produced in 1921, refers to Antioquia's "most interesting racial problem," avowing that the Jewish theory "is certainly borne out by the characteristics of these people, who are light complexioned (many having blue eyes and fair hair, even among the lower classes)" (1921, 38).

If we look at colonial Antioquia, it is hard to imagine how this ideology of racial purity could have arisen. In 1778, Antioquia had nearly nine thousand slaves, forming 19 percent of the population, a percentage equaled only by Popayán (19%) and inferior only to the Chocó (40%) and an absolute number surpassed only by Cartagena (approximately 9,600) and Popayán (approximately 18,700). (See table 1 in appendix A.) Among the free population, some 60 percent of the total, blacks and mulattoes were numerous. Parsons cites several censuses from 1778 to 1805 which show high proportions of blacks and mulattoes in the populations of Medellín, Santa Fe, Santa Rosa, and Guarne and concludes that "Negro blood must have constituted at least one third of the evolving Antioqueño strain" (1968, 52). When we turn to the present century, the black presence has by no means disappeared. The 1918 census, the last to include racial categories, classed 14.6 percent of the Antioqueños as black and 50 percent of them as mixed: even the "ethnically pure" Sonsón had 6 percent blacks and 40 percent mixed-bloods. Naturally, the census classifications are subjective ones, reflecting the opinions of the census taker and the respondent, but they can give us an approximate idea. Even if we subtract the blacks counted in the lowland mining municipalities of Antioquia from which "the white man fled" and the blacks of the Caribbean Urabá region, which was assigned to Antioquia only in 1905, *negros* still make up more than 13 percent of the population. It is worth noting, however, that Viejo Caldas (now the departments of Risaralda, Quindío, and Caldas), which was populated by Antioqueño colonists and then separated from Antioquia in 1905, had only

4.5 percent blacks. Brew (1977, 47) notes that the southward colonization movement involved almost no slaves, and this must be part of
the reason for this low figure.

The meanings that are loaded onto Antioquia as a place in Colombia barely include blackness, in contrast with the Atlantic coast region. The reason for this lies in a subtle combination of material,
cultural, and myth-making processes. The political economy of Antioquia structured the local racial order in such a way as to foment
processes of *mestizaje,* while the ideology of *blanqueamiento* superim-
posed on this a myth of racial purity. Going back to the colonial
period, when Antioquia was in its initial boom mining period prior
to 1700, it was a slave society much as was the Pacific coastal area:
thousands of slaves labored in the mines in large *cuadrillas* under the
control of a small nucleus of whites. As in other parts of Colombia
where slavery existed, there were rebellions and *cimarronaje* (slave
flight) as part of the slaves' reaction to bondage: Zaragoza, for example, was racked by uprisings in 1598, 1620, 1626, and 1659 (Alvarez
1985, 11); communities of escaped slaves (*palenques*) existed at Uré,
Guarne, and Remedios, and undoubtedly there were many other runaways scattered throughout the rivers and forests of the lower Nechí
and Cauca valleys (Parsons 1968, 51; McFarlane 1985, 139; Gutiérrez
Azopardo 1980, 42; West 1952). When the crisis in this lowland
mining area prompted a move to the highlands, mining and slavery
remained important, but "now the slaves were widely distributed as
family retainers and hands on the ranches and in small mine workings
scattered through the hills" (Parsons 1968, 52). Fabio Botero, writing
about the municipality of Salamina, quotes Tulio Ospina to the effect
that the slaves "found themselves in Antioquia in good conditions for
their rapid assimilation to their masters in feelings and customs. Due
to the poverty of the latter, there were very few who owned more
than a small number of slaves, almost always domestic servants who
lived in the same house as their master" (1966, 31). Although this
probably presents an overly benevolent picture in which slavery is
used as a means of "exalting the master and the whites"—or at least
the Antioqueño ones—as good masters (Alvarez 1985, 3), it seems
clear that a system of slave relations in which the slaves were in
close contact with many whites must have encouraged a high rate of
miscegenation in the region (Wade 1986). Among the free population
miscegenation was also common: to start with, Antioquia had a substantial white population (17%), larger than, say, the provinces of the
Atlantic coast (11%), and although much of this group constituted
an elite, Parsons notes that, due to the scarcity of indian labor, "many
Spaniards . . . were forced into productive labor for their own ac-

count" (1968, 2), rubbing shoulders with blacks, mulattoes, mestizos, and indians. Tovar Pinzón also notes that although whites usually had a superior economic position in rural areas and that often a small number of them controlled large areas of land, there were substantial numbers of poor whites, living at quite close quarters with the other racial categories (1987, 378, 419). This was distinct from the Atlantic coast, where the white population was more concentrated in the towns and cities and where even poor whites sought to avoid manual labor (Juan and Ulloa 1772, 31). The indian population, on the other hand, was decimated quickly and drastically, declining to less than 6 percent of the regional population by 1778. The indians that did survive added to the developing racial mix, as their reservations were invaded by the free population (Parsons 1968, 49–50; Tovar Pinzón 1987, 413). It is clear, however, that the indian population had a relatively small impact on the evolving Antioqueño racial mixture. The end result, then, was that miscegenation by degrees physically diluted the black contribution to Antioqueño stock.

On top of this, there appears to have been a process whereby the free population began to be sifted into darker and lighter groups. The evidence of this today is that the lowland mining areas in the northeast of the region, around Zaragoza, Remedios, Caucasia, and the Nechí River, are significantly blacker in appearance than the highland areas. It seems probable that some part of the free population remained attached to mining activities in the lowlands, largely abandoned by the whites after the mining crisis: once located there, opportunities for miscegenation would have been limited. It may also be the case that there was a tendency on the part of these people to avoid white society and set up as independently as possible. Meanwhile, another part of the population retained closer links with white society: Restrepo (1952, 51) mentions that after emancipation in 1851, Antioqueño slaves, "far from giving themselves over to idleness, continued to work in the mines for pay," and archive work in progress indicates that many slaves freed in individual cases of manumission (most commonly when the slave bought him- or herself out of slavery, Alvarez 1985, 19) retained links with their former owners (Alvarez, pers. com., April 1986). These individuals would clearly be in the highland areas where white interests lay and would also have been much more drawn into processes of race mixture. It is the highland areas that supplied the colonists who pushed southward into Caldas and Tolima—with hardly any slaves to accompany them—and whose rapid proliferation in the relatively salubrious temperate climate outpaced that of the blacker people in the hot lowland valleys (Parsons 1968, 53). Miscegenation in the highlands was greater, fueled by the rapid mixture of many whites, few indians, many blacks, and a majority of mixed-bloods who initially had a great deal of black heritage that became progressively diluted in the old highland areas, and even more so in the slave-free, newly colonized areas farther south.

This may help to explain why there are many fair-skinned people "even in the lower classes" in highland Antioquia; what it does not explain is the virulent ideological denial of blackness in the mythology of *la raza antioqueña*. This is connected to the larger Colombian, indeed Latin American, process of *blanqueamiento*, whitening, which includes the physical act of looking for a whiter spouse to ensure lighter-skinned offspring, the dissociation of oneself from characteristically black cultural forms, the reiteration of blackness as something poor, ugly, bad, and the denial that the taint of blackness is part of one's heritage. In Antioquia, a large part of the population which was black or descended from blacks was involved in a powerful process, not just of race mixture but of *blanqueamiento*, linked closely into dominant white society in the highlands and moving further away from blackness with every generation. The particular nature of Antioqueño political economy and demography meant that the blacks and mulattoes were scattered and rubbed shoulders quite closely with the fairly large white population; but the low status of blackness was still a potent force, and in Antioquia, as elsewhere, blackness occupied a lowly position in the social hierarchy. For the Antioqueño blacks and mulattoes both the motive and the means existed: the pressure to escape blackness was pervasive, and the opportunities for renegotiating one's identity away from the shameful status of being colored were relatively abundant. At the same time, as from about 1800, the very group to which blacks and mulattoes had contributed in such numbers was involved in the whole colonization movement with the concurrent emergence of a powerful identity of racial and cultural particularity. Logically, the *blanqueamiento* process with its denial of blackness became intertwined with the development of a mythology of ethnic and racial distinctiveness, leading to the negation of the black contribution to *la raza antioqueña*. The peasants were not just aggressive colonists, they were also in many cases descendants of blacks and mulattoes who had gradually escaped the low status of blackness: when they asserted their identity as *paisas*, they simultaneously did so as people denying their black heritage. The development of a powerful regional identity inevitably included a racial dimension. The assertion of dynamism and forcefulness went hand in glove with a negation of blackness, since blackness was seen as the very opposite of these attributes.

If black history and experience in Colombia has been characterized by two opposing forces, one encouraging concentration of blacks and affirmation of blackness, the other encouraging the dispersion of blacks and the negation of blackness through *blanqueamiento,* then Antioquia, and its offspring neighbors of Risaralda, Quindío, and Caldas, are examples of the latter process taken pretty nearly as far as it can go. And it was inevitable that in creating a mythology about themselves the Antioqueños should appeal precisely to ideas about *raza* to express what they felt themselves to be: whatever the role of accusations of Jewish origins, this appeal was also an expression of several generations of heavy race mixture in the morally loaded form of *blanqueamiento,* a specifically racial ideology.

Antioquia is a region that has at once a dynamic economy, a rather whitewashed population, and an assertive ethnicity combined with an ideology that denies blackness. It is high up on the ladder of moral, material, and racial value, and this mediates the relations that exist between its inhabitants and the Chocoanos, whether in Unguía or in Medellín.

In the course of research in Medellín, I made the acquaintance of a woman, a civic leader in one of the city's working-class barrios. At one point, I spotted a photo of her mother on the wall, an old black-and-white picture. The woman in the photo, although her hair was covered, looked to me like someone who might easily be classified as "black" by many Colombians; she was from Giradota, a municipality within the metropolitan area of Medellín. I asked if, in fact, she had been *negra.* "No, more like indian" was the reply. Tact forbade further investigation, but I later spoke to a black woman, a Chocoano, in the barrio who had known the other's mother: "She was as black as I am; it's just that her children came out quite white, so they don't like to admit it." Giradota was probably originally a settlement of free blacks and mulattoes: significantly, the 1918 census classes its population as 30 percent black.

5

The Atlantic Coast

Moreover, it was agreed and ordered, that no black man or woman should dare to go off and leave the service of his masters, on pain that the black man or woman that so fled and left service for a full two weeks, should incur a penalty of one hundred lashes . . . and after having been given these, that the said black should remain during that whole day bound to the pillary so that the blacks should see him. Moreover, if such a black man or woman who had fled and was absent from his masters should not return, and should be brought back to the service of his masters, one month after having gone absent, he should have his genital organ cut off . . . , which having been cut off, he should be placed in the pillary of this city, so that the blacks might learn from this example; which sentence should be done publicly, where everyone may see it, and which should be carried out rigorously, in view of its great convenience.

It was Christmas, 1986, and I was in Cartagena, along with many other *cachaco* tourists, taking a break from fieldwork in Medellín. We were at a party in the house of Rosalba, the sister-in-law of a Costeño friend with whom I shared a house in Medellín. The house was right on the outskirts of Cartagena, in a working-class neighborhood of unmetaled roads, flat, open, dusty spaces, cement-block bungalows with packed-earth patios, palm trees, and chickens. Areas where plots had been sold off by the government for people to build shaded indistinguishably into areas where people had invaded. As in most work-

Epigraph: Decree governing the treatment of runaway slaves in late sixteenth-century Cartagena. Quoted in Escalante (1964, 113).

ing-class areas of Cartagena, the majority of the inhabitants were black or clearly of black heritage. Attesting to their ubiquity in Colombian society, race and region did not fail to make an appearance that night. Our group was an ambiguous and mixed one: there was myself, a gringo, but who might pass for a *paisa;* there was a black woman, of Chocoano origin but born and raised in Medellín, who spoke with a *paisa* accent, making her a paradoxical *paisa negra;* there was also an uncomplicatedly white woman from Medellín who spoke as befitted her color; and another woman from Medellín, daughter of a Chocoano mulatto mother and a white father, who "came out" white enough to make her regionally-racially unambiguous, despite her mane of very ringlety hair.

We were stared at strangely on the dance floor, initially oblivious of the fact that it was, at that time in Cartagena, considered correct at the start of a number to stand by your partner and talk or look uncomfortably at your shoes, for at least thirty seconds and preferably somewhat longer, before actually beginning to dance. Our impetuous manner of reaching the dance floor and getting straight down to it immediately marked us out as strangers. It was also not considered necessary to sit down between each number—a rule rigidly adhered to in the Chocó and customary in Medellín—and people hung around on the dance floor waiting for the next record. Fashions in music were also in advance of those of the interior of the country—doubtless an age-old trait of port towns, but especially of Cartagena, with its access to the bubbling musical basin of the Caribbean. We were surprised to find salsa, traditionally connected with Puerto Rico, Cuba, Panama, Venezuela, and thus also with Colombia's Caribbean coast, practically ousted from its favored position, whilst it was still a burgeoning vine in the interior, entwining the most distant barrios of Medellín and Bogotá. Instead, other Caribbean music was clearly considered in vogue by the teenagers managing the stereo system: soca (soul/calypso mix), Haitian music, pop music from the English-speaking Antilles, some reggae—but still, of course, the inimitable Colombian *vallenato,* accordion music from around Valledupar, derived originally from the rich tradition of Costeño folk music genres and now a national commercial success.

For a moment, a salsa record came on—and was then rejected. Rosario, the *paisa negra,* eager for some salsa, called out, *"Colocalo, ponelo"* (play it, put it on). Apart from her strong Antioqueño accent, she also used a grammatical form called the *voseo* (an archaic familiar second-person singular), often associated with Antioqueño speech. There were loud hoots of derision from the crowd of young black Costeños around the record player; sarcastic imitations of her accent came back at her. Rosario was somewhat at a loss and put their reaction down to their being a bunch of vulgar Costeños, but the roots of this momentary confrontation were complex and deep-set. As we may unravel a witty remark, its power drawn from submerged realities, but only wholly true in the fleeting moment of its aptness, so we may crystallize these transient moments into more simplified ideas. Here was a person, black and therefore one of them, but at the same time Antioqueño and therefore the opposite to them, throwing her weight about in a party that belonged to them, ordering music that had first been Costeño territory and which had only later become popular among the *cachacos*. Here was an Antioqueño who thought she knew better than they did, as did all Antioqueños, because they considered themselves not black (although, of course, they really didn't know better, especially about music), but this one was black herself, so who the hell did she think she was? A black who thought herself better than other blacks? The reaction of the young Costeño men to this was a classic display of Costeño *mamagallismo*. *Mamar* means to suck (or suckle, as an intransitive verb) and to gobble up but also to suck dry, that is, take advantage of something. *Gallo* means rooster or cock (with the phallic connotations of the English term), and figuratively it means master, expert, or someone who is or wants to be in charge. It has overtones of "cockiness," too: *levantar el gallo* figuratively means to put on airs. In a fairly literal sense, then, *mamar gallo* means "taking advantage of the boss," that is, leg pulling or, in the English colloquialism, "taking the piss." Rather like the latter phrase, it implies undermining someone's claims to superiority and even subverting authority as a whole by consistently refusing to take it seriously and thereby challenging its legitimacy. It can also mean to deceive people by leading them on, making them believe the false or incredible, tying their endeavors up in knots, subverting their authority, and thus making them a figure of fun. In Fals Borda (1979, 155A), for example, it is mentioned that the town council of colonial Mompox *mamaba gallo* in the case of a local marquis by refusing to recognize his title and authority. In the example of Rosario and the salsa record, *mamagallismo* was employed to subvert the whole hierarchy of region and point up the contradictions of race which were evident in this case. It challenged any hint of a claim, albeit inadvertent, to superiority on Rosario's part and asserted an underlying value of egalitarianism among blacks.

An incident like this, of minor proportions, hints at many things—the way race and region manifest themselves in interaction, some underlying sense of egalitarianism among blacks. What I want to draw attention to here is the opposition established between the Atlantic coast region and the interior, specifically Antioquia, an opposition that is re-created over time through, in this case, changing fashions in music and dance. The distinction is hierarchical partly because of regional development and material wealth and partly because of color and putative ancestry. *La Costa*, as the Atlantic or Caribbean coast is frequently called, has a heavily mixed population but also an obvious heritage of blackness, some concentrations of people who are fairly unproblematically "black" in terms of local and national classifications, and also a reputation of blackness. But it is not nearly as black as the Pacific coast, and both people from the interior and the Costeños themselves classify the Pacific region as the location of "real" blackness. *La Costa* is ultimately ambiguous in the nation's semantic and racial landscape. It is black, but not *that* black; it has many people who might be easily categorized as black and classify themselves as such, but also many who might fall outside the flexible bounds of that category while still suggesting a good deal of black parentage; and it has many who would be more likely to be classified as mestizo and white than as black or mulatto. As we will see when I examine the frontier context of Unguía, the presence of the Costeños in the area has a particular significance for the Chocoanos, acting, as it were, as an exit channel from the more unambiguous nature of Pacific coast blackness.

In this chapter, then, I look at the history of *la Costa*, revealing how race mixture operated there and how a certain reputation of blackness—particularly when seen from an Andean perspective—has evolved. *Mestizaje* as a physical and cultural process was structured in *la Costa* by economic, demographic, and political factors in a way that contrasts somewhat with Antioquia. Physically, despite widespread race mixture, black and indian blood remained a much more obvious presence, due mainly to a smaller proportion of whites and a larger proportion of indians. Whitening processes, although present, had a less powerful impact than in Antioquia. Culturally, there were more strongly developed forms of black resistance, which gave black culture a more powerful impact on Costeño society.

Race Mixture in la Costa

The 1912 census for Bolívar (then equal to present-day Bolívar, Sucre, and Córdoba) gave 21 percent blacks, 20 percent whites, 10 percent indians, and 49 percent mixed-bloods—not so radically different from Antioquia's 15 percent blacks, 30 percent whites, 1 percent indians, and 50 percent mixed-bloods, with 5 percent not specified. Clearly the category "mixed-blood" (*mezclado*) hides more than it reveals, and there is no doubt that the general impression that one receives today is of a darker population in the coastal departments than in Antioqueño territory, indicating that black (and indian) blood has not been as diluted over time and that processes of race mixture operated which differed in some respects from those in Antioquia.

In 1778, slaves were 8 percent of the population of the provinces of Cartagena and Santa Marta (see table 1 in appendix A). They were widely distributed throughout the region, although half of Cartagena province's 9,603 slaves were less than fifty miles from the city itself, and other concentrations existed around Mompox and in certain areas along the coast itself. (See McFarlane 1977, 372–77 for a local breakdown of the 1778 census.) Indians were a large 18 percent of the population, and their distribution was patchier: two principal concentrations were west of the Sinú River (where there was no one but indians) and around what is now Sincelejo. The whites were 11 percent of the population and, although concentrated in the larger towns—such as Cartagena, Mompox, Lorica, and Santa Marta— were also spread throughout the province. As in Antioquia, these three groups had by this time mixed extensively to form a free mixed group that was 62 percent of the total: in this case, however, the indian component was much greater.

The regional economy was based principally on the hacienda, a land- and labor-extensive institution, raising livestock and growing food for a mostly regional and interregional market. Colonial Costeño society has been characterized as a "seigneurial" society (Fals Borda 1979, 30B), with its white aristocratic elite based in Cartagena, Santa Marta, and Mompox, owning some of the largest properties in New Granada and dependent on a subservient labor force of slaves, indians and *libres* of all colors which they tried to control principally by monopolizing the land (Meisel Roca 1988). During the colonial period, this was virtually impossible, but after independence capitalist stock raising, new grasses, and barbed wire made ever-greater inroads, and the predatory latifundia of the region increasingly dominated landholding, consolidating a society in which large properties are more common than the national average (Posada 1983), landless laborers are more numerous (CIDA 1966, 134), and remaining frontier areas are characterized by transient processes of agricultural colonization carried out by small peasant farmers who are later replaced by larger operators (Fals Borda 1976; Havens and Flinn 1970; Parsons 1967).

Miscegenation was very common and had a number of sources, mainly related to the labor needs of the economic system. In many areas, the different races lived in close contact. The haciendas depended eclectically on slave, indian, and free labor (Fals Borda 1979, 66B). Slaves were not regimented into large mining *cuadrillas* but used mostly in domestic and agricultural work. Indians who paid tributary labor were sometimes given a plot of land and encouraged to stay on as permanent labor, a process that facilitated a change to the status of *libre*. This change could occur both through race mixture and by way of indians dropping, or being forced to drop, their indian status and thus merging into the ranks of the *libres* (Wade 1986). On the edges of and outside the hacienda lands, a few poor whites, free blacks, indians, mestizos, and mulattoes could be found together: as early as 1600, for example, they founded a village in the Mompox region (Fals Borda 1979, 62A). During a late eighteenth-century Spanish campaign to concentrate and control the scattered rural population *a son de campana* (within the range of the church bell), Jorge Palacios de la Vega encouraged miscegenation by herding together all kinds of people into new settlements in the lower Cauca region (Palacios de la Vega 1955). The purpose was to provide a labor pool for the haciendas. Captain Antonio la Torre y Miranda also founded forty-three new villages in the province of Cartagena (Groot 1953, 2:289).

But miscegenation did not dilute black and indian blood as much as in nineteenth-century Antioquia. There were less whites and more indians, and, most important, there was no equivalent of the rapid increase of the highland Antioqueño group of mostly nonblack, mixed-blood colonists which outgrew the more heavily negroid lowland Antioqueño group and created the characteristic Antioqueño strain. In *la Costa*, rather than blacks getting swamped by nonblacks, the poor whites who did mix in (Friedemann 1977a) and the richer whites who had black and mulatto lovers and mistresses (Gutiérrez de Pineda 1975, 282) were swamped by greater numbers of blacks and indians. The presence of a large number of indians was also of importance for the blacks. Throughout the colonial era, the Spanish legislated against black-indian mixture, often known as *zambaje* (Mörner 1967, chap. 4; Peñas Galindo 1988). Blacks were considered to be of more "vile" origin than indians, thus endangering the latter and quite possibly impeding attempts to evangelize them (Mörner 1967, 39; Jaramillo Uribe 1968, 57). An element of divide-and-rule was also behind this policy (Bastide 1971, 72; Jaramillo Uribe 1968, 57). The very existence of such legislation indicates that black-indian mixture occurred, however, and it also appears from the reports of colonial observers that the authorities were often powerless to prevent it (Jaramillo Uribe 1968, 58–59; Palacios de la Vega 1955). An important incentive was that the offspring of a slave man with an indian woman would be legally free (Peñas Galindo 1988, 53). For *la Costa,* Humboldt observed: "In no other place in the American world are there as many *zambos* as here" (quoted in Peñas Galindo 1988, 50). Groot in his history of New Granada writes that the population of the hinterland of Cartagena was composed of deserters, stowaways, runaway slaves, escaped criminals, and indians who, mixed together, had "propagated an abundant caste of *zambos, mestizos* and other shades, difficult to determine" (1953, 2:290). There were many instances of free black men found living with indian women, and rebel communities of runaway slaves occasionally attacked indian villages and were known to abduct indian women (Jaramillo Uribe 1968, 58–59; Palacios de la Vega 1955, 14; Fals Borda 1979, 55A; Friedemann 1980, 78). As a result of these processes, today in *la Costa,* although most people are mixed, there is noticeably more black and indian heritage apparent, and there are areas of former slave concentrations which are still populated largely by blacks and mulattoes— for instance, along the coastal belt, in towns such as San Onofre, Berrugas, Barú, San Bernardo, or the Playas del Viento. A further result of this contrast with Antioquia is that in the latter region the correlation between race and class has been heavily blurred by race mixture, such that even the lower classes are largely light skinned, whereas in *la Costa* there is still a generalized correspondence between color and class position.

Blacks and Black Culture in Costeño Society

As a result of a different colonial economy and demography, there are certain aspects of physical appearance which facilitate the construction of a racial identity for *la Costa* distinct from that of Antioquia. On top of this, there is no doubt that blackness had an important cultural impact on Costeño society, and this is evident when it is compared with Antioquia. In Antioquia, slavery was, relatively speaking, a "weak institution" (Brew 1977, 44). Despite the large number of slaves and the proportion of the population they represented, and despite the fact that the elite depended on them for both mining and agricultural labor, they were widely dispersed in small groups, and, more important, their gold production was only 20 to 30 percent of the total gold output, the rest being in the hands of the *mazamorreros,* a distribution that clearly autonomized this population while simultaneously promoting local commerce and trade as the gold panners exchanged their gold for other goods. By the first decades of the nineteenth century, free labor was already a greater force in Antioquia than in other slave provinces (Jaramillo Uribe 1968, 241, 245), and it was in Antioquia that the first antislavery legislation was passed when in 1814 Felix Restrepo promulgated laws freeing the newborn children of slave mothers, a law he later pushed through for the new republic in 1821. Whereas in 1778 Antioquia had almost four times the Audiencia's average of 5 percent slaves, this proportion decreased rapidly to equal the 1843 Colombian average of 1.4 percent (Brew 1977, 46; José Manuel Restrepo 1952, 2:175). Moreover, Ann Twinam mentions (pers. com., Feb. 1985) that her reading of the Medellín council records from the 1750s to the 1830s reveals almost no discussion of slaves nor preoccupation about them as a threat to security, a fact attesting to the absence of a solidary black slave group that was felt to endanger the whites. Although references to slave rebellion and flight can be found for Antioquia, these tend to concentrate on the lowland northeastern mining districts around Cáceres and Remedios (Gutiérrez Azopardo 1980, 38; West 1952, 86; Alvarez 1985, 12; Jaramillo Uribe 1968, 65).

In *la Costa,* although slaves were a smaller proportion of the total population and were also distributed about on haciendas and in urban households, mixed with other racial categories, the black presence appears to have had a greater social and cultural impact. This is clearly connected to Cartagena's role as the principal slave port of New Granada, but there are also indications of a greater concern over slavery and slaves than in Antioquia. When abolitionist movements began in Colombia, their most vociferous opponents were the slave owners of Popayán and Cali, where slavery was an even greater force, but the Costeño elite was also to be heard (Jaramillo Uribe 1968, 243). This suggests a stronger attachment to slavery as an institution than in Antioquia, where it faded out relatively painlessly. Free labor in Antioquia was not as much of a problem as in *la Costa,* where, as mentioned above, special expeditions had to be sent out to herd together the *libres* living in isolated areas.

A further indication is the fear of slave rebellion. In contrast with the Medellín council records, Cartagena—which like Medellín had about 18 percent slaves in the 1780s (Pérez Ayala 1951; McFarlane 1977, 372)—shows evidence of a greater concern about slave rebellions and slave flight (Borrego Pla 1973; Friedemann 1980, 80–82; Arrázola 1970; Jaramillo Uribe 1968, 67). Such matters struck fear into the hearts of the general public and were a constant cause of concern for the authorities. Black resistance occurred all over New Granada, including in Antioquia, but it was a particularly powerful force in *la Costa,* where the phenomenon of *palenques,* or rebel slave communities, was widespread.

Palenques. The whole *palenque* phenomenon seems to have been particularly powerful in *la Costa.* Among the studies on *palenques* the Costeño ones outnumber any others (see especially Friedemann and Patiño Rosselli 1983; Gutiérrez Azopardo 1980). This may partly reflect research effort, but it is clear that *la Costa* was a New Granadian center of black resistance to colonial rule. It is only possible at this stage to hypothesize about *la Costa's* importance in *palenque* history, but a central factor may have been the paucity of mining activities in the region. In areas such as Antioquia, the Pacific coast, and the Cauca Valley, there were many gold-bearing streams where slaves could pan on their own behalf on weekly holidays; with the proceeds they could purchase their freedom from their masters (Alvarez 1985, 19; Colmenares 1979, 99; Sharp 1976, 143, 154; West 1952, chap. 3). In *la Costa,* the opportunities for self-purchase were more limited, making *cimarronaje* a more attractive prospect.

Throughout the colonial period, *palenques* sprang up in many areas of Colombia, forming refuges for escaped slaves where specific forms of Afro-American culture could develop, and often harassing the authorities, landowners, and townspeople. Conflict was not, however, permanent. Some *palenques* won their liberty, some traded with nearby haciendas and received visits from priests (Friedemann 1980, 80–84; Fals Borda 1979, 67A), and Spanish attacks were only periodic; between times, their inhabitants must have led a more tranquil life. Fals Borda records that some villages of blacks grew up which were not fully fledged *palenques* but were doubtless fueled by *cimarrones* (1979, 71A), and he also notes invasions of isolated areas of huge, underexploited haciendas by a mixture of *cimarrones,* indians, and free people—whites, mestizos, blacks, and mulattoes—who presumably rubbed shoulders fairly closely (1979, 61A–62A). The settlements that Palacios de la Vega invaded in order to round up the inhabitants into Spanish-controlled towns seem to have been a similar mix (1955, 57, 64, 96), and, although Gutiérrez Azopardo refers to them loosely as *palenques* (1980, 42), they were clearly not formed only by escaped slaves. Local conditions must have been varied for different *palenques* and *cimarrones,* and this is reflected in the varying ways they have developed since the colonial period. One famous *palenque* of the Atlantic coast region, Palenque de San Basilio, has retained its cultural autonomy and its unique creole language into the present century (Friedemann 1980; Escalante 1954), other *palenques* have retained a tradition of independence and a specific identity—such as the Patía area on the Pacific coast described by Zuluaga (1986)—while the majority have disappeared, melding into regional cultures and processes of race mixture.

It is clear that *palenques* were an important phenomenon in *la Costa,* and they contributed to its black identity in two ways. First, they acted as places where miscegenation with the white population must have been restricted, thus maintaining a physical black presence. They were also places where Afro-American cultural forms could evolve with a certain measure of autonomy—not, of course, pure African "survivals" but new forms generated out of new contexts that included whites, indians, and Catholic priests. Price (1973, 26) suggests a "widely shared ideological (or at least rhetorical) commitment to things 'African'" as characteristic of these new forms (see also Mintz and Price 1976). Second, they had a symbolic function, representing the impact of the blacks on the region, both in colonial times, when ominous rumors of massive uprisings led by the *palenqueros* made the white citizens of Cartagena tremble in their beds (Borrego Pla 1973)—some contrast with the carefree attitude of Medellín's colonial city council—and today, when women fruit sellers from Palenque de San Basilio ply their trade to thirsty *cachacos* on the beaches and appear in the background on television commercials for holidays in the sun.

Cabildos.   Black resistance also used the medium of *cabildos* (Escalante 1964; Friedemann and Arocha 1986; Gutiérrez Azopardo 1980, 51; Bastide 1971; Friedemann 1978, 15; Arrázola 1970; Medina 1978; McFarlane 1985, 143). These groupings were found, under different names, throughout New World societies, and they took their precedent from the *cofradías* or religious brotherhoods which existed in Spain and which already included *cofradías de negros* (Friedemann and Arocha 1986, 38). In Iberian slave societies blacks, slave and free, were authorized by the colonial regime to create their own associations and were generally organized, at least nominally, on the basis of ethnic origin (Bastide 1971; Ortiz 1920, 1921; Russell-Wood 1974; Scarano 1979; Graff 1973). In Cartagena there were *cabildos* with names such as Arará, Angola, Mandinga, Carabalí, Mina, and so on. These groups were a kind of mutual aid society where the slaves and free blacks could legitimately congregate with an authorization to have dances and celebrations after the custom of their African communities. Bastide (1971, 9), referring to *cabildos* outside Colombia, suggests that they may have been the result of a divide-and-rule tactic by the Spanish, or alternatively the spontaneous association of blacks

88

for their own purposes; the latter would apply mostly to free blacks, since slaves would only be able to associate spontaneously in secret. Whatever the motives of the Spanish, it is clear that the blacks used the *cabildos* to organize themselves, sometimes to plan rebellions and escapes (which were sometimes also betrayed by members of other, rival *cabildos*), and to carry on African-derived dancing and music as well as religious and magical practices, usually under a cloak of Catholicism but nevertheless persecuted by a suspicious Inquisition. There are reports from Cartagena of the church authorities confiscating the *cabildos'* drums, of citizens complaining about noisy drum battles between rival Carabalí *cabildos,* and of a city governor banning all *cabildo* activity, fearful of a rebellion (Escalante 1964, 153). *Cabildo* status was uncertain: on the one hand authorized and on the other persecuted. In some countries, the basic *cabildo* system persisted and evolved, although it no longer split blacks up into nominal ethnic groups. In Brazil there are a series of *candomblé* religious sects named after African towns and regions; equally in Cuba there are many Afro-American associations—practicing various forms of the worship of African and other deities—which have evolved from a basis of *cabildos* (Ortiz 1921). In Colombia, the *cabildos* have disappeared, except for the Lumbalú Cabildo of Palenque de San Basilio, nowadays only active in funeral rites. The *danzas de negros congos* of the Barranquilla carnival also developed from the *cabildos*. These are groups of costumed and masked dancers whose processional dance dramatizes traditional motifs (Friedemann 1978, 16; Friedemann 1985a).

Most of the limited research that exists on *cabildos* has focused on *la Costa,* specifically Cartagena, although there is mention of *cabildos* for other areas in Jaramillo Uribe (1968, 70) and McFarlane (1985, 143). Bastide (1971, 99) notes that there was more *cabildo* activity in cities than in rural areas, due to the concentration of slaves there, and especially in port towns such as Montevideo, Lima, Buenos Aires, and Cartagena, where large quantities of *bozales* or African-born slaves arrived. It is probably the case that *cabildo* activity was more pronounced in Cartagena than elsewhere. Although the *cabildos* have left few traces of their former presence, there is no doubt that during their existence they provided semisecret settings for the development of Afro-American culture, even if this did not take on the more obviously African-derived character of Brazilian *candomblé,* Cuban *lucumí,* or Haitian Voodoo religions. This was especially so in the realm of music and dance, which constituted, after all, the *cabildos'* principal activity. In Costeño music, African influence is most evident in rhythm and accentuation, off-beat phrasing, overlapping call-and-response patterns, and in the important position of the drum among the instruments. Guillermo Abadía Morales (1983) classifies Costeño music as black and mulatto, while José Ignacio Perdomo Escobar states that *cumbia,* a traditional genre of Costeño music, "has the same roots as *cumbe,* a dance of African origin" (1963, 281). Abadía Morales also affirms that *vallenato,* another traditional genre, is mulatto in origin (1983, 212), although most authorities accept a tri-ethnic origin (e.g., Londoño 1985, 128). Ocampo López (1988, 183) emphasizes the polyrhythmic structures, the call-response singing, the collective nature of the music and dance, and the social significance of dance as African-derived features of Costeño music.

The syncretism that produced Costeño music is complex, but the black influence is clearly noticeable and, more important, is *seen* as a critical feature of Costeño culture by Colombians in general. Dances such as the *mapalé,* with its fast, frenetic beat and its frank eroticism, although only one among other, more sedate Costeño dances, do much to reinforce this image. Following is a description of this dance by the turn-of-the-century Colombian novelist Carrasquilla in his work *La marquesa de Yolombó,* set in mid-eighteenth-century Colombia (1964, 2:65). Ironically, Carrasquilla is writing about the Antioqueño town of Yolombó and its slaves, an area now notably devoid of black culture.

> The *mapalé* is delicious. There are twelve dancers: they form up in rows, negroes on one side and negresses on the other; they raise their candles to an equal height with a single movement; they cross, they alternate, arms interlace, the flames unite. Face to face, eyes rolling, lips vibrating, they magnetize each other. They mark the rhythm with expert feet, now forwards, now backwards. They embroider and trace without drawing apart an inch. They rise up, they shake, they bend, they crouch. . . . The little windmill spins and spins in a whirl of flames. They break apart suddenly and continue as before in pairs. The culmination is supreme. They shake their hips in convulsive agitation; their breasts tremble as if they were jelly. Those mouths pant, those bodies twist and turn, gleaming with sweat, eyes, earrings and necklaces shine. Their bodies embrace in a frenzy, they turn to bend, they turn to straighten; they support themselves with their arms, throw their breasts backwards; they hurl away their candles and they are finished. It is the apparition of distant Africa, which they carry in their blood and which their eyes have never seen; it is a rite performed before a cruel and grieving Eros. Oh fire! you who burn thus in the dark wax of the rustic hive, as in the snowy brilliance of the golden bees.

The erotic overtones of the description are quite plain. Words such as delicious, vibrate, tremble, culmination, convulsive, breasts, pant, shine, frenzy, and finish take on an unmistakably sexual connotation in this context. They interplay with images of heat and fire to create a link between blackness, sex, and heat. The last two sentences complete the image. The invocation of Eros and the mention of rites not only specify the sexual element but are also suggestive of superstitious primitive ritual. The appeal to Africa reinforces the notion of primitiveness, while this, plus the mention of blood, and the image of dark wax in a rustic hive create a feeling of an instinct, deeply embedded, concealed, and rooted in the past.

Music and dance do not exhaust the realms in which black culture has made an impact on Costeño society itself or its image in the eyes of others. Family structure, while similar to that in many other areas of Latin America, also has some specific features, often associated with other black areas of the New World, such as polygyny, series of overlapping unions, frequent common-law unions, and matrifocal households (Gutiérrez de Pineda 1975; Dussán de Reichel 1958; see also Whitten 1974; Friedemann 1974; Pollak-Eltz 1974). The real causes of these traits are far from clear (MacDonald and MacDonald 1978; Bastide 1971, 31), but in Colombia, Costeño family organization is seen from the perspective of the more strongly Catholic interior as "disorganized" in much the same way that black family structures have been subject to criticism in other parts of the Americas. In the religious sphere, Price (1955) suggests that the funerary rites and concern with the dead which he observed in a Costeño village may also be connected to African ancestor cults, and doubtless, if one delved into folk healing and traditional medicine, more evidence could be unearthed. My point is not to trace African retentions but to draw attention to how black culture has manifested itself quite noticeably in *la Costa*. Blacks evolved a tradition of resistance which grew alongside, and later merged with, indian and poor mixed-blood resistance. They did this partly through *palenques*, partly through *cabildos*, partly through attempts to live independently of white influence in areas where they mixed with poor whites, indians, and other *libres*. As in Antioquia and the rest of Colombia, Spanish dominance and *blanqueamiento* meant that regional culture took on Catholic and Spanish forms to a large extent; but within that general process, black culture was a major current flowing into popular Costeño society.

In the Atlantic coast region, then, blackness became a part of regional identity through processes the particularity of which is most evident in comparison with Antioquia. The latter, despite having a greater proportion of slaves than the former plus large numbers of free blacks and mulattoes, effectively physically lost and ideologically covered up a black identity and relegated it to the hot lowland mining districts in the northeast of the department, considered to be unrepre-

91

sentative of *paisa* identity and *la raza antioqueña*. In *la Costa*, black culture had a much greater impact partly through less physical dilution of black heritage and also because Costeño society engendered traditions of black resistance which counterbalanced to some extent the usual processes of *blanqueamiento* which affected all of Colombia. In both areas, these processes were related to the economy, politics, and demography of the region. Systems of labor and the closeness of racial conviviality they encouraged, population ratios, gold-panning opportunities, slave flight in search of freedom: these were the main factors that affected the progress of *mestizaje* and black nucleation and dispersal in each area.

But blackness is often equivocal and ambiguous in Colombia, and *la Costa* is no exception. In contrast with Antioquia, its blackness seems more evident; and discourse about the region from the country's interior tends to assume a certain blackness for it. This is partly because many *cachacos* visit Cartagena and the coastal beaches where the people are blacker. It is also because Costeño troupes presenting traditional coastal music and dance to audiences in the cities of the interior tend to be made up of people easily categorized as blacks by *cachacos,* a phenomenon in which is reflected the subtle interaction of the supply of and demand for "blackness," with *cachacos* expecting blacks and the Costeño dance troupes assuming such expectations. And finally, it is so because a "black" coast fits neatly into categorical oppositions between "the interior" and "the coasts," Atlantic and Pacific.

On the other hand, *la Costa*'s place in the nation's semantic landscape is not as definitive as that of the Pacific region. It has great intraregional diversity, with some areas and some classes much lighter skinned in appearance than others. It is highly urbanized, and although as a region it is not as wealthy and developed as many areas of the interior of the country, it is plainly more so than the Pacific region. The Costeños themselves, while alive to the presence of blackness in their region, or in some cases identifying themselves as *negros,* do not see *la Costa* as a black region in the same way as they do the Pacific zone, home of *los verdaderos negros,* the real blacks. To this extent, *la Costa* has an ambiguous status, and in the chapters on Unguía I show the significance of this ambiguity for the Chocoanos.

The black identity of *la Costa* regenerates itself from continuing Caribbean developments as well as from its own black history: so much is obvious from the Christmas partygoers in Cartagena and their taste for Caribbean music. Although Rastafarianism has not made much impact with its very radical black discourse, and reggae has a limited popular following, other Caribbean styles are fashionable. And, of course, the United States is not much farther than Jamaica, as the following anecdote illustrates.

On the beach in Cartagena, we were assembling towels and bags, ready to leave. Fernando, the *barranquillero*, was putting on his shoes. A young black man, an itinerant seller of sunglasses and other knick-knacks, was making a last few sallies up and down the beach. He approached us and began a spiel, despite an evident lack of interest on our part. In his characteristic Costeño accent, Fernando called to him, *"Nada, viejo cuadro."* He replied, *"Nada, viejo brother,"* and turned on his heel and left. Roughly translatable as "Nothing doing, old mate" and "Nothing doing, old brother," the exchange captures two opposing faces of the same thing. *Cuadro* (literally "square" but also "cadre") is a Costeño term that derives from the old *cabildos;* in Palenque de San Basilio it refers to age groups, and it is also used to denominate the Barranquilla carnival dancing groups (Friedemann 1978, 16; Friedemann and Patiño Rosselli 1983, 50). "Brother," on the other hand, is clearly a black North American import. To establish his credentials as a local, to create a superficial solidarity with the seller and thus avoid the sales talk directed at us, the *cachacos*, Fernando used a term (and an accent) which marked him out as a Costeño. The seller indicated his acceptance of this tactic and its meaning by using a term that responded in kind even though it referred to other notions and experiences of black identity. Both terms depended primarily on establishing a common regional identity; but Costeño regional identity is heavily loaded with connotations of blackness, and, although the terms derive from different histories, both take their meaning from specifically black histories. One term looks back, albeit unconsciously, to *la Costa*'s own history, the other across the Caribbean to other notions and experiences of black identity. Between them, they established Fernando's status as a local who didn't want a pair of sunglasses.

6

The Chocó:

Rain, Misery, and Blackness

It may be that contact with active people, and the rapid progress that places rich in minerals always make, will draw them [the blacks of the Chocó] out of the stupidity, lethargy and abandonment in which they live and make them, with work, find a way to imitate them [the active people]. As the white race spreads itself over the high cordilleras in search of minerals, and finds them in the headwaters of the Atrato, the Andágueda and their tributaries, only then will Quibdó have a promising future, since this city (virtually abandoned to the apathy of the blacks) will then be a way-station for goods and merchandise destined for those who have settled in the heights.

The Chocó and the Chocoanos are the central focus of this study. In terms of the national racial order, the region is unambiguous: peripherality, poverty, and blackness are central characteristics of its position. In this chapter, I look at how these three features intertwined in the history of the region and examine the historical structuring of miscegenation and blackness by regional economic, political, and demographic factors. The outcome in this case was quite different from that in Antioquia or the Atlantic coast region, due to the region's position as an inhospitable peripheral frontier zone. I look first at images of the Chocó, which, although they are those of outsiders, nevertheless capture real aspects of the region, both past and present, and are particularly important insofar as it was outsiders' experiences and perceptions of the Chocó which played a major part in determin-

Epigraph: Agustín Codazzi, geographer and cartographer, reporting on the Chocó in 1853, as part of the Chorographic Commission's reconnaissance of the Republic of New Granada (Comisión Corográfica 1958, 328).

ing its development. I then look at how the blackness of the region was constituted over time.

Images of the Chocó

It is common knowledge among Chocoano schoolchildren that they live in the second rainiest place in the world. Cherrapungi, India, an otherwise little-known location, enjoys some renown in the Chocó, since it has the dubious reputation of being the world's wettest spot. It is noted in the *Guinness Book of Weather Facts and Feats* (Holford 1977) as having a mean annual rainfall of as much as 489 inches, while the Chocó stations of Quibdó and Andagoya are listed in *World Climatic Data* (Wernstedt 1972) as having 280 and 268 inches, respectively. There are other odd places in the world where rainfall in fact exceeds that of the Chocó—for example, Mount Wai-'ale-'ale on the Hawaiian island of Kauai (451 inches a year)—and even within the Pacific region there are places that equal it, but the Chocoanos' claim to a silver medal in the rain stakes is not to be easily quashed with mere facts, perhaps because of their region's position as the persistent loser in the history of Colombia's development.

Gaspar Mollien, speaking of the Chocó in the 1820s, remarked:

> The west north-west wind which blows daily on these coasts, violently impels the clouds against the mountains [of the western cordillera], where they accumulate, break and daily pour down torrents of water which supply the infinite numbers of rivers with which the country is intersected in all directions. . . . The continual humidity which prevails in the Chocó renders the climate . . . very supportable, and at the same time very unhealthy . . . the strongest constitution is undermined; all Europeans fall ill . . . the inhabitants of the Chocó have not fine days to console them in their poverty; the rain daily inundates their retreats, and covers with mud the spot they occupy; their canoe is perhaps the most healthy, if it be not the driest place where they can live, and they accordingly pass all their time in it. (1824, 303, 305)

Jorge Brisson, exploring around Bagadó in 1895, describes persistent rain, recurrent soakings, and perpetual dampness as he and his team slid and skidded their way across the area's broken terrain in search of gold deposits. Another visitor described some decades later how he was constantly "sliding from one tree root to another, buried in the mire, exhausted from perpetual gymnastics and soaked with the rain that never ceased to fall" (Jorge Alvarez Lleras, quoted in Velásquez 1983, 81).

What we gain from these descriptions is an idea of the Chocó as viewed from afar—as a savage place where nature is at its most inhospitable, where "iron rusts, leather rots, wool and cotton decompose" (Velásquez 1983, 60), and the "strongest constitution" is corroded. One detects the melodrama and exaggeration of the outsider in these descriptions, and what undoubtedly exists here is the view from the inside and from the outside: on the one hand, melodramatic amazement, and on the other, the much more prosaic acceptance of those who live there on a day-to-day basis, an acceptance that can include ironic amusement at—or even satirical disdain for—the outsider's sensationalism, discomfort, and weakness. I found this out when I went to the yearly Quibdó patron saint festivals, the Fiestas de San Pacho. I caught typhoid there, and after my recovery, one Chocoano friend commented to another, laughing, "Peter forgot he wasn't Chocoano. He followed the processions under all that sun; he stayed up all night and danced in all that rain. He thought he was Chocoano, but within a week he was finished."

It was not only the rain and nature's inhospitality that characterized the Chocó, as seen from outside. It was also the poverty and miserable living conditions of its inhabitants. Mollien observed that "gold [was] found wherever it [was] dug for" but noted:

> In the midst of all these riches, man is poor and miserable, it is only on the eminences which are met with from time to time on the banks of the rivers that he has built his dwelling, raising it upon pillars. . . . It is impossible to grow culinary vegetables in the natural soil, because the humidity would destroy them; they therefore erect a flooring of bamboo several feet above the earth which they cover with a thick layer of earth [in which they grow the vegetables] . . . maize, sugar-cane and bananas might be grown in abundance if the constant dampness of the soil did not hinder the inhabitants from burning the forests which cover it. . . . Their huts are uninhabitable sties . . . the slight roof is no defense against the rain. . . . The inhabitants of the Chocó are therefore very miserable. (1824, 304–6)

Cochrane found Nóvita a "miserable town" and "the people miserably ignorant," while Quibdó, although "far superior," was also "a miserable place" (1825, 2:417, 425, 439, 441). Parry, describing the expedition of the conquistador Balboa down the Atrato River in 1512, reckons that they got "as far probably as the neighborhood of Quibdó, the modern capital—if so grand a title can be applied to so miserable a place—of the Chocó" (1979, 118). Agustín Codazzi, head of the Chorographic Commission that mapped the new republic in the early 1850s, connected climate and economy, reporting to the governor of the Chocó: "The hot climate, extremely humid and rainy, allows this race and its mixtures nothing more than agricultural and mining work . . . and since they refuse to work, on the pretext of being free, naturally there is no work nor public wealth" (Comisión Corográfica 1958, 324).

Misery and an inhospitable climate and terrain were linked to a third feature, blackness, since the vast majority of the region's population was black, and together these three constituted the major impressions made on visitors to the Chocó, an impression characterized by negative evaluations and a certain amazement at the way people could live in the region.

Today these images are still current among Colombians who live outside the region. Gabriel García Márquez, writing a series of newspaper articles on the Chocó in 1954, remarks on its continued lack of communications and comments that as a result "the journey to the Chocó has been for one hundred years a somewhat fantastic adventure which, even as an adventure, is yet to be discovered" (1982, 144). He goes on to describe Quibdó, which, with its "unfinished church, patched with tin and its decimated municipal park looking like the remains of an earthquake," has the appearance of "an encampment in the jungle." Its features forcibly remind one "of what Quibdó is not in any sense of the term: an African village" (1982, 145).

Poverty is the main theme of García Márquez's sympathetic and sensitive articles. Rain, however, can hardly escape mention, and he notes that it "rained implacably" for nine days while he was there (1982, 146). Carlos Caicedo. Licona in his vehement book *Chocó por dentro* complains that of all the myths propagated about "an indomitable jungle, swarming with venomous snakes, alligators and cannibalistic indians, their children prostrated with malaria, under the never-ending rain," it is "the rain which has served as an excuse and a justification for abandonment to the point that a Liberal ex-president, a disciple of geographical determinism, cried out in Quibdó that his economic talents had left no fruitful traces during his term of national transformation, because the rain had prevented it" (1980, 51).

Blackness goes virtually without saying. Ramón Carlos Goez remarks, "The truth is that we know nothing about the Chocoano blacks, except the fact of their black skin, for which we despise them" (1947, 140).

On a more popular note, I asked students in a Medellín secondary school to write about their images of the Chocó, whether they had been there or not. Most were ignorant of the Chocó, but all concurred in describing it as "very poor . . . neglected by the government . . . inhabited by black people . . . unhealthy . . . [the people] suffer from hunger and illness due to poverty." Some thought it "a dark region, like its inhabitants . . . unpleasant . . . a nasty place to live . . . like the rest of the country, but less civilized." Others, some of whom had actually been there, thought it "pretty . . . very good because it produces a lot of food . . . a beautiful city [sic] . . . rich but unexploited . . . a fun atmosphere . . . a nice place." One noted tersely that "not all the race is black," while another recounted, amazed, "Not everyone is 'black' like we think, where I went there were honestly no black people . . . it seemed fantastic to me"—he had been in an area, east of Quibdó, previously belonging to Antioquia and populated by Antioqueños, which had been put under Chocoano jurisdiction in 1905 in exchange for the Urabá region. His experience there was "like seeing a Tarzan film in which you are in an unreal world, full of fantasies, flora and fauna." Although there is variety in these responses, induced particularly by firsthand knowledge, there is no doubt that the overall image conveyed is that of a poor, black, remote, and peripheral area.

Slavery and Race Mixture in the Chocó

The intertwining of blackness, poverty, and a climate seen by others as inhospitable is not just a matter of images. It also constitutes a great part of the history of the Chocó, since the rich gold deposits of the area, although legendary, were mostly removed by a few white people to more hospitable climes. Most of the white mine owners lived in distant towns, but some lived in the Chocó, and in 1852 Mario Espinosa wrote:

> Nowhere are there schools, nor public nor private establishments, nor workshops, nor convents, nor barely any offices. They live amidst the mud and the weeds, like the pigs and with them; they feed on the plantains of the countryside and the fish of the rivers, rewarding themselves on big days with a hand's-breadth of hung beef brought from the Cauca; they plunge in, greedy divers in this sea of heat, of humidity, of miasmas and of insects, risking their lives and endangering their health in order to accumulate at any cost and with all possible speed, with slave labor, great wealth which they then go and enjoy elsewhere: this, and nothing more, is what the miners of that country [i.e., the Chocó] have done, after which they abandon it without leaving a monument to pity, nor a trace of civilization, nor a souvenir of gratitude, nor a sign of good taste, of decency, or of rationality. (quoted in Velásquez 1983, 54)

Colonial settlement in the Chocó was limited to an area constituted by the eastern tributaries of the Atrato and San Juan rivers, between Sipí and the Bebará River (West 1957, 105). Within this area, the exclusive interest of the whites was in gold mining, plus a small amount of commerce, some of which consisted of the contraband of gold, illegally exported without paying the "royal fifth" tax, and luxury goods, imported also avoiding taxation. Settlement was an impermanent affair: mining camp location was subject to the vagaries of gold production, and the towns were small and ill equipped, since the wealthy mine owners were mainly absentee landlords with their fine houses in Popayán and their rich haciendas, worked by slaves and indians, in the Cauca Valley. "The region remained a mining frontier on the fringe of developing centers of commerce, education and authority in New Granada" (Sharp 1976, 3; for the Chocó see also West 1952 and 1957; Sharp 1974; Córdoba 1983; Colmenares 1979; Velásquez 1983). In 1778, for all fifteen thousand inhabitants censused by the authorities—there were doubtless many more *cimarrones* and indians outside their reach—there were a mere two dozen clergy, some of whom owned their own mines, worked by slaves. Education was practically nonexistent, and in 1824, when Cochrane was in Nóvita, he tried to procure a book to read "but in vain, although [he] was in the first house in the place." If the administrator where he was staying "had never read the Bible or the Testament," so much less a black whether slave or free (1825, 425).

Mining was the principal activity. In 1778, slaves were 39 percent of the total censused population, a proportion double that of any other New Granadian province. They were organized into *cuadrillas* that sometimes exceeded a hundred slaves and with 90 percent of the slaves in *cuadrillas* of more than thirty slaves (Sharp 1976, 115). In the early eighteenth century, most of these were *bozales*, slaves brought directly from Africa rather than born in Latin America, and they were mainly put to work in the labor-intensive placer mines that used only rudimentary tools and running water to extract the gold. West (1952) states that up to a third of the slaves in mining camps also worked growing crops for the immediate needs of the camp, but it is probable that in the Chocó the large indian population (37% of the total), which was exploited for food production and for the provision of canoes and special aqueducts to run water to mines distant from a river, reduced the number of slaves working in agriculture. The treatment of slaves was very much up to local administrators and overseers. Legislation was piecemeal and contradictory until 1789, when a more comprehensive code was established, but even then it was not necessarily known to everyone and much less enforced in inaccessible areas such as the Chocó. Legislation also existed to control the use of indian labor, but indians were nevertheless often ruthlessly and illegally exploited in the Chocó, frequently by the colonial officers themselves (Sharp 1976, 99). However, slaves were seen as capital assets and therefore had to be maintained with reasonable care. Food tended to be scarce, consisting principally of plantains, maize, and salt; meat was in short supply. However, slaves worked five days a week for their masters, and the other two they had to themselves, so they could hunt, fish, grow a little sugarcane (from which they sometimes made alcoholic drinks), and pan gold on their own behalf to buy clothes and tobacco or to save towards buying their own freedom. For the later eighteenth century, Sharp found that male-female ratios were fairly equal, one-third of slaves were married, another third were under 15 and a certain number (in some cases between a third and a quarter of the *cuadrilla*) were over 50 (1976, 122–25). Women were also used as labor in the mines, where they participated in most stages of the mining process, although they were especially valued in the last stage of washing the gold-bearing sands in the *batea,* a shallow wooden bowl.

Manumission was fairly common, although in most cases it was a question of self-purchase. Of 472 manumissions recorded between 1721 and 1800 in Popayán, the administrative center for the Chocó, 71 percent were self-purchased (and of these, by women more than by men) and only 29 percent spontaneously given by the masters, some on their deathbeds or to old slaves (Colmenares 1979, 99). Some masters contested the slaves' legal right to self-purchase, but Sharp records one instance of a court upholding this right (1974, 95). Free blacks formed a relatively low proportion of the population in 1778 (21%), compared with Antioquia (59%) or Cartagena (64%), but by 1808 they had grown to be 61 percent, having increased from slightly more than three thousand to about fifteen thousand individuals through natural growth and the manumission of slaves; their representation in the total was also increased by slight diminutions in the numbers of indians censused and of the slaves, some of the latter having been transferred out of the area in response to declining gold productivity (Colmenares 1979, 87; Sharp 1976, chap. 10). Free blacks were relatively unassimilated into the economy by the local colonial system. A very small number owned their own slaves, but almost always less than the five required for admission to the miners' guild (Sharp 1976, 116). Some free people joined the army in racially segregated regiments, while others worked in the mines as free labor. They were not welcomed by the slave owners, who feared their influence on the slaves, and this problem also affected free black farmers who tried to sell food to nearby mining camps. In general, opportunities for employment were scarce since official positions were reserved for whites and education was restricted for free people. Above all, the possibility of an expanding service sector was remote given the tiny white population (2 percent of the total) outnumbered by indians and blacks. Thus most *libres,* rejected by a discriminatory white society, simply retreated to remote areas of the forest where they grew plantains and maize and panned gold for the few purchases they needed (Sharp 1976, 150–53).

The free population lived in a dispersed settlement pattern along the riverbanks. Visiting in 1801, Carlos de Ciaurriz reported back to the king that the area had "no other resources than the *vegas* [patches of alluvial soil] . . . separated from one another along the rivers and on these [were] scattered the mulattoes, *zambos* [black-indian mixture] and free blacks of these districts" (Ortega Ricuarte 1954, 276). There must have been some links with colonial society since, he continues, some blacks engaged "in commerce, providing with their crops the miners and the people of other rivers," while the majority panned gold and some also fished and hunted. Gold clearly acted as a force integrating the free blacks into the economic system, since it had to be sold or exchanged for consumables, and in the last instance this transaction took place with merchants or miners, but it is also clear that colonial society was a small enclave in the Chocó which had repercussions less intrusive and widespread than in *la Costa* and much less so than in Antioquia.

As in other regions where slavery was a major presence, resistance emerged in the form of rebellion and *cimarronaje.* Velásquez (1983, 71) cites several examples of rebellions by indians and by blacks in the Chocó. The investigations made after the 1728 uprising in Tadó, which led to the execution of four blacks, revealed that the cause was "the oppression" in which the masters kept the slaves, "with so much work and punishment and so little food" (report to the king, quoted in Velásquez 1983, 71); the slaves had days off on which they could pan gold and save towards self-purchase, but equally they exchanged this gold dust for food and other items, provided at inflated prices by the mine owner, which made their work another source of income for their masters. Sharp (1976, 158) also found evidence of several rebellions and continued slave-master tension. *Cimarronaje* had a particular form. Whereas in *la Costa* slave flight typically gave rise to *palenques,* in the Chocó these seem to have been uncommon. There is mention of *palenques* farther south, around the Patía River (Nariño), near the Saija River (Cauca), or near Tadó (Friedemann and Patiño Rosselli 1983, map 3), but in the Chocó it seems that runaways tended to live in a more dispersed fashion, partly, perhaps, because this made detection more difficult and attack less likely and partly because settlement along the Chocó's rivers tended to be dispersed in any case. The *cimarrones* must have led an existence rather different from that of their cousins in *la Costa,* some of whom had visits by priests to their *palenques,* maintained trade links with haciendas, and pressured the authorities for their freedom: like the Chocoano free blacks, the *cimarrones* from the gold mines probably lived in the jungle, rather isolated from colonial society.

Given the nature of Chocoano society at this time, there was a very limited amount of race mixture, evident today in the relatively few people of mixed race and the vast majority of blacks. The whites, for example, numbered 300 persons in 1778, of which 183 were males, and, especially as white women probably contributed little towards race mixture, the opportunities for miscegenation were clearly limited. Given the minority position of the whites and the highly regimented nature of the slave regime, it was also in the interests of elite political control to maintain as definite a division as possible between the whites and the blacks. Furthermore, many free people lived away from the centers of colonial society and therefore did not mix at all with the whites. In contrast with *la Costa* where *zambos* were relatively common, black-indian mixture in the Chocó was relatively infrequent, and all contemporary accounts of relations between the two groups describe a certain antipathy, mediated by relations of *compadrazgo* (godparenthood), trade, and the exchange of certain services; the indians have retreated more and more into the distant headwaters of the rivers as the blacks have increasingly spread to the rivers' lower courses and deltas (Whitten 1974, 50; Córdoba 1983; Atencio Babilonia 1973, 88–90; Friedemann 1977b). Although the blacks learned much from the indians in terms of adaptation to the local environment, each group established a society in which ethnic distinctions were maintained and which was not broken into by colonial administrators such as Palacios de la Vega in *la Costa.*

In *la Costa* and even more so in Antioquia, both slaves and free blacks were needed in and were part of the colonial economy. This implied greater social propinquity, more integration, and more race mixture. In the Chocó, colonial society had little room for freed blacks and kept slaves in a strict *cuadrilla* regime. This together with local demographic structures—themselves determined in large part by the nature of the slave regime—powerfully influenced the nature of race mixture in each region. Interestingly, and in contradiction to ideas about the whites' need for free labor being the factor that gave rise to the appearance of a free mixed category in lowland Latin America

(Harris 1974), in the Chocó free blacks quickly grew to constitute 61 percent of the total population, despite being of relatively little use to the whites. The growth of a free category, then, was a force that—as in the United States—had to be actively repressed if it was to be kept to a minimum, rather than something that needed to be actively created by the elite for its own purposes. In the Chocó, and in many other regions of Latin America, the legal framework gave some space to manumission, although this was only codified in 1789 (Bowser 1972, 25). More generally, the whites in the Chocó, and elsewhere, hardly had the capacity to police a system so tightly as to reduce a free category to U.S. levels. What is pertinent is that a greater need for free labor tended to integrate blacks more and increase race mixture. The Chocó demonstrates that manumission and miscegenation are separate, though related, processes and need to be kept apart analytically (Wade 1986).

The Chocó after Independence

Although the first abolitionist legislation was passed in 1821, shortly after the republican victory over Spain at the Battle of Boyacá in 1819, the Wars of Independence (1810–19) had de facto been a massive liberating force for the slaves. First the royalists enlisted the indians and the blacks against their republican masters both in Venezuela and in New Granada; then Bolívar, the Liberator, turned the tables and played the same trick on his adversaries. Both forces declared free those who would join up—Bolívar forced the issue by obliging all free males over 14 years of age to join up under threat of being returned to slavery (Gutiérrez Azopardo 1980, 77). Clearly, the blacks acted principally as cannon fodder in these changing coalitions, but some also rose to quite high positions in the armed forces, and, in general, the mayhem caused by the wars took a heavy toll on slave owners, both by "freeing" their slaves and by undermining their enterprises with constant confiscations of lands and assets. But the impact of the wars was regionalized. Thus in Antioquia by 1825, there were 5,348 slaves forming 5 percent of the population, and in Cartagena slaves were only 4 percent of the total; while in Popayán, the main slavocracy of the country, there were still more than twelve thousand slaves, 14 percent of the total, and in the Chocó, a region controlled mostly by the Popayán slave owners, slaves were still nearly 30 percent of the region's population (Fernando Gómez 1970). In areas such as the Pacific coastal region, comparatively isolated from revolutionary upheavals and where slavery was the mainstay of the economy, it is clear that not many slaves had the opportunity to enlist. Nevertheless, some did, and as a result of this and the 1821 legislation freeing children born to slave mothers, slaves decreased in numbers both absolutely and proportionally; by 1851 they were only 3.4 percent of the population of the Popayán and Cauca areas combined and only 3.9 percent of the Chocó's population. Some slaves were being sold to Peru, where abolition came later (Gutiérrez Azopardo 1980, 85), and doubtless others were taking advantage of the political convulsions of the new republic and fleeing their masters' mines and haciendas, but there must also have been a constant process of manumission on an individual basis until general emancipation in 1851.

The reasons behind abolition are, predictably, complex and subject to debate, but in the Chocó, at least, any argument that free labor would prove more efficient certainly did not hold water. In contrast with Antioquia where ex-slaves turned to free labor apparently without much trouble, in the Chocó—and indeed wherever the slave regime had been most deeply entrenched—there was a definite tendency for the freed slaves to avoid working for whites. Emancipation thus constituted the "death blow" for large-scale mining in the region (Restrepo 1952, 95, 211). Foreigners who visited the area unanimously reported on its great mineral wealth, as Restrepo shows at some length (1952, chap. 5), but labor was a fundamental problem due to the "character of the freed slaves [who] continued to pan gold for themselves in the best spots and where the least labor was required, with the single purpose of attending to their daily needs; but as these [were] not great and their ambition still less, they gave themselves over to the idleness that characterize[d] them" (Robert White, an observer of the 1880s, quoted in Restrepo 1952, 95). Cochrane observed in 1824: "[The free blacks] are too lazy to work the mines, being perfectly contented if they can secure a sufficiency of plantains and corn for subsistence" (1825, 2:420). Brisson noted in 1895: "There is a shortage of hands: every negro has his little mine where he works a few days a week (when he urgently needs to) with his family, and he prefers to make little but live freely and work on his own account. Seldom does he resist a permanent occupation" (1895, 151). Agustín Codazzi saw progress for the province in the form of a law obliging the masses to work. There was a "shortage of hands," and the blacks were content to fulfill their necessities, which, in any case, were "almost none" (Comisión Corográfica 1958, 323–24). And later, in 1920, a Colombian newspaperman found that the American mining company at Andagoya tended to employ blacks from more distant parts of the Chocó and even from Jamaica, while the locals preferred "to pan gold and platinum in the rivers, since with two days work they [could] generally obtain enough to keep themselves the other five days of the week" (Cruz 1921, 11). The whites saw the blacks as simply lazy, but it is likely that given the nature of slave regimes in the region, blacks opted for greater independence and avoided wage labor. In addition, freed blacks in Colombia found themselves hedged about with restrictions on vagrancy, social reunions, commercial transactions, and even on how they could spend their money (Gutiérrez Azopardo 1980, 86; Cuesta 1986, 44): but these restrictions could only apply if the black was working for an employer or within the ambit of administrative control.

After independence and emancipation the Chocó was left largely to the blacks, and race mixture remained at a minimum. The whites confined themselves to small urban centers, such as Quibdó and Nóvita, and although they owned a few mines, they tended to concentrate on commerce: "In the iron coffers pile up the gold and platinum which the merchants obtain from the negroes who come from distant rivers to buy on Saturdays and Sundays" (Brisson 1895, 128). Of course, there were also blacks and mulattoes in these towns who lived at close quarters with the whites—Mollien called the mulattoes "the patrician class" and noted that some of them were slave owners (1824, 307)—but the vast majority lived along the Chocó's myriad rivers, farming, mining, fishing, and hunting and keeping clear of the whites: "They run and hide, probably from fright at seeing our white faces, something which they cannot be accustomed to, at least the women and children, most of whom cannot have moved from these places" (Brisson 1895, 138).

Rain, misery, and blackness were the three things that stood out for the traveler to the Chocó, and their congruence has been no accident. The whites never settled in the place because it was, for them, unpleasant and unhealthy; for their purposes, impermanent settlement sufficed for mining enterprises, and settlement in the area's small urban centers was sufficient since they could engage in lucrative commerce without having to invest much in infrastructure or public services of any kind. The blacks remained there precisely to avoid the whites and because colonial society outside the area was as unaccepting of them as blacks as they were unprepared for it after years spent slaving in the mines. The area was relegated to them and left to itself, although it continued to provide a reserve of natural resources for outside entrepreneurs and a local white elite. In this way, as a result of the demographic, economic, and political factors characterizing its history, the Chocó became a locus of black community, black resistance, and the reelaboration of black culture.

7

Heroes and Politics:

Quibdó since 1900

A los que nacen procesados.

I am disturbed when I hear of blacks who are opposed to my ideals and then become the executioners of my own race and of the workers. It seems to me that they disown themselves, are ashamed of their own mothers, and subconsciously long for the times when our forbears paid the *derecho de pernada* and our grandparents [endured] abject subjection by the master satyr, ignorant and severe.

The history of Quibdó since about 1900 provides a very neat and precise window on the Colombian racial order. From the particular vantage point created by the Chocoano coincidence of region and race, we can see a specific version of the more general pattern of coexisting *mestizaje* and discrimination. We see black community and resistance and correspondingly polarized, hierarchical, and discriminatory black-white relations. But we also see black adaptation to white society, facilitated partly by white acceptance, and the fragmentation both these imply for black solidarity; and we see the conditional nature of white acceptance. Throughout, the lowly position of the

Epigraphs: (1) "To those who are born accused"; part of the dedication of the book *Memorias del odio* (Memories of Hate) by the Chocoano Manuel Saturio Valencia (see Velásquez 1953, and below); (2) Diego Luis Córdoba, quoted in Rivas Lara (1986, 35); *derecho de pernada* refers to a feudal custom in which the lord put his leg upon the bed of two vassals who were being married (it is presumably related to the *droit de seigneur*). Córdoba refers in this way to sexual use made of slave women by their masters, an implication reinforced by the reference to the "master satyr."

106

Chocó in the racial order is maintained, not intact but in relative terms.

In early twentieth-century Quibdó, there was an important opposition between black and white. There was a very exclusive and discriminatory white elite that held the reins of power and wealth. Most blacks were poor and of low status. But, as one might expect in Latin America, things were not unambiguous. Not all whites were rich, and there was also a black "elite," based mainly on mining, which had adopted a lifestyle similar to that of the white elite; and these blacks were accepted—in a very conditional way—as social acquaintances by the whites. A category of mulattoes of diverse origins also existed, and a disproportionate number of them occupied a superior social position. Some blacks would adapt by adopting the lifestyle and educational standards associated with the white elite. This adaptation might also be connected with race mixture, although the latter could occur without cultural assimilation or upward mobility. There was also a degree of white acceptance which could take various forms: helping mulatto offspring or giving patronage to some blacks. Black upward mobility could be accepted, but it was a conditional acceptance, the condition being that whites should remain basically on top and that blacks should "know their place."

I start this chapter by looking at a particular historical, but also somewhat mythical, character, Manuel Saturio Valencia. His life history shows how blacks could rise, aided by some whites (although opposed by others). However, Valencia pushed his luck too far and transgressed certain norms. Nemesis was the outcome. This case study illustrates some of the basic themes of this book: the interweaving of black nucleation and black assimilation; the conditional nature of acceptance.

Manuel Saturio Valencia

Manuel Saturio Valencia is a black folk hero in the Chocó. In Quibdó the name can be seen emblazoned over the portals of schoolrooms and cultural centers, and a local newspaper was named after him. He is seen as a black rebel who fought against oppression by white society. He is a reminder of how things were, how far they have come, and how far they have still to go.

There are varied accounts of the life and works of this folk hero and quasi-mythological figure. *Memorias del odio* (Memories of Hate) edited by Velásquez (1953) is apparently the last writings of Manuel Saturio Valencia before his execution in 1907 (he was the last Colombian to be legally executed, although many question the legality of it), and it describes his life in a slightly haphazard way; it may or may not have been tampered with after his death by the authorities or his enemies. *Mi Cristo negro* is a carefully researched novelistic biography by Teresa Martínez de Varela (1983), a Chocoano woman, which may or may not contain a good deal of dramatic elaboration by the author.

Saturio was born in Quibdó in 1867 of poor parents, his father a mulatto, his mother a black woman. The early details of his life differ somewhat in the two accounts, but it seems that Saturio's poverty prevented education until the Capuchins arrived in 1878, ending a long period of virtual ecclesiastical absence from the region. Saturio's name soon appeared in the choir lists. With the monks he obtained his education, literary and musical, as did many others after 1884, when another group of monks arrived and opened a small school where pupils of any color were admitted. By the age of eighteen, Saturio was already a political figure, organizing Conservative party meetings and confronting members of Quibdó's white elite in public discussion, something unheard of at a time when this elite monopolized political and economic power. Like his father, Saturio was a Conservative, while the majority in Quibdó, white or black, were Liberals, but Saturio also represented himself as the leader of the black race in a battle against white oppression.

Impressed by Saturio's scholarly and linguistic talents, the Capuchins sent him to Popayán to complete his studies, and there he made friends among the powerful white elite. Through the patronage of a white friend he was allocated a job in the Quibdó bureaucracy in 1888 at the age of twenty-one, later rising to become *juez de rentas* or public revenue judge in the 1890s. Around this time, although the whites were the political and economic elite and they maintained a very exclusive social circle, not all the blacks were poor. Teresa de Varela mentions "blacks who had thrived and gained much social experience . . . their parties were of a standard to match those of the gentlemen of the Carrera Primera [First Avenue]," and they dressed, ate, and lived in a way that rivaled the white elite. First Avenue, or La Primera, was the symbolic center of white power and wealth. Running along the Atrato riverbank, where boats from Cartagena brought the finest European imports and took away gold, platinum, and some agricultural products, La Primera was dominated by the wooden three- and four-story houses of the white elite, with the ground floor dedicated to commerce and the upper floors to living quarters. Here they would hold aristocratic balls with fine liquors and food, served by black maids from fine chinaware emblazoned with the family crest.

The blacks who, according to de Varela, managed to rival these living standards would have made their fortunes from mining (Córdoba 1983, 53) and some commercial activities, but it seems unlikely that their economic basis was on a level with the white elite and more probable that they could occasionally put on a ball or party equal in some respects to those of La Primera.

In 1889, the country was convulsed by the Thousand Days War in which the Liberals tried to oust the Conservatives from power. When the Conservatives finally regained control in 1903, Saturio was reinstated as *juez de rentas*. Next, according to accounts of his life, Saturio becomes the accountant's assistant in a new business established by the Meluk brothers, two of the Syrians who at this time were establishing commercial enterprises all over Colombia: one of these men gives him credit to start up a small business of his own on La Primera. Soon after, through the influence of his Popayán friends, Saturio is appointed *juez penal* of Quibdó (criminal court judge), an unusually high post for a black man. Meanwhile, two events spoil the progress of his career. First, Saturio has an affair with a woman of the white elite, who also happens to be the sister of a sworn enemy. According to de Varela, this woman later becomes pregnant. This jeopardizes his relations with the white community, which are in any case uneven: although he has support in some quarters, he has bitter opponents in others. Second, he learns that a black woman he was planning to marry is in fact a half sister, since her father had had adulterous relations with his mother, a revelation that throws him temporarily into an abyss of despair and alcoholism.

From then on Saturio finds himself besieged by his enemies' plots: they write defamatory poems against well-known figures on the walls of public buildings and attribute them to him. His white lover has the baby, but her brother arranges to have it done away with. Saturio goes a bit crazy, drinking inordinately and preaching on the streets, and eventually his enemies arrange his removal from office. Not content with this, they decide to finish him off and conspire to frame him with an intentional arson charge, which at that time carried the death sentence.

Quibdó was duly set alight on 1 May 1907, though it was not severely damaged; Saturio was arrested and imprisoned and, on 7 May 1907, was publicly shot by a firing squad. Teresa de Varela presents all this as a massive plot, with details of names and places— an account supported by other oral versions I heard of the history. In *Memorias,* on the other hand, Saturio recounts how he was being tortured daily during the period he was writing his memoirs, until, finally unable to stand any more, he confessed to the crime, although he does not confess convincingly to the reader in the narrative itself. Instead he sees himself as a victim, not necessarily of a plot, but of the society that oppressed him and engendered in him the hate that was the cause of his undoing. "Thinking of common rights, I wanted to govern like the whites. Their power prevented me. They molded me, but the clay would not obey." And he ends by accusing his judges, "I am of your making, the precise imprint left by your conduct" (Velásquez 1953, 84, 87). The two accounts give rather different impressions of Saturio Valencia. In *Mi Cristo negro,* he is a hero, a martyr, virtually blameless, a man whom women, white or black, covet for his looks, charm, and talent. In *Memorias,* he accuses himself of favoritism as a judge, of vindictiveness and underhand tactics against his enemies, of arson, of hate; he mentions several spells in jail which never appear in the other version. The *Memorias* version is perhaps more human, but it is also suspiciously favorable to his enemies and the dominant white elite.

Quibdó at the turn of the century was clearly no Latin American "racial democracy" whichever version of Saturio's history one takes, but it was also quite a complex society. Although blacks were generally servants or were expected to occupy a servile position, there was also a small black elite that had some economic power and was bent on education. A black man such as Saturio could make important friends among the whites and through them obtain administrative posts and commercial credit. However, Saturio went too far for the white elite. The cause of his downfall is ambiguous to a certain extent. He was, of course, a Conservative in a Liberal town, and he also had enemies among the blacks. But it is also crucial that he wanted to "govern like the whites," while his relations with a white elite woman certainly caused conflict. Blacks were still expected to know their place.

The following poem is attributed to Manuel Saturio Valencia by Miguel A. Caicedo (1973), and the heavy irony and mock naivety with which it treats the idea of *blanqueamiento* satirize the arrogance of white pretensions to superiority. Alongside the irony, bitterness shows through, and the net effect is even tragic: a black man trapped in a white world that defines whiteness as virtue and blackness as a moral defect. The phrase *mandarme a blanquear* literally means "have myself whitened," as one would send washing to the laundry. The literal impossibility of this makes its mock ingenuousness all the more painful. (The orthography of the poem departs from normal Spanish orthography in the poet's attempt to convey a Chocoano accent.)

A yo que soy inorante	For I who am ignorant
Me precisa preguntá	It is necessary to ask
Si el color blanco es virtú	If the color white is virtue
Pa' yo mandáme a blanquiá	So that I can whiten myself
Pregunto al hombre leal	I ask the faithful man
Porque sabé me precisa	Because I need to know
Si el negro no se bautiza	If the black is not baptized
En la pila bautismal	At the baptismal font
Si hay otra ma principal	If there is another more important
Ma patrás o ma palante	Further back or further forward
Ma bonita o ma brillante	More beautiful or more brilliant
Me darán un punto franco	Will you tell me frankly
A yo que soy inorante	I who am ignorant
De un hombre y una mujé	From a man and a woman
Todos somos descendientes	We are all descended
Por qué al negro sólamente	Why is it only the black
Con desprecio lo han de ver?	Who is looked upon with disdain?
La misma sangre ha de ser	It must be the same blood
Aunque el negro . . . singular,	Although the black . . . strangely
Siempre lo han de colocar	Is always put
En un lugar separao	In a separate place
Si el negro no es bautizao	Perhaps the black is not baptized
Me precisa preguntá	I need to ask
Negro fue San Benedito	Black was Saint Benedict
Negras fueron sus pinturas	Black were his paintings
En la Sagrada Escritura	In the Holy Scriptures
Letras blancas yo no he visto	White letters I have not seen
Negros los clavos de Cristo	Black were the nails of Christ
Que murió en la Santa Cruz	Who died on the Holy Cross
Será que bajó Jesú	Could it be that Jesus came down
Por el blanco a padecé?	To suffer for the white?
Sólo así podré saber	Only thus could I know
Si el color blanco es virtú	If the color white is virtue
Cuando tengamo que dale	When we have to give
A mi Dios estrecha cuenta	To God a strict account
Cómo el negro va a pagá	How can a black pay
Por el blanco las ofensas	For the white's offenses
Si al negro no se le encuentra	If for the black can be found
Un delito que culpá?	No crime of which he is guilty?
Me dirán si esto es verdad	Tell me if this is true

Que'l blanco no tiene pena	That the white has no sin
O si es que no se condena	Or if he's free from condemnation
Pa' yo mandáme a blanquiá	So that I can whiten myself

Quibdó: Changing Racial Stratification

The story of Manuel Saturio Valencia reveals how an individual black man could advance socially; how that advance depended on white patronage and on adopting the lifestyle and educational standards of the nonblack world; and how it was conditional upon his still "knowing his place" in relation to the whites. For the blacks and mulattoes of Quibdó, above all the richer and better educated ones, the latter condition became increasingly onerous during the twentieth century, and major upheavals ensued. For all the changes, however, some underlying patterns were reproduced, albeit in altered form.

Because the history of Quibdó in this century is only very partially written (in, for example, Miguel A. Caicedo 1977), I talked to some of the town's older inhabitants, and what follows is mostly taken from interviews with Dr. Felix Arenas, Chocoano mining engineer and ex-mayor of Quibdó (taped interview, February 1987, Medellín), and with Miguel A. Caicedo, Chocoano poet, novelist, and folklorist of the Chocó; Cesar Rivas Lara, Chocoano university lecturer and writer; Emilio Bechara, one of the last Syrian merchants remaining in Quibdó; and Judith Ferrer, one of the last residing members of an old white elite family that has a reputation for having been one of the most exclusive (all interviewed with tape recorder and/or notes, March 1987).

If we look back to Quibdó in the 1920s or 1930s, it was a smallish town lying next to the Atrato River. It was connected primarily to Cartagena and other ports of the Caribbean coast whence came imports—a large quantity of which were European—which gave the elite their lifestyle. Many of the elite were also educated in Europe. There were also connections with Antioquia, but a serviceable road did not open until 1946, and the agricultural produce from Antioquia's southwest came in on mule trains. Socially, there were two main groups, the blacks and the whites, and the latter were represented basically by the elite.

The white elite was made up of the descendants of older colonial Spanish settlers, of families who had come from the Cauca Valley at some indeterminate time (probably after independence), of some Antioqueño merchants, and, from the early 1900s, of *los turcos*, the Syrian immigrants who, increasing in numbers after the First World War, came to control a large part of Quibdó's trade, owning some forty stores. Generally speaking, this elite was commercial in orientation, buying gold and platinum from the blacks and selling all manner of goods both to them and to the whites.

The relation of the white elite to the blacks was essentially that of master to servant, but there was also a certain amount of race mixture. For the traditional white elite this was nearly always between white men and their black mistresses or servants, the men also keeping up a legitimate family with a wife from the white elite. Caicedo mentions some cases in which this relation was open enough to be fairly common knowledge, and, according to him, Rodolfo Castro, Saturio's archenemy, died in the arms of a black woman. In the event of pregnancy, the black woman might be made to abort; alternatively the child would not be socially recognized by the father, that is, would not receive his surname. In some cases, however, the child would be recognized, thus spreading the elite surnames into the black lower classes. The *turcos* were different in this respect: being mostly single men, they found their wives among the white elite, but they also recognized all their children by other women; as Emilio Bechara said, they recognized whatever was "*sangre de uno,*" one's own blood. Clearly, social recognition opened the way for more material claims to be made on the father, and some of these mulattoes were able to rise socially: one governor of the Chocó, Alonso Meluk, was the son of a black woman from the San Juan Valley and a Syrian merchant. (One recalls Mollien's comment about the mulattoes being the "patrician class.") In addition, although no one talks about them much, there were also whites who did not belong economically to the white elite: minor public employees and small merchants, the latter probably increasing in numbers as the Medellín-Quibdó road opened the way to more Antioqueño immigration after 1946. For these people, the social constraints on the recognition of children resulting from unions with black women would have been less restrictive.

The black group had its own elite, which, if Teresa de Varela's account is true, must have been present for some time. Although these blacks adopted the lifestyle of the whites, the exclusiveness of the latter put strong conditions on the blacks' social pretensions, causing a reciprocal attitude of pride and introversion. Felix Arenas commented: "They were legitimate Chocoanos, blacks, of African descent, and they gained their position through education and because they amassed modest fortunes with work, with mining, agriculture, and commerce. They sent their children to study in Cartagena and Medellín, and they made their own elite, as closed in as the whites, closed in against the whites." According to Caicedo, their pretensions caused them to look down on the rest of the black population, emulating the whites to the extent of adopting the ideologies of *blanqueamiento,* even if actual race mixture with the white elite was very rare. He remarks: "The situation was difficult. They would separate themselves in order to be on top of the other blacks. They tried to rival the white elite in importance. It's something that leaves a rather bitter taste: that they, in view of the bad position of the other blacks, didn't want to be black anymore but considered themselves white."

In addition to the black elite, there were the mulattoes. The 1918 census classifies 24 percent of Quibdó municipality's population as *mezclado,* mixed, with 9 percent white and 61 percent black, plus 6 percent others. Much of the mulatto category would have been poor, but a disproportionate number had a superior position. Mulattoes could take this position not necessarily because they faced less social discrimination from the whites, but for two specific reasons. First, they could make use of the potential benefits of having a white, and hence generally wealthy, father. This, even in cases in which paternity was not socially recognized, could have material advantages, giving the mulatto a start in life. Second, blacks who became successful through their own efforts and/or through white patronage might, despite obstacles, manage to marry lighter-skinned people, giving rise to mulattoes who received the benefits of some family wealth and access to a good education. This was difficult in the face of a very exclusive white elite but accelerated from about the 1940s, when blacks started studying and living outside the Chocó. The mulatto elite group occupied an ambiguous position between the whites and the blacks. Like the black elite they attempted to distance themselves from their black heritage, an attempt backed in their case by actual race mixture. Cesar Rivas observed: "The Chocó has always had a problem, which is that the mulatto . . . has not identified himself with the blacks, but instead has tended to identify with the whites, and the whites have rejected him. . . . At bottom, the mulatocracy of Quibdó has never identified with the black group."

Outside the sphere of actual race mixture, there existed links of *compadrazgo,* godparenthood, between whites and blacks.

> It was perfectly common for someone to ask a richer person to carry their child [i.e., at the baptismal font]. The *compadrazgo* system estab-lished links that crossed the barriers: the house servant would ask her master to baptize her child. And many of these children were educated by the white families. For example, I have a friend, M, who was edu-cated by the Meluk family. His mother was a very respectable woman who worked for the Meluk family, and her children were baptized and raised with the Meluks and the Alumas. And still today they maintain

relationships with the descendants of those families who live in Medellín, Cali, and Bogotá. (Felix Arenas)

Not even at the level of entertainment did total exclusiveness prevail. Caicedo (1977, 36) records that "dances were the favorite sport in those days," and in Quibdó there were two blacks—but *"negros distinguidos"*—who held dances, Victoriano Parra and Victoriana Mayo. The former did so on Sundays with a record player, and he charged one cent a dance; students were the main participants, but everyone could and did attend, blacks and whites. The latter held two sorts, *bailes populares* and *bailes de la crème* ("as they used to call them," says Caicedo). Blacks and whites went to the *populares,* while the white elite and a few *negros distinguidos* went to the fancier occasions. Private functions were, however, more exclusive.

On the black lower class there is, predictably, little information. In 1929, there were four thousand people in Quibdó, and apart from two ice factories, two cinemas, a jail, and a hospital there was little else (Gutiérrez 1929). Clearly, then, there was not much demand for black labor, even when in the 1930s there also appeared small workshops producing candles, pasta, fizzy drinks, soap, and clothes (Caicedo 1977). The blacks were mainly domestic servants, stevedores, and carters, toters, and carriers of all kinds; they were also artisans, miners, and farmers. By all accounts, their relations with the whites were of a servile nature: pretty well any white could order a poor black to carry a bag or run an errand and expect to be obeyed. Black maids could not sleep on beds or use the same crockery and cutlery as their white masters. Felix Arenas recounts that "if a black was going along the sidewalk and some whites came the other way, either he got off or they got him off." In commercial and employment transactions, the blacks essentially had to accept the terms offered by the whites who did the accounts, especially since the majority were illiterate.

Education for these people was minimal. The church took care of some of this, as in Saturio's case, and by 1929 an Escuela Modelo for the primary education of poorer children had also been in existence for some time. But the good schools and secondary education were reserved principally for the whites: in 1912, nuns founded La Presentación for girls, and in 1915 El Colegio Carrasquilla was established for boys, with its own primary school annex. Photos of the pupils of both schools in 1929 show a couple of black faces (Gutiérrez 1929), but fees were high and both schools had a reputation for exclusiveness.

This general picture held in its basic form until the middle of this century, but from about 1930 important changes began to occur. According to Judith Ferrer, an old survivor of a white elite family, someone, for whatever reason, "planted the seed of hate," causing a "racial complex" that manifested itself in the desire of the blacks to be equal to the whites, a desire that also showed that they no longer "knew their place." Before, "everyone knew their place," and there was no "resentment." Relations between blacks and whites were cordial; the white girls had friends among the girls from well-off black families, but they did not invite them to their parties, nor would they be invited to a black party: "everyone knew their place."

A main cog in the mechanism of change was another Chocoano hero figure, Diego Luis Córdoba, born in 1907 (Caideco 1977; Rivas Lara 1986). And the main driving force behind the process was education. Like many of the better-off blacks of the period, Córdoba had been educated in Medellín and Bogotá, principally in law, and—like Saturio—was an exceptional scholar and linguist. He was also politically ambitious both for himself and for his people, as Saturio had been, and yet still at that time "in Quibdó there was no law, there were no elections; the people didn't participate in anything, and the whites took all the decisions at their own convenience" (Caicedo). The legal framework existed for proper electoral procedure, but the white elite basically decided amongst themselves on the distribution of jobs and power. Now, however, there was an increasing number of educated blacks who were no longer willing to let this situation prevail. Córdoba returned from the interior to Quibdó in 1933, having already achieved national status as a radical student leader. At the time, the Chocó was subsumed electorally under Antioquia, and when he failed to become an Antioqueño Liberal candidate for the position of representative to Congress in the 1933 elections—a member of the Quibdó elite was favored over him—he started his own party, Acción Democrática, later to become the existing Cordobismo, which quickly gained the support of the black masses, plus most of the black, and some of the mulatto, elite. They shouldered their way into the political arena and won seats on the city councils; they also gained the support of some of the white elite. Emilio Meluk, a lawyer, for example, thwarted by the rest of the elite in his objective to enter the race as a candidate, "got so annoyed that he called all the people to the central square by his house, and told them their rights and all about the political abuses that were being committed. And the people began to think that there should be proper elections" (Caicedo). Córdoba was elected as an independent representative for Antioquia to Congress, and Acción Democrática gained power and got its people into the local administration. Córdoba declared himself a socialist, but his concern was also firmly with the blacks and the Chocó: "My battle has not been to declare a war of blacks against whites, but to claim for the blacks equal opportunities in the economy, in education, in training and in social consideration, in the regency of the Chocó" (quoted in Rivas Lara 1986, 35).

With the help of Vicente Barrios Ferrer (father a white Antioqueño, mother a black), a member of Acción Democrática and director of education in Quibdó, the two boys' primary schools, rich and poor, were mixed in 1933, and "this was the first effective blow against the aristocracy" (Caicedo 1977, 61). It should be remembered that people such as Córdoba himself had studied at the Carrasquilla school prior to that moment: the blow had been gathering force for some time. Later, new schools were created for both girls and boys in Quibdó and Istmina. The exclusive convent school, La Presentación, retained its elitism but lost popularity and by 1971 had closed. Outside Quibdó, the new Chocoano political force now also had access to grants from the political machine for their high school graduates to study in the interior, creating a new influx of blacks from humble backgrounds with talent and expertise. The white elite laughed and ridiculed their servant class as it began to be educated, but the tide was now turning faster, and some of the whites began to leave Quibdó for Cali, Medellín, and Bogotá. As the blacks took over the administration, white women often found themselves as secretaries to black bosses, and this offended their sense of propriety. More generally, the blacks as a voting majority simply began to oust the whites from the available jobs. In 1947, Córdoba pulled off an unprecedented political coup by pushing through legislation making the Chocó, until then an intendency, a full department. He achieved this against the wishes of some congressmen and despite the legal minimum requirements for this status of two hundred fifty thousand inhabitants and five hundred thousand pesos of annual income, which the Chocó could not match. This move expanded the local bureaucracy greatly and gave more room to the growing educated black community. The process was a slow one, spread over three decades, and the final blow came in 1966 when a big fire burnt down most of La Primera, destroying a great deal of what remained of the white elite's commercial enterprises. The time when "everybody knew their place" had gone.

Continuity and Change

But this is no fairy story, and "happily ever after" is not the ending. For the blacks in the Chocó, politics, the administration, and public

117

A suburb of Quibdó, a city that has expanded rapidly in recent years.

services are the principal sources of employment for educated people, while at the same time the amount of goods and services to which the region has access is very small, since (according to official figures for the 1970s) the Chocó commands the smallest departmental electoral population in the country and contributes less than 1 percent of Colombia's gross national production. Its political and economic clout is therefore very small, its share of the pie accordingly diminutive, and there is not nearly enough to go around. Thus opposing factions emerge which fight over the existing resources, try to get their people into the administration, and, in some cases, try to pocket a portion of the resources for themselves. Marco Tobias Cuesta, Chocoano lawyer and municipal councillor of Quibdó, puts it thus: "The inept governing class [of the Chocó] constantly tangles itself up in fratricidal wars, not now about centralism or decentralization, but about who can take the biggest portion of the bureaucratic pie" (1986, 70).

Felix Arenas likewise speaks of "permanent internal fighting that makes good administration impossible." When Córdoba's party started—initially as Acción Democrática, later as Cordobismo—it was a Liberal tendency, for all Córdoba's socialist leanings. Almost straight away an opposing Liberal group formed under the Chocoano

Adán Arriaga Andrade. "He was a mulatto but considered himself white, and he took up arms against Diego Luis Córdoba. So Adán Arriaga, who was from Lloró, his father an outsider and his mother a black, allied himself to La Primera with the whites, while Diego Luis Córdoba gathered together the blacks" (Cesar Rivas Lara). "The elite needed someone with the capacity to confront Diego Luis Córdoba," remembers Caicedo, and a mulatto such as Arriaga was a good candidate at that juncture. When Arriagismo ended, another opposition group emerged under Ramón Lozano Garces; his son, Jorge Tadeo Lozano, still heads this faction, known as Lozanismo. Although the real makeup of these factions is complex and generally obeys the ups and downs of local politics, there is a traditional association of Cordobismo with the blacks and the opposing faction— currently Lozanismo—with the mulattoes. Within the Conservatives there are also at least two groups.

The blacks triumphed, but it has been a partial, not to say a hollow, victory. They won political control of their own region, and they won some education (although in rural areas illiteracy is still high). But politically they are fighting over a small pie, and education prepares them either to leave the department or to be a well-educated idler at home. As Felix Arenas's son said when he visited him in Quibdó: "Everyone you say hello to is doctor, doctor, doctor: here everyone is doctor." (In Colombia this title is often used for people with a first university degree.) "The University of the Chocó is generating a time bomb . . . there was a time when the Chocó supplied the country with teachers, and today some of the graduates of the university manage to get a job as a teacher, although not as a professional; but the great majority of these graduates are walking the streets of Quibdó with a professional's ambitions and no chance of a job. What do these poor people have? Frustration, hate . . . they are an ill-fated 'elite' that will one day create a serious problem" (Felix Arenas). So although education is a matter of pride and the family house "has diplomas on the walls from the front room through to the kitchen" (Arenas), it is again a conditional victory.

This fact is recognized by many of the black and mulatto political elite that replaced the old white upper class. Felix Arenas gives a good sense of the frustration of a local political regime whose power and scope is limited by the basic dependence of the region as a whole.

We have wasted the opportunity [that education has given us]: we are good executives, solvent professionals outside the Chocó, but in the Chocó it's as if we become forgetful, dulled. The ones to blame for the backward state of the region are ourselves, because we have left the

119

place. Perhaps if some of us had stayed, others would have stayed with us. And what happens is that the person who graduates from university and goes to the Chocó on a permanent basis loses his frame of reference, the habitat begins to appear fine to him, and the same thing happens to oneself as well. In less decent terms, you arrive in the Chocó, and within three months filth smells like perfume. And I'm not saying that the people there are mediocre, because there are many professionals there, and the universities don't give away degrees. . . .

You sit down with any of us in Quibdó, with the most important people, and they're on about nothing else but politics . . . and about how we're going to organize a party, a meal, the girls, and this and that. And if you're not in that game, you're completely out of phase. They are the most intelligent and best-educated people in the country, and if that intelligent, well-educated young man stays in the interior, he makes a good living. Why does that talent become unproductive in the Chocó? It has to be because of the very structure of the Chocó, and because there we all minimize ourselves. That's why, even though it may be hateful, social classes are inevitable, because at least they create the reaction of trying to be better than your neighbor. People lose their aspiration, and they make do with any old thing. In three months filth smells like perfume. The first few days the atmosphere feels heavy, and then you begin to get used to it; and you go past the puddle in the street and get splashed, and that's normal. Because the opium is there: and the opium is to more or less finish your work for the day, meet up with your girlfriend, nice and pretty, drink a few *aguardientes,* and have a party. And one's friends talk about petty things, about politics and worthless trifles, but never about important things that are of any benefit to the region.

Notice here how "politics" is equated with entertainment and activities of little importance: it is commonly heard that "politics" does not exist in the Chocó, but only "politicking." There is also a whole complex history of economic dependence and central government neglect behind this, and to a large extent the current political situation in the Chocó is a result of that. Without real economic power, the politicians are liable to become involved in a local, introverted game that has little impact on the region's fate. What this extract conveys is the sense that it is impossible to get anything significant done in the Chocó, that initiative becomes suffocated, that aspiration is drowned. Perhaps the price of economic dependence is precisely this sense of impotence.

Also noticeable is the lack of concern of most Chocoano politicians with issues of black resistance and protest. Their interest lies overwhelmingly in working the political machine of patron-client relations to get access to bureaucratic benefits. As such they fight against one another for a voting clientele, and there is no attempt to mobilize electoral support on issues of black identity. In the Chocoano context of the 1930s, with the political control of a mostly black region entirely in the hands of a local white elite, the bureaucratic changes that occurred were based partly on a localized black mobilization. But the initial phase of protest which had some degree of racialized opposition, albeit an ambiguous one, has defused as upwardly mobile blacks have become part of a clientelistic political system that emphasizes competing vertical linkages. This is largely due to the inherent difficulties of mobilizing a political clientele around blackness—even in the Chocó—when ambiguity about who is and is not "black" is the result of centuries of institutionalized race mixture. In a national context of official mestizo-ness, organization along racial lines is very hard to legitimate—only the indians have been able to do this with some success (see chapter 17, where I look at black mobilization in more depth).

In the Chocó, the ambiguities of black mobilization are also reinforced by clear continuities in the racial dimensions of stratification. Still today, the top posts of Chocoano politics and administration are occupied by mulattoes and other light-skinned mixed-bloods. The only black governor of the Chocó has been Ramón Mosquera, from 1966 to 1968. This is partly because the "mulatocracy" that already existed when Diego Luis Córdoba started his movement was clearly in a good position to take over the top bureaucratic places, while it was only the white elite that was gradually pushed out or which left of its own accord. It is also due to a marked tendency of the higher echelons of the administration to marry white women. Diego Luis Córdoba himself, a black man, married a white Antioqueño woman; Ramón Lozano Garces, already a mulatto, although of humble origins, also married a white woman; Adán Arriaga did likewise. In many cases, the most educated Chocoanos live and work in the interior of the country where the opportunities are and where political activity is carried out—although they may return to the Chocó to fill a post from time to time—such that their choice of spouse inevitably tends towards a woman of the surrounding social milieu. But a motive of *blanqueamiento* is hard to discount, and it is in any case impossible to avoid the symbolic connotations of marrying in this way, no matter what the personal motivation might be.

Racial differentiation has also been maintained in another way in the economy. The old white elite moved out, but as they did so, a new white group moved in—the Antioqueños. They had been around in small numbers for many years, but when the Quibdó-Medellín road opened in 1946, the influx increased. Their purpose was commerce, precisely the niche being vacated at that time, and today they own the majority of the businesses in Quibdó, many of them small enterprises. The blacks have some small, and one or two larger, concerns, but they are outnumbered by the *paisas*. The question of why the Chocoanos have filled the political but not the economic space left by the outgoing white elite is a complex matter. In part, it is because the Chocoanos have less available capital than do immigrant merchants, but this is certainly not the only cause, since many Antioqueños arrive with minimal resources. In addition, the Chocoanos have very little in the way of commercial experience, having been excluded from that sphere of activity, and, perhaps more important, the aspirations of those who have some capital tend to be directed towards education: the aim is to turn one's children into professionals—doctors, teachers, lawyers, and so on. The Antioqueños, in contrast, have a very commercial tradition, and among the emigrants from Antioquia commercial aspirations are paramount. They establish a foothold in Quibdó with a small capital investment, they form a tight-knit group within which mutual aid and cooperation assist each merchant (who also has good contacts in Antioquia whence are imported many of the goods the merchants sell), and they establish a majority control over the commercial sector.

In this sense, the wider economic structures of the nation reasserted themselves even in the context of the exit of the old white elite. The blacks still have little real power or wealth. Much of the political elite is noticeably lighter skinned than the majority. The whites control much of the dynamic commerce. There are some differences, of course. Many of the new immigrants are of plebian origin, resulting in a reduction of the hierarchical nature of black-white relations. Equally there are more blacks with some access to bureaucratic salaries. Although both blacks and whites tend to socialize and form unions within their own ethnic networks, and much of the limited miscegenation that exists continues to be of an informal nature, the greater economic overlap between blacks and whites does give rise to mixed marriages or stable unions. In short, the whole double dynamic of black adaptation/resistance and white acceptance/discrimination has softened with changes in the local economic, political, and demographic structures. The local racial order was, at the beginning of the century, a highly hierarchical system, although, as was typical of the Colombian racial order as a whole, not characterized by total segregation and discrimination. The oppressive nature of the local order plus the increasing integration of some blacks into the national arena through education effected a change in this order. But since the reins of real economic and political power escaped the blacks, the racial order of today shows some continuity with that of past decades and dovetails easily with that of the nation as a whole.

Expressions of Chocoano Identity

Despite the lack of explicit mobilization around blackness, there are some manifestations of a regional identity which shed light on the question of racial identity and the possibility of its overt articulation. There have been two major civic strikes, centered on Quibdó but encompassing the rest of the region. The first was in September 1954, when the dismemberment of the Chocó was proposed in Congress. Gabriel García Márquez (1982, 143) was in Quibdó at the time and reported on the reaction of the Chocoanos as they went out into the streets for more than four hundred hours of continuous demonstrations and speeches, made occasional processions around the city, ate "tinned food, a few fried plantains, a little hurriedly cooked rice," and sang "Lamento Chocoano" (a popular regional song) in a way reminiscent of the Mexican revolutionaries' "La Cucaracha." After eighteen days of protest and political maneuvering, the good news came through—no dismemberment after all.

The second was in 1987, when the government announced a National Rehabilitation Plan to extend aid and development projects to deprived areas of the country. The Chocó was not included, and the local population, incensed at this, organized a large-scale civic strike that paralyzed the entire region for days. Eventually, President Barco agreed to include the region, with the result that a Plan de Acción, 1988–1992 was formulated, although its concrete achievements are far from evident.

In neither of these strikes did there appear to be an overtly racial dimension. The focus for solidarity was clearly the region, and the target of the movement was clearly central government. Any ideas about racial discrimination as a problem were apparently muted, although people have expressed them to me in conversations about the plight of the Chocó. As usual, then, public mobilization around an overtly racial identity is absent, and the racial element remains an unspoken corollary of regional protest.

The same pattern is found in another example of regional identity: the annual patron-saint festival of Quibdó. The Fiestas Patronales de Quibdó, dedicated to San Francisco of Assisi, affectionately known as San Pacho, require a good deal of stamina and dedication: they last at least two weeks and may go on for a month—depending on one's inclination and stamina—and they involve extensive drinking, dancing, and dressing up, with rather less emphasis on religious obser-

123

vance. One of the messages constantly reiterated throughout the fiestas concerns the lamentable indigence of the Chocó and its exploitation by others, and although one sees Antioqueños enjoying the fun along with the rest, and while it is true that they help to finance the costs, the fiestas are nevertheless unequivocally established as an event that belongs essentially to the Chocoanos and expresses *their* identity, *their* feeling of exploitation, and *their* sense of injustice. Little overt antagonism is directed against the Antioqueños in this process, but in the carnival floats that graphically bewail the Chocó's situation, they are implicitly included in the exploitative forces at work, and occasionally one hears comments such as that of a friend of mine: "Well, they're a bit stingy with their contributions to the fiestas, but they're the ones who *se las ponen de ruana* [put them on as a poncho, i.e., have great fun]." In this way, the fiestas embrace the nexus of relations between the Antioqueños and the Chocoanos without directly addressing the issue.

The organization of the fiestas in their present form began in 1929; prior to that there had simply been a celebration of some sort on the fourth of October, Saint Francis's saint day (Velásquez 1960b, 21; Villa 1985). From 1929, Quibdó's principal barrios (neighborhoods) were each given a specific day prior to the fourth for their own procession and festival. In 1957 there were eight such barrios; in 1986, when I witnessed the fiestas, there were twelve. By then, some newer barrios had also tagged their own parties onto the main structure of the event, without being given a special day by the central fiesta committee, which wants to prevent the fiestas becoming even longer than they already are.

The essential unit of the fiestas is each barrio's day. The morning is dedicated to finalizing the preparations, which have been going on for weeks: the *disfraz* or processional float is perfected, and street decorations are finished. At midday, the previous barrio's representatives come and ceremonially hand over the *bastón*, or wooden staff, which officially opens the new barrio's proceedings. The *disfraz* begins its rounds of the city, along a standard route that takes in all the other principal barrios, accompanied by a horde of people, usually dressed in bright colors and T-shirts printed with a barrio motif, the barrio flag bearer, the *bastón* carrier, and at least one *chirimía*, a small band composed at its simplest of a clarinetist, a bass drummer, and a cymbals player but which may expand to include a snare drummer and other wind instruments (see Perdomo Escobar 1963, 342; List 1980, 575). The procession dances rather than walks, *aguardiente* bottles are passed around, and people sing and call out catchphrases in unison. In each of the eleven other barrios the whole show pauses briefly outside

Horn players in a *chirimía* band during the Fiestas of San Pacho, Quibdó, 1986.

the house of that barrio's main representative as a mark of respect. The sun burns down, or occasionally the rain pours, and the whole tour lasts until about six in the evening.

At this point there is a lull in which people rest and get ready for the night. Meanwhile, the more religious-minded take the barrio's own image of San Pacho to the church, where a mass is read. The image remains there until morning, when there is another mass, and it is then returned to the barrio. From about eight o'clock there is a big street party in the barrio, plus numerous house parties. Everyone plugs in his or her stereo, and many are put out on the sidewalks; a few giant sound systems are rented and put at strategic points on the streets so that at least in certain areas one rhythm prevails. People dance in the street, move from house to house, and stand around and talk. In the small hours *sancocho* or *mondongo* (types of stew) are usually served in people's houses.

The overall structure of the fiestas has a typical beginning-middle-end form. On the third of September at midnight all the barrios, their flags, and the bands go around the city, announcing the fiestas. Then there is a lull until the twentieth of September, when everyone gets

125

together outside the church and tours the city again. The next day the twelve barrios begin their festivities and proceed in order: Tomás Pérez, Kennedy, Las Margaritas, Las Esmeraldas, Cristo Rey, El Silencio, Cesar Conto, Roma, Pandeyuca, La Yesquita, Yesca Grande, and Alameda Reyes. There is a certain seniority, with the oldest and "strongest" barrios coming last. On the third of October, all the *disfraces* come out together and are judged by the central committee. At three o'clock the following morning, the city tour is made singing a special hymn to San Pacho in each barrio, and there is a mass at dawn. On the fourth, the church finally has its own day, and its statue of San Francisco is carried through the city in reasonably respectful silence, with the clergy intoning liturgies and prayers: alcohol is notable for its absence. Finally, on the fifth, the barrio flags all get together and close the fiestas with a round of the city.

The fiestas are a vehicle for political protest, for the Chocoanos' view of themselves as a social and racial unit in the nation's political economy. The *disfraces,* for example, are a public and outspoken means of political protest. Each *disfraz* is a large, usually animated model, moved from within by a person who manipulates strings and pulleys. The themes covered are varied, but nowadays certainly the majority of them concentrate on social issues. In 1986, for example, one barrio's float showed a solitary old man and symbolized "the Loneliness of the Old"; another depicted a young man smoking drugs, descending into a giant ashtray and arising from the ashes with a skull instead of a head (this was largely financed, not surprisingly, by the government antidrug campaign); another was essentially an advertisement for the Chocó's charity lottery, which financed it. But the remainder were more politically oriented, showing the Chocó as a huge breast being sucked on by the rest of the country; showing a Chocoano being mangled by a rapacious spider or, in another case, menaced with horrible rotating blades; showing high technology turning the agriculturalist into an unemployed layabout (not especially relevant to the Chocó's own situation); lambasting the Chocoano politicians for their inept efforts to relieve the region's poverty. One *disfraz* showed a map of the Chocó being dismembered by encroaching spiders from the neighboring departments of Valle, Risaralda, and Antioquia. This *disfraz,* recollecting the 1954 threat of dismemberment and the tremendous response of popular solidarity and regional pride it called forth, concurred with several others in depicting the Chocó as a vulnerable but succulent morsel surrounded by rapacious and bloodthirsty enemies. Nevertheless, enemies are rarely specified, and in the 1986 *disfraces* there was no explicit antagonism directed at the

Antioqueños—whereas the Chocoano political elite was pilloried in several exhibits.

The fiestas are organized and run entirely by the Chocoanos, and the Antioqueños play virtually no part at this level. Each barrio has its committee, and there is a central committee as well which takes care of the larger, more communal events. Velásquez noted that in 1957, although the election of these committees was democratic, the great majority of the members were blacks (1960b, 22). He mentions further that "the whites, simple observers, [did] not take an active part in the work of the people" (1960b, 24), and although it is no longer true that "white men do not . . . participate in the rejoicings" (1960b, 21), it is still true that they do not cooperate in their organization. However, then, as now, they paid their contributions. In 1957, the central committee secured a quota of twenty pesos each from most of the major commercial establishments, owned principally by Antioqueños and other whites. Similarly today, although sources of funding are various (the lottery, antidrug campaigns) and include small Chocoano businesses and quotas paid by the local inhabitants, the Antioqueños also pay up, and the *disfraces* are emblazoned with the names of their businesses as well. Although I do not know what percentage of the total budget they contribute, their patronage is doubtless why more outspoken comments are not made against them.

But in the end it runs deeper than this. The Antioqueños do not escape a public browbeating simply because they pay their quotas. Any attempt to mobilize a public collective opposition to the Antioqueño presence, although in theory it could be directed along purely regional lines, would almost inevitably bring to light questions of race, since one of the reasons Antioqueños are resented in Quibdó is that they are thought to look down on the blacks. Any argument that the Chocó belonged by right to the Chocoanos would in any case have to contend with claims that "Colombia belongs to the Colombians," and such an argument would be doubly difficult if it involved articulating a racial identity. So while a *regional* identity is plain enough in the fiestas, its claims directed at general targets such as central government or the rest of the country rather than at the Antioqueño presence, a *racial* identity remains implicit. Although it is perfectly possible to hear Chocoanos comment about the racism of the Antioqueños, or to hear disparaging remarks about "the blacks" from some Antioqueños, this hardly translates into a politicization of racial identity, except insofar as this is implicit in the expressions of regional identity which I have described. The very structure of Colombian race relations contains forces that undermine an explicit mobilization around black identity, and this reinforces the public silence about blackness and racial discrimination which fits in with a national racial order built simultaneously on ideas about mixedness and the inferiority of blackness.

When Jairo Varela, Chocoano singer and leader of the well-known salsa band Grupo Niche (*niche* means black in popular parlance), sings about the Chocó, he chooses a river, the Atrato, as the focus of his song. The river is a vital cultural focus, especially in rural areas. People settle along it and often identify themselves geographically with reference to it rather than a village. It provides the means of transport; it provides for drinking, washing, mining, and fishing. It is a social focus, like the town square in the interior of the country: children play, women wash clothes, people bathe and stand around and talk, canoes and boats arrive, people congregate for journeys. Even in Quibdó, the Atrato and its small affluent the Cabí play this role, since due to the shortage of piped water many people bathe and wash there. The principal bars and hotels are also located along the waterfront, not to mention the market, the church, and many official buildings. On Sundays, excursions invariably consist of a visit to another river to drink, eat, and bathe. "It is no wonder, then, that [the Chocoano] sings to . . . the three-meter pole he calls a *palanca,* to the flat paddle called a *canalete,* to his boat made from a single length of tree trunk, which he baptizes with the names of *canoa, potro, champa, piragua,* and *chingo*" (Velásquez 1960a, 19). Varela's song expresses some aspects of the regional identity which I have been talking about (Varela 1983).

Atrato viajero	Atrato the traveler
Que el Señor creó	Created by God
Atrato viajero	Atrato the traveler
Que mi alma llevó	That took my soul away
Ancho y caudaloso pasas	Broad and abundant you flow
Lento en tu viaje retratas	In your slow journey you portray
El dolor que injusto llevas	The pain you unjustly bear
Poco a poco hasta el mar	Step by step to the sea
Y pensar que todo quieres	And to think you want it all
Como yo	The way I do
Y cambiarlo todo quieres	And that you want to change it all
Sé también	I know as well
Un día, sabes, mi Atrato	One day, you know, my Atrato

Sin querer te descubrí	By chance, I came upon you
Cauteloso en un recodo	Cautious in a bend
Triste tus aguas vi	Sadly I looked upon your waters
Y paraste en tu camino	And you paused in your journey
Viste el sino	You saw your fate;
Con tus propios ojos	With your own eyes
Ver como el destino	See as destiny sees
Y tu madre una montaña	And your mother is a mountain
Busca el cielo y verás	Look for heaven and you'll see
Por qué no tu?	Why not you?
Por qué no yo?	Why not me?
Hijos del mismo Citará	Sons of the same Citará
Y pensar que tu pasado	And to think that your past
Fue mejor	Was better
De caciques de mi raza	From leaders of my race
Su portal	Your gateway was made
Hoy todavía te rinden	Still today pay you tribute
Aguas claras sin par	Clear waters without equal
Cientos y más	Hundreds and more
Como el Neguá	Like the Neguá
Como la sangre va a la mar	Like blood flows to the sea
Como son cautivador	Like a captivating tune
Pasas de nuevo como el sol	You pass once more like the sun
Volverán las golondrinas	The swallows will return
A posar en su habitat	To alight in their abode
Y en verbena, voladores	And during celebrations: fireworks
Compás de cuero y tambores	And the rhythm of drum skins
Subiendo farallones	Climbing your hills
De ti somos tus cañones	We are your canyons/cannons (?)
Y poder cantar	And to be able to sing
De orgullo gritar	And cry out with pride
Yo soy aguajero, señores	I am a waterman, gentlemen
Yo soy atrateño	I am an Atrateño
Tengo, tengo alma de aguajero	I have the soul of a waterman
Refrain:	
Orgulloso soy atrateño	I'm proud to be an Atrateño
Por eso les digo que soy el vocero	I tell you I'm the spokesman
(Refrain)	

129

De esta tierra linda	Of this beautiful land
De esta tierra amada	Of this beloved land
(Refrain)	
Y me siento sanjuaneño	And I feel Sanjuaneño
Aunque soy quibdoseño	Even though I'm Quibdoseño
(Refrain)	
Y mi voz como el sinsonte	And my voice like the mockingbird
(Refrain)	
Deja su canto sincero	Leaves its sincere song
(Refrain)	
Y mi protesta que hoy	And my protest that today
No ha quedado en cero	Has not been fruitless
(Refrain)	
Soy de Beté, soy tanguiseño	I'm from Beté, I'm Tanguiseño
(Refrain)	
Dale a la champa	Get going with the canoe
Que me voy pa' mi casa	Because I'm on my way home
(Refrain)	

(Glossary: Citará is the old colonial name for Quibdó, derived from the name of an indian *cacique*. Here, as in "leaders of my race," there is an ingenuous attempt to identify the indians with the blacks as common descendants of the same ancestors. The Neguá is a tributary of the Atrato. Swallows are a seasonal feature: in Quibdó they congregate in their thousands on the telegraph wires. The use of the word *cañones* in the sixth verse is difficult. Varela seems to be trying to conjure up the image of streams of people feeding into the Atrato like tributaries. Notice the play made with place names: Varela claims several local origins—the San Juan Valley, Beté, Tanguí—although he is from Quibdó himself.)

The lyrics, although a little incoherent in places, echo some of the feelings about the Chocó which I have been discussing—a sense of regional pride (with little explicit mention of race); a sense of injustice and pain, here with a hopeful but inchoate yearning for a better future; the vitality of fiesta. And flowing through it all, the Atrato, patient, everlasting, a captivating melody, a wise sovereign paid tribute by a hundred subject rivers, the ancestral unity behind the local riverine allegiances of the people of the Chocó.

8

The Chocó:

Poverty and Riches

The Pacific hardly exists for us, and our very vast western coast continues to be limited to the two advance posts opened centuries ago, when the Panama Canal had not yet brought its economic revolution to this part of our world. In a century, not a touch of civilization, not an opening in the jungle, not a port has been created and given to humanity to enrich the inheritance of Colombians.

The greatest contradiction of the Chocó is poverty amid wealth: "In the midst of all these riches, man is poor and miserable" (Mollien 1824, 304). It is second nature to any Chocoano to recognize that the region is a rich one, not only in minerals but also in agricultural wealth: the idea is axiomatic. And yet the poverty of the vast majority of the Chocoanos, in town and country, is palpable. The answer to the riddle is also common knowledge: neglect and exploitation. The riches have been channeled out of the region, mostly by outsiders, often whites, and the region has been left to wallow in its own under-development. Gabriel García Márquez noted in 1954, in his series of newspaper pieces on the Chocó: "The departmental comptroller, the shoeshiner, and the black girl who serves in the hotel explain in different words, but with the same arguments, why the Chocó has not progressed"; "the Chocoano goes to school where every day he is told, in mathematics or civic education, why the Chocó is the most abandoned, the most forgotten, and the poorest of all the departments"; "any plantain-loader . . . would go up onto the balcony and improvise a speech in which he explained why the Chocó was not,

Epigraph: From a speech by ex-president Alberto Lleras, given in Cartagena, 1945.

131

and how it should become, the number one exporter of plantains in the country" (1982, 145, 163–64). The answer, as recorded in 1954 by García Márquez, was the absence of a decent road. The answer is, in fact, more complex than that, if only because a good road can let in yet more people to cart off the region's resources, but certainly at that time, the road and its absence served as a symbol of the Chocó's neglect by central government and its historical condition of isolation and inaccessibility. It is not just a question of neglect and isolation, however. The Chocó, and especially Quibdó, may give the impression of an area closed off from the rest of the country, bottled in on its own. But in fact the area has never been totally isolated—on the contrary, there have always been forces hard at work, extracting its resources. Road or no road, the gold, like the waters of the Chocó's many rivers, has found its way out.

In chapter 6, I outlined the historical processes whereby the Chocó had become a poor black region: these hinged on the nature of the slave regime and the character of colonial society there. *Mestizaje* and discrimination were structured by these processes, producing a region in which discrimination was marked and physical race mixture was limited. This went hand in hand with minimal colonial settlement and enduring poverty. Blackness, environment, and poverty formed a self-reinforcing triad. The whites did not effectively settle the area because it was inhospitable for them and isolated. The local colonial society either enslaved blacks or rejected most of them as freed people. The blacks constructed their own lifestyle, which, consciously or not, did not provide the labor which the whites wanted. So the whites continued to avoid settling the area, seeing it as inhospitable and its populace as lazy and refractory. Thus race mixture remained limited, discrimination powerful, and the economy undeveloped.

If *mestizaje* and discrimination were structured by the regional conjuncture of economic, demographic, and political relations in colonial times, the same continues to be true today, and part of the reproduction of the Chocó as a black region is orchestrated by the economic relations within the region and between it and other regions. Discrimination and fairly distinct black/nonblack oppositions exist partly as a result of the continued presence of the small exclusive outsider population that controls much of the extractive and commercial activities of the region. But the relation between blackness and economic relations is not one-way, and part of the reason the Chocó remains poor is because it is black. Nor is the black/nonblack opposition straightforward in economic terms: as in the case of Quibdó, the nonblack monopoly is not complete, and some black Chocoanos also achieve some upward mobility.

Outline of the Chocoano Economy

If we look at the Chocó from the late nineteenth to the early twentieth centuries, we see a society in which the slave-based mining economy has collapsed, and the blacks are mainly dispersed along the region's jungle rivers, living a subsistence lifestyle and generally avoiding wage labor. The blacks have migrated steadily down the rivers that run into the Pacific, where, outside the main mining zone, they depend more on agriculture (maize and plantains are the staples), fishing, and, around the river deltas, the taking of shellfish. They have also moved down the Atrato River into its middle and lower reaches, where agriculture and fishing are again the principal activities. Mining remains important principally in the San Juan River valley and around Quibdó. There are a few small towns that still harbor a white elite with political and commercial power, with a surrounding group of free blacks and mulattoes, a small number of whom are also cashing in on commerce and mining at fringes of the whites' monopoly.

The Chocó has always been connected to outside markets, which, via intermediaries who are commonly merchants, channel out the raw materials it possesses. These have concentrated largely on gold in the past, but there is, in fact, some variety: Brisson (1895, 3–4) encountered black rubber gatherers in the upper Atrato area; rubber was also an important resource in the lower Atrato Valley for a period earlier this century, along with *raicilla* (ipecac root), *tagua* (ivory nuts), and tropical hardwoods (Parsons 1967, Wade 1984). Whitten (1974) notes the importance of mangrove bark collection in the coastal belt for the production of tannic acid. Generally speaking, it is probably a little-recognized fact that agriculture produces more value in the gross internal product of the Chocó than does mining (DANE 1985a, 122; see also the reports of the Banco de la República for the Chocó), and, of course, some of this product is marketed outside the region, notably bananas, plantains, coconuts, and rice. Dried fish is also exported to Cartagena, although most of it moves within a regional market from the Atrato to the San Juan River basin and to the towns. Timber is still a major export, mostly originating from the middle and lower Atrato. Although apparently and in many ways truly isolated, the Chocó has important avenues of trade: the Atrato River is plied by boats going to Turbo and Cartagena; the river deltas and maritime settlements are linked to Panama and Buenaventura, an international port only two hours by road from Cali; Quibdó is linked to Medellín, and recently a road has been completed between Tadó and Pereira. Thus certain areas—mainly settlements on principal maritime and fluvial routes, plus the central Quibdó zone linked by road—are connected to outside markets, the influence of which penetrates via these settlements to more inaccessible zones.

These links with the larger economy are crucial in reaching a general characterization of the economy of the Chocó. This can be defined as "economic marginality" (Whitten 1974, 4). The Chocó lies on the periphery of a national and international system that makes fluctuating demands on its natural resources—even gold, a perennial interest, has been subject to great market fluctuations. The region is exploited in an essentially sporadic way, according to the dictates of outside demand and natural resource availability. Meanwhile it retains a relative autonomy vis-à-vis centralizing forces of state-sponsored development (Whitten 1974, 5).

The routes that link the Chocó to outside markets have been the conduit through which the sporadic demands of the national and international economy have been made. These routes are also the ones through which manufactures and other articles are imported, items that are effectively exchanged for the gold and forest products. This creates what Whitten and Friedemann (1974) have called a "marginal purchasing society," that is, a society where the locals purchase imported goods and sell the natural resources that they extract.

The merchants and intermediaries form a critical link in this system. They are the nodal points that purchase primary products and sell imported commodities. Their activities may extend beyond the simply mercantile. They may directly own mines and land (for example, for logging purposes or agriculture). In more recent times, they have also begun to own processing machines, such as rice huskers, sawmills, and mining equipment, thus increasing their control over the productive process and introducing a more capitalist element.

These intermediaries, or, as they are commonly known, *patrones,* are not uniform figures: they can control a varied set of resources ranging from sawmills to bars, shops, canoes, outboard motors, and chain saws; they may be big or small and accordingly able to control different numbers of enterprises. In addition, they are not all outsiders. Although the majority, especially the larger ones, are usually Antioqueños (or other nonblack immigrants), there are some Chocoanos who occupy this role as well. As we saw in the last chapter, Quibdó had a number of fairly well-off blacks and mulattoes, many of whom, especially among the blacks, relied principally on mining and agriculture, and today the same situation still prevails, with one or two blacks also having entered the commercial sphere in Quibdó as more than simple petty traders. The same applies for areas outside Quibdó. Even here, some of these Chocoano intermediaries are the light-skinned mulattoes of the Chocó's politically dominant group—Yépez

Henao (1985) notes the case of two brothers of a former acting governor of the Chocó who owned a sawmill and a rice-husking machine in a small middle-Atrato settlement. And some of them are blacks: logically the blacks tend to start with less capital, or political connections, and are therefore smaller fish. Especially in rural areas, these Chocoano intermediaries tend to be tied into networks of kinship, godparenthood, and friendship based ideally on reciprocity but which tend to become a more one-sided drain on resources when a particular person or family enjoys economic success. These networks thus act as a leveling mechanism, in a way that does not generally affect the immigrants. (See chapter 17 for other aspects of this; see also Whitten 1974 for a model of black vertical mobility.)

These merchants and intermediaries rely heavily on the advancing of credit to the producers of primary commodities or the workers of their own enterprises. In 1943, the Contraloría General de la República commented on the predominance of a "consumption economy" characterized by the absence of capital and the centrality of the merchant, and noted how this tied into a classic consumption-production pattern in which credit (i.e., advances of goods) is used for subsistence during production, rather than for the expansion of productive capacity itself (1943, 336).

The advances system, as common now in mining and other economic activities as in 1943, is a well-known form of transaction in many less-developed areas of Colombia and Latin America in general. It is often characteristic of indian-colonist relations east of the Andes, where, for example, indians may be advanced articles such as machetes, shotguns, and outboard motors in exchange for, say, coca leaves or rubber. It is a form with a long history in Latin America, but its status is uncertain. While some have seen it automatically as "debt bondage" and an expression of exploitation, others have pointed out that it can testify to the autonomy of the person accepting the debt and to the problems of the creditor, who, to obtain labor or primary commodities, has to proffer incentives in advance (Bauer 1979). As I pointed out in chapter 6, a constant complaint of outsiders about the Chocó, after emancipation and still today, was the shortage of ready labor. The simple existence of a system of advances is not in and of itself unequal and exploitative. The extent of exploitation depends on local conditions and on the degree to which the creditor has a monopoly on the cash and goods he or she offers and can enforce payment of the debt. The debtor's assessment of the value of his or her work relative to the goods on offer is also a crucial factor in fixing exchange rates, and both ignorance, or inexperience, and the strength of desire for imported goods are intervening variables here.

The merchants' wealth in the Chocó accrues not simply as a result of an automatically exploitative advances system (although doubtless in many cases it is such), but rather as a result of their position as nodal points in the regional economic system. In the past, because of the limited communications routes and because the merchants were frequently part of a definite racial group with links to the extraregional economy, a quasi-monopolistic control could be exerted over trade. It was this control that would allow the imposition of unequal terms of trade. In the Chocó, the degree of control has decreased over time as more Antioqueños migrate in, competing with one another; as communications improve; and as some Chocoanos become merchants and intermediaries. But there is still a strong element of commercial monopoly managed by outsiders, and this implies the persistence of an exploitative system. Moreover, the breakup of this monopoly does not necessarily imply improvement: the type of enterprise which increasingly penetrates the Chocó in terms of logging and mining is still controlled mainly from outside, brings little benefit to the region as a whole, and is environmentally very destructive.

Mining.   Mining early this century was carried out mainly by the free blacks; their gold eventually gravitated to market centers where it was bought by merchants, who in return sold imported goods to the gold panners. After about 1920, these merchants are increasingly Syrian immigrants, not only in Quibdó but also in other mining towns such as Condoto, a flourishing commercial center in the 1940s, now displaced by Istmina, which is connected directly by road to Medellín. There are also some mines owned by richer people, whites and some blacks, who have them worked by free labor. Felix Arenas describes the system that operated around Quibdó, which he characterizes as exploitative in nature:

> The work force was based on the *cuadrilla,* as in the colonial era, and the workers were paid practically in kind; there were also some wages, but very little. The workers were always indebted, because they were given food and so on in advance, and then they brought in the gold [in exchange]. These people [the whites], almost feudal . . . got a concession [of mining land] from the government and then sent in a local overseer and laborers who did the work: "I'm the owner of this. You work, and I'll buy what you produce. Meanwhile, I'll give you clothes, food, etc." And they always fixed the accounts in their favor: they bought cheap and sold expensive, and the workers always ended up owing them. So the miners were linked to a specific *patrón:* complete dependence.

This system of advancing goods also characterized the straightforward sale of gold by independent panners to the merchants. In this way, gold was constantly being channeled out of the Chocó, leaving as its principal beneficiaries a merchant class that has scarcely left any investment in the region.

Techniques in mining were rudimentary, and as late as 1943 the Contraloría General de la República remarked: "In the Chocó there reigns a total absence of an industrial mining tradition. . . . The poor miners of the Chocó, unlike those of Antioquia or Nariño, are not acquainted with the mechanical *batea*, . . . the hydraulic pump, or the small-scale monitor" (1943, 326–27). It relates this to the fact that a good deal of mining is carried out by women who intersperse part-time gold panning with their domestic activities. Censuses from 1951 to 1973 still show that one and a half times as many women are occupied in mining as men (DANE 1986b, 676).

Mining is currently concentrated in the San Juan Valley, around Tadó, Istmina, Condoto, Nóvita, and Sipí, although it is also practiced in some areas of the middle Atrato (see Moncada Roa 1979, Abad et al. 1982, and Friedemann 1974 for studies of mining). It is an activity that takes many forms: women may wash the alluvial gravels alongside the rivers on their own or in small groups of two or three. Larger groups, generally loosely based on kinship, work in *minas de agua corrida* (running water mines), in which water from a small artificial reservoir fed by rain and/or streams is released through a channel that has been dug down to gold-bearing layers. The water washes away loose earth, while stones are removed by workers; eventually the remaining heavy sands are panned with a *batea* (a shallow wooden bowl) to extract gold and platinum. More recently, the powerful water jets of *motobombas* (gasoline-driven water pumps) are being used to simultaneously excavate and wash the earth. There are also *minas de hoyo* (pit mines), in which a large pit is excavated down to gold-bearing layers; a human chain with *bateas* removes mud and earth for later washing, while another chain removes the water that collects at the pit bottom; again, *motobombas* are now generally used for the latter task. Finally, *zambullido* is sometimes practiced by women: this involves diving down to the river's bed and filling a *batea* with gravels and sands, which are then washed for gold. Nowadays this is not common, and instead *dragetas* (mini-dredgers) are employed which use powerful pumps to suck riverbed material to the surface and pass it down a washing chute that traps only the heaviest sands and metals.

This kind of mining is essentially subsistence activity. Returns are regular in the sense of nearly always providing something, but unstable in that they may fluctuate wildly. Often a newly exploited area may yield well for some time before becoming exhausted as far as these methods are concerned. The advances system functions in min-

A woman excavating (*guachando* or *covando*) with a metal-tipped pole (*ba-rretón*) to remove gold-bearing dirt for panning in a wooden bowl (*batea*). This is the most rudimentary form of mining, often done individually, although also in small groups.

ing, as it has done for centuries, but the link between credit and debt-payment tends not to be as specific as in, say, logging. Instead, the miner simply buys on credit at the local store and pays off the debt when she or he can: the miner may not even sell the metal to the store owner but instead to itinerant gold buyers who tour the mines or even to the Banco de la República if there is a branch nearby (e.g., in Condoto or Quibdó). In areas of less infrastructural penetration, where the monopoly is stronger, the local merchant tends to control both buying and selling, and the dependency link is more direct. Mining is an activity in which the Chocoano intermediary is to be found. He or she may have some mines and a small shop that he or she uses to supply advances to workers and other smaller miners. Increasingly today such a person would have one or two *motobombas* or perhaps a *drageta,* obtained on credit from a retailer.

There have been some changes in the mining sector connected to the impact of this new technology. Mining production by large-scale companies has decreased rapidly since about 1970 (see below), while overall gold production in the Chocó has been steady or has increased since 1979, indicating that the small and medium-sized producers are producing more gold. Meanwhile, the proportion of the economically active Chocoano population engaged in mining fell from 29 percent to 19 percent between the 1951 and 1973 censuses, while the fastest-growing sectors were services, commerce, and construction—essentially urban-based activities (DANE 1986b, 676). In general, there is evidence of an overall rural-urban shift in which the increasing mechanization of mining probably plays a part.

The capitalization of mining is of uncertain economic status. On the one hand, it is not just outsiders who own these machines: although a *motobomba* costs about U.S.$1,500 and a *drageta* about U.S.$6,000, many Chocoanos have been able to purchase one of these machines. Logically, as with the *patrón* role, richer Chocoanos and also outsider Antioqueños tend to own more machines, but especially with the *motobomba,* its price is low enough to permit many people access to it. The problem is that a single *bomba* does not generally produce enough to do more than maintain subsistence: once the gold is split up and the gasoline paid for, profits are on average rather low (Abad et al. 1982, 48). Intermediaries who own, say, several machines and a store are in a better position to increase their incomes; but when these are Chocoanos, they find themselves weighed down with obligations to relatives, friends, and compadres who want a place in their mining teams or goods on extended credit from their stores. Mining enterprises, especially the *minas de hoyo,* tend to absorb labor even when this is technically superfluous: relatives tack themselves on and win a share of the output such that the mine becomes a collective insurance system run on a kinship basis (Abad et al. 1982). Every Chocoano is located in a complex web of reciprocity and exchange of goods and services which is crucial for subsistence (see chapter 9) but which tends to act as a leveling mechanism on upward mobility. The web can be constricted to reduce outflows and allow some mobility, but norms of reciprocity are also heavily policed by an ethic of equality (see chapter 17; Whitten 1974). This, of course, is a problem that the Antioqueño merchant and intermediary does not experience in the same way. Thus, while apocryphal tales abound of the miners who make millions of pesos in a few weeks, this mining mythology does not represent the reality faced by most Chocoano miners. The few Chocoanos who manage to attain the position of intermediary may significantly increase their incomes, but the majority experience minimal or no change.

Mining in the Chocó has a second, capital-intensive side that has proved of even less benefit to the local blacks. This is the story of the infamous Chocó-Pacific Mining Company (see Melo 1975; Cedetrabajo 1984; Caicedo Licona 1980). At the end of the nineteenth century, Henry Granger, a North American, obtained titles to mining areas around the San Juan River. Soon after, the Anglo-Colombian Development Corporation also obtained titles to adjacent areas which conflicted with Granger's; they negotiated, merged, and created the South American Gold and Platinum Company (SAGAP) in 1916 with a subsidiary, the Chocó-Pacific Mining Company based in Andagoya, controlling operations in the Chocó. SAGAP expanded operations throughout Colombia, and when it merged with the International Mining Corporation (IMC) in 1963, it controlled 76 percent of Colombia's precious metal production. Over its lifetime the Chocó-Pacific generally produced between 65 and 75 percent of the Chocó's gold, equivalent to 10 percent of the national total (Cedetrabajo 1984, 8, 71–72). It used large-scale dredgers, powered by a small hydroelectric plant built in 1921, but by 1972 production had declined greatly, due fundamentally to exhaustion of gold deposits in the area of their concession.

During the period up to the early 1970s, the company operated from its headquarters in Andagoya, where it established a small, independent town "with everything that civilized living, morality, and hygiene demand," including ice production, electric light, and telephones (Cruz 1921). The precincts of the compound were not open to local blacks except in their capacity as workers and servants, and only a handful of Colombians—whites and mestizos from the interior—worked in the offices. When Gabriel García Márquez visited the town in 1954, he recorded the bitterness, the tension, the "sordid social battle," the feelings of injustice which infected the air around Andagoya as the poverty-stricken blacks watched the company dredgers haul out tons of gold and platinum, leaving only useless, barren piles of stones, eating away areas that they themselves used to mine on, and, according to them, encroaching on areas outside the company's legal concessions (1982, 170).

In 1974, as part of the nationalization of Colombia's mines, the IMC sold Chocó-Pacific to a Colombian mining consortium who re-

A view of a dredger, part of the fleet once owned by the Chocó-Pacific Mining Company, working the Suruco River near Andagoya in 1987. Inside the wire-fenced cage, the finest sands are periodically washed for gold dust. Beneath the chutes, women collect waste sands in *bateas* and canoes to extract the minute remaining traces of gold.

named it Mineros del Chocó. Production was low, and there were obscure maneuvers with certain company funds. Losses were continuous, and in 1977 the company was eventually handed over to Chocoano management in the guise of a workers' cooperative under the direction of Jorge Tadeo Lozano, the political boss who appeared in the last chapter. The dredgers were in bad repair, gold deposits were low, and now management problems became acute. The fund for retirement pensions and severance payments seems to have disappeared, and it is virtually the unanimous opinion of the local populace that Lozano and his team lined their own pockets in one way or another. Debts mounted, the workers went on strike several times, and they tried to sue the company: the operation was a shambles. In 1984, the government stepped in, and, after some reluctance on its part, a new, half-state, half-private company was created, the Empresa Nacional de Metales Preciosos, which is still functioning. In 1986, gold production was 3,086 ounces troy, compared with the Chocó-Pacific's lowest production of 16,557 ounces in 1972 (Melo 1975, 112; Dario Cújar, company employee, pers. com., April 1986).

Logging and Fishing.   Logging concentrates around the middle and lower reaches of the Atrato River (municipalities of Riosucio, Bojayá, and Quibdó). Timber extraction in this area takes two basic forms. On the one hand, big timber companies have government concessions on certain areas of forest, use a wage-labor force, and simply sack the region's hardwood resources at will, using bulldozers, chain saws, and sawmills. There are six main companies of foreign and Antioqueño ownership, and the timber goes to the interior of the country or abroad (Córdoba 1983, 104). On the other hand, the system of advances is very widespread. Reports compiled by Colombian investigators working under the current Dutch development plan for the Chocó, which describe the situation in the middle Atrato Valley, document the extensive nature of this system (see Yépez Henao 1985, 1986; Valencia Chávez 1984, 1985). A local *patrón*—who quite probably has a small logging permit and owns a shop, a bar, some motor canoes, and a couple of chain saws—fronts food and other goods to a black peasant who goes off for several months into the forest and cuts timber using his own or the *patrón*'s chain saw and a couple of helpers; meanwhile these men's families are also semidependent on the *patrón*, who gives them goods on credit. During the cutting period, the group may return briefly for more goods and/or to add a substantial increase to their debt with a visit to the *patrón*'s bar. The timber may be left as *tucas*, or logs, in which case the loggers then float the timber downstream, a process in which, depending on local and seasonal conditions, it may be necessary to use the *patrón*'s conveniently available canoes as tugs; this adds yet more to the debt. The logs go to a sawmill, the owner of which is usually a *patrón* himself. Alternatively, the timber may already have been sawn into planks with a chain saw, in which case it is transported by canoe and sold by the *patrón* direct to the boats that ply between the Atrato River and Cartagena. The accounts are then added up and settled, and the loggers may find themselves with a mere pittance, penniless, or even owing the *patrón*.

Fishing is a major activity in this area of the Chocó. During the *subienda,* when fish swim upriver to mate, there is large-scale fishing in the rivers, and fish is sold fresh to Quibdó or dried and salted: either way it is sold to intermediary traders who ply the Atrato between Quibdó and Cartagena and who are often in a position to dictate their buying prices, given surplus production and poor communications about the state of the market. During the rest of the year, whole families may move away from their settlements to temporary shacks on the *ciénagas,* or lakes, where they spend several weeks fishing. If a woman has small children, she may remain in the settlement, while her man goes with another woman to assist him during the time he spends away: polygyny of this kind is not uncommon (Yépez Henao 1985). The advances system also operates for fishing. Local *patrones* advance food for trips to the lakes and nylon line, hooks, and lead weights for fishing. Similarly, advances help along other economic activities: for example, Cartagena boats give advances for maize and rice crops.

Development in the Chocó

The situation of the department remains lamentable. The recent government study on poverty in Colombia found that nearly 83 percent of the Chocoano population had "unsatisfied basic needs," making it the third poorest region in the country, after the distant Amazonian intendencies of Vaupés and Guainía (DANE 1989, 45). Life expectancy in 1986 was between forty-two and forty-seven years, compared with a national average of sixty-four years; there are about ten thousand inhabitants for every doctor, most of whom are concentrated in the towns anyway, whereas nationally the ratio is two thousand to one; infant mortality is three times, and overall mortality four times, the national average; and child malnutrition is common in rural areas (Cifuentes 1986, 19). Thirty-nine percent of the population over 10 years old is illiterate, more than three times the national average—this relation holds for both urban and rural zones—although in the intercensal period 1973–85 illiteracy dropped from 43 percent to 39 percent. School attendance rates are lower than national ones, as are rates of completion of primary schooling. Education, however, is highly valued, and in García Márquez's oft-quoted, but clearly not very accurate, phrase, "By any means possible, although they may have to get up at dawn and travel several kilometers on foot or by canoe, the Chocoanos get to school every day" (1982, 163). In 1972, the Universidad Tecnológica Diego Luis Córdoba was opened in an attempt to brake the exit of aspiring professionals from the region, an effort that has been only partly successful, since those who do qualify there find it hard to get a job in the department. Increasing education tends to foment emigration (Sanders 1970). About 70 percent of the population is rural, more than double the national average, and lives isolated from roads, electricity, and piped water supplies. According to rather old 1959 figures—no agricultural census has been conducted since then—only 1.3 percent of the Chocó's area was used for agriculture and pasture; "uninhabited" jungle made up 60 percent of the total area. This situation has changed somewhat over the years: there are now more schools, hospitals, and health centers than, say, twenty years ago, but the changes do little to alter the Chocó's position relative to the nation—illiteracy, for example, has increased relatively despite an absolute decrease.

In simple terms, the Chocó has given but has not received. This is partly because much of what it gave went abroad, first to Spain and then to the United States, and partly because its resources have been largely channeled out through commercial networks that link it to other regions of the country, in many cases with Antioquia but also with Cartagena. There are black and mulatto *patrones* involved in these networks, but they are few in number, and their mobility is often restricted by kin networks. When a more solid degree of upward mobility is achieved by blacks, they or their offspring often end up in the cities of the interior of the country, as I noted in the last chapter. Meanwhile, the Chocó has also been neglected by central government because it wields little political and economic clout at the national level and also, I would argue, because it is ideologically peripheral: it is populated by blacks and considered ecologically inhospitable, and thus it ranks low in the national hierarchy of development priorities. The region appears to be an appendage to the nation which is manipulated in larger political and economic strategies: the case of the Mining Company off-loaded onto a workers' cooperative when production had declined is one example. Another is the Parque de los Katios, established near the Panamanian border, at the behest of the United States, as a sanitary cordon against foot-and-mouth disease (see Caicedo Licona 1980, who sees more devious and complex U.S. geopolitical strategies behind this natural reserve).

The two main development plans that embraced the Chocó have achieved nothing, remaining almost entirely on paper (DNP 1961; DNP-CVC 1983). Even such concrete endeavors as the so-called Plan

Chocó begun in 1969, financed partly by Dutch aid and administered by Codechocó (Corporation for the Development of the Chocó), allocated 70 percent of its 1969–74 budget to roads that have never actually appeared or are still only half-constructed (Codechocó 1970): "The results of the Plan Chocó cannot be found anywhere" (Chocoano senator, Ismael Aldana, quoted in *La República*, 25 March 1979, 5). In 1979 the Dutch, precisely in recognition of the Colombian state's neglect of the region, initiated a more comprehensive program managed by their own people in conjunction with Codechocó, consisting of primary health care and forestry programs and DIAR (Desarrollo Integrado Agrícola Rural), an integrated rural development program that implemented rice growing, pig raising, and similar projects (Netherlands Ministry for Development Cooperation 1984). This is not the place to assess the results of the the Plan Holandés, as it is known, which have undoubtedly been partially successful: suffice it to say that internal politics and factionalism, emanating largely from Codechocó (the director of which changed eleven times in political machinations between 1979 and 1987), have taken their toll on the efficiency of the program, while, although the agricultural projects in the middle Atrato attempt to bypass intermediaries and the advances system, both these elements continue to function strongly there.

Overshadowing the plans for the Chocó is a still more recent and extremely grandiose plan for a "New Pacific Dimension for Colombia" (Office of the President 1988). Envisaging the Pacific basin as a new area of global development, and determined to cash in on Colombia's strategic position between the Pacific and the Atlantic, the government has had plans drawn up for a Pacific port about 100 kilometers south of the Panamanian border; a road, rail, and pipeline link between this and a new port in the Gulf of Urabá; the completion of the Pan American highway (from the border, via the Pacific port and Bahía Solano to Tadó and thence to the interior of the country); and various schemes to develop fishing, mineral, and forestry resources. The plan states that the interest in the area shown by the state and the private sector "may imply 'progress and development' in itself, but if it is not properly planned and rationalized, there will be a threat to the environment and the local population." Hence there are proposals for "the introduction of appropriate technology, permanent crops, strengthening of community and the formalization of land ownership" in order to modernize and protect what is misleadingly, but tellingly, described as "a totally natural economy" (Presidency of the Republic of Colombia 1989, 118–19). Whether the plan itself comes to fruition depends, of course, on international finance. If it

145

does, whether or not the "threat to the local population" is success-fully countered is difficult to predict. To judge from past efforts on its behalf, the prognosis is by no means optimistic.

In its 1943 report on the Chocó, the Contraloría General recom-mended more government intervention and increased immigration but added: "What the government should specifically try to prevent is this mass of immigrants dedicating itself to purely commercial or specula-tive business, which does not leave as profound an imprint as those enterprises which claim the land as the proper means of their develop-ment" (1943, 336). However, immigrants—whose entry is eased by a tendency to see development as improving communications with the interior of the country—continue to specialize in (and largely monopolize) commerce. When they do turn to enterprises that claim the land, it is generally with purely extractive ends in mind.

In the racial order of Colombia, blackness occupies a low status. Nowhere is this clearer than in the case of the Chocó: black, poor, underdeveloped. In this chapter, I have outlined some of the forces that keep it poor, in relative terms, at least. These forces are primarily economic and political, and this is easy grist for the mill of those who claim that a "racial democracy" can legitimately be said to exist in Colombia because the forces that keep blacks at the bottom of the racial order appear to be purely "class" factors, as opposed to "racial" factors. This type of argument tends to pose class and race as equal but opposite principles, the contribution of each of which to any given situation of inequality can be measured and compared. In my view, outlined in chapter 1, race and class cannot be opposed in this way, since they have different analytical status: rather, we should examine how racial dynamics are structured by material forces, while at the same time helping to orchestrate those forces. The blackness of the Chocó region was created by the economic interests of a colonial elite, but its blackness, or rather the perceived significance of this trait, is also involved in the reproduction of its poverty. As I show in detail in the case of Unguía, the white/mestizo immigrant population that controls many economic resources discriminates against the Cho-coanos for being black, "untrustworthy, lazy, unprogressive"; they maintain their own position partly through an ethnic exclusiveness built on ideas of Antioqueño dynamism and nonblackness; and they justify their presence and activities in the region in terms of its being a part of Colombia (thus one more region of a democratically available mestizo nation) which is nevertheless inhabited by blacks deemed "un-progressive" (in a hierarchy of material and racial value). Such dis-crimination might suggest the possibility of political mobilization by

146

blacks to protest not simply as a region, but against racial discrimination. But as I showed in the last chapter, such mobilization is highly problematic, not only because of the clientelistic nature of politics which fragments solidarity and co-opts political leaders but also because of the difficulty of mobilizing around a stigmatized and ambiguous category. Leaders may voice protest at the region's abandonment by central government, but they rarely mention race. And yet racial discriminations play a role in the region's continued poverty.

Attempts to reduce the situation of the Chocó to explanations based uniquely on class factors or forces of uneven regional development are thus inadequate because they fail to see how racialized identities intervene actively in the orchestration of these factors. One concept that has tried to take account of this intervention in theorizing racial or ethnic and economic inequalities, particularly when they have a regional dimension, is that of internal colonialism (e.g., González Casanova 1971; Blauner 1972; Hechter 1975). This concept is by no means unproblematic, and as Hechter (1975, 33) points out, there is little agreement on what internal colonialism actually is or whether it is a specific type of unequal regional relation. In radical black American discourse, it has assumed a rhetorical function (Blauner 1972, 82), while Stone notes that some see it merely as a misleading analogy; Omi and Winant (1986, 50), for example, class it as "an analogy which was politically and not analytically grounded." Stone concludes that there are no definitive conclusions about the broad merits of the thesis (1979, 253, 258). As Roberts (1978, 82) points out, the internal colony model, by focusing on regional isolation and monopolistic control, can mask the actual forms of integration which connect a peripheral region to core areas, while Wolpe (1975) and Yinger (1986, 34), among others, also suggest the dangers of tending to see the internal colony and its colonizers as two homogeneous groups, glossing over internal class differentiation—a view that would greatly oversimplify the internal heterogeneity of both the blacks and the non-black immigrants in the Chocó.

The characteristics outlined by Hechter and others are, however, highly relevant to the Chocó. Generally, internal colonialism refers to a situation in which an ethnically identified category, often spatially segregated, is in a structured relation of economic, political, and cultural subordinance to another ethnically identified group that promotes its own interests in the region. Commerce tends to be monopolized by members of the core; the peripheral economy is forced into "complementary development" to the core and is dependent on it; the economy of the region relies on one or two primary export commodities; movement of labor in the region is influenced strongly by outside forces; a "cultural division of labor" exists in which the subordinate people occupy the lower occupational strata; there is a relative lack of services and a low standard of living; and there is discrimination (Hechter 1975, 33; see also Blauner 1972, 83–89; González Casanova 1971, 221–51). For the Chocó, there is less obviously the set of special political and legal relationships noted by Hechter and Blauner which enforce economic dependence. Since the old white elite was expelled, the Chocó has officially been a normal part of the national polity, and the Chocoanos run their own administration. Even so, as we have seen, this power is extremely limited, especially when it comes to directing or implementing economic change.

Given the vagueness of the concept of "internal colonialism," I would not choose to use it as an exclusive theory, but it does have the advantage of highlighting the role of ethnic or racial categories as active principles. Wolpe (1975) argues that "in certain conditions" racial ideologies are related to the conservation and exploitation by capitalism of a precapitalist mode of production, whether inside or outside state boundaries. Whatever other problems such an analysis might have, it reduces racial categories to an effect of the exploitation of a labor force. However, within a single discourse about blackness, Antioqueños may exploit black labor, colonize a territory where blacks live, marginalize blacks from the development they control, and cooperate with them in a limited, often paternalistic fashion. For the Chocoanos, discourse about race can encompass both opposition to nonblack immigrants, and processes by which upwardly mobile blacks become associated with the nonblack world. This discourse is internally heterogeneous and adaptable and impinges on a wide variety of different economic relations. But it also has a common basis in rooted ideas about the relative positions of blackness and whiteness. It is difficult to see how such a discourse can be reduced to the epiphenomena of a set of economic relations.

III

Chocoanos

on the Frontier

and in the City

9

Unguía:

History and Economy

The Antioqueño, always active and enterprising, will not be still and will cross the cordillera in order to devote himself to the cultivation of food crops and to take advantage of the great market which will present itself to him.

Unguía is located in the Urabá region, an area in the most northwesterly corner of Colombia, near the Panamanian border, comprising the zone around the Gulf of Urabá. During 1982, in the process of reconnoitering the Atlantic coastal region of Colombia in search of a field site in which I could study relations between blacks and nonblacks, I came across the town of Turbo, the economic center for the area around the gulf. Here, in one town, were collected together people of the three regions that have been my principal concern so far: the Chocó, Antioquia, and the Atlantic coastal region. By chance I was staying in the same *pensión* as a young Chocoano man, Evelio, who worked on the boats that plied between Turbo and the small towns on the western side of the gulf, which belongs officially to the Chocó, while the eastern side belongs to Antioquia. I accompanied Evelio one day to Unguía, a small town reached from the gulf by way of the Atrato River, a lake, and several smaller connecting waterways. On seeing it, I made an almost immediate decision to make the place the site of my first fieldwork.

I lived in Unguía in rented accommodations for about a year. My central interest was in race relations between blacks and nonblacks,

Epigraph: Agustín Codazzi, writing in 1853, predicts the Antioqueño colonization of the Chocó (Comisión Corográfica 1958, 327).

Looking onto a main street in Unguía on a Sunday morning in 1985. The two-story house belongs to one of the town's wealthiest Antioqueño merchant-landowners.

but the presence of the Costeños complicated matters—as it turned out, in a very interesting way. In a frontier town most people were bent on betterment, and my research inevitably focused on patterns of economic relations and relative upward mobility. Ideas about regional origin, racial identity, and culture interweaved in complex ways with economic relations, and I tried to untangle their interactions. My methodology consisted largely of interviews with individuals and/or their families, finding out how they had got to their current position, their networks of economic and social relations, who they employed, were employed by, or cooperated with, what their children were doing, what they thought of Chocoanos, Costeños, or Antioqueños as friends, employees, employers, workmates, or simply as a presence in the area. Naturally, a few people became central informants and supplied information about others and in more depth about themselves: these included Chocoanos, Antioqueños, and Costeños of varying economic status. I also collected data from the local Agricultural and Stock-Raising Institute and from the municipal land records. Using hired assistants to help, I did a basic questionnaire on a random sample of households, covering about two hundred of the total of more than four hundred which made up the town at that time. This enquired about age, sex, education, occupation (and rather naively about income), and about the regional origin of the respondent, and her or his partner, parents, and grandparents. It also asked the interviewer to classify the respondent's "race" as white, black, mulatto, or mestizo. Given the ambiguity of racial classification, this was a dubious exercise, but it gave me some idea of how my interviewers, mostly black secondary school students, classified people of different regional origins: Antioqueños were overwhelmingly classed as white or mestizo, Chocoanos as black, plus some mulattoes, Costeños as mostly mulatto and mestizo. Finally, I asked the local secondary school students to write about their impressions of Chocoanos, Costeños, and Antioqueños. This gave me some textual information on such matters as stereotyping and the Chocoano reaction to the Antioqueño presence.

Participant observation was, of course, crucial, and from this I picked up a great deal of information about economic and ethnic relations and the manipulable nature of ethnic categorizations. I worked in the mines with Chocoano friends, helped a black stevedore friend loading and unloading 80-kilogram sacks of maize, stayed on the richest Antioqueño farms, spent hours sitting in people's shops and their doorways, taught English to a couple of teachers, played basketball with local teams, and went drinking and dancing in the dance halls. During all this, I formed a relationship, classed locally in due course as that of *novios* (boyfriend/girlfriend), with a local Chocoano woman of about my age who, at that time, ran the town's nursery school. Although it was not my reason for forming the relationship, the effect not surprisingly was to aid my integration into some sectors of the community, particularly the Chocoanos and the Costeños (see Wade, 1992). All this, then, formed the methodological basis for the analysis of Unguía.

Unguía is tied into the process, noted in chapter 3, by which peripheral areas occupied by blacks become increasingly integrated into the national economy through waves of frontier colonization which are basically controlled by nonblack people from more central regions of the country. In the process, the local economy becomes more differentiated, with the blacks generally concentrated in the lower echelons of society. Concomitantly, however, channels are opened up for economic advancement, cultural change, and race mixture. In the local context, the dynamics of Colombia's racial order operate: black adaptation, but also black community; nonblack acceptance, but also discrimination.

The Urabá region is a particularly interesting case study of this general process, because it involves more than the confrontation between black Chocoanos and white/mestizo Antioqueños which is characteristic of most of the Chocó region. The Costeños are present in large numbers on both sides of the gulf, and they blur the division between the Antioqueños and the Chocoanos. In effect, Urabá as a whole is for the Chocoanos a location where blackness can be dispersed and diluted, both physically and culturally, and it is through the Costeños, rather than just the Antioqueños, that a good deal of this occurs.

History of Urabá

The position of Urabá as a channel for the dispersal of blackness derives principally from its uncertain regional affiliation. In terms of the Colombian sense of place, the Urabá region is very ambiguous. Almost until independence, the whole area was in the hands of the Cuna indians, who traded with Dutch and English pirates and with the smugglers who took the Chocó's gold out via the forbidden Atrato River route (Parsons 1967). After independence, in the political upheavals of regional power distribution, the area swung backwards and forwards between three legitimate claimants: the states of Cartagena, Cauca (which included the Chocó), and Antioquia. Between 1831 and 1905, the zone changed hands six times. Much of the area was administratively Chocoano for a long time (as part of the Cauca state), while the population, even on the western side of the gulf, was Costeño with some Chocoano additions. But in 1905, Antioquia finally got its longed-for "corridor to the sea," and slowly and laboriously a road was built from Medellín to Turbo, opening finally in 1954, dramatically increasing the influx of Antioqueños from the interior who had previously been present in small numbers, and sealing the hold of Antioquia over what had until then effectively been Costeño, and to a lesser extent Chocoano, territory (Parsons 1967).

It is difficult to say to whom the area belongs: for if the eastern Urabá is officially Antioqueño, it is only so since 1905, and in 1930 Luis Gaviria could still remark of Turbo (1930, 108), "The population is generally of negroes who—oddly enough!—do not consider themselves Antioqueños, as indeed is the case in all of Urabá. The whites they call 'Antioqueños' and respect them more out of fear than any other sentiment." Some of these blacks originated from the Chocó, migrating down the Atrato, and some from *la Costa* farther east, migrating along the coast itself; whatever their origins, they consider themselves Turbeños and hence Costeños rather than Antioqueños. Meanwhile, on the other side of the gulf, in territory still officially

Chocoano, it is the Costeños who actually founded most of the villages there—the majority of the Chocoanos there are immigrants from the upper Chocó area farther to the south (Parsons 1967; West 1957, 105, 107; Montes 1975; Granda 1977, 55, 201; Wade 1984, 54). And finally, it is the Antioqueños who now run both sides of the gulf economically, if not politically on the Chocoano side.

Economically, the zone has been, and still is to a large extent, a frontier zone of colonization with a boom-bust cycle once based mostly on raw material extraction and now stabilizing into a pattern in which small colonists open up the land and are subsequently pushed out by the expansion of cattle-raising latifundism (see chapter 3). During the nineteenth and early twentieth centuries, there was exploitation of rubber, ivory nuts, ipecac root, tropical timber, and some gold; between 1921 and 1947, Syrian immigrants established a sugar mill near Sautatá, and in the 1930s an Antioqueño firm cultivated bananas for a couple of decades near Acandí, both towns on the western side of the gulf (Parsons 1967; Valencia Chávez 1982; Fernández Gómez 1976). All these activities came and went, but some of the colonists and merchants they attracted settled and formed villages that also depended on agriculture, the small surplus production of which was shipped to Cartagena and Quibdó. The major boom came in the 1960s when a U.S. fruit company began a program in the Urabá Antioqueño and there was a banana bonanza that suddenly and massively increased immigration to the area from all sides (Bolívar n.d.; Parsons 1967). Although this boom too has lost some of its impetus, Colombia has become a world-ranking producer of bananas, most of which still come from Urabá. Meanwhile, agricultural colonization continued on both sides of the gulf, and capitalist cattle-raising enterprises began to move in, buying up land and pressuring the small colonists who clear the land and make way for the bigger cattle farms. Nowadays, the area is violent and wild, a frontier cattle town with conflicts generated by latifundia pressures on smaller farmers, by cattle rustling and the cattle ranchers' revenge, by the presence of guerrilla forces in the more remote areas and the army's tactical maneuvers there, by the small-scale cultivation first of marijuana and then of coca leaves, with all the usual drug-running violence that such activity entails.

The Local Economy of Unguía

The participation of Antioqueños, Chocoanos, and Costeños in the local economy has been broadly in tune with their traditions and economic powers. In Unguía, for example, the Costeños settled early this century, migrants from *la Costa*'s seaboard towns where blacks and mulattoes predominate. They exploited raw materials and engaged in farming, stock raising, and trading. The odd Antioqueño merchant was also around early on, even before the Medellín-Turbo road, purchasing gold, timber, and other forest products. The first Chocoanos were after the gold of nearby Cuqué, an old colonial mining area (Groot 1953, 2:227), and they also engaged in some trading and agriculture. As colonization stepped up, this initial low level of differentiation became more marked, quite soon taking on the profile I encountered in 1982.

The Antioqueños range from day laborers, through small and midsize farmers who grow maize and raise cattle, to large-scale capitalists with farms of over 1,000 hectares and more than a thousand head of cattle (see tables 2 and 3 on land and cattle holding in appendix A). Equally, they range from small merchants to individuals with the largest commercial establishments—the latter usually have cattle farms as well, making them a small nucleus that controls the best part of the area's wealth. The top posts in the national government organizations (the credit bank, the cattle institute, the hospital, and so on) are also filled by Antioqueños. The Costeños form the backbone of the rural labor force, and they are also small and midsize farmers—outside the Unguía area there are also occasional cases of rich landowners from the latifundia of *la Costa*. A sprinkling of Costeños have commercial interests as well, generally on a fairly small scale.

The Chocoanos participate little in farming and cattle raising, being represented in that sphere by a small nucleus of related individuals plus a few others. They are a major element in gold mining, although this has been subject to a boom-bust cycle. They are the majority of the public employees (teachers, nurses, municipal officials), since these appointments are mostly made from Quibdó. They perform most of the services and manual labor activities of the town—construction, loading and carrying, stevedoring in the small port, washing clothes, selling cooked food on the streets—and they also generally run the town's dance halls. One effect of this distribution of economic activities is that in the town Antioqueños, Costeños, and Chocoanos are present in roughly equal proportions, while in the countryside Costeños and Antioqueños predominate.

There is no definite ethnic occupational segregation but rather a pattern of certain occupational tendencies. The class structure of the town crosscuts ethnic considerations—it is possible to find Antioqueño washerwomen and miners, or Antioqueño, Costeño, and Chocoano rural laborers working together on a weeding contract, or the odd Chocoano with a little grocery kiosk—but within that structure

156

there are clear patterns of ethnic grouping and interaction, and in the context of the expansion of economic opportunities which the colonization of the Urabá Chocoano represents, it is clear that the Antioqueños are doing best and the Chocoanos the worst, with the Costeños somewhere in the middle.

This, of course, is no simple matter of racial discrimination, although this has a role to play, as we shall see later; these patterns are also the outcome of the histories and traditions of each regional group in the context of their interaction in the local economy. In essence, the Antioqueños come from a region more integrated into currents of national development. Their background tends to be more urban and to have a population better educated and with greater commercial and entrepreneurial experience and spirit; they tend to be dynamic migrants with high aspirations, and a number of them have greater access to capital and credit. In contrast, the Costeños are frequently landless laborers, peons, and small colonist farmers, with less education or commercial experience, who have been pushed westward by the predatory expansion of *la Costa*'s land-extensive cattle latifundia (see Fals Borda 1976, 41; Parsons 1967, 71; Havens and Flinn 1970, 44, for descriptions of this colonization process). Some of their number, however, have some capital or a certain amount of education or commercial experience. The Chocoanos, on the other hand, come from a predominantly rural background, with very little access to capital, a weak agricultural and commercial tradition, and a poor educational system. Although the presence of many Chocoano teachers and employees in Unguía appears to belie this overall profile, their influence has little impact on the Chocoanos' position in the main spheres of the local economy.

People have thus taken a position largely determined by the insertion into the historical process of frontier colonization of the cultural and economic capital they have brought from their region of origin. At first, the opening up of the frontier zone is brought about gradually by Chocoano and Costeño immigrants who establish a fairly relaxed pace of life, redolent in people's memories with images of peace, sharing, and simplicity. Whatever the images, the reality is soon that of a previously quite isolated area of fertile land, rich in natural resources, being rapidly linked into the national economy. With this, land-hungry colonists arrive from both *la Costa* and Antioquia, and, particularly among those from the latter region, there are people bent on making their fortunes, who have commercial and even quite urban backgrounds, sometimes with access to capital and/or credit. Arriving just at a time when the area's link to their home territory has improved vastly via the Turbo-Medellín road and when its local economy is taking off, such people find good scope for their enterprises: there is land, timber, gold, immigrants to sell things to and whose crops need a purchaser. Although most Antioqueños are small farmers and shop-keepers, some put together an eclectic commercial and landholding venture, quickly expanding into cattle raising—the real wealth of the region—and in a short time become quite wealthy individuals. A noticeable feature is that more than half the fifteen or so Antioqueños who control most of Unguía's land and cattle arrived in the area with minimal resources. Others, however, come with a small amount of capital and buy their way into the same enterprises, and some well-endowed capitalists move in and start creating large-scale cattle-raising enterprises. In all this the Antioqueños collaborate with one another, building on their ethnic identity of *paisa*, and in some cases there is a kind of patronage between the richer and poorer Antioqueños which opens to the latter an important avenue of economic advancement through employment, credit, and cooperative ventures. This helps account for the impressive upward mobility of some of the Antioqueños and the near monopoly they now have on commerce. Although Antioqueño merchants were present from an early date, they did not monopolize the trade in ipecac root, rubber, ivory nuts, rum, cloth, timber, rice, and so on; in those days, links were with Quibdó and Cartagena, and Chocoanos and Costeños also traded. Now, the Antioqueños manage virtually all the trade, and links are principally with Medellín; they maintain close links with Antioquia, importing cheap manufactured goods from Medellín's factories.

Many Costeños are landless laborers and small labor contractors doing pasture fumigation, fencing, and other farm work, but many are also small and medium-scale farmers who hold onto their land and have successful cattle-raising and farming ventures. However, they do not achieve as good a position as the Antioqueños for a number of reasons. They are less oriented towards commerce and thus tend not to diversify in the typically Antioqueño way; in addition, even the relatively wealthy Costeños tend to have less access to capital than the richer Antioqueños. The Costeños come from an agricultural tradition of expansive latifundism and temporary seasonal crops, which has fostered among the poorer Costeños a more nomadic, colonist attitude to land than in Antioquia, where small coffee farms are tenaciously held on to. Around Unguía, they tend to locate their farms on lower, flatter land than the small Antioqueño farmer, who is used to mountainous terrain: they thus lay themselves open to pressures from larger, mechanized landed interests that prefer this land.

The Chocoanos find themselves largely pushed out of the main sectors of the economy. In addition to being on average a very poor group and therefore susceptible to being bought out by larger, more vigorous interests, their formation is one in which land is used for shifting cultivation, legal titling is minimal, boundaries are agreed on by eye, fencing is virtually unknown, agricultural surplus is small, and "there is still a long way to go before land is considered a commodity" (Gutiérrez de Pineda 1975, 241). Equally, they come from a background of little commercial experience, in which outsiders and whites have almost always dominated commercial ventures. Although they previously participated in trade around Unguía, and while some would still like to break into the Antioqueños' monopoly, they were not able to compete with the combination of capital, commercial connections, entrepreneurial zeal, and in-group cooperation which the *paisas* represented. Now their commerce is rather peripheral: the selling of cooked food on the streets, tiny grocery kiosks, one or two shops selling clothes and other sundries. Instead, they rely on mining, an unstable occupation, often allowing no more than subsistence. They also rely on urban service occupations, and they run one or two dance halls. The only field they convincingly control is the political one, as they do in Quibdó, where the Antioqueños also dominate commerce. Thus most of the administrative jobs appointed by departmental authorities are filled by Chocoanos, although top-level posts appointed by national bodies are occupied by Antioqueños. The distribution of these jobs, particularly in the municipal administration, depends on political contacts, and it is thus also the Chocoanos who run the local branches of the Cordobist, Lozanist, and Conservative parties, maintaining links with these groups in Quibdó. For many Chocoanos, education is the great hope; but once they are educated, there is a good chance that they will have to emigrate, since the jobs in the Unguía public sector for which their education prepared them are limited.

Chocoanos also rely heavily on the family. Naturally, family and kinship connections are important for people in all regions of Colombia and especially for migrants. For the Chocoanos, kinship networks of a flexible nature form a crucial aspect of subsistence. One of the central adaptations to the economic conditions of the region is a good deal of mobility. There are long-term migration patterns that began in colonial times as the blacks moved down rivers to the north, south, and west and also left the region for Panama, the Atlantic coast, and the interior (West 1957). Recently, there have been moves towards the Chocó's urban nuclei and more than ever to the cities of the interior. More important, there is what Virginia Gutiérrez de Pineda describes as a "continuous cyclical agricultural movement, complemented by fishing activities, hunting and gathering of forest products, plus the

159

sporadic work of mining [which] move the coastal dweller of the Pacific littoral from one place to another in a permanent nomadism" (1975, 242). A development plan diagnosis reiterates: "For the people of the Chocó there is no truly stable activity. When it suits them they are miners, oarsmen, woodcutters, wage-laborers or farmers" (DNP 1961). In its study of the economy of the Chocó, the Contraloría General de la República (1943, 274–76) noted the constant transhumance of the Chocoano peasant, who moved seasonally exploiting different resources (gold, fishing, agriculture).

This mobility is by no means random. Whitten (1974, 76) links it partly to the boom-bust economy of the region: as rubber or *tagua* or *raicilla* markets collapse, or gold prices fluctuate, the peasants shift part of their cash-earning activities into other spheres, often physically moving in order to do so. While some of the mobility is related to external markets, some of it is also cyclical. Valencia Chávez (1984) notes that mining in the Murrí area of the middle Atrato often implies movement, since during the drier period, *verano* (December through March), people make two-week trips to mine and fish in the river headwaters, while in *invierno,* the wet season, some men and many women mine in areas lower down the river, and agriculture occupies a good deal of time. Fishing also often involves month-long trips to lakes during the wetter season (Valencia Chávez 1985; Yépez Henao 1986).

The work of Whitten (1965, 142; 1974, 158) and Friedemann (1974, 1985b) highlights the importance of kinship networks in organizing mobility. They show how people use kin links within a large and flexibly constructed cognatic kindred to legitimate claims to residence, land, reciprocity, assistance, and so on when they choose to move. Land tenure is mostly based on a system whereby river communities have communal lands, usually untitled, within which individual families have a right to their own plot as well as communal lands. These rights can be claimed in different places according to a person's kinship links such that the arrangement allows a good deal of flexibility of residence (Friedemann 1974; West 1957). Kinship provides an extensive network around which people can migrate, exploiting different resources, and indeed the network spreads beyond kin to include putative kin (i.e., nonkin treated as kin), ritual kin (i.e., compadres), and also friends and paisanos (i.e., someone from the same town or village as oneself). These networks provide a resource that can be used to ensure subsistence, attach oneself to a mining gang, ask for a *batea*-load of good pay dirt, recruit labor for logging parties, obtain goods on credit from a small store, and so on. These networks can also act as a leveling mechanism on Chocoano upward mobility. Resources are spread out from earners and owners via kinship networks in a centrifugal fashion, so that many benefit from few. Those who have little shops may find themselves hampered by friends and relatives who ask favors or buy on credit and cannot pay but who are difficult to refuse.

Among the Chocoanos in Unguía, I found patterns that reflected these types of kinship arrangements. Household structures, for example, were typically more flexible than those of either Antioqueños or Costeños. Of the roughly eighty households that I was acquainted with, those of the Antioqueños and the Costeños were overwhelmingly nuclear in form. In contrast, almost two-thirds of the households of Chocoanos (including those born locally of mixed Chocoano-Costeño parentage) were extended, in the sense that people additional to the household head's nuclear family were also present. This was partly due to the fairly recent arrival of many of these Antioqueño and Costeño households and the more established nature of the locally born black families. In Antioquia and the Atlantic coast region, the extended household is not uncommon (Gutiérrez de Pineda 1975). But many of these Chocoano households were also relatively recent arrivals, and it is evident that flexible kinship networks tended to encourage the formation of households in which relatives came and went. By way of illustration, my friend Elean, who maintained two separate households with two common-law wives, quite often had additional relatives staying at one of the houses: the brothers of one of his wives, the former common-law wife of a cousin, and so on. Equally, the few small Chocoano shops tended to have many clients who were more or less closely related and who often owed money. Elean, for example, whose shop turned over about fifteen thousand pesos a week at that time, was owed fifteen thousand pesos by ten clients, all Chocoanos and many related, albeit tenuously, to him. Another such shop, run by a Chocoano woman, had a similar turnover and was owed about thirty thousand pesos by about fifteen clients, most of whom were relatives. In a place where there were many poor people, most shops sold on credit, and this included some of the larger Antioqueño establishments: in some cases they were owed between 50 and 100 percent of their turnover. But the owners of these shops thought that the Chocoanos were the least trustworthy of clients. One said that they were "disordered and careless," another that they were *pícaros* (rogues, villians, knaves); still another commented, "They've given me a hard time; I don't trust them." In the face of this suspicion, then, Chocoanos often found it easier to extract credit from another Chocoano, and preferably a relative. The problem was, of course, that these tiny operations were very vulnerable to the effects of nonpayment.

In sum, then, many Chocoanos tend to rely heavily on unstable and difficult economic activities and on moving around using kinship networks that have a "centrifugal" effect: resources are spread out from certain nodes of accumulation in a way that helps the subsistence of many but can pose problems for the upward mobility of a few (cf. Whitten 1969). In contrast, Antioqueño kinship networks have a more "centripetal" form: the family, extended or nuclear, forms a node for accumulation, and unproductive extra members are borne less willingly. As one well-off Antioqueño said of the needy relative: "We'll give him a helping hand, but we won't carry him."

Successful Chocoanos

From early on, however, there has been a small number of successful Chocoanos. The first notable Chocoano family was that centered on Cárdeno Chaverra, who arrived in 1937. He, and soon after his brother Eraclio, who still lives in Unguía, engaged in trading ipecac, gold, and cloth and later opened up farmland, exporting rice to Quibdó. Cárdeno was probably a fairly typical example of a small Chocoano *patrón,* with modest amounts of capital and some political connections in Quibdó. He himself began by assisting one of the first Antioqueño merchant/*patrón* figures in the area. He had children by a legal wife and three other women, and his estate was split up among these four women, only one of whom has retained a farm, in company with an Antioqueño partner. The children of his legal wife have all had a university education and no longer live in Unguía.

Today there is also a handful of some seven or eight relatively successful Chocoanos. Many of these belong to one loose aggregate of kin, the Machados, effectively a kindred in the sense of the bilineal descendants of a sibling pair—although still referred to locally as a *familia* (cf. Friedemann 1985b). A member of this kindred came to Unguía as a teacher and in 1960 had a total of 783 hectares of land titled near the town. This he later sold partly to an Antioqueño and partly to his father and an uncle. The sons and sons-in-law of the latter two now own and work the land in several adjacent farms. In contrast with the Antioqueño strategy of combining land and commerce, two of these Chocoano farmers combine Cordobist politics with landholding, thus spreading their interests and opening up other opportunities. There is also a certain amount of cooperation between these farmers which provides a safety net. There is a definite tendency to introversion within the kindred, in that their lands are contiguous, they collaborate a certain amount in farming activities, and many of them seek compadres (their children's godparents) within the kindred. Another case of Chocoano upward mobility is that of a locally born family of mixed Chocoano-Antioqueño descent whose current position is due to an Antioqueño father who handed down an estate with land, cattle, town houses, boats, and outboard motors. The farmers of these two families account for five of the seven Chocoano farmers with more than fifty head of cattle on their farms. A final case of Chocoano success is that of a well-educated man who worked as a construction contractor and, together with his Costeño wife and her inherited money, bought farms in Unguía where his father had previously established himself; this man was also politically connected with the Lozanistas and served a term as mayor of Unguía. His children have nearly all had a university education and work either in Bogotá or Quibdó. Success for the Chocoanos, then, is relative and infrequent: as landholders and cattle farmers, even these relatively well-off Chocoanos are poorly placed compared with the better-off Antioqueños and Costeños.

Unguía is a black area—although not unequivocally so—which has progressively come under Antioqueño domination. In the process, change and growth have occurred, but in ways that have not benefited the blacks as much as the nonblacks. In keeping with the patterns I have outlined in other contexts, however, not all blacks are poor, and a handful achieves a rather higher position, often with important inputs from nonblacks. In this chapter I have argued that differences in economic position between categories of people from different regions are due mainly to the varying economic and social baggage they brought with them. In the next chapter I examine how ethnic and racial categorizations are both reproduced and eroded and how these processes affect the positions of Chocoanos, Antioqueños, and Costeños in the economy. Ethnic and racial categorizations here are not simply specific to the local context but follow the pattern of the national racial order in terms of the coexistence of *mestizaje* and discrimination.

10

Unguía:

Ethnic Relations

I observed that in the staff of employees, people from the interior of Antioquia are not to be found. They have in fact been brought, but it was necessary to get rid of them . . . due to the bad treatment that they customarily used towards the local people. It seems to them that the indians and people of color obey no order which is not uttered as a shout . . . "Damned black" is the favorite expression deserved by the poor native. . . . In the majority of the population of these coasts, [there is] a subterranean resentment of the Antioqueño, in place of which there is a feeling of sympathy towards the Chocoano and the people from Bolívar.

In Unguía there is both *mestizaje,* physical and cultural, and there is differentiation. There is interaction across ethnic boundaries that are not strictly defined or policed, but there is also ethnic differentiation that maintains black community and white, or more accurately, Antioqueño exclusiveness and discrimination. This interweaving is basically structured by the way people are integrated into the local economy and how this affects the ethnic identifications they make of themselves and others. Thus Antioqueños tend to retain a strong identity and be exclusive and discriminatory because they have an economic position to defend and justify. For the Chocoanos, on the other hand, there are certain advantages to claiming a Chocoano identity—access

Epigraph: Comments by Father Luis de Santa Teresa on a colonization development scheme mounted near Apartadó, south of Turbo in the Urabá Antioqueño, in 1943, quoted in Severino de Santa Teresa (1957, 5:458). The "people from Bolívar" are the Costeños, and the locals get on well with both them and the Chocoanos, since most of them are, or are descended from, Chocoanos and Costeños themselves.

to the political machine and to subsistence networks—while it is also difficult for the majority of them to avoid being ascribed this identity. There is, of course, a mutually interactive process at work here. People do not simply claim a Chocoano identity in order to claim access to the political machine: they already have potential access if they are Chocoanos. Equally, people do not simply claim to be Antioqueños to defend an economic position: they already have potential privileged access to economic opportunities if they are Antioqueños. Race, ethnicity, and economics are intimately interwoven in the local context.

Basic Patterns of Ethnicity

I was faced with plenty of contradictory evidence on all sides: I saw a drunken Antioqueño screaming "black sonuvabitch" at Chocoanos with knives drawn, and I saw not only some Antioqueño men living with Chocoano women, but a few Chocoano men living with Antioqueño women as well. My Chocoano friend Elean, in whose tiny grocery kiosk I would spend many hours, told me of drunken fights with Costeños provoked by anti-Chocoano insults, and, at the same time, Chocoano-Costeño intermarriage was common. I came across Chocoanos, Antioqueños, and Costeños who held mutually antagonistic and disparaging views of one another—at times imbued with frankly racist images of blacks—and also easygoing interaction between people from different ethnic backgrounds.

As time went on, patterns began to emerge. It became clear that most people led most of their lives within a network of individuals of the same class status and the same ethnic affiliation as themselves. There were a number of economic and political interests that were structured along ethnic lines and which induced people to make clear their ethnic identity and loyalty. There were also processes of exclusion at work as the obverse side of this coin. On the other hand, ideas about race and ethnicity were more important to some people than others (for example, the richer Antioqueños); moreover, specific motives would induce people to form certain relationships across ethnic boundaries that were not rigorously defended in the majority of cases. All this was expressed in a discourse of ethnicity which used simple images, assuming nonproblematic divisions and differences, pointing to everyday features of food, clothing, accent, and typical behavior. Differences existed, and they were constantly reiterated in the classic language of ethnicity, a discourse of stereotypes, which does not necessarily make reference to a clear-cut system of exhaustive and mutually exclusive categories but may rather use relatively simple cognitive models, in this case one that had three prototypical images of Antioqueño, Costeño, and Chocoano as a fundamental framework with which to structure the classification of individual cases (cf. Lakoff 1987). The discourse of ethnicity is often based on remarks that derive from the unspoken, taken-for-granted knowledge of "typical" ethnic behavior and which allude to isolated characteristics in a practical context that illustrates the aptness of the allusion and implicitly discards as irrelevant all contrary instances. Thus in Unguía differences and identities could be established in the loyalties and intimacies of everyday relationships, and in the arena of public behavior, but they could also be constantly transgressed in particular instances without the basic tripartite model being dissolved. Underneath this, and interpenetrating with it, lay a more invidious discourse of race which, sometimes overtly, sometimes tacitly, touched on claims about the inferiority of blacks and the superiority of whites.

Early this century, ethnic distinctions, albeit slight ones, were made between the first Costeño and Chocoano immigrants. The latter were nicknamed *pizarros* (literally "black slates"), and the former *bogas* (the name applied to the boatmen who poled rafts and canoes along rivers and in coastal waters. Black Costeño *bogas* were well known for their work on the rafts that plied the Magdalena River: Peñas Galindo 1988). The Costeños generally came from the coastal fishing villages of *la Costa* and were mostly blacks and mulattoes; in 1921, a visiting priest described Unguía as "a little village of blacks" (Severino de Santa Teresa 1957, 5:166). There was very little competition between the two categories, and intermarriage was common. As immigration stepped up, the Costeños now came from the hinterlands of *la Costa*, around the Sinú River region of Córdoba: they were much more mixed in origin, being of tri-ethnic stock, and they came from an economic tradition dominated by latifundism and cattle raising. These people are commonly known as *chilapos*, a word said to denote indian ancestry and implying a somewhat pejorative picture of a rustic peasant. The arrival of these Costeños, together with Antioqueños and more Chocoanos, added salience to ethnic differentiation in the area, bringing into relief particularly the opposition between the original black Chocoano-Costeño nucleus, plus its newer Chocoano additions, and the virtually entirely nonblack Antioqueños, whose arrival was seen to galvanize the sleepy village peacefulness of before, bringing progress and modernity but also antagonism based on ethnic divisions and violence of a general sort. It was during this time that people remember incidents of violence taking place which had specifically racial configurations, although these were isolated events. Nowadays it is easy to elicit from people of different ethnic backgrounds descriptions that characterize the prototypical image they have of people of other ethnic backgrounds, and these characterizations are also manifest in everyday interaction. Such images are most mutually antagonistic across the Chocoano-Antioqueño divide. The Antioqueños tend to stereotype the Chocoanos as lazy, irresponsible, often dishonest, fun loving, and good mostly for physical labor. The Chocoanos, on the other hand, while often admiring the progressiveness and application of the Antioqueños, also frequently resent them as what they feel to be racist and rapacious intruders, aggressively and unscrupulously ambitious. The newer Costeños or *chilapos* bridged the Chocoano-Antioqueño divide, both as people racially intermediate between the Antioqueños and the blacks and as people defined as less "primitive" and therefore less lazy and more progressive than the Chocoanos in the hierarchy of Colombia's national cultural geography. The Antioqueños, for example, view them as more acceptable and trustworthy than the Chocoanos, and the Costeños frequently admire the Antioqueños as *gente progresista,* progressive people. In the local context, however, one could see an attempt on the part of the Chocoanos to subvert this hierarchy to their advantage. The newer Chocoanos included some teachers and various administrative employees who could boast some education: they were able to manipulate the rustic image of the *chilapo,* frequently observing that *el chilapo es bruto* (the *chilapo* is stupid), to throw into relief their own education, asserting with equal regularity that Chocoanos valued education highly. The Costeños, on the other hand, could always fall back on the power of a nationally recognized scale of values which gave the Pacific coastal region a lower, more primitive status than the Atlantic coastal region, and even black Costeños would sometimes disparage the Chocoanos. Interestingly, of course, the claim that *chilapo* connoted indian ancestry was a reference to the position of the indigenous population, which is considered to be virtually beyond the pale of "civilized" society. Behind these manipulations, however, the history of Chocoano-Costeño mixing in the area tended to defuse a radical confrontation of images.

Ethnicity in the Local Economy: Differentiation

People came to Unguía with different ethnic and racial identities, and with different economic and cultural capitals. The reasons why ethnic and racial categories continue to exist as differentiating forces are primarily due to the way ethnicity, race, and economic opportunity are interwoven. Ethnic difference is continuously reconstituted as part of ethnic inequality.

People of each ethnic category tend to occupy different, if somewhat overlapping, niches in the economy. The Chocoanos, as miners and public sector employees, are active in fields in which the Costeños and the Antioqueños have limited interests: some Antioqueños also mine, but their major presence in the mines is as traders; some Antioqueños are public employees and teachers, but they occupy posts distributed by national, not departmental, agencies. For the Chocoanos, ethnic identity can be a useful resource in mining. Although anyone is free to go along with a *batea* and pan gold at the river's edge, if one wants to work with a *motobomba* owner, or perhaps take a *batea*-load of ore-rich pay dirt from his or her working, claims to ethnic solidarity—or better, kinship solidarity—are a good strategy because they refer to a network of reciprocity into which both parties are inserted and on which both can expect to make future claims. In this sense, Chocoano ethnic identity helps a person to penetrate into the mining sector. In a more general sense, of course, being Chocoano means having access to the wider networks that Chocoanos use to travel and subsist and which, while based fundamentally on kinship, spread beyond that to ultimately include all Chocoanos, especially when outside the Chocó. Equally, in politics and the public sector, the Chocoanos generally occupy posts distributed by the departmental bureaucracy, and they maintain political links with Quibdó, the symbolic heart of the Chocó, in order to influence this distribution. This in itself keeps Chocoano identity alive in Unguía, but more generally it is clear that, whatever the infighting behind the regional configurations of Chocoano politics, to enter into the political machine of patron-client relations and bureaucratic string pulling, it is a great advantage to be a Chocoano, and preferably a "legitimate"—that is, a black—one. At the level of individual motives, it makes sense for Chocoanos in the political machine to distribute jobs and other goods and services to fellow Chocoanos, since these form their electorate and are more dependent on them due to lack of other opportunities. At a more categorical level, in view of the Antioqueños' control of commerce, both in Unguía and elsewhere in the region, the Chocoanos are loath to let them into the political game, and in truth, the Antioqueños generally have little interest in participating. They may occasionally resent the Chocoanos' control of local administration if it affects them directly through, say, taxes on business premises, but the money involved makes this a petty matter. The Chocoanos' identity is a resource for them in politics, mining, and, more generally, spatial mobility and subsistence: these economic factors influence the maintenance of black community in the area. Practically no one else is seriously attempting to encroach on these spheres that yield unstable and restricted benefits, and as a result the Chocoanos do not have to defend their ethnic niche with much exclusiveness or create a tightly bounded group.

The Antioqueños' position is somewhat distinct. There are now few Chocoanos and Costeños who are merchants, but this is not only because they come from regions with less entrepreneurial and commercial traditions: previously they traded in the area, but they have been largely pushed out by Antioqueños who defend a near monopoly. Part of the way they achieved this—aside from such factors as their superior access to capital and their greater experience in the commercial sphere—was to be exclusive with their capital, their trade contacts, their cooperative arrangements, and their private credit. They tend to restrict access to these things to their own people, and not only in a way that links people at the same economic level and collectively enhances their economic power, but also in a way that links poorer Antioqueños with richer ones. There is no definite distinction here in the way Antioqueños collaborate in the commercial as opposed to the landholding spheres, because the economically powerful Antioqueño nucleus has both commercial and landholding interests, and they have tended to expand both in an interdependent fashion. They may therefore give poorer Antioqueños access to a series of opportunities in both commerce and landholding, which, when taken advantage of, increase the overall Antioqueño share in the local pool of resources. The Antioqueños have a strong reputation for clannishness and ethnic esprit de corps. For example, a Costeño farmer said this of the Antioqueños:

> The Antioqueños who have money come here . . . and they become allies . . . and one comes here rich, and by the simple fact of another person being *paisa* as well . . . they're more regionalist . . . they help their *compañeros* [companions]. So if you're a Costeño who's come here poor, you have nothing to help your *compañero* with. . . . The *paisas* progress because their *compañeros* help them, they're already further on.

An Antioqueño farmer agreed: "The poorer Antioqueño starts off day-laboring. Then he begins to look around and see who'll help him. He goes on and on, he's crazy to find someone who'll give him credit, who'll lend him something so he can sow a crop; and then he goes and buys a piece of land. And the other *paisas* help him, because that's our instinct, to progress."

At least two major Antioqueño land and cattle owners started out as farm administrators for richer compatriots. Equally in commerce, they invest in enterprises together and lend one another money—not recklessly of course, but "the simple fact of being a *paisa*" is a basis—

the richer employ the poorer to administrate their businesses and may then give them a helping hand to get started on their own. As I mentioned in the last chapter, Antioqueño shopkeepers are cautious about trusting Chocoanos, and they are more open-minded with their compatriots. One commented that Antioqueños were "very dutiful" with their obligations; another, perhaps more realistically, said, "The *paisas* rob a lot, but the blacks . . ."

Antioqueños also cooperate with one another in other ways in the farming domain. Cattle can be raised *a utilidades* for example, a system in which one party with some spare capital buys young cattle and the other party raises them on a farm with spare pasture, covering the costs incurred: the profits of the sale of the cattle are then split equally. Clearly, this arrangement, as well as being mutually beneficial, gives the cattle raiser access to opportunities that could have gone to someone else. To the extent that Antioqueños control more capital and more cattle, they also control these opportunities; to the extent that they favor other Antioqueños for these arrangements, the latter benefit as against farmers of other groups. It is not true that the Antioqueños are totally exclusive in this respect, since there are cases of Costeños and some Chocoanos who have Antioqueño-owned cattle on their farms (see below), but in my interviews with farmers I found a definite tendency for the Antioqueños to favor other Antioqueños. Other cooperative arrangements in farm work exist in the form of different varieties of sharecropping agreements in which someone, with or without his or her own land, crops on another's land, plants pasture, and splits the harvest (usually maize). Again, although these kinds of arrangements exist both within and between the Antioqueño and Costeño categories, there is a tendency for these farmers to cooperate with people of the same ethnic identity as themselves. The few Chocoano farmers have almost no sharecropping arrangements except with other Chocoanos.

Exclusiveness also extends to the realm of marriage, common law or legal, and statistically speaking, the Antioqueños marry with people of their own ethnic origin to a greater extent than either the Chocoanos or the Costeños: in a random sample of 157 unions, the ratio of observed to expected intermarriage rates was 39 percent for the Antioqueños compared with 70 percent and 77 percent for the Costeños and the Chocoanos, respectively (see tables 4 and 5 in appendix A). This pattern is characteristic of all Antioqueños, but it is logically most marked among the richer families who can make economically advantageous marriages; it can also represent a means for slightly poorer Antioqueños to link themselves to a richer family.

There is no doubt that the Antioqueños avoid cooperating with the

Chocoanos and may even avoid employing them as labor. One of my central Chocoano informants, Elean, recounted that he once worked together with an Antioqueño on a house-building contract arranged by the latter with another *paisa:* the Antioqueño did as little as possible and in the end tried to pay Elean as if he had been employing him as a laborer. This is, of course, Elean's account of events, but Antioqueños themselves expressed their distrust of blacks. One Antioqueño farmer said, "We don't much like the black man, not because of his color, no, that's no shame; but because he's a real thief and is very lazy . . . and a liar: he'll go on his knees and swear to you that he's going to do such-and-such a thing—no way." An Antioqueño merchant and landowner alleged that the blacks were untrustworthy and also that they did not really know how to do business in a straightforward way, that they had a different "vision of the world" and that it made no sense economically to cooperate with them. In sum, then, the Antioqueños form quite a tight network. They cooperate with one another because both parties think that they will probably get a better deal that way: someone who is likely to understand them, to work hard and have the same aspirations as themselves. They cooperate less with the Costeños and very little with the Chocoanos. Logically, it is the Antioqueño nucleus of larger merchant landowners which represents the tightest group, since they have the most interests in common, but the rest of the category also has an important stake in Antioqueño identity.

However, *paisa* exclusiveness does not emerge in the local context simply as the collective outcome of individual strategies directed at maximizing access to economic resources. There is also a crucial sense in which the Antioqueños are defending an image of themselves which they value and for which they are famous: *gente progresista,* progressive people who work hard and are shrewd and successful. Progress in Colombian ideologies is pervaded with ideas about whiteness, or at least distance from blackness and indianness, and is also redolent with images of the highland interior and its urbanism. The Antioqueños in Unguía are virtually entirely nonblack and present a very light-skinned appearance; they maintain strong links with their homeland in the interior of the country and in some cases, especially among the richer people, have urban backgrounds. They play the role of the harbingers of change, progress, and civilization, brought by whites from the interior to the benighted and distant regions of the country inhabited by blacks and indians (there are still several small indian reservations in the Urabá Chocoano; Baracaldo Aldana 1977). Interestingly, an official 1977 report found that Unguía was quite "urban" in outlay and mentality, despite its small population of about two

171

thousand people (Dobyns and González 1977). In effect, the Antioqueños have come to dominate the central streets of the town with large, two-story, well-finished houses-cum-business premises. People in Unguía make half-ironic remarks about *la calle del comercio* (commercial street), but they are half-serious as well: the Antioqueños have virtually created a commercial sector in the town, true to their role as the bringers of progress. The social exclusiveness of the Antioqueños is an expression of this image of themselves, of their claims to a superiority defined by color, urbanism, and economic success. To mix freely with everyone would be to jeopardize this position.

What is more, the very presence of the Chocoanos and their generally subordinate economic position brings into prominent relief the Antioqueños' claims about the nonblackness of the *raza antioqueña* and their superior entrepreneurial abilities, claims that simultaneously reiterate the blackness of the Chocoanos, imposing on them an identity that, because of its lowly position in the national hierarchy, the Chocoanos would not necessarily lay claim to with the alacrity of an Antioqueño upholding the fact of being *paisa*. Antioqueño and Chocoano identity cannot, naturally, be disengaged from national hierarchies of color and cultural geography: one reason why *paisa* identity can be a strong focus for solidarity is that it has a high status at a national level; conversely, Chocoano identity is more problematic in this respect.

Ethnicity in the Local Economy: Mestizaje

The economic specialization and stratification along ethnic lines which exist in Unguía are the result of a complex mixture of past traditions and contemporary interactions in which people and groups have vested, but varying, interests in maintaining an ethnically articulated stake in certain economic networks. The Antioqueños have the most to defend in terms of economic and cultural value, and any *paisa* has, on average, more chance of making a succulent catch by casting a net of ethnic claims than a Chocoano or indeed a Costeño. Ideas about region, race, and cultural origin are therefore more significant and useful to them. They are relatively less useful to the Chocoanos since they entail more meager, but nonetheless vital, benefits, but they are still of great significance because *others* discriminate against them on these grounds.

For the Antioqueños and the Chocoanos there are particular structures in their relationship to the local economy which tend to foster nonblack exclusiveness and discrimination, and also black community. But these do not affect all Chocoanos and Antioqueños equally, nor are they the only elements in the picture. There are also factors that encourage *mestizaje* and the crossing of ethnic boundaries, or their neglect.

A major influence in this respect is the presence of the Costeños. As a category, the Costeños have little in the way of an economic niche which they defend against others. They have few stakes in the commercial sector and are generally only small and medium-sized farmers: there is therefore less chance of benefiting from the position of richer members who control a wide range of opportunities. They tend to predominate in the farming labor force and among the contractors who recruit working parties for specific tasks such as fencing or fumigating pastures, but as in the Chocoano case, this is a field of activity which few others encroach on. Whereas the Antioqueños and, to a lesser degree, the Chocoanos have specific reasons for claiming their particular identities, and whereas both are involved in a racial and cultural opposition that the Antioqueños engineer principally to their own advantage, the Costeños have few such interests, and they are also intermediate in that opposition. As a result, the Costeños have relations of various kinds with both Chocoanos and Antioqueños. Much of the intermarriage involving Chocoanos is with Costeños (see table 4 in appendix A), and from earlier times this has given rise to a category of locally born mulatto Chocoanos who are as much Costeño as Chocoano in terms of personal identity. On the other hand, many small and medium-sized Costeño farmers associate and cooperate with Antioqueños.

This Costeño presence has particular repercussions on the nature of black adaptation to the cultural mores of the encroaching nonblack world. Although black community is a force in Unguía, fostered by politics and subsistence strategies and by the exclusion they experience at the hands of many Antioqueños, it has to be borne in mind that the whole Urabá area has been steadily coming under the sway of Antioqueño culture. Unguía as a town is now literally shaped by Antioqueño priorities. Antioqueño culture is identified with progress, modernity, and development, as well as with whiteness, and it stands in contrast to Chocoano culture, which is identified in national hierarchies with primitiveness and backwardness. Local blacks therefore come under pressure to adapt culturally to avoid stigmatization as primitives. This can be accomplished for some by their control over or participation in the education system as the local teachers. It is also evident in Unguía that cultural changes are occurring under the influence of Antioqueño dominion—changes towards more "urban" and "modern" forms in, say, house construction or dress, with wooden and palm thatch houses being replaced by cement block and corrugated iron, and shoes replacing bare feet. These are changes that are occurring all over the Chocó in its growing urban nuclei, where national culture has the greatest impact. In Urabá, however, there has long existed the possibility for Chocoano migrants, and more particularly their children, to begin to identify themselves as Costeños rather than Chocoanos, both through intermarriage and through the simple claiming of a Costeño identity by virtue of long residence in the area. Chocoanos can thus associate themselves with a region and a culture considered less primitive, more urbanized, and more developed—and less black—than the Chocó. This strategy utilizes the prestige values attaching to national hierarchies of cultural geography: it appeals to an intermediate category in precisely the hierarchy that also locates the Antioqueños on a higher rung than either the Chocoanos or the Costeños themselves, and which gives them a position of authority in the redefinition of the local cultural milieu. In this sense, by virtue of its ambivalent position between the Chocó and *la Costa,* the Urabá region is a zone through which Chocoano identity and blackness can be diluted, dispersed, and transformed in the context of the increasing impact of national society which Antioqueño dominion represents.

In addition to the intermediate position of the Costeños, which facilitates actual race mixture and the transformation of ethnic identity, there are also more specific reasons why people form relationships across ethnic boundaries and encourage *mestizaje.* Take marriage, for example. Many of the men who come to Unguía are single men. The single women in the town are locally born daughters of Chocoano or Costeño families, some of whose sons have migrated to more urban areas. Over time, the Chocoano and Costeño men have intermarried with Costeño and Chocoano women, and their daughters, a kind of Costeño-ized Chocoano hybrid, are mates for other incoming migrants, including a handful of single Antioqueño men (see table 4 in appendix A). In this case, an Antioqueño's acceptance of a black—or rather a mulatto—mate is influenced by the constraints of the migration process and affects principally poor young male migrants. The richer Antioqueños do not form these kinds of unions, or if they do, only in a more informal manner and perhaps parallel to a formal union with an Antioqueño wife.

In the economic sphere, there are also reasons for crossing or ignoring ethnic boundaries. Neighboring Antioqueño and Costeño farmers may, for instance, cooperate for reasons of convenience. More interestingly, a few Antioqueños had cattle *a utilidades* with some of the few successful Chocoanos. Because of lack of capital these Chocoano farmers have spare capacity on their farms of which other farmers, better endowed with capital, can make use if necessary. However, the conditional nature of nonblack acceptance is manifest in these cases. When faced with the examples of the successful Chocoanos, the Antioqueños would say that they were *chocoanos apaisados,* Antioqueño-ized Chocoanos, who had had experience of the world outside the Chocó and had learned other ways. This was true to some extent of the Machado farmers (mentioned in the last chapter), who had indeed gained experience outside the Chocó; even so, these individuals were still unequivocally Chocoano in identity and affiliation. Whatever they had learned, however, could not be accepted by the Antioqueños as a legitimate aspect of being Chocoano but had to be arrogated to themselves as the only real bringers of progress. They would also say that the cattle on their farms mostly belonged to *paisas,* or in other words that these Chocoanos were tagging onto Antioqueño economic success. Only if a Chocoano is *apaisado*—that is, is considered to have in some way overcome the general condition attributed to blacks as a category, an achievement itself attributed to Antioqueño influence—can he or she be trusted to the extent of forming a cooperative economic link.

From the point of view of the Chocoanos themselves, links with nonblacks and the nonblack world are often a corollary of economic success, and this is in fact a structural feature of black upward mobility. Looking at the successful Chocoanos described in the last chapter, there is a clear connection between success and nonblackness which characterizes these cases in one form or another. Several of the farmers of the Machado family have economic links with Antioqueños and Costeños who keep cattle on their farms or have *a utilidades* arrangements with them. The Machados have generally based their progress on retention of land and cooperation within the kindred (cf. Whitten 1969), but their own resources are nevertheless limited, and much of the cattle on their land was bought with nonblack capital. In this case, there is little link with *mestizaje* as a process, since only one of the men has a white wife and all of them are firmly embedded in Chocoano social networks, but it illustrates quite clearly black dependency on nonblack capital and the need for blacks to form links with nonblacks if they are to progress. Engaging in physical or cultural *blanqueamiento* is a further step, but already there is a basis from which to make this move. In the other cases, the link between success and nonblackness is more obvious. The Chocoano who became successful in the 1940s, Cárdeno Chaverra, had nine legal children who have benefited from his success in terms of their higher education, which mostly took place in the interior of the country; several of them now also live in the cities of the interior. In the other two cases, in which a Chocoano man married a Costeño woman, and a Chocoano woman married an Antioqueño man, success was predicated on Costeño or Antioqueño capital. In both families, those mulatto children who have married all have spouses who are the same color or lighter than they are. In the case of the Chocoano-Costeño family, all the children lived for long periods in Bogotá while they studied for higher degrees: some of them still live there, while two others have been drawn back to the Chocó via their father's political connections and the job opportunities these opened up.

Generally, then, upward mobility and *mestizaje* tend to operate together, the structural conditions for this lying in the fact that possibilities for success are managed by nonblacks and/or located in the nonblack world. This does not mean that all *mestizaje*, physical or cultural, is determined by patterns of personal economic success, since the presence of the Costeños opens up a number of channels for *mestizaje* less linked to individual fortunes—although this is within the context of the upward mobility that the Antioqueño presence has produced for the locality as a whole. It does show that upward mobility structures patterns of black *mestizaje*.

The school is a further instance in which ethnic differentiation is minimalized, although the causes here were more connected to young Antioqueños temporarily embracing Chocoano and Costeño culture than being in a position to conditionally accept it on their own terms. The locally born children of Antioqueño families are outnumbered in the schools, partly because Antioqueños send some of their children back to Antioquia and partly because they have had less breeding time in the area. In a sample of ninety-eight secondary school students in Unguía, only fourteen were Antioqueños. An analysis of "best-friend" relations among these students, compiled by a teacher at the school, showed that people formed friendship with little regard for ethnic identification and that young Antioqueños befriended Chocoanos and Costeños. Interestingly, this was despite the fact that, in answers to questionnaires, the students showed themselves to be completely familiar with the stereotypes with which people from the different ethnic categories typically described one another, and the Costeños and the Chocoanos tended to classify the Antioqueños as racist. The special circumstances of the school environment effectively quelled a tendency to reproduce the ethnic differentiation of which the students were fully cognizant. The Chocoanos and Costeños were actually numerically dominant, and most of the teachers were also Chocoanos, having been appointed by the Chocoano-controlled bureaucracy, and the Antioqueño students had little incentive to maintain any exclusiveness if they wanted to participate in the youth activities of the town.

There is even a sense here in which the Antioqueño youth actively embraced Chocoano culture as it was presented to them in Unguía, that is, in a form already adapted to a changing cultural milieu. In a small town such as Unguía, most of the social activities of the teenage cohort were centered around sports and dancing, both realms that were controlled by Chocoanos and Costeños, both because of their numerical preponderance in the younger generation and because the dance halls were run by Chocoanos who played genres associated particularly with the Atlantic and the Pacific coastal regions—salsa and *vallenato* (see chapter 15, where I discuss both these genres, and music as an aspect of black culture). In order to enter into their cohort's social world, and especially in order to form relations with the opposite sex (usually of an informal and transient nature), it was indispensable for the younger Antioqueños to go out dancing in a small dance-hall world that was basically black territory. Here it is less a question of Antioqueños conditionally accepting an adapted form of blackness than of them embracing black community for the qualities it is seen to offer—the possibility of black culture holding a certain attractiveness for nonblacks. However, the shadowy dividing line between conditional acceptance and the embracing of blackness is revealed by the increasing integration of these Antioqueños into their parental ethnic networks as they grow up, become more oriented to work and marriage, and perhaps move out of the region.

In Unguía it is the process of colonization which structures the dynamics of the Colombian racial order as it emerges in the local context. Black community and nonblack discrimination; black connections to the nonblack world through *mestizaje* and nonblack acceptance of blacks: all are structured by the way Chocoanos, Costeños, and Antioqueños relate to the local economy and the particular interests and motives of individual people which arise from and transform that relation.

Black community is fostered by Chocoanos making use of ethnic and kinship affiliations for subsistence and political strategies in the context of a local economy dominated by nonblack interests that tend to be biased against them. White discrimination is encouraged by the positive advantages of ethnic clannishness and by the status accruing to those who can adopt the role of a civilizing presence. Black adaptation is structured by the Costeño presence, which provides an intermediate racial and cultural category to which the Chocoanos can relate themselves, and by the nature of black upward mobility, which is almost inevitably linked to the nonblack world. The overall cultural ethos of the zone, once defined largely by the Costeños and to a lesser extent by the Chocoanos, has been increasingly controlled by the Antioqueño presence, which emphasizes progress, development, and modernity, and the persistence of cultural patterns typical of a rural Chocoano milieu is subject to disparagement. Finally, nonblack conditional acceptance is influenced by such factors as the need of some Antioqueño immigrants for mates, by the need to find farms with spare carrying capacity for cattle, and by the position of locally born young Antioqueños in the local school and in the activities of their cohort. In the latter case, the lack of power of the young Antioqueños in their immediate situation prevents them laying down the rules for conditional acceptance, and instead (even if only temporarily) they embrace black culture for the social qualities it holds for them.

In all this, while the local racial order is structured by the relation of people to the local economy, the former is not reducible to the latter, and there is a reciprocal relation between them. Antioqueños also fight to maintain color and regional reputation as values in their own right, and being identified with that color and reputation can give potential access to privileged opportunities in the local economy. Chocoanos may, especially via the Costeños, distance themselves from blackness and black culture as low-status elements, and distance from blackness, cultural or physical, may bring favorable reclassification (e.g., as a *chocoano apaisado*) in the eyes of those with greater control of resources. Values attached to race and ethnicity have arisen in the historical emergence of the Colombian racial order, and, being already constituted in the context of Unguía, they act as forces that, while structured by the local political economy, can actively intervene in it.

Meanwhile, the local situation tends to reproduce the larger racial order, not only in terms of the values this encapsulates, but in terms of its hierarchies of wealth and power. It is here also that we can see the sense, outlined in chapter 3, in which a social system is constituted and reproduced in a spatially regionalized form, with local conjunctures being generated from overarching structures and themselves contributing to the reproduction of those structures. The overarching, historically given structures of region, race, and class which exist in Colombia determined that in Unguía Costeños should be mostly poor mixed-blood agricultural colonists pushed from their territory by the expansion of capitalist haciendas; that highland Antioqueños should be mostly white and mestizo with experience of aggressive colonization, commerce, and entrepreneurship, and that among their number should be some with considerable capital assets; and that Chocoanos should be poor blacks with little in the way of such experience and assets. In the local conjuncture of these larger structures, people interact in a way that tends to reproduce those structures: the Chocoanos, for example, are on average losing out in the overall expansion of opportunities which the colonization of the area entails, and this is partly due to their lack of preparation for competition—a difficulty embedded in the long-term colonial and neocolonial structures of exploitation and discrimination which have affected the Chocó—and partly to the direct exclusion they experience at the hands of the Antioqueños. In this sense, an overall racial stratification is maintained, seen from national perspective.

There are, of course, forces at work undermining that stratification: the Chocoanos are benefiting in an absolute, if not in a relative, fashion, and a few of them are doing quite well. There are also important processes of race mixture under way: although the Antioqueños are rather exclusive in their social relations, and especially in marriage, some of them form relations with Chocoanos, and for the latter group, the presence of the Costeños, with whom they intermix a good deal, forms a significant avenue of *blanqueamiento*. The colonization of a part of the Chocó by Costeños and Antioqueños thus opens up certain channels of escape from poverty and blackness. But it is important to bear in mind that these forces have been undermining the racial configurations of social stratification since the beginning of the colonial period in the form of regionalized processes of race mixture, manumission, and the occasional advancement of colored individuals: what is happening in Unguía is not new. The question is whether this type of small-scale current of osmosis out of the poor black category will eventually destroy the racial inequality of the class system—so far, time has not improved the position of the blacks in Colombia, and any improvements tend to have negated blackness itself.

11

Medellín:

Working in the City

Every reasonably well-off family had one female slave, at least, in domestic service; the cook was always a black woman. These city slaves had a much better time than those on the haciendas, who lived a life of hard work and were treated in some cases with great cruelty. There were masters of terrible fame, who used to threaten servants who would not behave well. It was enough for an easygoing master to say to his servant: "I'll sell you to Master so-and-so," for her to mend her ways at once.

In the next two chapters, I examine in detail the position of Chocoano migrants in the city of Medellín. I have examined the interweaving of blackness and race mixture historically in three regions, and nowadays in Unguía, a frontier zone where national ideologies of progress, development, and *blanqueamiento* encroach on a peripheral black area and where the spatial process of colonization is also a nexus of race relations. Now I look at a context in which migration forms the nexus of race relations, and blacks from a peripheral area place themselves in the symbolic heartland of national ideologies of progress, development, and *blanqueamiento*.

The migration of Chocoanos to Medellín has a double aspect. On the one hand, the majority of them are simply poor migrants to the city, and they face the same problems of housing, work, transport, health, and coping with urban institutions as any other migrant of similar means. In this sense, then, they participate in national processes of rural-urban migration and urbanization. On the other hand,

Epigraph: Description of Cali in 1789, from the novel *El alférez real,* by Eustaquio Palacios (1942).

180

these processes are part of the increasing spatial integration of the national territory in which regions that occupy different positions in the hierarchies of race, power, and culture are brought more closely into contact. In Quibdó, Antioqueño migrants are nonblack entrepreneurs in an underdeveloped black city; in Unguía, Chocoanos lose their tenuous grip on the area to encroaching Antioqueño society. In Medellín, the Chocoanos are blacks in a nonblack city—and nonblack with the vengeance of a region with a whitewashed black history. They are not simply migrants but come from a region classified nationally not just as rural, in the way rural Antioquia is contrasted with urban Medellín, but as unremittingly and completely rural, primitive in its backwardness. Blackness therefore tends to suggest to nonblacks images of the most gauche country bumpkin—an evocation that has to be fought with "civilized" behavior—and this is linked to other stereotypes of blacks as inferior, nonprogressive, lazy and disorganized, images that can survive the overcoming of a rustic identity. As a result of this, the Chocoanos form a specific group with their own ways of adapting to the urban environment, even though these are within the overall pattern of migrant adaptation. The encounter of the Chocoanos with the Antioqueños in Medellín is not just a rural-urban one but also another step in the historical dynamic of being black in Colombia, of coping with a dominant nonblack world by engaging in a dialogue with it in which blacks, understanding the image of them held by nonblacks, try to subvert that image, adopting the discourse and behavior of the nonblack world. Or, equally understanding the image, they try to create or rather re-create their own black world with its distinctive discourse and behavior—a response understood by the nonblack world as confirmation of their impression that the blacks refuse to "integrate."

Chocoanos as Migrants in Medellín: Basic Patterns

Medellín, *ciudad de la eterna primavera,* city of the eternal spring. It was once a small colonial town where wooden houses thatched with palm leaves surrounded the central market square, the muddiness of which was only cobbled over in 1857. Now Colombia's second city, with nearly one and a half million inhabitants, it is a major commercial and industrial center whose central square, the famous Parque Berrío, is towered over by several vertiginously high multistory banks and submerged in the constant exhaust fumes of a hundred buses that pass through the cramped city center en route to distant neighborhoods, the destination also of the migrants who leave the countryside and smaller towns of Antioquia to swell the city's population in search of economic betterment. Medellín has a growing and dynamic economy, partly because it is also a major center for the country's cocaine economy; and between the mafiosos and the common thieves and muggers—not to mention the increasing violence of right-wing death squads—the city has acquired a reputation as one of the more dangerous places in Colombia.

On 23 October 1850, the emancipation of the slaves was celebrated in the Parque Berrío, when 133 of them were given letters of freedom (Olano 1939). Nowadays the blacks who congregate there on Sundays are mostly domestic servants, Chocoano women who work in middle- and upper-class Medellín homes. Their black Antioqueño cousins are forgotten in the image of the city, because the Parque Berrío is the symbolic center of the *raza antioqueña,* birthplace of "all self-respecting Antioqueños who are worthy of the name" (*El Colombiano,* Tricentenary Collection, 30 October 1975). In terms of the country's cultural geography, Medellín is also *la capital de la montaña,* the capital of the mountains, where blacks are strangers from the hot lowlands and where the *ritmo paisa,* the *paisa* rhythm, holds sway, imbuing commerce and industry (and death) with a fast-moving efficiency.

Chocoanos in this city deal with employment and housing in ways characteristic of migrants in general. They generally find work in the types of jobs which occupy most migrants to the city: domestic service for women, the construction industry for men, and the "informal sector" for both sexes, specifically the sale of food and drink on the street. Like other migrants, they try to consolidate their economic position and, when possible, educate their children. Some achieve a certain upward mobility into a relatively secure working-class position, which others remain at a more precarious level; some return home. In any case, they make use of networks of contacts with relatives, friends, paisanos, and neighbors to help them in their strategies for survival and progress, as do other migrants. Equally, like other migrants of similar economic status, a minority of Chocoanos solve their need for housing by invading unused land in ecologically marginal locations or by renting rooms in tenement blocks and other low-income dwellings. More commonly, they buy small plots sold by landowners or semilegal urban developers who subdivide larger holdings; or they buy a skeleton dwelling from a "pirate urbanizer" whose products do not conform to municipal regulations; or they may get a plot or a house through the government housing agency, the Instituto de Crédito Territorial (ICT), which they pay off in installments; some also save enough money to buy a house outright. These processes place the majority of Chocoanos in working-class neighborhoods that exhibit varying degrees of consolidation, from newly formed shantytowns to areas with paved roads, public services, and houses with plastered facades. A minority have the means to buy or rent a house in a middle-class neighborhood. As homeowners of all kinds, they—like others—construct or improve their dwellings in a piecemeal fashion, usually with their own labor and helped by relatives, friends, and neighbors.

Yet factors specific to the Chocoanos make their position different. They suffer a certain amount of discrimination in the employment and housing market; they sometimes form certain nuclei of settlement, often where a Chocoano-run dance hall functions or used to function and which are points of congregation where Chocoano culture holds sway, if only temporarily; they have a particularly strong and dense network of mutual aid and information which goes beyond kinship and local ties of city neighborhood or Chocoano river/village loyalties to include all Chocoanos as an ethnic-racial group. This ethnic network has certain key concentrations, including the nuclei of settlement and also certain bars, city locations, and one or two associations. The network also has more rarified parts where families or individuals maintain few links with other Chocoanos: as is the case with many migrants, with the passage of time they integrate into the city and lose contact with original networks and old paisanos from their home territory. In the case of the Chocoanos, however, this process is viewed by them not simply as adaptation to the city but also as assimilation to the nonblack world; as a process of *blanqueamiento,* it may attract criticism and accusations of betrayal and desertion. This is frequently connected with economic consolidation such that upward mobility, even on a small scale, tends to take on meanings that belong to a discourse of race and ethnicity.

Methods and Sources in Medellín

I lived in Medellín for about a year. I started out renting a room in a city center house, once the home of a middle-class Medellín family, which had been converted into rooms-to-let: the owners occupied a couple of the best rooms at the front, and there were nine other rooms with a total of about twenty-five people in the house. Some rooms were cubicles partitioned off with hardboard, and a couple of retainers who did cooking and cleaning slept on the floor in the kitchen. From there I moved into a rented room in La Iguaná, an invasion settlement near the city center which had a significant Chocoano population. Despite being an invasion settlement, it had some parts dating from the 1940s which were well consolidated—although not, for all that, better regarded by the middle-class housing that surrounded it and saw it as a den of crime, vice, and poverty. The house I was in belonged to a Chocoano, Luis Urrutía, and his wife, Delfa, the oldest Chocoano residents of the settlement. It was a two-story house with piped water and electricity, and the lower story, at least, had plastered walls and tiled floors. From there, I moved into an outlying consolidated working-class barrio (neighborhood) called Aranjuez where I rented out a flat with Carlos Pino, his wife Noris, and their two children. Carlos was a black from Turbo, his father a Chocoano and his mother a local Turbeño woman. Noris was also from Turbo but was more mixed in appearance, with long black hair and light brown skin, a person who would not readily be classed as "black" in Medellín or elsewhere. In this house, everything was legal, power cuts were only occasional, and bills for water, light, and telephone were delivered monthly—in contrast with La Iguaná, where power cuts were frequent, many people paid for electricity by an ad hoc system of charging, many did not pay at all, and there were only a couple of public phones and no mail deliveries. If I had stayed in Medellín, doubtless I would have participated in the next stage of the housing process which occurred when Carlos got his own house from the government's Instituto de Crédito Territorial: it was a structure in *obra negra,* an unfinished state, which could then be improved by plastering the walls, tiling the floor, painting, adding another story, and so on.

The Chocoano presence in Medellín was very varied, and I gathered data on a number of fronts. Through a number of contacts, made originally via friends in Unguía, I visited Chocoano families in their homes all over the city and carried out interviews on their life histories, social networks, and experiences in Medellín. I focused on specific sites of Chocoano nucleation by living in La Iguaná, a locale with probably the highest concentration of Chocoanos in the city, and there I interviewed both Antioqueño and Chocoano families. I also interviewed families in other barrios with obvious concentrations of blacks, usually pursuing contacts made via different city authorities, some involved directly in housing, some in other forms of community organization. I had particularly close contacts with Desarrollo Comunitario, the Community Development office of the municipality which dealt with upgrading low-income settlements. Planeación Social (the municipal social planning office) and Colcultura (the local branch of the Colombian Institute of Culture) also proved a useful source of contacts and information. I had contacts with black- and white-run organizations for domestic servants, the former of which was also a meeting place for Chocoanos from all walks of life. And living with Carlos Pino was an invaluable entry into the Chocoano and Costeño networks in the city. Gradually, my own network expanded so that it included Chocoanos and Antioqueños all over the city and from a variety of classes. For example, knowing Chocoanos in La Iguaná was a fairly sure way of finding a mutual connection with a great many of the Chocoanos in Medellín, at least the poorer ones: if they didn't live there themselves, or hadn't done so in the past, there was a good chance they'd have friends or relatives there. At the same time, from a mixture of written and oral sources, I learned about the city as an urban place and set of processes, about the construction industry, domestic service and other "informal sector" activities, about local politics and education, about bars, clubs, and music—all this was necessary to conceptualize the Chocoanos in the city.

A brief account of statistical sources is also necessary here, since this and the next chapter rely on a common statistical basis. A principal source for statistics has been the government's 1981 Estudio de Población, which took a 10 percent sample of the city's households and quizzed their occupants on general and labor characteristics. The Departamento Administrativo Nacional de Estadísticas (DANE) sold me a copy of this data set, and I have been able to rework it to analyze the position of Chocoanos in the city. The survey collected a total main sample of 122,000 people. For convenience, I picked out all the households containing a person born in the Chocó and cut the households containing no Chocoanos to a quarter of their original number, giving a total sub-sample of 31,704 people, of which 55 percent were born in Medellín, 34 percent in other areas of Antioquia, and 9 percent elsewhere. The 712 Chocoanos were 2.2 percent of this subsample and 0.58 percent of the main sample. Of these 712 Chocoanos, 670 were over 12 years old and thus subject to questions about labor force participation; 415 were actually working at the time.

Other statistical sources for Medellín came from censuses carried out by Desarrollo Comunitario, a municipal agency dealing with "subnormal" barrios. They had information on two city center invasions that also happened to have substantial Chocoano populations, La Iguaná and Moravia (see fig. 1 in appendix B), and which they planned to upgrade. Again I was able to rework these censuses for my own purposes. La Iguaná, censused in 1985, had, out of a total of 1,130 families, 141 Chocoano families (12%), and I took a third of all non-Chocoano households for purposes of comparison: data were recorded for each dwelling, for the head of each household in the dwelling, and for their spouse/companion. Moravia, censused in

1983, had a total of 3,031 families with 108 Chocoano families (4%): data were recorded for each dwelling and all its occupants, although often only reliably for the head of household.

The city sample and the Iguaná sample are internally differentiated in ways that affect comparison of the Chocoanos with others. In the city sample, the Chocoanos represent a younger group (41% under 25, compared with 25% of immigrant Antioqueños) and a poorly educated group (65% with primary education or less, compared with 56% for immigrant Antioqueños). Unfortunately, no data were available for time spent in the city. In La Iguaná, their educational status was similar to that of Antioqueños, immigrant or otherwise, but they were a more recently arrived group, both in the city as a whole (62% Chocoanos vs. 56% Antioqueño immigrants had less than ten years city experience, the difference being greater for women) and in the barrio (84% of Chocoanos vs. 60% Antioqueño immigrants had been in the barrio less than ten years). They were also a younger group (58% were under 30, vs. 26% of immigrant Antioqueños). These differences had to be borne in mind when assessing the Chocoanos' occupational and income-earning position. In the city sample, the Chocoanos were a poorer group on average, and this also had to be taken into account when assessing their housing situation. In the Moravia data, the Chocoanos' profiles with respect to age, education, time in the barrio, and income are broadly similar to all others: with these data it was not possible to separate out Antioqueño immigrants from city-born people and other immigrants. In analyzing all these data, I try to give as accurate a picture as possible, making appropriate comparisons and controlling for variables where feasible, without presenting scores of tables. I do not give levels of significance but, unless otherwise stated, only present results that are taken from tables in which the chi-square test shows a significance level of 0.05 or less. This is a limiting factor particularly for the Iguaná and Moravia data, where *n* is small for the Chocoanos and controlling may reduce it even further for, say, a specific age group.

Domestic Service

Domestic service is one of the principal occupations for Chocoanos in Medellín. In general, in Latin America, domestic service occupies many women relative to other Third World countries, and, according to Boserup (1974), this is due to the availability of cheap female labor plus a middle and upper class for which domestic technology is still rather costly and yet which is large enough to create a high demand for service. It is also the case that women urban migrants in Latin

186

America often outnumber males, and the job market in domestic service may be a causal factor here. The close juxtaposition of the Chocó, a poor region inhabited by blacks who since colonial times have fulfilled service roles, with Medellín, a city with a quite large commercial and industrial middle and upper class, clearly encourages the migration of black women, who as blacks and as women fit neatly into ideologies that define service as both a black and a female role (cf. Cock 1980; Radcliffe 1990; Gaitskell et al. 1983; Chaney and García Castro 1989, 7). In fact, there are more Chocoano women than men in Medellín, and, although a skewed sex ratio is common for the city as a whole, it is much more biased for Chocoanos than for other immigrants to Medellín. Related to this is the fact that Chocoanos are overrepresented in domestic service, even when compared with Antioqueño immigrants of the same age and educational status.

In the city sample, women were 67 percent of all Chocoanos, while only 58 percent of Antioqueño immigrants were female, compared with 54 percent of all city dwellers. This bias was more pronounced among working Chocoano women, who outnumbered working Chocoano men sixty to forty, roughly the obverse of the ratio for the working Antioqueños, immigrant or city born. Of the approximately 2,740 people counted as "domestic employees" in the main sample, 159 were Chocoanos (6%), and of these, the vast majority were young (under 25) women. Of the 415 Chocoano workers, male and female, nearly 40 percent were female domestics; of the 261 working Chocoano women, 60 percent were domestics. Comparative figures for Antioqueño immigrants are a mere 9 percent and 24 percent, respectively. Controlling for the fact that, relative to working Antioqueño women, working Chocoano women are generally badly educated and that many are young, their relative overrepresentation remains pronounced: significantly, it is greatest among women with primary or some secondary education, which means that even Chocoano women with some education concentrate more heavily in domestic service than Antioqueño women with the same education. The Iguaná sample of household heads indicated that a biased sex ratio is more characteristic of low-income settlements than of the city at large. For household heads and their partners, women outnumbered men by fifty-four to forty-six for immigrant Antioqueños, and by sixty-one to thirty-nine for Chocoanos. Despite more equal sex ratios, Chocoano concentration in domestic service was even more pronounced, with 51 percent of the 59 Chocoano women household heads in domestic service compared with 19 percent of the 37 Antioqueño women household heads. (If all women are included, not just household heads, the figures are 31% for Chocoanos and 6% for Antioqueño immigrants.) Again, controlling for the fact that the Chocoano women are more recent immigrants and are a much younger group than their Antioqueño counterparts does not alter the size of this difference, and even older Chocoano women or those who have been longer in Medellín proportionally outstrip their Antioqueño counterparts, although by a lesser margin (31% vs. 13% for women with more than ten years in Medellín; 40% vs. 17% for women over 25). Thus, although some Chocoano women leave service as they grow older, many remain. The Moravia data again reinforce this picture, with females outnumbering males among both Chocoanos (fifty-nine to forty-one) and others (fifty-two to forty-seven), but with 52 percent of all Chocoano women in service compared with 26 percent of other women over 18 years old. (Inexplicably, occupational data were not recorded for people under 18 in these data.)

Chocoano women who work as domestics generally leave the Chocó for economic reasons (Mena 1975), a combination of difficulties at home, plus the possibility of earning a cash income in Medellín: sending remittances home is common practice (Mena 1975). In addition, for the younger ones, their work frequently gives them their first opportunity to dispose of at least some money as they please, and this independence, albeit severely limited, is attractive. It was not unusual among the women I interviewed, who were or had started out as servants, to find that they had migrated because they "felt like it." In a great many cases, domestic service was a kind of entry into the urban world: a young woman could get to know the city and find her way around from the relative security of a middle-class home. As she became more experienced, she could pick up positions that paid more or had better conditions or perhaps allowed her time off for school or vocational classes. In the great majority of cases, the women lived in their employers' houses and at some point would contract some kind of relation with a man, nearly always another Chocoano, and have a child. This led to a number of possibilities. She might leave live-in domestic service and set up home as a housewife with her man, almost certainly in low-income housing. From home she might continue to work on a daily basis in domestic service or selling cooked food in the streets, a generally more flexible arrangement for a mother; if her man left her, she would be forced to do this, at least until she found another partner. This horizontal move from domestic service to street selling is a common strategy and has been noted in other countries (Bunster and Chaney 1985; Smith 1989). Coping with children under these circumstances is clearly a major problem, in the resolution of which women often made recourse to neighbors, friends, or relatives; it was not rare, however, to shut children in the house

188

all day, with the eldest sibling in charge. Frequently, children would be taken back to the Chocó and brought up there by the woman's family; this would leave her free to carry on as a live-in domestic. Some women would also pay to have their children looked after by another woman and see them only on Sundays. In general, for the women I interviewed who lived with their children in their own accommodations, whether or not a man was present, life in the city had started in domestic service and progressed—as they saw it—to a situation in which they had a family and usually a dwelling, albeit in some cases an illegal shack in an invasion settlement. In many cases, the progression was tangible—having started with nothing, they now had consolidated dwellings and children at school, even at university; in these cases, however, a man with a steady job had usually been present. In this sense, domestic service is a mode of incorporation into urban life, as Jacklyn Cock (1980, 307) observes for South Africa, and it may also be a channel for upward mobility, as Margo Smith found for Lima (Smith 1973; cf. Smith 1989). Nevertheless, there is no way of knowing how representative these women are of all the Chocoano women who enter domestic service: after all, some return to the Chocó, and many continue to work in domestic service even as mothers. In effect, about a third of Chocoano domestic servants have been in service for fifteen years or more.

Statistical data on domestic service were also obtained from the Colombian Association for Population Studies (ACEP) which had a legal aid program for domestics. Their archive had basic data for some 1,120 women, collected mostly between 1984 and 1986, out of which I selected all the Chocoanos (103) for comparison with a sample (228) of the rest, of which 84 percent were Antioqueño immigrants. The Chocoanos were about 9 percent of the total sample. (It is pertinent to observe that the women who register with ACEP are a self-selected sample.)

These data showed that Chocoano domestics were roughly the same as the others in terms of education (about 80% had primary education or less), income (about 90% earned less than the minimum legal wage, with about a third earning less than half that), and age (although, since Chocoanos over 40 are underrepresented among immigrants in general, they are underrepresented among servants too). However, the Chocoanos had some specific features.

1. More Chocoano women had been working in agriculture or mining before entering domestic service (45% vs. 15%); in contrast, while 61 percent of Antioqueños had previously done housework, another 16 percent had had a more urban

occupation (e.g., waitress, cleaner, operative) prior to service, compared with only 2 percent of Chocoanos.

2. A further difference was that many more of them (80%) were live-in servants than the others (54%).

3. Yet fewer of them (33%) were single than the others (53%). Instead, they more frequently had relations of *unión libre,* common-law marriage, with a man (17% vs. 6%) or were single mothers (34% vs. 22%); marriage was almost the same for both groups (12% vs. 10%).

4. In agreement with this, fewer (33% vs. 55%) had no children, and more (49% vs. 27%) had more than two.

Regional differences in gender relations here mediate women's relation to the class system (cf. Gaitskell et al. 1983). In Chocoano gender relations and family structures, unions are often more consensual than in other areas of the country, and these unions are not necessarily permanent. People, especially men, tend to be quite mobile as they move around exploiting changeable and unstable income opportunities, and they may change their partner several times during their life span, giving rise to what Whitten has termed "serial polygyny" (Gutiérrez de Pineda 1975; Friedemann 1974, 1985b; Whitten 1974). Thus women tend to head families and have to work independently of men more frequently than in Antioquia, where marriage for a woman more frequently means withdrawal from the paid labor force and dependence on a husband (see also Bohman 1984). Chocoano women are thus often obliged to earn a living, and one option is to continue to work as domestic servants, despite having children or being in a union with a man. Since only 8 percent of them said they lived with their children, versus 24 percent of others, they clearly either sent their children back to the Chocó or had them with other relatives, or possibly in paid care, in Medellín.

For all domestic servants, personal contacts are vital for finding work: for the Chocoanos this assumes particular importance, and they make very limited use of employment agencies. Virtually all of them find a position through an aunt, a cousin, a sister, or, failing those, a Chocoano friend. In a great many cases, their first visit to Medellín is in the company of an older female relative (classified as *tía,* aunt) or a female relative of the same generation (classified as *prima,* cousin), who takes them along after a visit home at Christmastime. There is a tight network involving the black servants and, parallel to this, another network linking white middle- and upper-class women to their friends, neighbors, relatives, and colleagues.

Each "maid-madam" relation is a point of articulation between these networks, and this creates a very direct link between Medellín's upper and middle classes and the rivers and villages of the Chocó.

The network linking the Chocoano women—which is, of course, part of the Chocoano network in general—does more than find them an initial position. The women change jobs quite frequently, looking for better conditions or to escape a household they dislike, and the network functions as an ongoing employment exchange. The congregation of black women in the city center on Sundays is an important focus in this respect, but this function of the network is also a more continuous process carried out over telephones, in Chocoano households and in the houses of *las patronas,* the employers. The network is also a source of aid and support: friends and relatives can supply a place to live while looking for work, lend money and clothes, give advice and support in case of problems with a *patrona* or a boyfriend, and, crucially, it can help with child care. Here the fact that the network stretches back into the Chocó is of vital importance, since many women take their children back to the Chocó to be looked after. The women maintain fairly close links with the Chocó, generally returning there over the Christmas period.

The position of domestic servant, while it may be an entry into the urban world and, perhaps, social mobility, is ultimately a degrading one. Of course, there are cases in which the maid is treated as "one of the family" and given a certain amount of freedom, but she is a junior member and largely subject to the disposition of her employers. Generally speaking, the pay is bad and the hours long; women may be fired without warning, and the shadow of sexual harassment always looms. If this leads to pregnancy, a maid is almost invariably made to leave. Lack of information and education, plus the ease of replacing servants, means that these women can rarely enjoy the legal protection that exists for them (García Castro 1989; León 1989). The position is ultimately a servile one, and white images of blackness strongly associate black people, and above all black women, with the servant role. Several Chocoano women described domestic service as *humillante,* humiliating work, in which they occupied a role that was clearly inferior, even if generally they felt that they were reasonably well treated *as domestic servants.* In one extreme case, a black maid was fired ostensibly for having the same name as the employer's daughter; in other cases, the *patrona* rebuked the maid for wearing smart clothes to go out or for putting on perfume: *la muchacha,* the girl/maid, was "getting above her station." Part of this is due simply to status differences between maid and *patrona,* but there is also a strong idea that black women in Medellín are servants and should remain so: young black women students, for example, recounted that Antioqueños sometimes automatically assumed that they were domestic servants. This is to some extent a reaction that stems from the most public face of the Chocoano female presence in the city. As one newspaper article put it (*El Mundo*, 2 March 1986, 5), "By eleven o'clock [on a Sunday morning] the Parque Berrío is theirs." But there is evident exaggeration here, since the blacks only form a small percentage of the total crowd in the Parque Berrío. Again, the director of the ACEP program estimated that 30 percent of her clients were Chocoanos and that this underestimated their participation in domestic service: in fact, the figures from the ACEP 1984–86 data and the citywide 1981 sample are 9 percent and 6 percent, respectively. The Chocoano female presence in domestic service is exaggerated in people's perceptions, and this is due not simply to the overall visibility of blacks in Medellín, specifically black women servants, but also to the idea that all black women are domestics and that domestic service is an appropriate domain for black women.

In terms of political economy, domestic service is not just a luxury but, like all domestic labor, plays an important part in the reproduction of the social body. It is socially necessary labor, even if the so-called domestic labor debate has generally concluded that it cannot legitimately be termed "productive" in the strict Marxist sense of contributing to the creation of surplus value: domestic labor produces use values that are consumed within the household (Smith 1978; Vogel 1983, 23; García Castro 1982; cf. Burton 1985). Nevertheless, it is necessary to view domestic service in a wider perspective. In domestic service, women (and sometimes men; see Hansen 1986) are paid to do other households' domestic labor; in doing so, they free these households' women from some of the domestic labor culturally assigned to them in the sexual division of labor. These women can engage in simple leisure or a variety of roles in the sphere of cultural or economic production: Saffioti's (1978) Brazil study showed that many female employers take paid jobs. They can do this to the extent that domestic service is cheap. Obviously, the economic roles these women may perform when released are ones that the domestics cannot perform due to lack of skills or education (or because they are discriminated against) and are ones that earn more than domestic service costs. From the employing household's point of view, the benefits of domestic service can include more leisure for its female members, the social status that accrues from having servants, an increase in the family income if the women members work, and an increase in family status due to the women's social and cultural activities (anything from giving dinner parties to charity work). It may also be the case that the release of women into certain segments of the paid labor force depresses wages there, while middle-class discontentment is defused by the possibility of wives working for salaries that are many times greater than the wages they pay their servants (García Castro 1989, 117). All this depends on the cheapness of domestic service and thus on the exploitability of the people who do it. The stage is set for this by traditional definitions of domestic labor as women's work and thus as nonproductive (in the popular, as well as strictly Marxist, use of the term) and nonremunerative. The group that does this work for others consists of, most typically, females whose rights, earning power, and education are legally and/or socially restricted; migrants from rural backgrounds, whether in a national or international context, whose qualifications and skills are low and whose rights may be restricted; and ethnic and racial minorities, who often suffer discrimination. Quite frequently, these populations coincide, as in South Africa (Cock 1980), or overlap, as in Medellín, where about 80 percent of domestic servants are female migrants and 6 percent of them black female migrants from the Chocó.

We can now see the role played in Medellín by the Chocó and its women. In essence, the supply of Chocoano women on the domestic service market helps keep the cost of service down, with the results noted above. Significantly, although Chocoano domestics are frequently mothers, they need to work, and they can remain on the domestic service market in Medellín because the kinship-based subsistence economy of the Chocó maintains a good many of their children. In this sense, the Chocó acts as a labor reserve that supplies cheap labor to Medellín, allowing mothers to stay and work in the city and also absorbing some of the cost of reproduction of a labor force, part of which will itself work in Medellín at a later date. (See Wolpe, 1972, for an analogous argument for the South African Bantustans.) In Medellín, Chocoano women have increased their representation in the domestic labor force: fifty years ago there were virtually none; now they are heavily overrepresented there compared with immigrant Antioqueño women. There are two basic factors behind this. On the supply side, the ability to off-load children onto the Chocó gives Chocoano mothers who have to work a competitive edge that increases their participation in domestic service. On the demand side, the prevalent image of black females as servants opens this particular job market to Chocoano women, just as it makes it harder for them to enter any other. This is not necessarily expressed in outspoken preferences for black maids: the important point is the pervasive idea of the appropriateness of blacks, and especially black women, for providing service.

Street Sellers

According to the citywide sample, after domestic service, Chocoanos are most frequently employed in a certain sphere of the commercial sector, to wit, the sale of cooked food, fresh fruit, and drinks in public places, a category popularly known as *ventas ambulantes* or ambulant sales (Bunster and Chaney 1985). It is usually a matter of a small barrow with a few crates of beer and *gaseosa* (fizzy soft drinks) and perhaps a bottle or two of *aguardiente,* served out by the shot with green mango or orange slices as a chaser; or a small stall with a charcoal brazier on which are heated *chuzos* (kebabs) and corncobs, or with a pan of oil for frying fish, empanadas (corn-flour and meat pastries), and *patacones* (slices of plantain), or with a gas-heated hot-plate on which are fried chorizos (sausages) and *arepas de chócolo* (sweet corn cakes); or a trayful of watermelon, mango, papaya, and pineapple, sliced into handy chunks. Sometimes there are slightly larger enterprises with chairs, tables, and awnings which provide a variety of food and drink, and occasionally one sees a small stall selling sweets and cigarettes, but the small-scale sale of food is most typical. These enterprises locate themselves in different ways. Generally they congregate around places of public diversion such as El Estadio, Medellín's largest football stadium and sports complex; the Palacio de Exposiciones, where shows and events are held; the Parque Bolívar, a small city center plaza with monthly art and craft markets; the Parque del Norte, an amusement park; or the Pueblito Paisa, a tourist reproduction of a rural Antioqueño village. Some enterprises have a regular spot in these places, while others move from place to place; still others cater to the ordinary city center trade or to more suburban night spots. Wherever they go, the sellers of *chuzos* and chorizos have an irregular timetable, usually most active on weekends, with occasional midweek events. Some sellers go farther afield, visiting nearby towns and villages on the occasion of their annual patron saint festivals.

The citywide sample has no specific categories that select this type of activity, but next in importance for the Chocoanos after domestic service is a category that includes *ventas ambulantes* with other shop employees (8% of the employed Chocoano work force). There is also another 4 percent under the rubric of "merchant-owners": since most of these people run enterprises classified under "small-scale commerce and the distribution of food," and since virtually no Chocoanos in Medellín have their own shops, these are almost certainly people with their own small operations selling cooked food. In the citywide sample, the Chocoanos are not overrepresented in either of these categories, even though the activity is an important one for them.

In the Moravia and the Iguaná samples, domestic service still employs the greatest number of Chocoanos (47 and 44 people, respectively), despite being samples of people with their own or rented accommodations. In second place came the construction industry (with 36 and 44 individuals), and in third, *ventas ambulantes* (with 20 and 28 people in each barrio). Only in La Iguaná were the Chocoanos overrepresented in *ventas ambulantes* compared with others (17% of Chocoano household heads vs. 8% of Antioqueño immigrant household heads), but there are indications that this drops out when education and time in the city are controlled for (the numbers become too small to allow significant comparisons). La Iguaná is located very near the Estadio sports complex, and many of the Chocoanos, and the Antioqueños, in the barrio go there to sell food and drink on weekends.

There are several reasons why the Chocoanos tend to concentrate in this particular activity within the whole range of street sales, and within the informal sector as a whole. First, it is an activity that requires little investment or risk. Although some of these stalls, those with chairs, tables, several stoves, and a wide selection of meats and other fried foods, do represent a substantial investment, few Chocoanos own such enterprises, and instead they tend to concentrate on smaller-scale endeavors due to their general status as poor immigrants. Second, the sale of cooked food is an intermediate step between the domestic sphere and commerce proper: the elements and skills needed in it are easily commanded and easily reintegrated into the domestic sphere should the enterprise fail or a change in occupation take place. The sale of cooked food represents a half step into the commercial world, without confronting a host of unknown risks and processes. Third, and connected to this, the sale of street food is particularly apt for many Chocoano women who come to Medellín: this is partly because such an activity is like an extension of the kitchen in terms of skills and experience and partly because it is a fairly flexible occupation that can be adapted to the lifestyle of a single mother who has to look after her home and children. The Moravia and Iguaná samples, although not the city sample, show that Chocoano women are more frequently employed in this kind of activity than Antioqueño women, compared with their menfolk: for the Chocoanos, roughly equal proportions of working women and men are in this activity, while for the Antioqueños the percentage of women involved is about half that of men. In my experience, both in these barrios and citywide, the sale of food in public places is typical of poor, single Chocoano mothers. Clearly for these women, subsistence may be precarious: I came across families that survived on what the mother made one or two days a week.

Given the overall economic and social position of the majority of Chocoanos, the sale of street food represents a viable strategy: it requires minimal investment and risk and permits a good deal of flexibility. Equally, however, the returns are low and unstable and the hours long and antisocial, often involving work on Sundays and long into the night. They are, of course, joined in this position by many Antioqueños, immigrant and city born, who sell prepared food and drink on the streets, although many of this group also make up the other categories of street merchants, offering newspapers, vegetables, clothes, shoes, pens, nailclippers, flowers, bootleg music cassettes, secondhand ironmongery, a shoeshine or shoe repair, cigarettes, sweets, posters, books, magazines, balloons, toys, cheap jewelry, umbrellas, stationery, lottery tickets, or a chance to weigh yourself on a bathroom scale.

Construction Industry

The third major source of employment for Chocoanos in Medellín is the construction industry, in which they are proportionally overrepresented compared with Antioqueño immigrants of roughly their age and educational status. Within this industry there are several levels, and the Chocoanos tend to concentrate in some and not in others. At the lowest level is the *ayudante* or helper, equivalent to an unskilled laborer. Next comes the *oficial,* or general-purpose builder, who is able to lay bricks, plaster walls, tile bathrooms, and so on. Also located at this level are electricians, plumbers, carpenters, and painters. Usually there are no qualifications to define this level: an *ayudante* may learn on the job until he feels confident enough to start on his own. Above these is the *maestro de obras,* or general foreman, usually an ex-*oficial,* who gives the *oficiales* their orders, and at the top is the *ingeniero* (engineer) or an architect who is in charge of the whole operation. Within this schema are the *contratistas,* contractors and subcontractors, who range from large-scale businessmen who subcontract out to more specialized contractors who run smaller building firms, to individual *oficiales* who seek out small jobs on a site or in private houses; *contratista* is also used to refer to unskilled individuals

196

who, for example, get contracts digging huge holes with picks and shovels for the foundations of buildings more than five stories in height.

Chocoanos are, in the great majority, *ayudantes* and *oficiales* the latter generally being small *contratistas*, rather than employees of a building firm. Typical is the small *oficial* with a few *ayudantes* who does small private building jobs or small contracts on a site. The unskilled *contratista* who gets digging contracts is also a common figure. Significantly, the foundation holes that the gang digs are referred to as *pilas*—the same term used in the Chocó for the artificial reservoir dug above a mine working to provide running water for a *mina de agua corrida* (see chapter 8)—and there are obvious parallels between the *cuadrilla* mining gang and the digging gang. These *paleros*, shovelers, may also be day laborers who stand at certain spots— just by La Iguaná, for example—where dump trucks pass by to collect them for work shifting earth and debris. Almost no Chocoanos are *maestros*, and I came across no Chocoano *ingenieros*.

Work as an *oficial* or *ayudante* is very unstable: a man would count himself lucky to work as many as six months in a year; *paleros* sometimes spend whole days waiting in vain for a truck to pick them up. In this situation, contacts and information are vital, and the building trade has its own spots in the city center where people meet to exchange news, pick up tips on work, and find *ayudantes* or *oficiales* to do contracts. Naturally, the Chocoano network also operates here, and it is very common for a Chocoano *oficial* to have other Chocoanos as his *ayudantes* and for a Chocoano *contratista* to have Chocoano *paleros* on a digging contract. This is partly because other Chocoanos are part of the immediate social network, but there is also a positive preference: "There's greater understanding between paisanos, especially in the language: you can talk fast and they understand you," said one Chocoano builder. And there is some distrust of Antioqueños: "The Antioqueño thinks he's really smart, so when he works with a Chocoano, he tries to put one over on him." However, it is also true that, in a city in which Chocoano-Antioqueño relations are typically those of subordinate to superior, the construction industry does present occasional examples of the opposite, when a Chocoano *oficial* employs Antioqueño *ayudantes*.

The citywide sample shows an overrepresentation of employed Chocoano men in the construction industry compared with employed male Antioqueño immigrants (20% vs. 11%). The Iguaná data reflect this even more strongly (49% vs. 17%), and the Moravia data also confirm the pattern (18% vs. 6%), although they can only compare the Chocoanos with all others, not just immigrants. The latter data break construction workers into maestros, *oficiales,* and *ayudantes* and show that workers split roughly equally between *oficiales* and *ayudantes* for both categories. There is just one Chocoano maestro. If age and education are controlled for in the city sample, the Chocoano overrepresentation remains in a slightly more marked form for people under 40 years old and for those with less than completed secondary education. On average, Chocoano men in Medellín are older and better educated than Chocoano women, so controlling in this way is less necessary and has less impact on patterns of overrepresentation. In the Iguaná data, controlling for age and time in the city again does not diminish the basic pattern of Chocoano overconcentration in construction.

The construction industry is an expanding one, both nationally, where the population occupied in it has risen from 3.5 percent of the economically active population in 1951 to 6.9 percent in 1985, and in Medellín, where the proportion of the employed male population in this activity rose from 9 percent to 13 percent between 1977 and 1985 (Camacol 1986; DANE's National Household Surveys) and where the area under construction has risen steadily, doubling between 1980 and 1986 (Camacol 1986). This reflects a number of trends: rural-urban migration and a growing urban population creates more demand for housing, and even the urban poor employ some paid labor for their housing needs. The reorganization of the city center and the municipality's construction of housing schemes also generate new demand. And the cocaine trade, centered on Medellín, also generates a demand for luxury housing. The construction industry absorbs a great deal of unskilled labor and gives excellent opportunities for learning on the job; there is almost no control on qualifications, and building firms subcontract out between 60 and 70 percent of their work: this represents a fairly open market. Nevertheless, there is an oversupply of unskilled compared with skilled labor, and firms have a problem fulfilling their need for skilled people (Camacol 1986). So, although the construction industry is theoretically easy to enter, there is strong competition within it. An indication of this is the fact that wages in construction are consistently only 70 percent of those in manufacturing industry. The influx of black male migrants from the Chocó clearly plays a role in all this: they are part of the oversupply of unskilled workers and of builders with basic skills, and their presence helps keep wages in the industry down, maintaining a pool of cheap labor for the expansion and remodeling of the city.

Other Occupations: Teachers, Policemen, and Professionals

Domestic service, *ventas ambulantes,* and construction are the major occupations for Chocoanos in Medellín, but in smaller numbers Chocoanos are also to be found in other occupations. There is a handful in manufacturing industry, which is otherwise the sector that employs most men and women in the city: generally, the Chocoanos do not have the experience and the skills needed to work in industry. An even smaller number work in commerce, outside the *ventas ambulantes* field: I came across just two who worked as sales representatives in established commercial firms. However, there are two occupations in which the Chocoano presence is notable: teaching and the police force.

In the days when Diego Luis Córdoba and Vicente Barrios revolutionized education for blacks in Quibdó, several *escuelas normales,* or schools designed to produce teachers, were created, and since that time many Chocoanos, taking advantage of one of the few opportunities open to them, have trained as teachers and found work either in the Chocó or very often outside their department: they are often found in the most isolated and distant regions, such as Guainía and Meta in the Amazon basin. At one point in the mid-1980s, eleven of the fourteen *jefes de núcleo* (a person in charge of several schools in a district) in Meta were Chocoanos. In Medellín, too, there are a good many Chocoano teachers, without their being overrepresented in this category, according to data in the citywide sample (4% of Chocoanos vs. 4% of immigrant Antioqueños vs. 3% of city-born people). Being a *profesor,* or teacher, carries a certain amount of status, and it is clear that, economic considerations apart, this is attractive for the Chocoanos, who in this fashion chip away at the racist stereotype of the black as primitive and uncultured. During much of my stay in Medellín I lived with Carlos Pino, who was a *profesor,* and I learned that, whatever the status involved, a teacher's salary gave little room for maneuver, partly because it is low by any standards and partly because the government is notorious for delaying payment and holding back extras for months on end: there are constant strikes just to get the basic salary paid. I used to socialize with Carlos and his other teacher friends, Chocoanos and other blacks from Turbo, who would meet in the center of town in the evenings for a drink or two and to exchange rumors on whether that month's pay was coming through.

Interestingly, there are clear gender differences between Antioqueños and Chocoanos in their participation in the teaching profession. For the immigrant Antioqueños, teaching is a mainly female profession, occupying 8 percent of women in the city sample and only 2 percent of men. Comparative figures for city-born Antioqueños are 5 percent of women and 2 percent of men. For Chocoanos, however, 5 percent of men teach compared with only 3 percent of women. One explanation may be that men tend to monopolize occupational positions that, from their point of view, are seen as advantageous (cf. Beavon and Rogerson 1986). For Chocoanos, teaching is a good option, hence men tend to enter into it where they can; for Antioqueños, it is relatively less so, and it becomes a feminine occupation.

Rather like teaching, the police force represents a good economic opportunity for a Chocoano man: with a little secondary education and a six-month training course, he can have a steady, if modest, income and the status of authority. In the Chocó itself, this represents an important advance, and the Chocoano trainees who go to the police training school in Medellín generally like to return to the Chocó if they can; the Antioqueño lieutenant in charge of training there in 1986 said: "To be a policeman in the Chocó is like being a professional here: they say so themselves." In that year's course, the graduate trainees were 11 percent Chocoano, 48 percent Antioqueño, and 41 percent from other areas of the country: clearly, the police force was an attractive proposition.

The small nucleus of Chocoano professionals is an interesting case: they are well-educated people, not infrequently quite light skinned, usually from families in Quibdó which have some resources there and which have been able to finance their children's studies up to university level, generally in such fields as law, medicine, dentistry, and accounting. The unusual thing is that they are not significantly underrepresented in the city sample in the various professional categories (5% for both Chocoanos and immigrant Antioqueños vs. 7% for city-born people). This is a reflection of the importance of education for the Chocoanos and also of how education for the Chocoanos tends to draw people out of the Chocó: in order to qualify in these professions, Chocoanos have to study in the interior, and since the opportunities for employment in the Chocó are limited, they often try to work in the cities of the interior as well.

The Chocoanos' Position in Medellín

From the citywide sample, two things at least are clear. One, the Chocoanos are a rather younger and somewhat less-educated group compared with Antioqueño immigrants. Two, the women concentrate heavily in domestic service and the men in construction compared with Antioqueño immigrants, even when age and educational status are controlled for. Both domestic service and construction yield low and/or unstable incomes, as indeed do *ventas ambulantes,* but the data on income are very hard to interpret. In the city sample, between 40 and 50 percent of working respondents declared zero income, and anyway accuracy and candor in this matter are always in doubt. The available data show the Chocoanos as a low-earning group, with a third earning below the minimum wage compared with a mere 5 percent of immigrant Antioqueños, but removing domestic servants from the sample (whose low wages are partly, but not wholly, due to many being live-in employees) almost removes this disparity, suggesting that the Chocoanos outside domestic service earn practically as much as other Antioqueño immigrants, within the limits of trustworthiness of these data. It is significant that removing domestics from the sample also balances the Chocoanos and the Antioqueño immigrants almost completely with respect to age and education.

For La Iguaná and Moravia, settlements on the lowest rungs of Medellín society, where the Chocoanos are broadly matched with other residents in terms of education (although they form a younger, more recent group in La Iguaná), the data show the same occupational patterns, although most of the domestic servants in these samples are day, not live-in, workers. Again the Chocoanos' income profiles roughly match those of Antioqueño immigrants in La Iguaná or those of all others in Moravia. In the Iguaná data at least, the great majority of household heads declared some income, although in Moravia 70 percent of respondents declared no income.

If we take the data on income seriously, along with the other data, there are a number of conclusions. One, a small minority (about 10%) of well-educated Chocoanos are well placed as professionals or somewhat less well placed as teachers. Two, given their education and experience, a majority (about 50%) of Chocoanos enter the job market in its lower echelons but compete and achieve reasonably equally relative to Antioqueño immigrants at those levels, although they concentrate in specific sectors within them. Three, a large minority (about 40%) of Chocoanos are female domestic servants, often young women, and, although they are on equal terms with other domestic servants, the burden of child care is greater for them, and they depend more on kinship and ethnic networks to cope with this. If we reserve judgment on the income data, the above conclusions hold, except that we have no idea as to how equally the Chocoanos are in fact performing: the data on housing quality in the next chapter may indicate that they are in fact performing slightly worse.

There are two more general considerations. The first is that the vast majority of Chocoanos can only compete, especially initially, at the lower levels of the occupational ladder: nearly 70 percent are employed in domestic service, construction, and *ventas ambulantes*. This is clearly connected to their background and the historically determined social and economic characteristics of the Chocó. In this sense, the Chocó as an underdeveloped region is clearly providing cheap, unskilled labor to the developing urban economy of Medellín. While migration from the Chocó to Medellín may represent a step up the ladder of regional value, being a move into a relatively developed, urban, central, and nonblack locale, the chances of significant upward mobility are limited. Chocoanos enter what has often been referred to as the "informal sector," and although there was at one time a vogue—still current in some circles (see De Soto 1989)—for seeing this "sector" as a thriving center of potential capital accumulation, critics have tended to concentrate on the exploited and subordinate position of many people working in this type of activity. This approach points out that the informal sector, or more precisely, certain specific groups within this heterogeneous and vaguely bounded descriptive category, have positive functions for the so-called formal sector, or again more precisely, for certain dominant capitalist or state sectors (Roberts 1978; Burgess 1979; Moser 1979; Bromley 1979). This line of argument can verge on a teleological functionalism that reifies the "needs" of capital and ignores possible contradictions between different capitalist and state interests (Gilbert 1986). However, recent work has given greater rigor to the concept of the informal economy, and clearly a sector of the economy which escapes official regulation, whether due to the absence of such legislation or the lack of its enforcement, does have specific relationships with, and functions for, specific interests in the regulated sector and in the state bureaucracy (Portes, Castells and Benton 1989). For example, self-help housing and community servicing saves government expenditure on these services and reduces housing costs for the urban labor force, keeping wages down (Gilbert and Gugler 1981, 113). Some industries use an outwork subcontracting system or use dependent workers disguised as independent workers in order to pay lower wages and eliminate costs associated with secure, permanent employees (Roberts 1978, 116; Bromley 1979; Portes, Castells and Benton 1989). Street vending of food has a less obvious role to play here, but it arguably reduces the cost of reproduction of the labor force, both manual and white-collar. In any event, this type of approach severely undermines the idea that work that escapes official regulation is an open road to upward mobility: much of it remains at the level of subsistence because of its subordinate relation to the regulated economy.

The second consideration is that racial discrimination may be restricting the access of Chocoanos to occupational opportunities. This is, of course, hard to prove. For example, the fact that Chocoano men concentrate heavily in construction, much more so than immigrant Antioqueño men of similar age and education, is not in itself proof of racial discrimination. Although construction is an unstable occupation, the income data cannot support the contention that Chocoano men earn less than Antioqueño men. Therefore Chocoanos may concentrate there due to preference and the operation of the ethnic network. However, there is a strong argument that the concentration of Chocoano workers in domestic service indicates a relative exclusion of them, especially the men, from other occupations. This is a contentious issue, since it might be objected that this concentration could be more related to unspecified factors internal to the Chocó which push more women out to Medellín than men, and to Chocoano family structures that tend to engender a relatively large number of single-mother families in which the woman is obliged to find work to support her children. Rather than Chocoano men being excluded, Chocoano women are simply working more than Antioqueño women, who instead tend to be housewives. This is undoubtedly partly the case, but there are three factors that support the exclusion hypothesis. First, according to 1973 census figures, Chocoano men are as numerous as Chocoano women in Antioquia, if Medellín is excluded: they went at that time, and still go, in large numbers to the Urabá zone banana plantations where they worked principally in the heaviest manual labor, the digging of drainage ditches (although it appears that nowadays they are less specialized). Men leave the Chocó on a par with women, but they do not end up in Medellín. If opportunities were open in Medellín, as they were for women in domestic service, surely they would also have migrated to the city in larger numbers. In fact, the main opening for them then, as now, was construction and *ventas ambulantes,* notoriously unstable activities. Second, Chocoano women who are married to, or living with, a man work more frequently than Antioqueño immigrant women in a similar position, and although this could be due simply to different attitudes towards women and their role in the home, or to the different contributions men make to the family budget, it also suggests that Chocoano men are at a disadvantage in the job market and depend more on women's earnings. Third, there remains the very obvious concentration of Chocoano women in domestic service. They do not participate in other occupations as much as immigrant Antioqueño women: for the latter, white-collar administrative jobs, commercial activities, industrial jobs, and seamstressing all occupy greater proportions than for Chocoano

203

women, even when age and education are controlled for. This certainly suggests the impact of racial discrimination, since domestic service is unquestionably a low-earning and low-status occupation.

This is not conclusive evidence. Counterarguments would (a) attack the absence of data on time spent in the city, which would be an important control factor in the citywide sample; (b) point out the generally agreed-upon inferior quality of the Chocoano education system compared with the Antioqueño system; and (c) note how ethnic networks can create concentrations in certain occupations. But the evidence presented here has to be taken in conjunction with the evidence of the Chocoanos themselves.

One black woman student, born in Medellín of Chocoano parents, reported that she was rejected at an employment agency with the words, "We don't place blacks here." Previously, when unsuccessful in job applications, she had always thought of other reasons for her failure, although the specter of racism was in the back of her mind, but this time, "I felt as if a bucket of cold water had been thrown over me." For her, it was a particular case: the agency a disreputable one, the man in charge rude and ill-mannered; she did not see it as a symptom of a more widespread phenomenon. A Chocoano physician, however, was more skeptical: "Things are difficult in Colombia, and above all in Medellín; you have to fight your way through. There's a structural aspect that nowadays is quite clear." He was referring to the Antioqueños' ethnic exclusiveness, which limited the access of the Chocoanos to the institutions, public and private, which they controlled. He had studied medicine in a university in Medellín, teaching as he studied, and after a practical year in the Chocó he found himself unable to get his foot back in the door, despite the necessary qualifications and good political contacts in the right places: he could get only short-term replacement contracts from the Social Security Department until he became a partner in a practice established by another Chocoano physician. He admitted that Antioqueño exclusiveness probably affected other non-Antioqueños apart from Chocoanos, but, while this is true, it is also a fact that the Chocó is the fourth largest source of immigrants to Medellín, after Valle del Cauca, Risaralda, and Bogotá. Since Risaralda and the northern Valle del Cauca are within the Antioqueño cultural sphere of influence, it is Bogotanos and Chocoanos who are liable to bear the brunt of *paisa* exclusiveness. In addition, Antioqueño exclusiveness is hardly separable from their ideas about the *raza antioqueña,* which defines itself in opposition to blacks, so it is inevitable that ethnic exclusiveness based on regional identity overlaps into racism.

Instances of direct, overt discrimination are fairly unusual, and it is clear that discrimination is not systematic and generalized. Indeed, some Chocoanos denied that racism existed at all. Others, however, were certain that it did, or had. In the words of one Chocoano woman,

[In the 1950s,] people looked at a black person like something strange, like a ghost or something from another world. But nowadays there's not much [racism] because people of 20 or 25 years old have lived among the blacks . . . it's not strange for them. There are still one or two people [who are racist], but. . . . You have to understand that in those days, in a rich barrio, you didn't feel bad; but you went to a poor barrio and you felt more like sinking into the ground. But people have changed.

Nevertheless, people still reported deprecatory remarks, looks, and attitudes. There is a basic assumption that a black person is of low social status, and this has to be specifically contested. Carlos Pino, for example, found that in the school where he taught he was more than once mistaken for the janitor by Antioqueño parents: "They denied me a certain social position simply because of the color of my skin." Equally, young black women found themselves identified as domestic servants irrespective of their real status.

By the nature of the racial order in Colombia, racial discrimination against blacks is not systematic. There are, however, strong indications that Chocoanos are generally admitted to servile and manual occupations and that they encounter dissimulated resistance when they try to break out of these roles. This would help account for the striking concentration of Chocoano women in domestic service, which is otherwise hard to fully explain. It also fits in with what many Chocoanos reported on the assumptions made about blacks which classed them as low status, uneducated, and so on (see also chapters 13 and 14). The critical problem here in amassing evidence of racial discrimination is, of course, the nature of the racial order itself. Individual mobility is accepted conditionally, and discrimination is not systematic. Blacks are seen as inferior, but the qualifications and background of the vast majority in any case only suit them for the type of work which is assumed by many nonblacks to be appropriate for them. The tiny number of blacks who challenge these preconceptions can be accommodated on an individual and conditional basis. Thus overt discrimination is only likely to occur where not only is there relative clarity about blackness and nonblackness, but there is also a competitive relation between aggregates who can identify each other in these terms, or there is a perceived attempt by a "black" to challenge what are felt to be the conditions of acceptability. Competition was perhaps clearest in Unguía, where an Antioqueño frontier mentality involved clearly racist elements; but as the next chapter shows, it has also occurred in specific contexts in low-income settlements in Medellín, although the competition was about territory and cultural authority rather than jobs or wealth.

12

Medellín:

Living in the City

Haunt of Chocoano drums. Dance floor of Pacific blacks. You too were sentenced to death! The pickax has no mercy. And much less when it's a question of a crowd of blacks, bright and smiling, dedicated to the most unproductive thing in the world: dancing. . . . The black women, like defenseless stains in a city that did not know them nor will ever know them, took refuge in more distant dens where the air was heavy and the happiness an artificial decoration. Now it was prostitution. The Street of Drums sounds no longer . . . because the music, the blacks and the happiness have sunk.

Although Chocoanos tend to concentrate in certain types of employment, the black presence tends to manifest itself more plainly in the realm of consumption rather than production. Concentrations of people easily identifiable as "black" in the Medellín context occur in certain locales, and where this has happened, confrontations and antagonism have sometimes developed. When faced with black community taking an assertive and vocal stance, the working-class Antioqueño reaction has been hostile and has generally pushed blacks into adapting their behavior. The majority of Chocoanos, however, do not live in such locales and instead are widely dispersed around the city.

Epigraph: From the Medellín newspaper *El Colombiano,* in its series of pullout features for the three-hundredth anniversary of the city, 30 October 1975. The writer refers to a part of Bolívar Avenue in the city center, where Chocoanos used to congregate in bars to drink and dance. Some of their haunts were destroyed when the avenue was widened. However, contrary to the impression given by the writer, they continued to congregate there (see chapter 15).

The Parque Berrío, symbolic and geographic center of Medellín, seen from the top of the Banco de la República, which occupies one side of the square.

Chocoanos in the Urban Space of Medellín

The history of Chocoano migration to Medellín largely mirrors the overall processes that characterize the growth of the city. After about 1920, Medellín began to grow rapidly, spurred first by industrialization in the city, then by the 1930s depression and low coffee prices, and later, after 1948, by La Violencia, the waves of civil violence between warring Liberal and Conservative factions which affected the whole country. Equally, the classic causes of rural-urban migration, such as polarization of landholding and the concentration of resources and services in the city, had a continuous effect. Within the city, from about 1920, a split began to develop within El Centro, the city center, between a traditional, more upper-class area around the Parque Berrío (prior to 1892 a typical provincial town marketplace) together with its neighbor, the Parque Bolívar, and a newer, brasher, dirtier, and more lower-class area around Guayaquil, the location of the new marketplace, the train station, the bus terminals, and hundreds of cheap hotels, pensions, tenements, brothels, small shops, and bars (see fig. 1 in appendix B). Here was the arrival point for the new immigrants, and it was an area looked down upon by the "ancestral Mede-llín" (Viviescas 1983). Nevertheless, both zones partook of and con-tributed to *paisa* identity: the Parque Berrío continued to be a symbolic center of Medellín and Antioqueño identity, where any "self-respecting" Antioqueño was born, figuratively at least; but Guayaquil, now a *zona de candela*, a zone of fire (gunfire and heat), was also the "synthesis of the mightiness of a race" (Upeguí 1957), bursting with Antioqueños of rural origin, teeming with commercial ventures and wheeling and dealing.

Around 1950, the city decided to implement a Pilot Plan, designed by foreign architects, which envisaged the transformation of El Centro, in search of a city center that would "personify the driving spirit of the Antioqueños" (José Luis Sert and Paul Weiner, cited in Planeación Municipal 1980). Fundamental to this was the breaking up of Guayaquil, dispersing its transport and market facilities to more distant locations, building new roads and avenues through it, and constructing a new administrative center on a spot known as La Alpu-jarra, a zone surrounding the now disused railway station and occu-pied until 1982 by a small shantytown invasion settlement also known as La Alpujarra. The whole area of Guayaquil acquired commercial value, and the cheap hotels, tenements, and pensions began to be replaced by workshops, ironmongeries, and auto-parts stores—a transformation that is still in progress today. The low-income dwellers of the area took several different routes. Some went into nearby city center areas that had escaped these changes, converting them into tenement zones. Many went to a neighborhood called Barrio Antio-quia, just outside the city center, which in a rather absurd 1952 decree had, without warning, been declared the only official red-light district in the city and was taking over some of the functions of the old Guayaquil. And many more dispersed to the more peripheral barrios, where they invaded, bought plots of land or skeleton dwellings, or rented accommodations (CEHAP 1986, 81). The inhabitants of La Al-pujarra shantytown, along with other city center invaders, were moved into municipal housing schemes in various outlying barrios, where they paid for dwellings, if they were able, in monthly install-ments. This dispersal coincided with the increasing growth of the city's *barrios populares*, a euphemistic term covering consolidated working-class areas, peripheral invasions, and pirate urbanizations. By 1930, invasions, illegal subdivision, and sale of urban lots had already be-gun, and from 1940 their number increased rapidly, fed by rural mi-gration as well as by the poor displaced from the city center. Today, the city is surrounded on most sides by ever-growing low-income settlements of various kinds; only in the southeast is this ring broken by the elite suburbs that house the rich families who once reigned over the ancestral center of Medellín but retired in the face of noise, pollution, insecurity, and overcrowding. The city authorities estimated in 1985 that there were some fifty thousand people living in what they term *barrios subnormales* (Mosquera 1976; Planeación Metropolitana 1985).

Chocoano emigration focuses in order of importance on Medellín and Cali, the Urabá banana zone, Bogotá, and the Atlantic coast cities (DANE 1985b, 122–28). Migration to Antioquia in significant numbers has been quite recent: as late as 1930, most of the journey had to be made by mule, and a reasonable dirt road did not open until about 1946. According to the national censuses, there were 3,811 Chocoanos in Antioquia in 1951; 10,174 in 1964, and 18,490 in 1973, rising from 0.3 percent to 0.6 percent of the total population. Figures on Chocoanos in the municipality of Medellín are very scarce: the 1973 census gives a figure of 5,978 (0.5%), and a 1981 population study of a 10 percent sample of the city (DANE 1985b, 126) gave an expanded figure of 7,423 (0.6%), with another 885 estimated in neighboring municipalities within the Metropolitan Area of Medellín. The accuracy of these figures is, of course, open to question, and it is quite possible that they are underestimates. Nevertheless, the 1981 study does cover all barrios, including peripheral and illegal ones, and does explicitly include live-in domestic servants, both categories that would include many Chocoanos and that one might otherwise suspect would be badly covered.

In the 1950s, the Chocoanos had small concentrations of settlement near the Guayaquil area—specifically in an area called La Bayadera—in small zones of tenement buildings; this area was also a center for diversion and dancing on Sundays, when the black domestic servants had their day off. Other Chocoanos dispersed straight out into the more outlying consolidated *barrios populares,* and, of course, a great many were live-in domestic servants in middle- and upper-class barrios. With the slow transformation of the inner-city tenement zone and the transfer of people and activities between it and Barrio Antioquia, the latter became a new focus for Chocoano settlement, although others clung on to islands of tenement buildings which still survive today, and some, along with Antioqueños, invaded the nearby Alpujarra land belonging to the railway station and built shacks that were only finally removed in 1982 in a resettlement program.

Chocoano settlement in Barrio Antioquia was accelerated by the location there in 1963 of the headquarters of the Association of Chocoanos Resident in Antioquia, founded in 1962 by a group of Chocoano professionals as a social, mutual aid, and educational society.

The association held dances and other functions and gave classes in sewing, first aid, and so on, directed principally at the black domestic servants. Shortly after, other Chocoanos in the barrio started up dance halls, and the neighborhood became a focus for Chocoanos, who would come from all over the city to dance and meet their paisanos on Sundays. Many also rented rooms in the tenements that were increasingly appearing. The black servants suffered a good deal of abuse on the streets of the barrio from the local youth, who would shout racist insults, run off with the women's umbrellas, and generally make life unpleasant for them. Things came to a head in the late 1960s when Chocoano settlement was at its peak, and the civic leaders of the barrio, who had already fought strongly, but with only partial success, against the 1952 decree making their neighborhood a red-light district, started a quiet campaign among the owners of tenements and rooms-to-let to restrict Chocoano settlement there. The civic leaders considered the young women in particular to be loud, foul-mouthed, and bad mannered, and the landlords had already had problems with several women crowding into a room let out to one person. This campaign braked Chocoano settlement, while many of those who already lived there, like other tenement dwellers and rentees, began to move out in search of their own homes, whether on invaded land or in pirate urbanizations. Barrio Antioquia had passed a phase of its life: from a quiet working-class neighborhood of the thirties and forties, it was suddenly converted, in the 1950s, into a red-light district, becoming a barrio with a noisy and energetic nightlife, full of bars, cheap tenements, prostitutes, and high livers; towards the end of this period, in the 1960s, figured the Chocoano dance halls and the crowds of blacks who came to dance on Sundays. By 1986, all the black dance halls had closed, and only a score of Chocoano families remained; equally, the barrio's status as a red-light district had passed—it had since become a center for petty drug dealing and small-time drug mafiosos, whose vendettas still occasionally rack the neighborhood.

Nowadays, Chocoanos are distributed widely over the city, a process of dispersal which has always existed alongside their concentration, temporary or long term, in certain areas such as Guayaquil or Barrio Antioquia. They live mostly in the barrios populares, in the more consolidated areas; they also live in less consolidated, more peripheral barrios formed by accretive invasion or illegal subdivision and pirate urbanization (barrios that, in time, tend to consolidate and upgrade themselves with help from the municipal authorities and political patronage); and they also live in the two remaining city center invasions that have not been eradicated, La Iguaná and the zone known as Moravia, in the center of which is located what was until recently the municipal garbage dump (see fig. 1 in appendix B). A small minority also live in middle-class areas that roughly correspond to their economic status. Nevertheless, the sociospatial relationship of the Chocoanos to the city is not simply a result of their primary condition as poor immigrants, most of whom have little education or city experience. The Chocoanos also form ethnic enclaves in some of the barrios where they live, and, as was the case in Barrio Antioquia, music and dance are often a focus, sometimes simply in the form of a private house commercially used for dances on weekends. These ethnic enclaves are points of congregation and exchange of information, and they can also act as places where Chocoano culture is reproduced, albeit in forms that would appear altered to a Chocoano "back home." In this sense, these enclaves are foci where a new urban form of black culture is being elaborated.

The localized concentrations in the outlying barrios or in the city center invasions may be noticeable only to those who live or work thereabouts, but the concentrations in El Centro are visible to all. There on Sundays many Chocoanos, especially the domestic servants, congregate on the steps and low walls around and in the Parque Berrío to pass the time of day and exchange news. Nearby, a few bars have been colonized by them, and the strains of *vallenato* accordion music from *la Costa* blast from jukeboxes over tables where hardly a white face is to be seen, except for those of the Antioqueño staff. Along the way a little, another group of bars vibrates with earsplitting salsa music, and again the blacks congregate there, although as salsa has become fashionable music among the younger Antioqueños as well, there are more white faces to be seen in these places. It is in the very heart of Medellín that the black presence is felt most publicly: the usually invisible army of black maids dispersed around the city suddenly becomes apparent (while their Antioqueño sisters remain unnoticed in the Sunday crowds); the groups of black men loafing on corners—as are so many other Antioqueños—spring to the eye. Right where all "self-respecting" Antioqueños can claim to trace their roots, there also are the Chocoanos, a contrast that has not failed to attract the attention of the local press. A reporter in *El Colombiano*, a Medellín newspaper, wrote thus: "The Chocó has inundated our main recreational centers in Medellín, above all at weekends and on holidays. On these days, they take over the steps of the Banco de la República, the Parque Berrío and the Parque Bolívar, the Zoological Gardens, the shopping malls and other places of recreation throughout the city, where the dirtiness of the streets and avenues can now be noticed." Further on, he refers to "the bad habits, excesses, lack of culture and the vulgarity of some Chocoanos . . . with no curb on their instincts" (16 July 1986, 13A).

I would occasionally drink with Chocoano and Costeño friends in one of the Chocoano bars, El Salón Suizo, and on one occasion took some photos there for purposes of illustration—an act that could not help but draw attention to me, especially as a white. Twice I was challenged by Chocoanos who objected to the sensationalist reports they had seen in the papers and which poked fun at the blacks: luckily, I was able to convince them of my serious intentions. Recalling how, a few minutes after I entered the Suizo for the first time, gunshots were puncturing a ceiling already peppered with bullet holes and how a knife or two appeared shortly after—all of which was noise and no action—or recalling the odd fight I had witnessed between a couple of young Chocoano women over some romantic attachment, I could see the scope for cheap sensationalism if the newspapers wanted to pick on the blacks' supposed lack of culture, even though in Medellín such incidents are of daily occurrence all over town.

El Centro is a critical focus for the city and has been ever since the Spanish imposed on Hispanic America their classic town plan with a central plaza around which were located the main institutions of power and authority: the church, the administration, and the houses of the wealthy citizens. In Medellín, El Centro has seen the class conflict between the "ancestral Medellín" and the new, pushy Guayaquil, in which the rich finally moved out of an increasingly congested and polluted center to quieter, leafier suburbs, leaving to commerce, the banks, and the city authorities the job of pushing out the less prestigious elements to more peripheral barrios. But El Centro is still a zone where these divisions are acted out: Guayaquil is not dead but still full of loud cantinas, cheap hotels, and prostitutes; Calle del Sapo, Toad Street, near the old railway station and a few minutes' walk from the Parque Berrío, is still full of decrepit tenement blocks where poverty-stricken people live, eking a living out of the city center. And El Centro is, naturally, the scene for public political discourse—union rallies, party political meetings, demonstrations. Everyone must pass through El Centro, not just because all the buses pass through there, not only because the city administration is there along with a hundred other city institutions, but also because it *is* the city in its essence. And just as it has reflected the city's class divisions in its spatial arrangements, so now it reflects racial divisions: it is in El Centro that temporary black enclaves form and blacks claim their own space in the city and its life. It is here that they are seen by the city's "owners" as alien and even as a threat to public morals. Naturally, what one sees in El Centro hides as much as it reveals. In the same way that the division between ancestral Medellín and Guayaquil hid the real interdependence of the two and the latter's increasing power to define the nature of urbanism, so the apparent segregation of the Chocoanos in the city center masks their dispersal into the city's economy and urban space and their impact on its culture in terms of the spread of music and dance from the Caribbean and *la Costa*.

Chocoanos and Housing in Medellín

For most people in Medellín, as in other Third World cities, buying a finished house is not a standard procedure: whether one invades land, purchases a plot, or buys a concrete base or a skeleton dwelling from a pirate urbanizer, a legal urbanizer, or the state, housing oneself and one's family is a slow process of consolidation and, often, expansion as the dwelling grows to accommodate more people. This creates a tremendous variety of housing in the city which nevertheless obeys a basic sectoral zoned pattern (see fig. 2 in appendix B).

Locating the Chocoanos in this variety is by no means easy, since they appear over the whole spectrum of that variety: the places where they are obviously concentrated in small nuclei of settlement are in the poorest areas of the city, but this is deceptive because, proportionally, there are more Chocoanos dispersed around the city in reasonably consolidated working-class barrios (see fig. 3 in appendix B). Generally speaking, the greater the concentration, the poorer the area, whereas the greater the dispersion, the higher up the urban scale the barrio, until middle-class levels are reached where blacks are a tiny, widely scattered minority.

Housing Quality: The Chocoanos' Position. Chocoanos in Medellín live in broadly similar housing conditions compared with other immigrants. However, the data show that Chocoanos live in slightly worse, or more insecure, housing than Antioqueño immigrants, even when some other intervening variables are controlled for, such as time in the barrio, age, and education. But it is ultimately unclear how much of this is due to lack of capital or income and how much to discrimination in the housing market, or certain preferences on their part. My own conclusion is that the major factor is lack of disposable resources; discrimination does exist in the realm of housing, but it has a particular form characteristic of Latin America. I found evidence of it in sensitive areas such as the room-renting market, where renters lived at close quarters with rentees and had close control over the allocation of accommodations. I also found some evidence of it directed against better-off Chocoanos who tried to locate in higher-class barrios, although this seems to have been more characteristic of an earlier period of Chocoano immigration. And finally, as the case studies in the following section demonstrate, I found it manifested against black communities that made their cultural presence felt.

In La Iguaná, it is clear that many Chocoanos live in the worst-housed areas of the barrio: 40 percent of them live in the area upriver from Seventieth Avenue, and another 30 percent downriver from Sixty-fifth Avenue (see fig. 4 in appendix B). These are both recent areas of invasion and contain the least-consolidated housing. However, the Chocoanos' concentration in these areas is primarily due to their relatively recent arrival in the barrio, and if this is controlled for, the discrepancies in general housing conditions between them and Antioqueño immigrants become statistically insignificant. General housing conditions in this context refers to the census enumerators' classification of dwellings as rancho (shack made out of planks, waste materials, etc.), "transitional," or "consolidated."

The Moravia data are similar in some respects and different in others. The zone comprises different sectors, with two rather older invasion areas dating from the 1960s, a new invasion area actually on top of the central garbage dump which dates from about 1976, and several other areas dating from about 1975 which were illegally subdivided and sold off by a family that was renting the land at the time. The first of these sectors, called Fidel Castro, is one of the oldest and most consolidated sectors: only 20 percent of the dwellings are ranchos. Of the 108 Chocoano families in Moravia, 25 families (23%) lived in Fidel Castro. Sixteen of these lived in three adjacent houses, the owners of two of which rented out accommodations. The second sector, El Bosque, despite its age, had some of the worst housing in the zone, with 60 percent ranchos and only 25 percent of houses in a consolidated state; it was very overcrowded and haphazard in layout, with open sewers running alongside and under dwellings: 30 percent of the Chocoanos lived there. The third, La Montaña, is on top of the now disused and grassed-over "mountain" of garbage which, at the time of the census in 1983, was still the municipal rubbish dump: the housing there was 90 percent ranchos. The rubbish hill itself is, of course, an unstable base for housing, and the authorities, who were upgrading this barrio, have tried to remove much of this housing. Thirty-four percent of the Chocoanos lived in this sector. Although Chocoanos are not overrepresented as invaders, having bought much of their housing even in sectors originally invaded, their general housing conditions are significantly worse since, despite being overrepresented in Fidel Castro where housing is relatively good, their presence there is in overcrowded rented accommodations, and they are also overrepresented on La Montaña and in El Bosque where housing is very bad. If we look at homeowners, Chocoanos are more frequently housed in ranchos than others (66% vs. 54%) and have less dwellings in a "transitional" phase (16% vs. 18%) or in a consolidated state (18% vs. 28%). With these data, no controls are applicable, since the Chocoanos' profiles in terms of time in the barrio, age, education, and declared income are broadly the same as for others.

The city sample census allocates every block to a socioeconomic stratum, graded one to six (see fig. 2 in appendix B). The data show that, while the Chocoanos broadly follow the pattern for immigrant Antioqueños, they are marginally worse off. (For all the following figures, domestic servants living in their employers' houses are excluded.) While almost half (46%) of both categories live in stratum three, "medium-low," Chocoanos are overrepresented compared with the other category in stratum one, "low-low" (6% vs. 3%), marginally so in stratum two, "low" (32% vs. 30%), and are underrepresented in stratum four, "medium" (15% vs. 17%), and in strata five and six, "medium-high and high" (1.5% vs. 2.6%). Both categories are worse off than city-born dwellers. Controlling for age and education does little to alter this pattern; especially noticeable is the fact that the percentage of Chocoanos in stratum one is consistently twice that for Antioqueño immigrants, except for people with secondary or some further education, among whom there are no Chocoano stratum-one dwellers. It is also noticeable that these Chocoanos are overrepresented in stratum-three housing and underrepresented in stratum four, suggesting that even well-educated Chocoanos are living in areas not entirely consonant with their educational status. A critical shortcoming here is the absence of data on time spent in the city, which must affect housing standards in an important fashion: controlling for age is the only available alternative, and its relevance is shown by the fact that older Chocoanos' housing is better that that of their younger fellows, as is the case for everybody in the sample. The data also show that Chocoanos legally own their own home less often (56% vs. 62% for immigrant Antioqueños) and rely more on renting and de facto possession (i.e., invasion, etc.). Last, the data show that working Chocoanos are more frequently in the inner-city tenements (5% versus 0.5% for immigrant Antioqueños) and in ranchos and *viviendas de desechos,* dwellings made from waste materials (4% vs. 2%), and that less live in a private house (74% vs. 82%). Although the numbers are small, this last pattern remains when age and education are controlled for. Virtually all the Chocoanos living in tenements live in two houses in a small inner-city area, Colón, a surviving remnant of the Guayaquil tenement areas.

In sum, leaving aside domestics living in their employers' houses, although most Chocoanos live in what is, for Medellín, average housing—that is, strata two and three in the one-to-six hierarchy—their overall situation is rather worse than that of Antioqueño immigrants, even when age and education are controlled for. The only data on income available from the city sample indicate that, outside domestic service, Chocoanos earn almost on a par with Antioqueño immigrants, so controlling for income would have little effect. In fact, controlling for income is almost meaningless, since the numbers of those who declared an income are too small to allow significant results. The data from La Iguaná show that Chocoanos have bad housing in the barrio as a whole, but probably not when compared with other immigrants who arrived there at the same time as them: however, more of them did invade their plots. The data from Moravia show that the Chocoanos have inferior housing, even in the context of this generally poorly housed zone.

There are a number of possible explanations for these patterns. First, time in the city could be a crucial control that the citywide data do not include and which is not adequately compensated for by controlling for age. The Iguaná data show the importance of controlling for time in this way, but even here hints of discrepancies remain, and in any case the Moravia data are independent of time. Second, Chocoanos are a poorer group and can spend less on housing than can Antioqueños of similar age and education, despite partial evidence to the contrary from the incomplete income-earning data. It may be that housing itself is a better indicator of economic status than declarations about income. Third, Chocoanos are not poorer but attach less importance to housing or have different housing preferences and thus appear as a more poorly housed group. Coming from a region where a good deal of housing consists of wooden structures on stilts, they may be less averse than Antioqueños to living in a wooden dwelling classifiable by census takers as a rancho. Connected to preference is the possibility that an ethnic network of information and solidarity draws some Chocoanos to live near one another, despite inferior housing conditions. Four, various discriminatory mechanisms restrict their access to the housing opportunities appropriate to their age, education, and income.

Trying to assess racial discrimination in distributive processes from the results of those processes is, of course, notoriously difficult, since many factors intervene in distribution outcomes. Eliminating all other factors, such as time in the city, income, or access to capital, is impossible with the data I have. The wide spread of Chocoanos through much of the city in conditions broadly similar to those of other migrants suggests that direct discrimination does not operate to any great extent in such areas of the housing market as house renting, house purchase, accretive invasion, or pirate urbanization. The differences noted above are probably due primarily to lack of disposable income among Chocoanos. However, by investigating one allocation process itself, I did find evidence of direct discrimination in the room-renting market, probably one of the most sensitive areas of the housing market, since these rooms are often in private houses. I recruited a group of eight blacks, made up of Chocoanos, children of Chocoanos born in Medellín (who therefore spoke with Antioqueño accents), and one Costeño; and a group of eight Antioqueños. As far as possible, I matched these two groups for age, educational status, and social status as apparent from their general appearance (color aside, of course); there were equal numbers of men and women in each group. I then gave each person a number of room-to-rent advertisements and left them to telephone the house and, if possible, arrange a visit. They were instructed to leave the renter with the impression that they would take the room and would phone later to confirm. After leaving, they filled in a short questionnaire about the visit. Later I phoned every house, partly to check that it had been visited and partly to cancel their offer. The idea was to see if the blacks got more refusals than the Antioqueños, assuming that the rate of refusals for reasons unconnected with color (e.g., the room had been taken between the initial phone call and the visit) would be randomly distributed. The experiment was conducted on two successive Saturdays. The results showed that out of forty-one visits made by blacks, they encountered eight refusals (20%), while the Antioqueños made thirty-four visits and were refused only once (3%). The black men encountered slightly more refusals than the women. Several times the refusals towards the blacks were reported as being done evasively or with some hostility and rudeness.

This simple experiment is important because it gives direct evidence of discrimination by some Antioqueños against people whom they could easily classify as "black." Even though these individuals were clearly not rough country folk fresh from the Chocó, there was a significant tendency to simply reject them. The conditionality barrier of acceptance in this context was quite high. And although it goes beyond the limits of this experiment, the suggestion arises that other Antioqueños discriminate in other contexts in a similar fashion. The crucial point does not seem to be simply admitting blacks into the home, since black domestics are widely accepted. Rather, it is a matter of admitting people stereotyped as "black" into socially autonomous and equal positions, as opposed to servile, dependent, and symbolically "junior" positions. This admission is not excluded—as we have seen, racial discrimination is not systematic—but it is restricted. It also tends to be conditional, and in Medellín, especially in the earlier years of Chocoano immigration, the conditions could be quite stiff. One of the few middle-class Chocoanos, for example, gave the following testimony:

> When I came from Quibdó, I'd bought a house in El Estadio [mostly stratum-four housing], and I had to leave the area because frankly they made life impossible for me there. I'd gone into a white barrio . . . people who had a certain economic status and who looked down on me. And I had to sell the house and go somewhere else. My children would go out, and they'd make life impossible for them. When I arrived, they'd shut their doors, despite the fact that economically I had what was needed. I had a house, a car, my children were studying, and I was a professional like any of them. I realized that that wasn't my milieu, and I had to leave. And that's happened to a lot of paisanos. Of course, nowadays, many have prospered: there are blacks, paisanos of mine, who are economically well-off and live in very select areas.

This man now lives in a stratum-three neighborhood farther away from El Centro. At that time, then, middle-class Medellín residents had no time even for someone roughly on their own economic level.

Black Communities in Medellín

Discrimination in the housing market is typical of Latin American racial discrimination against blacks in general: it is individualistic, unsystematic, and nongeneralized. As the case of Barrio Antioquia and the following case studies show, it is also tied into the overall dynamics of the racial order, which means that discrimination is generally directed at black community, which is perceived by nonblacks as not assimilated to their cultural mores.

La Iguaná. La Iguaná is the most obvious and dense concentration of Chocoanos in the city. There are barrios where there is a greater number of families present, but they do not represent such a large proportion, nor are they so densely concentrated. The barrio began as a settlement in the 1940s. The first settlers were gravel diggers who extracted sands and gravels from the river La Iguaná and who built dwellings on land near the river ceded to them by a local owner. Gradually, others invaded the land along the river's banks, and by 1963 the settlement had expanded to include about one hundred families. Municipal attempts to control invasion and restrict dwellings to easily removable wooden structures coexisted with community organization and attempts to consolidate. In this, the residents had various allies, including the municipality itself, which, although it never officially recognized their title to the land, grudgingly gave permits to build in certain zones after a flood wiped out part of the barrio in 1971 and then in 1973 to build permanent dwellings. Between 1972 and 1974, after many petitions to the secretary for health and to the Public Services Department, electricity, water, and sewerage were installed in a rudimentary fashion in the community using the inhabitants' labor. The church helped from an early date to finance a community building that functioned as a chapel and a school, and in 1983 a new school was built with community labor and finance from the Conservative party politicians, the archdiocese of Medellín, the drug trafficker Pablo Escobar, the city council, the city's Community Action Department, the armed forces, and a Swiss charity.

By this time the barrio had a tripartite structure, according to time of invasion (see fig. 4 in appendix B). The settlement followed the river's banks and was crossed by Sixty-fifth and Seventieth avenues, between which was the oldest, most consolidated sector, with the school, the church, and most of the shops. Downriver from Sixty-fifth Avenue was a rather newer area that nevertheless had some consolidated dwellings, since Sixty-fifth had only been pushed through the barrio in 1984. Upriver from Seventieth Avenue was a sector called La Playita (literally "Little Beach"), a substantial part of which consisted of wooden shacks on stilts, practically over the river itself, although, where possible, residents had constructed in more solid materials.

In 1986, when I was living there, the municipality, through its agency Desarrollo Comunitario (Community Development), was trying to negotiate an upgrading plan for the barrio which consisted of canaling the river to obviate its periodic and disastrous floodings, reorganizing the layout of the barrio, installing proper services, and giving legal title to land. There were also plans to build two roads on either side of the barrio, for which the river's canalization was an obvious prerequisite. The left-wing housing action organization, Provivienda, which had a branch committee in the barrio, saw this as a long-term plan to make this little working-class nucleus accessible to the city's commercial interests, valorize the land, and open it up to pressure from urban developers and other capitalist ventures, thus eventually pushing out the present inhabitants, who would no longer be able to afford to live there or would succumb to attractive cash offers for their land. Every community in Colombia has a Junta de Acción Comunal, a Community Action group, a body elected locally but instituted and constituted on a national basis by government prescription. This group in La Iguaná took a more moderate line, seeking to negotiate a settlement that would guarantee as much protection as possible for low-income inhabitants and restrict disturbance of the barrio's actual layout. They tended to argue over specific details rather than contest the plan as a whole. Canalizing the river, for example, inevitably meant relocating the dwellings situated right on its banks, and there was discussion about exactly how this should be done. Moreover, La Playita was not included at all in the plan, mostly, it seems, because a planned road went right through it, and there were demands—albeit rather muted since the local Community Action group members all lived in the part that was to be upgraded—that this area be included.

During the time I lived in La Iguaná, it was still regarded as an alien element, dangerous and immoral, by the surrounding areas, which mostly contained middle-class residential units, commercial areas, and some light industry. Whatever the real benefits that had been handed over by the city authorities after extensive lobbying by the community, the feeling of the place was that of confrontation, whether with the nearby National University, which had fenced off land previously used by the barrio's soccer team; or with the nearest residential unit, the guards of which ejected Iguaná children from its playgrounds; or with the state, which sent in, alternately, teams of social workers and surveyors, or armed raids of military jeeps, mounted with machine guns. An island of poverty in a sea of middle-class plenty, only a ten-minute walk from the city center, the barrio has grown up and progressed in spite of, or at most with the grudging and opportunist acquiescence of, its neighbors and the state, and the feeling one had when descending into its huddle of houses and huts—with symbolic aptness, the place was physically as well as socially lower than its surroundings—was that of entering a different world.

The first Chocoano family arrived in La Iguaná in 1966: Luis Durán Urrutia Mosquera, his wife Delfa, and their three children. It was in his house that I lived during the several months that I was in the barrio, and he told me about his decision to move from Barrio Antioquia on the suggestion of a compadre of his who lived there.

So my compadre says to me, "Compadre, why don't you find a way . . . paying rent is very tough. . . . I live there, so let's go there." The first year, the second year, I didn't want to; the third year, I came over to have a look—it was a Saturday—and after, I convinced my wife to come too. Listen, you know how much I got for the first ten years' *liquidación* [a retirement-cum-severance fund, cashable during employment]? Just over five thousand pesos. With that I bought the first roof tiles, and I'd come in the evenings and every Saturday to work on the house.

The secretary of the barrio's Junta de Acción Communal, Octavio Palacio, wrote a history of La Iguaná for a people's write-the-history-of-your-barrio competition run by Desarrollo Comunitario in 1986. In this Urrutia is quoted as saying, "As is the custom of our race, I took to having parties at the weekends. People would have a good time, because before, there was nothing like that to be seen. There was just a little shop run by Pablo Beltrán."

The arrival of the first Chocoano thus saw the establishment of the first *bailadero,* or dance hall, in the barrio. He would play music, sell beer and *aguardiente,* while Delfa cooked and sold fried food to the customers. This initiative excited the moral indignation of some Antioqueños who thought the place encouraged drunkenness and licentiousness among the young, but Urrutia carried on until about 1976 when he tired of the enterprise and because people were using the house to consume drugs. A more explosive source of conflict was his decision to participate actively in the local civil defense group in an effort to combat crime and vice in the barrio: he became a central figure in the group and was seen by some as little more than a police informer. Some attempts were made to kill or injure him, and his front door still bears the marks of the impact of many stones. Significantly, others in the group, Antioqueños, did not suffer these attacks, and it seems clear that the fact that it was a black man, an outsider—who seemed in any case to be encouraging new and immoral activities—who was setting himself up as the barrio's moral authority exaggerated the antagonism felt against him. Nowadays, he leads a quieter life, having also given up working with the civil defense group, and continues to work as a welder in the light engineering firm that has employed him for the last thirty years. He has one of the best houses in the barrio, and he rents out the second floor as four single rooms; the rentees tend to be Chocoanos, not due to a particular preference on his part, since Antioqueños also live there from time to time, but because the ethnic information network creates a steady flow of Chocoano tenants.

The next Chocoanos to arrive were to be the center of a collection of kinsfolk which developed over the seventies and the early eighties. The first members of this aggregate came in the late sixties, from rented accommodations in an outlying barrio called Zafra, also a nucleus of Chocoano settlement. Over time, various other kinspeople arrived until, by 1984, there were some twenty-five adult members of

222

the Rivas family, from Condoto, Chocó, who together with their children made up a group of some seventy-five blacks. In the chapter on the economy of Unguía, I noted how people moving around the Chocó make use of a flexible and widespread network of bilateral kin links in order to facilitate travel and subsistence (see also Whitten 1969, 1974; Friedemann 1985b). In the emergence of this localized aggregate of kin in La Iguaná can be seen the continuing use of these wide-ranging kin networks. Once a couple of members of the family were established in the barrio, others could use their presence there as a pied-à-terre. Naturally, the rights that could be claimed in this situation were not over land or mining territory, as in the Chocó itself, but having a relative in place made things that much easier, and in a couple of cases an incoming member had a piece of land ceded by an established relative. The kinship diagram in figure five (appendix B) shows the connections between the Rivas who live in La Iguaná. The first to arrive were the two related sibling sets made up of Socrates, Rómulo, and Alfredo Rivas Rivas and their cousins Manuel Santiago, Leofanor, and Gorgoño Rivas Rivas. Jesús Ibarguen Rivas is generally spoken of as one of the latter sibling set, being an *hermano de padre,* that is, a sibling who has a common father but a different mother. He, like some others in the diagram (e.g., Fabiola Rivas Hinestroza), has taken his mother's surname, a practice not uncommon in the Chocó, where consensual unions are very common and people may change partners a number of times during their lifetime. Mercedes Maya (1987, 92) notes the same phenomenon for the village of Bebará, Chocó, and attributes it variously to personal choice, a conscious rejection of the father if the latter was disliked or perhaps hardly known, a maternal decision stemming from conjugal animosity, and lastly, an imposition by the clergy who did not, and sometimes still do not, recognize the social paternity of an absent father. Other members of the Rivas family then joined these sibling sets, and the links that join them to the original invaders are flexible, wide-ranging, bilateral, and both affinal and consanguineal. In some cases, these links were of material advantage: Francisco Mosquera Benítez was ceded a piece of land by Gorgoño Rivas Rivas, who is his *tío* (uncle) by virtue of the half-sibling relation between Gorgoño and Francisco's mother. Sometimes the actual links are not known, although a distant relationship is recognized: Juan Lucio Asprilla Rivas, for example, is known to be related, but I could not ascertain the precise link even from well-placed informants. Despite the complexity of the actual relationships involved, people use a small number of basic kin terms: *primo/prima,* cousin, *tío/tía,* uncle/aunt, and *sobrino/sobrina,* nephew/niece, are very frequent terms and include a great number of

kinsfolk, while given the plethora of half-sibling relations, *hermano/
hermana*, brother/sister, can also include many relations. The terms
cuñado/cuñada, brother-/sister-in-law, include most affinal relatives
of the same generation. This classificatory use of a few kin terms eases
the tracing of relationships in a kinship system whose complexity
stems partly from the many half-sibling relationships caused by patterns of serial unions; it also facilitates the use of kin links to legitimate residence and claims on networks of reciprocity.

Kinship is, of course, important for the Antioqueños in the barrio
too, but it is noticeable that virtually no Chocoano is without some
kin in La Iguaná or arrived there without some kinship link, whereas
this is not so common among the others. Moreover, the largest Antioqueño family in La Iguaná, comprising some seventy-five people, has
a completely different structure, being made up of most of the bilateral
descendants of an initial conjugal pair who arrived in the barrio in
1958 from a rural Antioqueño village: their offspring have dispersed
throughout, and beyond, the barrio in a style very different from the
accretive growth of the Rivas family by the addition of *primos* and
sobrinos who migrate from the Chocó.

The Rivas formed part of the major influx of Chocoanos which
occurred around 1978: according to the Desarrollo Comunitario census, 70 percent of the Chocoanos arrived after this date. And just as
Urrutia had brought the first *bailadero* to the barrio in the form of
his front room on the weekends, with this new influx several more
houses began to take on this function. Both Manuel Santiago and
Gorgoño Rivas had small-scale *bailaderos* in their houses in the late
seventies, and the latter's still functioned in 1987. Altogether, of the
eight *bailaderos* that the barrio has had, six have been in Chocoano
houses (see fig. 4 in appendix B). The owners of the houses have
generally been well-known, older figures who have been in the barrio
several years and who have dwellings made out of brick rather than
planks. These houses are particular in the sense that there tends to be
minimal separation between domestic, ordinary social, and *bailadero*
functions. The *bailadero* operates in the main room of the house on
the weekend, usually only in the evenings and during the day on
Sunday as well; sleeping and cooking areas are therefore very close
by. When the *bailadero* is not operating, the main room acts as a kind
of "open house" where people, mostly Chocoanos, collect to play
cards and dominoes, share cigarettes, talk, watch television if there is
one, and just sit around. These *bailaderos* were, during the late seventies, a focus of ethnic conflict that both Chocoanos and Antioqueños
remember. This took the form of attacks by the Antioqueños, usually
the younger men, who would throw stones at the roofs of the houses

when the *bailadero* was operating. Occasionally, they would enter to provoke incidents; equally, some Chocoanos would retaliate against the stone throwers. Clearly, the Chocoanos were seen initially as a foreign and disliked element. Not only were they building their houses there, but their *bailaderos* attracted other Chocoanos from all over the city as well, just as the *bailaderos* of Barrio Antioquia had done in the 1960s; and just as this provoked a reaction there, so it did in La Iguaná. With time, conflict has quietened down, and I came across no overt antagonism of this kind. However, the Chocoano *bailaderos* in the central, consolidated part of the barrio, which is overwhelmingly Antioqueño, no longer function, except for that of Gorgoño Rivas, which is right on the edge of this sector. Instead, the other three current Chocoano *bailaderos* are in La Playita, where 40 percent of the Chocoanos live, and in the sector below Sixty-fifth where another third of them live. So reduction in conflict has been accompanied by a de facto segregation process: even though the Chocoanos do not form a majority in any of the barrio's three sectors, they form concentrations within each sector, and the *bailaderos* are precisely within these nuclei (see fig. 4 in appendix B).

This history demonstrates in a specific and local way the establishment of a black community, structured largely around characteristic patterns of Chocoano kinship and also around the institution of the *bailadero*. Nonblack reaction was hostile and antagonistic when faced with this community in its midst, and the outcome was a certain degree of de facto segregation, with the *bailaderos* locating in areas of the settlement where the Chocoano presence was strongest. As always, black community coexists with patterns of black adaptation to the nonblack world, and by no means do all La Iguaná's Chocoanos live in La Playita or the sector below Sixty-fifth, nor do they all participate in the *bailaderos* and associated activities. Typically, it is the younger, more recent immigrants who concentrate in La Playita and its *bailaderos,* while those living in the central sector tend to be older migrants. Nearly 80 percent of Chocoanos living in La Playita are under 30 years old, while of those living in the more consolidated central area, only 44 percent are under 30. Equally, 81 percent of Playita Chocoanos have been in Medellín for less than ten years, while the figure drops to 47 percent for those living in the central area. La Playita represents a niche in which black Chocoano culture is reelaborated in an urban context principally by younger, quite recent migrants and in which it is differentiated from Antioqueño culture.

The *bailaderos* are a focus of cultural differentiation. The atmosphere in Chocoano *bailaderos* is very different from that in the only Antioqueño *bailadero*—which would in any case prefer to be styled a *discoteca,* since the word *bailadero* has rather low-status connotations. The Chocoano places have a freezer, a sound system, and a couple of rough tables with a few stools and the odd upturned crate; they play only salsa and *vallenato* music, and most of the clientele is black. Often a good deal of the social activity takes place in the street outside the *bailadero,* where people talk and stand around, going inside to dance. This is especially true of young single women who do not have money to buy a drink: they will accept a *gaseosa* (fizzy drink)—or sometimes a beer, or more rarely *aguardiente*—from a man, who will then invite them inside to dance. The men who are at tables or standing inside tend to have more money to spend on drink for themselves and the women they have invited. Occasionally, one also sees women together paying for their own drinks, although this is more common in the city center bars such as El Suizo. (Compare Whitten's [1974, 103] description of the "saloon context" of the Pacific littoral.) In contrast, the Antioqueño establishment is a place specifically set up as a *discoteca* with colored lighting, chairs, tables, a separate dance floor, and waiter service; it plays a mixture of salsa, *vallenato,* ballads, and *música tropical* (usually popularized versions of traditional Costeño music, played by groups from both *la Costa* and the interior). The social activity associated with dancing takes place within the confines of the *discoteca;* although there are young men hanging around outside watching the action on the street and inside, there is not the same constant interchange of people from inside to outside, and women do not stand outside and expect to be invited to a drink outside and then a dance inside; lastly, the clientele is mostly Antioqueño.

The Antioqueño *discoteca* attempted to follow patterns defined by the city at large, from the center out to more peripheral neighborhoods. These are partly concerned with establishing divisions—inside and outside the premises, on and off the dance floor—which bound behavior. In the Chocoano *bailaderos,* the boundaries were far less obvious, with the limits of the dance hall itself spilling onto the street and there being little division between dance floor and a sitting area. These places seemed to transgress the urban norms of propriety to which the Antioqueño *discoteca* was aspiring.

The atmosphere in La Playita likewise has a distinctive flavor. The oldest part of this sector is on the highest and driest land and is mostly Antioqueño; the newer part is right down on the river and is mixed Antioqueño and Chocoano, with the latter predominating by about fifty to thirty households. One of the daughters of Urrutia, whom I knew from her frequent visits to her father's house, lived with her

The central pathway of La Playita, the least consolidated part of La Iguaná.

marido, common-law husband, and her child in a rancho in La Playita, and I used to go and see her there, since she was a main informant for kinship relations and general gossip and a facilitator for interviews with local residents. In the mornings, one could feel the Chocoano dominance of that little section with its houses and ranchos crowded along the narrow, muddy pathway. The women were out and about, sitting in their doorways, exchanging news, going to the corner shop, walking up and down with bundles of clothes to wash and with children hanging on to their skirts; they shouted at one another from their doorways, made barbed comments about their neighbors' sex lives, laughed uproariously; some walked around dressed in nightdresses, and if these were a little translucent, the odd loud comment might pass about that woman's knickers being a little on the skimpy side. Equally, in the afternoon card games there would be noise and shouting, loud disputes about scoring and betting transactions, rebukes yelled at importunate children. This type of behavior is *part of* lower-class black culture, although not necessarily synonymous with it, and appears to many Antioqueño residents to be typically *escandaloso* and *alborotado,* boisterous, noisy, rough, excitable, scandalous, and often too sexually explicit. For the Chocoanos, however, loudness is often the expression of well-being or confidence in oneself, and quietness is seen as indicating unhappiness or being ill at ease.

La Iguaná is a point of concentration for the Chocoanos, but in practice it is La Playita and, to a lesser extent, the part of the barrio below Sixty-fifth Avenue which take on this function. La Playita—also the name of a barrio in Quibdó—has a tightly knit group of Chocoanos, interlinked by kinship; it has two *bailaderos*—open houses that attract Chocoano visitors from all over the city on weekends, not to mention those who come to visit kin and friends; there Chocoanos feel at ease to behave in ways classified as *alborotado* by their Antioqueño neighbors; there one can find cases of Chocoano men with polygynous relations—in one instance, a man, a construction laborer, had two women living in adjacent houses, an unusual arrangement even by Chocoano standards. In short, it is a Chocoano community in Medellín.

Zafra. Despite being on the urban periphery and physically distant from La Iguaná, and despite a different history of settlement through the subdivision of a small landowner's territory for sale as individual housing plots, Zafra is a barrio that has a number of links with it. First, some of the Iguaná's Chocoano inhabitants rented there before moving to La Iguaná. Second, the process of its formation shares some similar features.

The barrio was originally a small, rural, agricultural settlement. In the 1970s, the area was caught up in processes of pirate urbanization, as landowners sold off plots to people who constructed their dwellings as they saw fit on the steep slopes of the hillsides. In the 1980s, there was some invasion on the margins of Zafra, but recently the area has found itself increasingly surrounded by middle-class housing schemes that, as in the case of La Iguaná, have isolated Zafra and its older neighbor, Sucre, as islands of poverty, looked down on as nests of petty drug dealing and crime by their richer neighbors.

The first Chocoano resident was a woman, Neila Ibarguen, cousin of La Iguaná's Luis Durán Urrutia Mosquera. Her brother lived in rented accommodations nearby in Sucre. She and her husband rented a house from an Antioqueño in Zafra in 1968, and she started a Sunday *bailadero* that attracted Chocoanos from other barrios. Her sister Dora, who had been working as a domestic, married a Chocoano man, a bus driver, and rented in a nearby barrio, helping her sister on Sundays. Soon after, Leofanor Rivas (now of La Iguaná) arrived, followed by some of his brothers and nephews and, of course, other Chocoanos. While many of these moved to La Iguaná after a few years, around 1975 Neila and Dora and their husbands bought their own houses, and in the latter's the Sunday dances continued. In 1973, another family, the Martínez, moved from Barrio Antioquia to Zafra, and between 1978 and 1981 the mother of the family rented a small place from the barrio's Community Action group to have dances on the weekends. As in La Iguaná, Chocoanos from all over the city would come to drink and dance.

The Antioqueños' reaction to this was similar to that in La Iguaná: young Antioqueños would throw stones and pick fights, a few local thieves would try their luck on the incoming crowd, the Chocoanos retaliated and defended themselves. Both Antioqueño and Chocoano informants identified Antioqueños as the initial aggressors. Eventually, Community Action refused to continue renting to the Martínez family, who then moved their dances to a more peripheral location in a place rented from a big Antioqueño family. But already the influx of Chocoanos had been braked: not long after this, the *bailaderos* all stopped functioning.

Another point of disagreement was the Chocoano *velorio,* or wake, in which the deceased's coffin is watched over before burial: thereafter, every night until *la novena,* the ninth night, some people congregate in the family's house and perhaps pray or more usually sit around and talk, tell stories, or play dominoes. The Chocoano version of this is traditionally more celebratory than the more pious Antioqueño version and especially on *la novena* includes more noisy dominoes, storytelling, drinking, and so on. In Zafra there was general disapproval of the way these *velorios* were carried on: as one Antioqueño graphically put it, "The bottle of *aguardiente* on top of the coffin— that was too much." Again, the Chocoanos were seen as *alborotados,* and this was also *falta de respeto,* lack of respect, not only for the dead but for the morals of the community at large. Older Chocoano residents remember occasions when the necessary permit from the local *inspección de policía,* a civil authority despite its name, was refused for Chocoano *velorios.* With time, the Chocoanos adapted their *velorios* to a form that provoked less censure from the Antioqueños.

However, the Chocoano presence still causes the odd ripple of discontent in the barrio. Outside the Martínez house, men gather, especially on Sundays, to play dominoes, and given the close proximity of the houses in this area, one or two of the Antioqueño neighbors regularly lodge complaints with the police about the noise this involves.

In contrast with La Iguaná, where a certain degree of segregation facilitated the persistence of black community, in Zafra the original Chocoano nucleus basically adapted its behavior to local cultural mores. This black adaptation, generally accepted by the Antioqueños there, was influenced in part by the fact that the number of recent young Chocoano immigrants to the barrio was then less than in La Iguaná and that many of the original black residents had moved away.

The same kind of reaction occurred in the case of a municipal relocation project in Kennedy for the inhabitants of the old city center Alpujarra invasion, in which there were about thirty Chocoano families out of a total of about one hundred fifty. In the new housing, there were complaints to the municipal agency from Antioqueños who alleged that the Chocoano women would come out of their houses in petticoats or the men in their underwear and so on. One Antioqueño woman recounted to me how she had seen a black man naked, washing himself in his backyard; she rushed into her house and bolted the door. The agency put pressure on the Chocoanos, and they adapted accordingly. The Antioqueño woman observed: *"Ya les da pena hacer todo eso"* (Now they're ashamed to do all that).

Nucleation and Dispersal

The stories of these two barrios, La Iguaná and Zafra, contain more ethnic hostility and antagonism than those of other Chocoano nuclei (with the exception of the older Barrio Antioquia nucleus), but in other respects they are typical: in all cases, chain migration based on loose and wide-ranging kinship is a fundamental feature; also very common is the presence of a *bailadero* or open house belonging to a well-known figure which acts as a center for social activities, including parties and dancing. In the other Chocoano nuclei I investigated— Moravia, El Rincón, San Pablo, Kennedy (see fig. 1 in appendix B)— these two features also appear.

But to talk of Chocoano settlement in Medellín simply in terms of nuclei would be highly misleading, since a majority of Chocoanos live in a much more dispersed fashion. Even many of the nuclei have adapted culturally more than in La Iguaná, and most of them are not as tightly knit as La Iguaná: in San Pablo, for example, there are two well-established Chocoano families, one of which ran a *bailadero* for six years and the other of which rents out rooms to tenants who are almost entirely blacks, but the other Chocoano families in the barrio are not linked by kinship to these families. And the majority of Chocoanos live in barrios where there is little in the way of black community, where contacts with the ethnic network are more occasional, the inflow of young migrants from the Chocó is reduced, and an Antioqueño milieu clearly predominates. So La Playita in La Iguaná, although a critical focus of Chocoano activity in Medellín, is an extreme case on a continuum that ranges from tight nucleation to dispersal.

Nucleation and dispersal are clearly intimately related to processes of black community and black adaptation. They are analytically distinct because simple physical dispersal does not inevitably lead to cultural assimilation into the new cultural milieu, nor does the latter necessitate the former. But, as the previous chapters have demonstrated several times, black community and adaptation, and likewise race mixture, are facilitated by nucleation and dispersal. In the context of a hierarchical racial order that nevertheless allows conditional acceptance, being surrounded by nonblacks and being immersed in a nonblack world increase the ease and likelihood of cultural change and race mixture. In this sense, spatial dispersal, genetic dilution, and cultural adaptation go together in the overall process that I term black adaptation to the nonblack world, just as spatial nucleation, the absence of race mixture, and the continuity of black identity together constitute what I term black community.

As in previous instances, the dynamics of the racial order in Medellín are structured by the local political economy and by the processes of living in the city as an urban space. The urban processes that concern us here are: first, the city's residential differentiation per se, the economic position of immigrant Chocoanos, and the processes of economic consolidation over time (which do not necessarily mean upward mobility out of the working classes); second, dependence on the ethnic network for practical purposes, as against gradual familiarization with urban networks and institutions; and third, the family cycle.

First, Chocoanos, like any others, are subject to the constraints imposed on them by the availability of housing. Chocoanos cannot necessarily live near one another or with relatives, friends, or paisanos simply because they so choose. This in itself restricts the possibility of nucleation and inhibits black community, especially given the small numbers of Chocoanos in the city. However, within the housing market there are certain sectors within which nucleation can occur more easily, and these are the sectors that tend to attract the poorer and more recent arrivals. In tenement blocks, in invasions that are in the process of formation, and in developing pirate urbanizations, there is sufficient flexibility to allow ethnically oriented locational choices to operate, whether these be actual preferences for living near other Chocoanos or choices made with information garnered from the ethnic network (see below). In these types of housing environment, people can effectively choose to locate near one another more easily than in already consolidated housing or in housing allocated via bureaucratic procedures. Thus poverty and recent arrival are conditions that facilitate the formation of Chocoano nuclei.

On the other hand, there are factors that encourage dispersal. In essence, greater purchasing power implies a relationship to the city's pattern of residential differentiation and the housing market that generally militates against forming residential nuclei. People tend to locate more in areas where Chocoano density of settlement is lower, not only because there are fewer Chocoanos at their economic level but also because there is less flexibility in the more consolidated sectors of the housing market into which they tend to move. Evidence from the citywide sample backs up the general relationship between more dispersed settlement and higher economic status; there is also a slight correlation between dispersal and age. (For these figures, domestic servants are excluded, since their residence in middle- and upper-class households distorts any analysis of spatial patterns.) For example, working Chocoanos living in "high-density" survey tracts (i.e., those with more than 1% Chocoanos; see fig. 3 in appendix B) are under 30 years old in 50 percent of cases, compared with only 33 percent of Chocoanos living in "low-density" tracts (i.e., those with between 0.1% and 0.5% Chocoanos). In terms of occupation, whereas 25 percent of Chocoanos in low-density tracts work in professional-technical occupations or as teachers, only 8 percent of Chocoanos in high- or middle-density tracts do so. Not surprisingly, housing quality for Chocoanos in the low-density tracts is higher than for the high- and middle-density dwellers. About 50 percent of each category lives in stratum-three housing, but a full 40 percent of Chocoanos in high-density tracts live in strata-one and -two housing, compared with 32 percent of Chocoanos in both middle- and low-density tracts. Accordingly, 29 percent of Chocoanos in low-density tracts live in strata-four and -five housing, compared with only 3 percent of Chocoanos in high-density and 20 percent in middle-density tracts. In sum, then, Chocoanos who live in areas with low densities of Chocoano settlement tend to be better off, have better housing, and be slightly older than Chocoanos who live in areas of high-density Chocoano settlement. These differences can be due to variations in economic means on arrival in the city, or they can be a result of processes of economic consolidation while in the city. The chances of economic consolidation, of course, depend on the relationship to the labor market, and, as I showed in the last chapter, these chances are limited. Generally, such consolidation as there is rarely means upward mobility out of the working class, and more usually it means securing a reasonably stable place in it, getting one's own home, and improving it over time. For example, many of the Chocoanos I interviewed in reasonably well consolidated areas had started life in the city in areas such as La Bayadera or Barrio Antioquia, barrios of dense Chocoano settlement, before moving to other areas. Both initial and emergent differences in economic status impinge on the Chocoanos in Medellín, and their impact leads to the same result. Greater access to economic resources or economic consolidation leads to physical dispersal: Chocoanos find themselves living in barrios with relatively few other Chocoano families and surrounded by Antioqueño neighbors. In the context of the Colombian racial order, these circumstances clearly facilitate black adaptation to the Antioqueño milieu.

The second factor that structures the Chocoanos' relation to the local racial order is their familiarization with the city and its institutions and the degree to which this facilitates independence from the ethnic network of contacts with other Chocoanos. The ethnic network is important because it supplies, or supplies information about, a great many things of fundamental importance, especially, but not only, to the recent immigrant. It can supply contacts, orientation in a strange geography of streets, avenues, "transversals," "diagonals," and "circulars"; it can supply work, accommodations on a temporary basis, and information about more long-term housing strategies; it can supply advice, loans, friends, potential spouses, a Chocoano doctor, places to have fun, laborers and employers, helpers for a communal work party for one's house, parties, music, and somewhere to get one's hair plaited *en trensitas* (in little plaits or cornrows). Chocoanos make use of the ethnic network to obtain these goods and services, and, especially among recent immigrants, this induces them to regroup with their paisanos. As we have already seen, most Chocoanos come via a kin link or, failing that, a link with someone from the same village or river as themselves. This immediately links them into an ethnic network. Of course, both these features are fairly typical of immigrants per se: they often migrate in a chain fashion and depend on kin and people from the same village and town to orient them and help them settle in. There are, however, some differences between the Chocoanos and others here. Kinship is more important for them than for other migrants, a factor that tends to create a tighter network. In addition, whereas the network for Antioqueño immigrants is basically village or town based, the network for the Chocoanos spreads out to encompass all Chocoanos—a phenomenon that also occurs among Antioqueño migrants to Quibdó or Unguía.

Over time, however, Chocoanos become familiar with the city and how to cope with it: they learn how to move around, about danger spots, buses, and the grid system of the city; which institutions deal with what; and how to go about getting work and looking for housing. The network of ethnic contacts which initially tends to supply information and assistance begins to become less fundamental in a

233

utilitarian sense, although it can remain important for information about scarce resources such as work and housing or for loans and other critical resources. Thus a Chocoano, if he or she chooses, can begin to leave the ethnic network behind as time gives him or her the experience to manage city life. It is significant in this respect that in a nucleus such as La Playita, 50 percent of the Chocoanos arrived after 1975, a fact that reinforces the relation noted above between recent arrival and nucleation.

The network is particularly relevant to patterns of nucleation because it mediates the relation between nucleation/dispersal and patterns of residential differentiation discussed above: it provides much of the information about housing with which people make the choices that are opened to them by their economic means. Gilbert and Ward (1982), for example, found that migrants in Bogotá tended to begin to concentrate in certain barrios according to their region of origin because of the way information about housing moved through regional networks after the migrants had arrived and initially settled. Equally, in the nuclei of Chocoano settlement in Medellín, I found that people had generally located through contacts with other Chocoanos, often relatives. In this sense, although the relation to the ethnic network is structured by the nature of the city's residential differentiation, the ethnic network itself feeds back into those patterns by supplying information about housing.

The third factor that structures processes of black community and black adaptation is the family cycle, which operates by influencing the impact of residential differentiation, although in a contingent fashion. Many Chocoanos who came as single migrants form unions with other Chocoanos and with Antioqueños and have families over time. The impact of this process on nucleation and dispersal can cut both ways, depending essentially on economic status. A couple with small children may decide to move out of rented accommodations and invade, or perhaps purchase, in a location that they learned about through the ethnic network. The Chocoano community in La Iguaná was indeed formed mainly by young families. Equally, a single mother will probably depend more than ever on the ethnic network for help with child care and economic assistance. On the other hand, a couple that has a relatively stable income may also be seeking extra living space to accommodate children. This may be an incentive to enter a more consolidated housing market, where, as before, there is less flexibility. It is only the decision to enter a more consolidated housing market—a choice ruled principally by economic status—which induces dispersal.

Black community and adaptation are thus structured by urban processes, and what emerges quite clearly from an investigation of the phenomenon of nucleation and black community is that it occurs in the poorest zones. Economic means are a crucial factor here and affect nucleation in two ways. First, it is in the context of settlements such as La Iguaná, Moravia, and Zafra that there exists the flexibility of choice of housing which allows a nucleus to develop. When people have greater purchasing power and want to move into more consolidated housing, they are more restricted in their choice of where they can go and the people near whom they can live. Second, the more recent immigrants tend to depend more on a network of other Chocoanos to find work, housing, information, friends, and diversion; as poor migrants their housing possibilities equally tend to be in the poorest, newest zones. Therefore, there is a tendency for more recent Chocoano immigrants to collect together in poor areas, due to their economic means and the operation of the ethnic network. Hence La Playita, Moravia, and Zafra are all fairly recent settlements, dating from the late seventies in terms of major Chocoano settlement. Youth, recent migration, and poverty are particularly evident in La Playita, and this is also clearly connected to its role as a vibrant focal point of Chocoano culture.

Nuclei and concentrations of blacks form as Chocoanos make recourse to their ethnic network to solve housing and employment problems in a city that often relegates them to certain lowly social positions. It is not only housing and employment that are at issue, as the Iguaná and Zafra cases suggest. Chocoanos also stick together in the process of living and re-creating forms of black culture, forms that are subject to disparagement and even hostile attack from Antioqueños. The relationship to the ethnic network is not simply a functional matter of to what extent a person depends on the Chocoano network to provide aid and opportunities in the urban environment; it is also a deeper matter of the person's relationship to being black, to black culture, and to the blacks, or more accurately, to the Chocoanos as a category within Colombian society. The racial order also has cultural dimensions that, although structured by the economic processes I have outlined, are not reducible to them but rather present themselves as a relatively autonomous dimension in which blackness and whiteness as cultural values compete unequally in the arena of the city and the nation. It is these cultural dimensions that I examine in more depth in part 4.

IV

Blackness
and Mixedness

13

Images of Blackness:
The View from Above

They have different customs from the Colombians, but they are ordinary people with different ways of living.

The *boga* of the Magdalena displays his prodigious agility and strength and exhibits his beautiful athlete's muscles, comparable to an ebony Apollo.

The material I have presented on Unguía and Medellín needs to be seen in the context of how people who claim certain racial identities that avoid the category "black" think about others whom they class as "black." In chapters 1 and 2, I outlined a perspective on blacks as propagated by an intellectual and political elite within a set of ideas about nationhood. Although this has the power to structure many people's ideas about blacks as individuals, as a category, or as a regional population, it is necessary to see how ordinary nonblack people in Unguía and Medellín think about blackness, or more specifically about Chocoanos. This reveals a good deal of complexity, which is nevertheless structured along lines that are by now familiar. In this chapter, I also reintroduce a notion mentioned in the first chapter, the idea of the power and fascination of blackness. This is a muted, but

Epigraphs: (1) An Antioqueño secondary school student from Medellín, writing about the Chocoanos; this was one of the very few instances in which someone implied that Chocoanos were not actually Colombians at all (cf. chapter 1). In this case, the implication undermines completely his neutral comments about them being "ordinary people."
    (2) Cordovez Moure, writing in the late nineteenth century, describes the black *bogas* (boatmen) who poled rafts up the Magdalena River (1957, 481).

I believe significant, theme in perceptions of blackness and one that affects the dynamics of cultural change.

Ideas about the inferiority of blackness were powerful in the colonial era and are not just a thing of the past: the cult of whiteness still exists today. Blacks almost never appear on magazine covers or in television advertisements that manipulate images of conventional beauty: their role is almost always touristic and folkloric. Richard Jackson (1976) notes a persistent ideology of the superiority of whiteness in the portrayal of blacks in Latin American literature. The whiter a child is born, the prettier he or she is held to be: I remember the comments made about the child of a white friend of mine in Unguía who had married a local mulatto woman: "Oh, he's come out all nice and light colored [*clarito*]." In contrast, *negro* and *feo,* ugly, are frequently paired terms. Christian symbolism, of course, is heavily loaded with associations of black with evil and lightness with good (Bastide 1967), and when Colombian blacks say that racism exists in their country, they often point out that the devil is portrayed as black skinned. Stereotypes exist which portray blacks unfavorably as lazy, disorganized, vulgar, dishonest, and often aggressive. Stock phrases reinforce this image: "If a black doesn't shit on the way in, he'll do it on the way out." This implies an ultimate untrustworthiness that may not be initially apparent, an impression reinforced by the damning *"negro tenía que ser"* (just had to be a black) when a black does something a nonblack considers typical of black behavior; or equally by the comment *"un mono es un mono, aunque se vista de seda"* (a monkey is a monkey, even when he dresses in silk). Clearly, racism exists, but, as the following material shows, it is neither systematic nor straightforward.

Antioqueños on the Chocoanos

On different occasions, I would get schoolteacher friends to assign their captive audiences tasks that involved writing about race and ethnicity. This resulted in three different sets of responses.

1. In Unguía, thirty-two students between the ages of 14 and 16 replied to questions about typical characteristics of Chocoanos, Antioqueños, and Costeños and about how the groups got on together in the town. Twenty-one of these students classified themselves as Chocoanos, four as Antioqueños, and six as Costeños. In terms of class, this sample was made up principally of students from poor, rural backgrounds, although their very attendance at a secondary school

indicates that they were not from the poorest strata of the town. These students all had firsthand experience of living in the same small town as, and being at school with, people of all three ethnic categories.

2. In Medellín, thirty-two Antioqueño students of about 14 years old wrote about their concept of the Chocó and the Chocoanos. The children in this sample had parents in mostly working-class occupations, with a couple of more middle-class ones (teacher, engineer).

3. An open-ended questionnaire was distributed by university student friends among Chocoano and Antioqueño acquaintances of theirs (mostly students at university level) which asked Chocoanos about their experiences as blacks in the city, and the Antioqueños about their impressions of the Chocó and the Chocoanos in the city: of these, thirty Antioqueños and nineteen Chocoanos replied (including two people born in Medellín of Chocoano parentage). The Chocoanos' fathers came from varied backgrounds (farmers, public employees, merchants, manual workers), while the Antioqueños' parents had mostly working- or lower middle-class occupations.

In what the Antioqueños thought about the Chocoanos, some of the complexity and ambiguity of ideas about race, not apparent in more uncompromising ideas about the need to whiten the nation and the rank laziness of the blacks, reveal themselves. The Unguía Antioqueño students thought the Chocoanos were lazy: "they like to get up late . . . they're not fond of getting rich . . . doesn't like to work . . . little initiative . . . little liking for work." On the other hand, they did enjoy a good time: "they're always happy . . . they like dancing . . . a happy spirit." (The Costeños did not mention laziness in describing Chocoanos: two said they were hard workers.) However, the Antioqueños were complacent about ethnic relations: cultural differences did not impede interethnic unions or general harmony in the town.

Students in Medellín generally had much less direct contact with Chocoanos, and few of them had ever been to the Chocó. Their impressions were thus usually derived indirectly. In some cases this was complemented by personal experience with a few Chocoano acquaintances or friends generally made through school or university. The secondary school students in Medellín presented a more varied picture than the Unguía students. About a third of them thought the Chocoanos were "vulgar and despotic . . . rude . . . egotistical . . . repellent . . . coarse . . . very primitive . . . unpleasant." A few less thought them "nice . . . hospitable . . . straightforward . . . friendly." Others simply characterized them thus: "normal, some friendly, others not . . . ordinary . . . some are good people, some are bad . . . they have the same rights as anyone else in Medellín . . . they're like us." Interestingly, only one said the Chocoanos were "not hard-working," while four mentioned that they "wanted to progress." About five noted that they "like music, they like to dance and have parties." Just over a fifth (not the same ones as thought them "vulgar," etc.) recognized that "many are rejected by the Antioqueños . . . there are people who reject them because they are black . . . they are kept to one side . . . society rejects them because they are a different color." One ingenuously noted: "They have little importance here because most of the high posts are occupied by whites, and since they are black [they don't occupy these posts]." Three observed that the blacks stuck together a lot, and one who lived in Castilla barrio, where many black families live, complained: "[they have] places where only those of the same race can go. In the block where I live, there's a Chocoano family: they don't like to have white friends. When they have a dance they won't let whites in."

In the last sample, mostly university students, their mixed opinions were again evident. About a fifth admitted to negative views about the Chocoanos, with one writing that they were "bad-humored, aggressive, wary about something, fearful . . . ungrateful . . . they only live for today, tomorrow does not matter to them. . . . They believe in herbs and witches," and another thinking that they were "bad-humored, resentful . . . aggressive . . . lacking drive in work." Another said that although the ones he had met were good people, most of the muggings he had witnessed had been done by blacks in a "dehumanizing" and "brazen" way. One referred to the Chocoanos consistently as *negritos,* the diminutive implying a rather condescending attitude, and said that they had "inspired distrust" in him until he met a black man who helped him out in a town in the Urabá region. One woman said that, although she had noted that blacks were a bit "easy-going in their personal cleanliness," she thought they were "people like any others." However, she recounted how her son at the age of 3, when given a bicycle instead of the tricycle he wanted, cried and said that the bicycle should be given to "those poor children," indicating the black children of a local Chocoano family who were playing in the street. "'Why poor?' we asked him, and he answered that they were *negritos* and that we should give them the bicycle." At age 5, she found her son before a crucifix, praying for a sister—as long as she was not black. Finally, when being entered for third year in a new primary school and faced with a black teacher, he said that he did not want to study there because he would have that teacher. She ends: "I wonder where such a deep-seated racism came from." Perhaps personal trauma had played a part here, but a full 45 percent of this sample recognized that racism existed in Medellín, so it would not be surprising if children picked this up. As just one example, a man wrote, "I have noticed that there is a certain position against people from the Chocó, but I think it is not the fact of being from the Chocó, but rather because they are of the black race. The number of Chocoanos in good jobs is very small; I think they have been discriminated against."

On the other hand, ten of these Antioqueños thought that Chocoanos were nice people, good friends, helpful, and so on; and four, breaking with traditional stereotypes, mentioned that Chocoanos were dynamic, progressive, and *superador,* determined to succeed. Five adhered to the view that all people were equal, whatever their color. Nine people mentioned that Chocoanos were *alegre,* happy, extrovert, and a couple noted that the Chocó was *muy fiestera,* party loving, or that a nearby Chocoano family "loves salsa and partying and loud music." In this sample, the idea that blacks are *acomplejados,* have a complex about their color, emerged three times in relation to the Chocoanos: "The men seemed to me *acomplejados* with respect to the Antioqueños." A secretary said that "if they have something to ask, they do it timidly, as if they thought they were going to be rejected." One woman wrote that she had had a black boyfriend for three years and had a black godson and commented: "I don't like the fact that these people have a complex about their color. The problem is, at bottom, in the blacks and not in society." Here, then, the blacks were the authors of their own misfortunes. Connected with this idea were a few comments about the Chocoanos being "an isolated colony with few relations with the other inhabitants of Medellín," although only in one case was this related directly to racial discrimination. Change and variation within the Chocoano group were also mentioned, with a few noting how Chocoanos' initial reactions of timidity and suspicion gave way to friendliness and helpfulness through a process of adaptation to Medellín, or how children born of Chocoanos in Medellín, although "they have roots, of course . . . adopt the position of the Antioqueños." One woman thought there were two types of Chocoanos in Medellín, nice people who studied university careers and "vulgar, rowdy and hypocritical" people from "*la sociedad popular.*"

This material highlights a number of central themes in the Antioqueño perspective on blacks which illustrate some of the basic arguments of this book about the Colombian racial order. There was open expression of negative images and stereotypes of Chocoano people seen as a category and seen as typically "black" people. Interestingly, this reaction was most prominent among the Unguía Antioqueños, who had the greatest direct experience of the Chocoanos and the Chocó in general. Despite the fact that their school environment displayed minimal ethnic divisions in social interaction, these students generally adopted the characterizations of blacks current among the majority of Antioqueños in Unguía, seeing them as lazy and unenterprising. This is the image that corresponds to a black frontier zone being taken over by a dynamic nonblack colonist population that sees the local people as incapable of progress.

The Antioqueño students in Medellín, of course, had a rather different experience of Chocoanos, rarely having related to them as anything but fairly isolated individuals—these students were not from La Iguaná, for example. Negative ideas about Chocoanos were less frequently expressed among secondary school students than among Antioqueños in Unguía, and even less so among university students. This corresponds to what many Chocoanos mentioned when I asked them about racism: that it was the product of "ignorance." But the real reasons are more complex. On the one hand, more educated people may indeed have (or at least express) allegiance to more egalitarian ideologies. On the other hand, the encounters of university students in Medellín with Chocoanos, if it was not with domestic servants, would tend to be with well-educated Chocoano students. Therefore, their direct experience of Chocoanos would be very different from that of Antioqueños in Unguía or in the low-income barrios of the city. Significantly, one girl who did live in Castilla, where a large number of Chocoanos live, reacted negatively to what she saw as their exclusiveness: "They won't let whites in."

Negative ideas still existed, however, and they centered not on laziness but on the Chocoanos' supposed unpleasantness: they were seen as uncultured, lacking in proper manners and urban sophistication. But there were also many neutral and positive reactions and some that broke with traditional stereotypes of laziness. Here, then, the complex of responses corresponded to a situation in which blacks are seen not as a category that is being pushed out of a colonized zone in the name of progress but rather as an uncultured and lower-class minority in the home territory. However, there is room for acceptance, and this is chiefly the product of relations of an individual nature, particularly with well-educated Chocoanos. There is a conditional acceptance of blacks who adapt to the mores of the nonblack world. Interesting here is the suggestion that adaptation includes forgetting completely about color and race as an issue. Any sensitivity about it

244

is easily classed as showing signs of being *acomplejado*. Indeed, I was surprised that this term did not crop up more often in these written responses, since the idea that blacks were sensitive or ashamed of their blackness emerged frequently in conversation with both Antioqueños and Chocoanos. *Acomplejado* is typically used about a black person who is thought to be ashamed of being black, but behind this lies a deeper significance. Blacks may say this about other blacks who they think are ashamed of being black, or alternatively if they think that issues of color should be ignored altogether. When used by nonblacks, the term nearly always has the latter sense. Being *acomplejado* effectively means drawing attention in some way to racial identity, whether by timidity or by attributing racist motives to others. A "well-adapted" black would, in contrast, have no such "complex," conforming instead to convenient ideologies about the insignificance of racism and racial identity in Colombian society. "Having a complex" thus implicitly undermines ideas of racial democracy but shifts the locus of blame from society at large onto the individual psychology of a black person. In line with this, remarks made about Chocoanos sticking together or being an isolated colony were rarely linked to observations about racism, this usually being presented as an unfortunate tendency on the part of others, due to their "ignorance." Equally, the perception that some blacks were *acomplejados* was generally understood as a slightly mysterious phenomenon and only occasionally linked to the actual probability of rejection. Here, then, Medellín is envisaged as basically an open society, although marred by some racism, in which blacks can be accepted if they behave "properly" and in which nonintegration is seen as the responsibility of the blacks, who choose to segregate themselves or lack confidence.

The Power of Blackness

The Chocoanos are seen as coming from a poor, neglected region that is at the bottom of the social scales of race, region, and power. Despite this, however, many respondents mentioned that the Chocoanos appear to be *alegres* and to enjoy having fun. Here we enter into a more subliminal and contradictory realm. For if the Chocoanos, and more generally the blacks, are seen as inferior or coming from uncivilized and inferior regions, their very position seems to give them access to things from which whites are alienated. Certain ideas about blacks, created and reiterated over time, can cut both ways: if blacks are irresponsible and disorganized—and therefore not to be trusted with anything other than simple jobs—then is this not also a blessed freedom from the burdens and anxieties of responsibility and gnawing worries about tomorrow? A white friend in Unguía remarked scathingly on how he had seen Chocoano students work for a while at some job, until they said "*ya tengo mi sábado completo*" (now I've got enough for Saturday [night]), at which point they stopped work. But another Antioqueño said, "Well, you know, I think they're happier than we are: always smiling, never a care." Or if the blacks, including the women, are particularly suited to manual labor, is it not "natural" that they should have strong, powerful, and well-formed bodies?

The step from powerful physicality to potent sexuality is, of course, a short one, and here other ideas edge in which link primitiveness and closeness to nature with an unrestrained sexuality. Saint-Hilaire said of indian women in Brazil that they gave themselves to other indians out of duty, to whites for money, and to blacks for pleasure (quoted in Bastide 1971, 74), and I found all over Colombia the idea, although not necessarily publicly expressed, that black women were *caliente*, hot, and black men sexually virile. Only some black women would play down black female sexuality, since this clearly impinged on their honor. This overlaps into another two-edged image about the family. In Colombia, relative to the interior of the country, areas such as the Pacific and Atlantic coastal regions have rather high rates of illegitimacy, consensual unions, series of consecutive unions between men and women, and polygyny. While scholarly studies have related this to historical and contemporary factors such as patterns of spatial mobility and the weak influence of the church (Gutiérrez de Pineda 1975; Friedemann 1974, 1985b; Pareja 1981; Barretto Reyes 1971; see also Whitten 1974), there is also a popular view that the "black family" is simply "disorganized" and improper (cf. Martin and Martin 1978; Engram 1982; McAdoo 1981). On the other hand, if blacks have a "disorganized" family life in which partners change frequently and men have more than one woman, does this not also say something about their sex lives? Both these images are double-edged: the supposed sexual powers may be a source of envy, but they can lead to accusations of immorality, especially against the women, and a "disorganized" family life can also be held to be a reason for lack of progress, since the men are said to be always after more women instead of working for a single family.

Physicality and sexuality are also linked through dance, because beautiful bodies that are prodigiously dexterous at guiding canoes in rushing rivers, or at gently panning away earth and sand so that only precious grains of gold remain, are also expert at dancing, and, as if the courtship of dance were not in itself enough, black dances are replete with "erotic movement" and "obscene words" (Cordovez

246

Moure 1957, 484) or with "shameless lubricity" (Samper, cited in
Peñas Galindo 1988, 59), or like the *mapalé* they are "a rite performed
before a cruel and grieving Eros" (Carrasquilla 1964, 2:65; see chapter 5). Carrasquilla's description is, however, nothing compared with
Bernardo Arias Trujillo's account of a black dance in his 1936 novel
Risaralda. Juancho and Rita are dancing the *currulao*, a Pacific coastal
dance "that is purely African":

> She shakes as if offering herself for pleasure, as if urging avidly to
> be possessed. He, in turn, quivering with desire, moves in the excited
> unrestrained way of the buck. . . . Her sensuous movements cause her
> savage and desirable breasts to undulate like spinning tops, their tips
> lewdly firm in a phallic-like erection, inviting and exciting the male to
> his own erection. (Translated and quoted by Richard Jackson 1976, 46)

This kind of treatment of black women in Latin American and Hispanic Afro-Caribbean literature is quite common, and the emphasis
is frequently on dance (see Venture Young 1977; Prescott 1985).

On a more prosaic level, in Unguía, where I was initiated into
the subtle skills of salsa and *vallenato* dancing, some Antioqueños
mentioned that they had at first been shocked by the local Chocoano
and Costeño dancing styles. There is a method of intimate dancing
described by the verb *covar*, a word used locally in mining to signify
the action of excavating a large hole with a metal-tipped pole, from
where gold-bearing gravels are extracted—the symbolism hardly
needs emphasizing. On the dance floor, the action is simply a close
dance, *en una sola baldosa*, on a single tile, in which the man insinu-
ates his thigh between those of the woman, as their hips and feet
move to the rhythm of the music. This kind of dance also occurs
in the interior of the country, where it is sometimes referred to as
serruchando, sawing, but it is more common in the Chocó or in *la
Costa*, where people participate in it at a younger age, and it does not
necessarily mean intimacy off the dance floor—to a greater extent
intimacy can be initiated on the dance floor alone. For all these reasons, Antioqueños tended to see it as rather licentious.

However, as one Colombian musicologist puts it, the music of the
coastal regions "heats the blood of the highland man, invades him
with irresponsible happiness and shakes him out of the prison in
which he lives" (Perdomo Escobar 1963, 277). In the interior of Colombia *música tropical*, which derives from Costeño and Caribbean
traditions, is also known as *música caliente*, hot music, and clearly
the various meanings of "hot," as in English, are not simply coinciden-
tal. So, if blacks waste their time, money, and energy on dance, music,
and fiesta, they may also be enjoying something from which the non-

black world is alienated and which it can yet recover, if only temporarily, via the blacks.

Of course, both faces of these double-sided images are culturally constructed: the reverse, so to speak, is no less an invention than the obverse; both have been hammered out in the history of relations between blacks, whites, and their mixed-blood intermediaries. The dynamic of construction is complex because it involves the intertwining of processes of a political and a moral nature. Blacks as a politically subordinate group could establish a world that was their own and constituted a de facto expression of exclusivity and separateness. As such, alien and apart, it was particularly able to take on the moral images that the nonblack world constructed upon it, which saw it as inferior and yet in some way endowed with potency. And this image of potency was built on the nature of the black world, which had inherited from Africa cultural forms that appeared to the whites sensuous and erotic.

The admiration for and fascination with black music and dance has a number of sources. If we look for a moment at images of black sexuality, it has been argued (Bastide 1961; Hernton 1965) that the sexual attractiveness of the black woman comes from the historical relation of dominance itself: since the white man could "use" the black woman without responsibility, she became the perfect sex object. Meanwhile, the black man's virility was, in Bastide's argument, an image created by the black man's real desire to revenge himself on white men by taking white women, or, according to Hernton, a white invention to justify the repression of black men as potential partners or seducers—and hence, if frustrated, attackers—of the white female and thus to deny them equality with the white man. I think these arguments, here somewhat caricatured, have some truth in them, although one would have to account for the fact that the indian population, despite being dominated and used sexually, albeit probably not in the same way, does not have the same sexual imagery surrounding it. But in any case, I am loath to completely reduce the fascination with black sexuality to underlying political relations. In the same way that Taussig (1987) has argued that shamanic healing powers are partly projected onto lowland jungle indians by other peoples, it seems to me that blacks in Africa or brought to the New World had certain cultural characteristics that made them good seedbeds for the cultivation of white colonial society's ideas about itself. The importance of music and dance in the black world was, and is, tremendously suggestive to a white culture that secretly fears its alienation from what it defines as baser, cruder aspects of life, even while it trumpets its achievements in more refined and "cultured" realms. There begins to grow in white society an ambivalent relationship to blacks in which they are seen as politically and morally inferior but at the same time possessed of special powers: images are projected onto black people and culture which are reflections of white society's relation to them and to itself. Of course, the blacks are far from passive screens for these images: not only did the seeds for this creation come from Africa itself and thus belong to them, but in the New World they have their own relationship to music and dance as well, and these can come to form a symbol of their own resistance to white domination and their own separateness from the white world—a separation that makes them seem all the more inaccessible and thus all the more fascinating. The possibility also exists for them to manipulate their understanding of the whites' understanding of them in order to reverse, albeit momentarily, the roles of domination and make the whites not only physically but morally slaves to their dexterity and prowess as dancers, casting them as clumsy outsiders in a small world of "natural" dancers or skillful sportspeople.

The role of domination in this dialectical process of construction of images is important in two ways. First, the whites have greater power to impose their own view of the matter: theirs can therefore be the official perspective. Part of the white view is, of course, constructed with a basis in their real material and political domination: the Chocó *is* poor and underdeveloped, for example. In addition, as will become evident, some blacks accept to a certain extent even negative images of themselves which are used to explain the Chocó's position, since these take on the status of facts that appear to be as self-evident as the material condition of their region. Second, the powers that the blacks are said to possess cannot be admitted to equal status with the powers that white society arrogates to itself: they are defined as base and crude, immoral and even evil, and must be kept down. The fact that this is all couched in a discourse of race is fundamental too. The discovery of physical difference and the creation of ideologies on that basis adds rigidity to hierarchical political stratification, since the symbol of social inferiority is a physical, and physically transmitted, one. And the idea of deeply ingrained physical distinctiveness also meshes perfectly with ideas about the physicality of dance, musical ability, and sexual power: *ritmo* (rhythm) and "hot blood" are construed as heritable qualities that, in the Colombian racial order, can be both diluted or preserved in the passing on from one generation to another.

These ideas are far removed from the written testimonials of Antioqueño students. But they are not so distant from remarks made to me

249

by both blacks and nonblacks in Unguía and Medellín about how blacks are sexually "hotter" or have music and rhythm "in the blood" or have "power and speed" on the sports field. Although the remarks generally had their positive and negative edges, one more prominent than the other depending on the context, when blacks delivered them there was more of a sense of pride and superiority, sometimes boastfulness, while when the speaker was not black, the space between the two edges was always more ambivalent, even if the remark was made with prejudicial intent. It seems to me that this ambivalence stems in some respects from the history of what some people in the white world feel about white culture and society and how complete these are or what is missing from them. The images that exist of blacks are social constructions, but the relationship to them is also a personal one: some people are more attracted and fascinated than others by black music and dance, just as only some people venture into the lowland jungles to get curing powers direct from the indian shamans, even though ideas about indian healing powers are widespread and advertisements for indian curers appear in the national press (Taussig 1987). The black realm is, perhaps, more difficult because of the more overtly racial ideology: it is fundamental that shamanism is an apprenticeship and that not all indians are masters, even though a nonindian shaman may inspire less credence than a "real indian"; in contrast, the discourse of race explicitly makes sex, music, and dance a natural "gift." The tendency, then, is for the white world to appropriate black powers as it can and transform them into whitened and more accessible versions for its own consumption.

The Rusticity and Potency of Chocoano Culture

Some of the ambivalence that emerges when images of blackness are examined also appears at the more specific level of Chocoano material culture. On the one hand, much of the culture of the Chocó is centered around ubiquitous, down-to-earth, day-to-day elements—the river, the canoe, the *batea,* the plantain—and the rustic, peasant nature of these items gives them low status in the national cultural hierarchy. Interestingly, representations of Antioqueño identity also rely heavily on symbols of rustic, peasant culture, but in this case, the context of these symbols gives them a rather different meaning. Antioqueño identity makes much of rustic, peasant accouterments, but whereas the Chocoano elements are more like an index, that is, they are part and parcel of Chocoano culture like smoke is of fire, the Antioqueño elements—the *carriel,* the poncho, the *aguadeño* hat, the rope-soled sandals—are not only this but have also been elevated to the status of symbols that represent Antioqueño culture as a synthetic whole, removed from its local peasant environment into a bustling national-level industrial, commercial, and urban one: in contrast, the Chocoano elements remain completely *rustic* in meaning. In his writings on the central importance of the canoe in Chocoano culture, Velásquez says, "When a man of the elite sees in what we have written an image of the barbarous past of the black, another of dark skin . . . will take it as a sign of the advanced achievements of the [black] race" (1959, 124), and such may be the case, but the fact remains that national culture defines Chocoano culture as primitive and Antioqueño culture as advanced, even though representations of the latter still make use of rustic symbols. The location of rusticity with respect to the regional culture as a whole is very different in each case. One can come into contact with the rustic, peasant side of Antioqueño culture in the comfort of a traditional Antioqueño restaurant in Medellín. To make contact with Chocoano canoes, one has to get into one on a Chocoano river. In other words, whereas the Antioqueños use rusticity to represent a culture that has become as much commercial, industrial, and urban as peasant, the Chocoanos hardly use rustic images at all in public expressions of their identity, while on the other hand, other aspects of their identity—canoes, rivers, *bateas*—actually *are* their peasant cultural baggage. Having rich economic and symbolic capital in the national hierarchy of values, the Antioqueños can afford to play upon the rustic elements of their culture, as if looking back benignly to a rosy past. Being themselves predominantly peasant, the Chocoanos cannot afford this luxury.

On the other hand, however, certain products from the Pacific coast have acquired national fame. One is the *chontaduro* (peach palm nut), the other a rather unusual fruit called the *borojó*, which belongs to the coffee family but is close in size to a large grapefruit, green and hard when unripe, brown and soft when mature. Both fruits are rather special. The *chontaduro* palm tree is completely bristled with long, extremely sharp spines; its fruit, once conquered, contains a large variety of vitamins and proteins; it must be cooked, however, or it will lacerate the mouth. The *borojó*, despite being a fruit, has the strange quality of never rotting—it simply gets softer and softer; it is consumed as a juice and also has a phenomenal quantity of vitamins and proteins; it has been reported by some researchers to have anticarcinogenic qualities. On the Pacific coast and in the interior, both fruits fetch high prices—and both are popularly believed to increase sexual potency and have aphrodisiac effects. I would argue that there is not merely a chance connection between the powerful fruits of the Pacific coast and a society where men have dozens of children by different women, women change male partners several times, and where the "music heats the blood of the highland man." It is a connection constructed by a culture fascinated by the sexual powers attributed to the blacks and, of course, reconstructed by the black men (if not so much by the women) in their understanding of how the whites have understood them.

14

Images of Blackness:

The View from Below

In New York, when I walk along the street, white women tighten their arms around their bags. I understand, but it gets real tiring.

Faced with the kind of images of blackness described in the previous chapter, which take their logical place in the overall racial order of Colombia, blacks react in ways that can always be made sense of in that order, whether or not the meanings they attribute to their own actions are consciously placed within it. In the context of an environment economically and culturally dominated by the Antioqueños, such as Unguía or, even more, Medellín, these reactions confront in an everyday fashion the possibilities of both racism and *blanqueamiento*. In this chapter, I examine some testimonies from the Chocoanos in Unguía and Medellín to see how they think about how the Antioqueños think about them.

Chocoanos in Unguía

Of the twenty-one Chocoano school students in Unguía, half agreed that Chocoanos in general were not of a progressive attitude of mind or were negligent or lazy. Six others stressed their ability for hard manual work, an observation that only partly contradicts the previous image in that, as one girl wrote, "the majority of Chocoanos work, but they don't progress." Half stressed that Chocoanos were *rum-*

Epigraph: Comment by a middle-class black New Yorker, *Independent,* 4 June 1990, p. 16.

253

beros, or party lovers, liked dancing, and so on. However, six also pointed out that education was a fundamental value: "With respect to the education of their children or their siblings, they are capable of working to the utmost [to achieve this]." Perhaps interestingly, one of the most dogmatic statements came from the rector of the school, a Chocoano himself, who participated in the exercise: Chocoanos were "negligent, lazy, extrovert, not progressive, fond of fiestas and other pleasures." One girl wrote:

1. Laziness. I say laziness because we Chocoanos, having land to work, are overcome by laziness, and we don't work but rather sell the land if possible in order to go to the city because we think the city is great and we're not going to work hard.
2. We don't like to progress, and instead we always live badly, even if we've got the means to build a good house.

There is a clear tendency here to adopt at least some of the images about blacks which are propagated by the nonblack world.

Their views about Antioqueños in Unguía were also ambivalent. On the one hand, more than half said they were racist: "they tend to be racist . . . they don't like to get together with Chocoanos . . . they think they're a bit superior." The *paisas* were also identified as dominant and overweaning: "they like to have the advantage . . . the *paisa* is always on top of the Chocoano . . . if there's a Chocoano who's living more or less well, they look down on him, because they think the Chocoano will get on top of them; they'll propose a deal to him so he won't finish what he'd thought of doing . . . the *paisa* is very racist, but he'll look for a Chocoano sometimes as a worker . . . most of them follow the old traditions, like that they can't associate with blacks because they'll turn black themselves . . . they have all the advantages, they fleece us day by day, with time I think they'll take over this town . . . they always want to be on top." Five Chocoanos noted that Antioqueños "are very fond of money . . . they have a desperate ambition to get money," while eight also emphasized that the *paisas* were aggressive and always involved in fights and problems. On the other hand, they also had some complimentary things to say about the Antioqueños: "progressive, work hard, overcome obstacles . . . helpful, do their best for the progress of the area, straightforward . . . collaborate with the town." However, although five mentioned their forward-looking approach, only a couple said that they were helpful and collaborative: the predominant feeling was of the Antioqueños as racist and aggressive intruders. The Chocoanos were also less complacent than the Antioqueño students about the harmoniousness of marriage and ethnic interaction, since as many saw problems in these respects as did not, usually pointing out the Antioqueños' racism as an obstacle to harmony.

These reactions highlight two things. First, a good deal of antagonism exists towards people who are seen as progressive and hardworking but also as exploitative and often racist. This is interesting especially in view of the lack of ethnic segregation within the school. Clearly, the particular circumstance of the Chocoanos' and the Costeños' dominance in the school did not soften their perception of the reality of town life. Second, despite this antagonism, there is still a tendency among Chocoanos to refer to perceived traits of Chocoano culture in a negative, blame-the-victim fashion. Antioqueños are resented in a particular, local way, but overall hierarchies of nonblack superiority and black inferiority in terms of "progress" are accepted at deeper level. Clearly, the pervasiveness of these hierarchies reinforces potential motives of *blanqueamiento* among the blacks themselves.

Chocoanos in Medellín

The Chocoano university students in Medellín were asked to write about their experiences in the city. (See appendix C for full transcriptions of selected written responses.) As before, there was a varied reaction. Out of nineteen replies, twelve women and seven men (which included two people born of Chocoano parents in Medellín), eleven said racism of some sort existed, with roughly equal proportions of men and women responding in this way. Racism could be a minor consideration: "they throw out unpleasant remarks because of my color . . . they call out *mono* [here "blondie," but also monkey] in the street . . . student colleagues look down on one simply because of being black . . . they shout out nasty things in the street." Or more severe: "people think black is the worst thing . . . they think all [black] women are cooks . . . blacks are discriminated against in educational establishments by the teachers and the students . . . they think Chocoanos are uncultured and immoral and you hear phrases like 'It's going to be difficult for him to leave his loincloth and come down from the trees' . . . they give us practically no opportunity, they try and exclude us from everything, giving us to understand that we are incompetent . . . they think that blacks are just servants and can't study or progress." One woman was approached by a man in the street and asked if she wanted work as a domestic servant. She replied, "Sure, if you'll pay the fees at the two universities where I study," at which the man "went pale and apologized."

But five others said that they had not experienced any racism: "I've had no problems with racial discrimination . . . I can't complain, because I've been treated well . . . I don't feel discriminated against, perhaps that happens to domestic workers who are looked on as of little importance . . . my life as a black person has been marvelous . . . I haven't felt the racial discrimination I was expecting." And many of those who did emphasize racism made qualifying remarks, pointing out that not all Antioqueños were racist, that racism was due to ignorance and lack of education, that Antioqueños accepted educated Chocoanos more. One commented: "More and more they are accepting the blacks in their society, because the blacks show their worth and people recognize this." Another said: "When you show them [student colleagues] that you have the same abilities as them, they accept you, but still with distrust." A couple noted that it was a question of regionalism more than racism, but one acutely noted that for the Chocoanos, regionalism, social discrimination, and racial discrimination all worked in unison. However, lingering distrust was detectable: "My Antioqueño friends accept me because they've got used to living alongside me, but I never trust them completely because they usually look down on other blacks"—here, precisely, is the individualistic acceptance of the black. Another said, "You register all the cases [of racism] and just don't take any notice." This hardening of the skin was a reaction I found frequently in my interviews with blacks. Also frequent in interviews were comments such as "*Yo trato con quien me trata, y no con quien no me trata*" (I have contact with whoever makes contact with me, and not with those who don't), a formula that clearly leaves all initiative in social interaction to the Antioqueños and avoids potential rejections as much as possible. So, if among those who emphasized racism there were qualifying observations, there was also a tendency among those who did not emphasize it to avoid the issue by turning their back on the matter. One or two also blamed the blacks themselves: "I think the Chocoanos feel bad here in Medellín because of their sour nature and because some are quite aggressive and foul-mouthed." Or, as one woman told me: "It's 30 percent a rejection from them and 50 percent that we ourselves withdraw."

Basic Patterns of Personal Identity

A pattern begins to emerge which is by now familiar. There is a clear ideological hegemony that underlies everyone's images of race and region: the white regions are more wealthy, more powerful, and healthier and therefore "more civilized" and "superior"; the black regions, and especially the Pacific coast as the blackest region, are seen as poor, underdeveloped, and "primitive." These images have the status of self-evident truths, and the power of the hegemony is such that some blacks accept ideas, linked into the hegemonic complex but at a more contestable level, about blacks being lazy and unprogressive in attitude. Firmly linked to ideas about race and region, but also going beyond them, is the powerful notion of blackness being a primary signal of lower-class status which has to be specifically renegotiated in particular cases in order to be avoided. However, crucially, racism is not thoroughgoing: there are opportunities for acceptance; not everyone applies stereotypes to blacks in an immediate or rigid fashion; the meaning of blackness can be recast more easily for some nonblacks than for others. Context makes an important difference. In Medellín, for example, where blacks are a tiny minority, there was evidence of greater conditional acceptance of blacks, especially well-educated blacks, than in Unguía, where they are a much bigger aggregate and the Antioqueños are in an important sense the intruders.

Blacks tend to take two main directions in the face of this situation, without there being a radical split between these alternatives. On the one hand, there is nucleation and black community, the elaboration of forms of black culture, and a certain resistance against assimilating nonblack culture wholesale. On the other hand, there is adaptation and more definite assimilation, perhaps eventually resulting in a union with a nonblack which will set offspring more firmly on this road. The former option tends to be associated with a strong awareness of racial discrimination and often with what the Antioqueños call being *acomplejado,* that is, having a "complex" about one's blackness. The second, while not necessarily denying racism, tends to play it down, emphasizes instead the need to adapt, and may blame blacks for their situation. These different paths, presented here in a simple fashion, are in reality complex processes, as previous chapters have shown. To begin with, they are structured by other levels, so that in Medellín, for example, these ethnic options are structured by urban processes: economic position, familiarization with the city, and family cycle influence choices in this respect. On a grander scale, the various economic, political, and demographic forces at work in the different histories of *la Costa,* Antioquia, and the Chocó have structured these ethnic processes in very different ways (see chapters 4, 5, and 6). Second, people can take up ambiguous positions with respect to these options, adapting in some ways but not in others. For example, some individuals may play Chocoano identity down in the company of Antioqueño workmates but reaffirm it in the presence of Chocoano kin or friends. Or again, a few blacks adopt an overtly political discourse about the positive value of black culture and the need for black consciousness, while others tend to live Chocoano identity in a practical, everyday fashion. Third, what counts as nucleation and black community or as adaptation is, of course, context dependent and historically variable: going to the Salón Suizo in Medellín is a form of black community in the context of the city, while the same people might be seen as culturally assimilated to Antioqueño behavior by their relatives back in the Chocó—it is a basic feature of ethnic identity that its markers and symbols have meaning in a specific context. This also derives from the nature of the cultural dynamics of the Colombian racial order outlined in chapter 1, in which what is "black," "white," or "mestizo" culture is subject to shifting claims and ascriptions in the context of hierarchical black/nonblack ethnic interactions. Fourth, these processes occur at different levels. They structure both individuals' choices and the history of the dynamics of black culture in general, although these levels are, of course, linked in a mutually generative relationship. Part of the argument of this book is that the historical patterns of race mixture and cultural transformation of Colombia's regions, and the contemporary patterns of these processes as seen in Unguía and Medellín, and the personal experiences of individual people with respect to their racial identity must all be understood within the context of the same basic order.

I explore the cultural dynamics of these two processes in more depth in the next chapters. Here I illustrate them with interview material that captures them at an individual level by showing the different orientations of two Chocoano students at the same university. The first, a man, has an attitude that, in the context of Medellín, falls within the black community option. This material is taken from an interview (March 1987), recorded partly by tape and partly by note taking. I have removed my questions and other extraneous matter and present the interview in a condensed form.

> The thing is that the Antioqueños have a contempt for blacks which comes from their childhood; it's really rooted in them, deep down. They see the black as a bad sort of person, a thief. If we treated the Antioqueños like they treated us, there would be a war on: they say to your face "a black is a black [and that's all there is to it]" . . . they let slip any old racist comment.
>
> The first years here were very tough. When I used to see a woman coming towards me shift her handbag from one side to the other [to forestall a possible theft], I used to feel really bad. I would try and cross the street to avoid it happening: I'd walk down the middle of the street rather than on the sidewalks. With time, you get used to it: you don't accept it, but it comes to be a daily thing, and you stop taking any notice—nowadays I'll go anywhere. In the university, it's different: you

study and show that you're a good student, and you earn respect—and people do respect you.

[But distrust remains:] I had a friend here and she was okay with me in the university, but once I ran into her in the street with her family, and she tried to avoid saying hello to me: I'm certain—because you can just tell—I'm sure it was because of being black. Another time, I was doing a course on accounting, and there was this Antioqueño girl who started to stick around with me. She would always sit next to me; when the exams came, she had my place ready right next to her. At first, I swallowed the story and I helped her, I'd give her the answers in the exams, I'd help her to study, and all that. And then, when she didn't need me any more, all at once *me trató de negro* [she treated me like a black, i.e., contemptuously].

If you go around with Antioqueño people, you become infected a bit with their own attitude towards the blacks, and you begin to think like they do and look at other blacks with scorn. At first, I went around with a group of Antioqueño friends, but I put the brakes on when I realized what was happening. And if you look at the Chocoanos who are always with Antioqueños, you can see the change in them over the years.

If you go to an Antioqueño house you feel timid, you're watching everything you do and you do everything timidly. But when I'm with three or four paisanos I feel good, I feel happy, free, like without any clothes. In the Suizo or among one's own people you can shout, behave as you're used to, use nicknames, call out to a friend from the other side of the room, and all that: you feel in your element. I think the people go there because they feel good there. And the domestic servants—in other places they whistle at them and make fun of them, so they go where no one whistles and no one makes fun of them.

This man is what many Antioqueños would call *acomplejado:* in their view, his interpretation of events would be oversensitive and inaccurate, too ready to ascribe to people motives connected to his racial identity. From his point of view, he senses their deep-seated and often dissimulated disrespect for him as a black—"because you can just tell." He is aware of the possibility of winning conditional acceptance through equaling or bettering the Antioqueños in the acquisition of values that they too respect, such as education, but he senses also the barriers behind this, especially at a personal, family level. Here, one may suddenly be *tratado de negro*. *Tratar de* means to address someone, and hence to treat someone, in a particular way: *él me trata de usted* means "he addresses me as *usted*," that is, with the polite personal pronoun and hence with respect. *Tratar de negro* is thus both to call someone a black (to their face) and to treat them "like a black," that is, contemptuously. It is interesting here that even this man, who would contest strongly the very premise on which this trope relies for its force—that to call someone a black is equivalent to disrespect—uses it to convey his meaning. However, the connotations of the term *negro* are quite complex and need elaborating in this context. To call someone a black to his or her face is not always taken as a sign of disrespect: its meaning is highly context dependent, which is not to say arbitrary. Indeed, in its various uses there is a central reference to inequality. For example, *negro* can be used as a friendly term of address to people easily classifiable as "black." The friendliness, however, draws its power precisely from the contravention of a more basic meaning: intimacy is implied by the ability to use a potentially derogatory term without derogation. The same goes for the term *negra* or *negrita* used as a sign of intimacy or endearment from men to women, including women who would not generally be classed as "black." In this case, a power difference between men and women is also asserted by referring implicitly to the power difference that typically exists between black and white. The connotations are of intimacy but also of paternalism, dependence, and service. Similarly, *negro* may be applied as a family nickname to a son or daughter with darker skin or hair than others in the family, even if the person would not normally be classed by others as "black." But in this context, the term tends to be used for members who are junior in a sibling set, thus again referring to hierarchical difference, this time of age. *Negro,* then, may not convey disrespect, but its various meanings as a term of address are underlain by a central concept of lower position on a hierarchical scale. It is to this more basic meaning that the woman in the anecdote above returned when she began to *tratar* this man *de negro,* the more basic level that underlies the conditional nature of nonblack acceptance.

This informant perceives that the process of black assimilation into the nonblack world can entail adopting disparaging attitudes towards blackness. A black person may be accepted by Antioqueños, but it is an acceptance conditional on adopting nonblack culture and attitudes, and inevitably this implies accepting ideas about black inferiority—ideas that may already be part of a black person's views about blacks as a category. Many blacks would see nothing exceptionable about this: some blacks *are* uncultured, they might argue, and cultured blacks have every right to look down on their untutored cousins. Others, construing blacks as, despite everything, linked together in some fundamental way, understand any attack on some blacks to include all blacks, and they see such an attitude as a hypocritical betrayal and/or a cowardly self-denigration. The latter approach is obviously strengthened by the very nature of racial identifications that inherently make evaluations of a categorical kind. The informant in this interview tends towards the second approach, and he rejects the adoption of Antioqueño attitudes to blacks, not by totally rejecting Antioqueño culture—which he inevitably adopts to some extent—but by purposely joining into the nuclei of black community which exist in Medellín—for example, the Salón Suizo. In this way, he participates in the perpetuation of black culture and makes a positive statement about its value and about his solidarity with other blacks.

The second person, a woman, has a rather different attitude. This interview material was recorded by note taking in March 1987 and is presented in the same way as the previous case.

> It's 30 percent that they reject us and 50 percent that we ourselves withdraw. I haven't felt any kind of rejection in the five years I've been here, but Medellín is really tough—friends tell you, you realize. They think that all black women are domestic servants: you get on a bus on a Sunday and they begin to ask you where you work, how much you earn, and all that. You say you're studying and they're surprised.
>
> It hasn't happened to me, thank goodness, but a lot of times when you get yourself a white boyfriend, it may be that you don't feel any kind of rejection from him, because love is created between the two of you, but with the family—it's a different story. They might like you as a friend, but right there in the bosom of the family—forget it. In Bogotá it's not like that, but here in Medellín in 90 percent of cases that's the way it is. I have a lot of admirers here—*cachacos* [people from the interior, i.e., whites], but I don't take any notice of them—because of the family.
>
> I go to dance classes, guitar classes, and so on, and often I'm the only black there. In the matriculation party here, I was the only black who came: the others said, "What a bore." So they withdraw out of fear of rejection. If it's one of our dances, it's nothing but blacks, there are no *cachacos;* and if it's a *cachaco* dance, the blacks say, "What a bore." But I don't withdraw: you have to link into the environment you're living in. In guitar and dance classes, I'm the only black.
>
> And if your paisanos see you talking with the *cachacos,* they start saying, "Now you don't want to talk to your own paisanos any more"—the comments start. But to have a little group of Chocoanos here and another little group of *cachacos* over there—that looks really bad.
>
> Take the servant girls. They come straight from the countryside and arrive here and say they're from Quibdó [i.e., the town]. And the people from the country talk in an irritating way and so on—so the people from around here think we're all like that. They come to a city like this straight from the country, and all at once they think that this is the life

for them. So they begin to talk differently and put on airs—I don't like talking to people like that. So I say, become a bit more cultured and then we'll talk.

This woman, although she admits the impact of racism, has an attitude very different from that of the man, whom she knows personally and in opposition to whom she is, to some extent, defining herself, although he was not present at the time. Her position is full of contradictions. She denies having felt rejection yet admits that people have taken her for a domestic servant on the bus. She insists that Chocoanos should make the effort to integrate and adapt, but she also purposely restricts her social encounters with men in order to avoid possible problems with the families of white boyfriends. Like the man above, she anticipates the limits to the acceptance that she is banking on, but her reaction is simply to continue attempts at fitting in. She interprets other blacks' separatist tendencies as "fear of rejection" (which ironically she admits to herself), which is equivalent to the accusation of *acomplejado,* without linking this to the actual rejection she herself knows to exist. Separatism to her is simply destructive, although, again, she actually practices it herself on a more intimate level. She resents the criticisms made of her by blacks when they notice her tendency to associate with Antioqueños. From the man's point of view, above, she is potentially becoming "infected" with the Antioqueños' attitudes. Indeed, her disparaging comments about the domestic servants and their "airs" would doubtless be interpreted in just this light by the man, who, in contrast, takes a much more sympathetic view of them, despite their class differences, and sometimes socializes in the same bar as them. For her, the idea is to become "more cultured"—which in this context also means more adapted to Antioqueño ways—and she sees no reason why she should identify herself with blacks in general just because she is also black. Domestic servants are one thing, she is another, and there is no essential equality between them because of their racial identity. Interestingly, she holds this view even though she herself has been identified as a domestic servant by Antioqueños.

There are great contradictions underlying this woman's ideas about herself, blackness, and nonblackness. The source of these is not some lack of insight or wrongheadedness on her part. She sees herself as a person like any other, rejects her own color as a locus of social identity, and wants to integrate into her surrounding social milieu. All of these are coherent stances. The contradictions derive from the nature of the racial order in which such stances are accepted and simultaneously denied or limited, in which blacks are made a social category and seen as inferior while they are also accepted "like any other person," but conditionally and without their blackness really being forgotten.

Another telling example of these different options is from a Chocoano family in La Iguaná. There were two daughters, both born in Medellín and largely raised in La Iguaná. One was lighter skinned and prettier, the other blacker and not so attractive. The latter lived in La Playita with a Chocoano common-law husband and was actively involved in the Chocoano networks in that part of the barrio, playing cards and bingo there in the afternoons and going to the *bailaderos* on the weekends. She also visited the Chocó from time to time with her husband. Her sister explicitly rejected the idea of a black boyfriend and said of La Playita, "I don't like living up there. They don't like me there, they say I'm stuck up and all that, but they're so *alborotados* [rowdy] there, and that smell of fish . . ." Her friends were Antioqueños, and she lived in the central part of the barrio, well away from the concentrations of Chocoanos. Some writers on Latin America have dismissed racism, saying that racial variation within a single family is too great to allow it: here race enters the very heart of the family. The lighter-colored daughter was firmly on the road to *blanqueamiento,* both social and, she hoped, physical. Her attitude was understood by many other blacks as a pretension to superiority and hence as a disparagement of blackness and black culture. The darker daughter was, in contrast, in the heart of black community, reestablishing links with the Chocó stronger than those her own parents had since allowed to fall into disuse. I would argue that the courses followed by these two women were strongly influenced by their own understandings of their location in the local racial order and the possibilities open to them there.

Cicatrices: Scars

Jairo Varela, Chocoano and leader of the well-known salsa band Grupo Niche, has a song, "Cicatrices" (Scars), which touches on all these themes, and its lyrics are indicative of all the ambiguity and complexity surrounding the two basic orientations I have outlined (Varela 1985).

Toda la gente que vino de Africa	All the people who came from Africa
Es de raza negra	Are of the black race
La misma que Ud. que no es negro	The same one that you, who isn't black

Le llama morena	Calls brown
Tal vez por pena, tal vez por decencia	Perhaps from pity, perhaps from politeness
Busque la manera	You seek a way
De no herir a este negro que un día	Not to offend this black who was once
Fue puesto en cadenas	Put in chains
Su actitud la perdono	Your attitude I will pardon
Mas no comparto con ella	But share it I will not
Pues hay otros que sin conocerme	Since others without knowing me
Se estrellan, qué pena	Ride roughshod, what a pity
Que me llamen negrito, lo acepto	To be called negrito I will accept
Lo acepto a poquitos	I will accept from very few
De pronto formo al alboroto	I may make a fuss
Depende del tonito	It just depends on the tone
Fueron años de dura lucha	There were years of hard struggle
Buscando un mañana	Searching for a future
Y agradezco el gesto que tuvieron	And I am thankful for the gestures
Personas hermanas	Of brotherly people
Que su sangre la dieron por una causa	Who gave their blood for a cause
Por mis derechos	For my rights
Y no es justo que ya cualquiera	And it is not right that anyone should
Olvide aquellos hechos	Forget these deeds
(Chorus)	(Chorus)
Adónde parará?	Where will it end?
El tiempo lo dirá	Only time can tell
Uno tenía herida sana	One had a healed wound
Y otro la destapa más	And someone uncovers [opens] it more
Yo les he pedido a Changó	I have asked Changó
A Changó y a Yemayá	Changó and Yemayá
Que no cambien mi pigmento	Not to change my color
Porque esto se va a acabar	Because this is going to end
Tiene que acabar	It has to end

Yo que de Africa lejana	I who from distant Africa
Me vine con mi tambor	Came with my drum
Trayéndoles un mensaje	Bringing a message
De lucha, paz y amor	Of struggle, peace and love
Han pasado cinco siglos	Five centuries have gone by
Que mi cuero aquí sonó	Since my drum first sounded here
Agradezco al cielo y a mi gente	I thank heaven and my people
Al pueblo que me esperó	And the people who waited for me

(Interjection: *Que no agite mucho la botella: porque con la tapa, se vuelan las manos.* Don't shake the bottle: the cap will blow your hands off.)

Da me fe, que la esperanza	Give me faith, for hope
En gemido se quedó	Lies groaning
Dame paz, que otro rumbo	Give me peace, for today my life
Hoy mi vida ya tomó	Has taken another path
Dame la gracia, que en tu seno	Give me favor, for one day
Algún día estaré	I will be in your heart
Dame amor, que yo esto en odio	Give me love, for I do not
No deseo terminar	Want this to end in hate

This song has all kinds of contradictory messages. On the one hand, there are references to African origins and qualified rejections of the condescending *negrito* and of the euphemistic *moreno* (brown) in favor of *negro* (black). Tellingly, he refers to the various possible meanings that the term *negro* can carry by identifying the tone of voice as the crucial indicator of context. There are also requests to Changó and Yemayá, Yoruba gods who, among other things, form part of Cuban *santería* and Brazilian *candomblé* ceremonies, not to whiten him since "this [the downtrodden position of the blacks] has to end." Ominous warnings are given to others not to "shake the bottle," that is, push the blacks too far, because an explosion might result. And pleas are made for faith because "hope [of respite] lies groaning." All this is clearly within the orientation that reaffirms blackness and its worth—here a central value is the African drum and its message. In these references, there is little indication of an attitude of assimilation, and nonblack society appears in confrontation with the black world. On the other hand, we hear that the old wound (i.e., slavery, or perhaps the fact of being black) has healed: only the activities of an unspecified other (e.g., a racist nonblack) uncover or reopen the scar. Here confrontation remains, but it is created unilaterally by nonblacks rather than by the blacks themselves. For the latter, better things await *en tu seno,* in the heart of society. Fraternal gestures from nonblacks are appreciated, and thanks are given to *el pueblo,* the people of Colombia, who waited for the blacks in their struggle. Finally, confrontation is abandoned in the last request for love and the avoidance of hate. This all seems to be located within the framework of adaptation and reconciliation. The song vividly captures both the reaffirmation of blackness and the desire for integration. This may be contradictory, but the contradiction is only in the context of the past and present orientations of black Colombians vis-à-vis nonblack society. Seen anew, there is no contradiction: Varela is simply asking for blacks to be accepted and integrated wholesale *as blacks.* He is, in effect, demanding the overturning of a racial order in which blacks are integrated only through a process of *blanqueamiento.*

15

The Black Community

and Music

Yo soy parrandero y qué? A nadie le importa.

In the context of the New World, Colombian blacks are relatively distanced from their African cultural heritage. Although Jairo Varela might address Changó and Yemayá in his song "Cicatrices," and while the black author and scholar Manuel Zapata Olivella might title his recent novel *Changó, el gran putas,* there is no contemporary popular tradition of calling upon African gods as there is in Cuba, Brazil, or Haiti—with the sole exception of the invocation of the Bantu god Calunga in the rituals of Lumbalú, the funerary society of Palenque de San Basilio (Escalante 1954; Friedemann and Patiño Rosselli 1983, 71). Rather, the main symbolism of black religious expression in Colombia is Catholic (Atencio Babilonia and Castellanos Córdova 1982; Velásquez 1961b; Price 1955). This is not to deny that there are many cultural features in Colombia traceable to Africa: the musical *style,* if not the form and the content, of much black music is very African (Lomax 1970; List 1980 and 1983, 566); the Congo dances and the masks of the carnival of Barranquilla clearly have strong African origins (Friedemann 1978, 1985a); Herskovits reckoned that magic and folklore in the Chocó were "quite African" in terms of his controversial five-level scale (1966, 53). Clearly the Africans imported into Colombia had a major impact on the evolution of Colombian culture, especially along the two littorals but also elsewhere (Friedemann

Epigraph: Roughly translatable as "I'm a party lover, and it ain't nobody's business but my own"; the opening line of a *vallenato* song that won particular favor in the estimation of my friend Carlos Pino.

267

1978; Escalante 1964; Arboleda Llorente 1950; Zapata Olivella 1967; Granda 1977). In keeping with nationalist ideologies of *mestizaje*, understood as *blanqueamiento*, African contributions to Colombian culture have generally been ignored, and recent investigation has done a great deal to uncover this (Friedemann 1984a); the fact remains, however, that "black culture" in Colombia is itself a tri-ethnic mix with strong Spanish and indigenous contributions and that the very overt Africanism of Cuban, Haitian, and Brazilian black culture is lacking (Price 1954).

"Black culture" is not, of course, a self-evident category. In Colombia, as in other Latin American countries with significant black populations, the culture of black people seems the same in many respects as that of nonblacks. Especially in Colombia, black culture is highly Hispanicized. This is to miss, however, the subtle ways in which black people, living in black regions, have molded their own cultural forms out of Hispanic cultural traditions, often with traceable African influences at work in the process. As with the category "black" itself, there are certain regional contexts in which the cultural patterns of black populations are distinctive. In the Pacific coast region, family structures, while similar to those of nonblacks in other areas, are rather different: for example, polygyny is not only present but quite overt, informal unions are more frequent, and so on. Patron saint festivals, again very similar to those of the interior, are distinctive: the church is a more muted presence, and music and dance have a more central place. Music and dance are themselves distinctive, as we shall see. Ultimately, there is no easily demarcated national "black culture" but rather localized cultures, with more or less African influences, practiced by people who are more or less "black." Hence, at its boundaries black culture is in a constant state of negotiation, and black and nonblack Colombians themselves use these cultural differences to help establish ethnic distinctions in specific contexts. In this sense, "black culture" is contextually defined. The absence of the strict racial boundaries of North American society has resulted in a less distinctive and certainly less "ghettoized" form of black culture, one that instead feeds into the nonblack world across blurred boundaries. But this does not mean that within Latin American culture black cultural forms do not have a specific and distinctive pattern. Blacks have elaborated their own culture using elements from all three initial cultures. Right from the start there have been important processes of regrouping and nucleation of black people, creating physical concentration and cultural crucibles for the construction of blackness within the New Granadian and then Colombian framework of *mestizaje* with its hierarchy of racial status.

In this chapter, I look at black community not simply as it is structured by mainly economic processes but as an aspect of black cultural identity which has emerged partly out of blacks being thrust together in certain regional and local contexts and partly as a de facto means of defense and a statement of separateness and resistance to domination, although the overtness and aggressiveness of this have varied over time. I use music as the cultural focus for this argument, seeing the process of musical syncretism or creolization as an arena for the cultural dynamics of the racial order; and I argue that what happens in Medellín with black community and music is a version of the larger-scale processes I outline for music in general.

Nucleation and Black Community

Nucleation and black community have taken different forms: *palenques* are a major one, along with *cabildos* (see chapter 5). On a larger and more continuous scale, nucleation has manifested itself through processes of the spatial distribution of race, wealth, and power: hence the concentration of blacks in certain areas, along the littorals and in certain areas of the two big river valleys of the Cauca and the Magdalena. Through complex historical processes, blacks are kept in or relegated to, but also may try to maintain their independence in, these areas. All along the Pacific coast, they were kept in the region by the Spanish until emancipation, when the area was left to them as an inhospitable and insalubrious area into which whites only dipped for commercial and extractive purposes: black labor was defined as refractory, unwilling, and lazy. The blacks were rejected by postemancipation republican society and largely stayed where they were, a choice made in a context of limited options. In the Atlantic coastal region, blacks were initially used in agriculture, cattle raising, and urban services. There was much more opportunity for race mixture, but those who remained black tended to concentrate along the coast itself or in the poorest barrios of Cartagena, or to a lesser extent in the low marshy areas around the river Magdalena: in each case, black people tended to take up, or be pushed into, niches that were ecologically rather marginal as far as the dominant white population was concerned, specifically the coastal strip, which is the only area, especially outside the towns, where blackness is a visibly predominant presence. In Antioquia, the blacker parts of the population concentrated in the lower, hotter mining districts of the northeast of the department, while race mixture whitewashed the highland blacks. In the Cauca Valley north and south of Cali, after manumission, while some blacks remained on the haciendas as dependent workers or tenants, many refused to work for the whites and moved away into more remote areas (Mina 1975; Taussig 1980a, 51; Friedemann 1976), although as time went on, the blacks became increasingly hemmed in by expanding haciendas and, after these, sugarcane plantations and were constantly badgered by hacienda owners seeking to combat their labor shortage.

In all these cases, the concentration of blacks has been the outcome of both black and white choices and has been intertwined with local economic, political, and demographic processes that influence the nature of the regrouping. In Medellín, it is possible to see the same pattern in the form of the kind of nuclei which I have already described, whether these are residential, like La Playita or Zafra, or temporary, like El Salón Suizo and the Parque Berrío on Sundays. These nuclei exist for the practical reasons I described in chapters 11 and 12. But these practical aspects are interwoven with the fact, signified precisely by the ethnic nature of the network, that the Chocoanos are black migrants to a "white" city. They come in awareness of the position of their territory in the national hierarchy, of their rough rural ways if they are coming from the countryside, of the way blacks and black culture are classified in the interior, and of the way the Antioqueños behave in the Chocó. They enter what is, in the words of one Chocoano student, "another world" for many of them. So their recourse to paisanos is not just because they are kin or because they come from the same village or river. They turn to paisanos for both utilitarian help and moral support because they are blacks together who may distrust, and be distrusted by, Antioqueños, although this is not inevitable, as I have already shown. Getting together in nuclei and creating dense, tightly woven patches within the whole ethnic network—which, after all, stretches way beyond these nuclei— is a means of constructing a defense for one's blackness and of creating another small world in which being black is again the normal state of affairs. Equally, there is also an attempt to create a world in which enacting black, or more precisely Chocoano, culture is a normal state of affairs as well. Recall the remarks made by the Chocoano student: "If you go to an Antioqueño house, you feel ill at ease, anxious about how you're going to do everything; if I'm with my paisanos, I feel free, happy. In the Suizo you can shout and behave like you're used to behaving . . . you feel in your element." I think it goes even further than feeling more at ease among one's paisanos: there is also an attempt to claim a cultural space in the city—whether in La Iguaná, El Centro, or El Suizo—which belongs to the Chocoanos and where they can define morality and social behavior by means of their own social processes. Of course, these are never, in fact, independent of Antioqueño society and culture: the point is that they should not appear to be totally dominated by them. In this sense, black culture is being defended in the very act of re-creating it within a black nucleus. This is not to say that Chocoanos purposively politicize their daily behavior into acts of resistance, but simply that behavior carries with it ideas, albeit implicit, about morality, social values, and personal identity, ideas that are necessarily located in relation to other sets of ideas with which they may be in conflict. Thus it is no surprise that some Antioqueños resist what they see as an attack on their cultural and moral authority, and they complain about Chocoano "invasions" of El Centro or stone Chocoano *bailaderos* in La Iguaná or Zafra.

But there are complex cultural dynamics at work here, because what is being re-created or defended is not some pure or objectively defined and demarcated "black culture," and black culture itself is subject to continuous change. Rural Chocoano culture is classified as *montañero,* literally "from the mountains" and figuratively meaning rustic and uncouth. Ridicule is aimed at the classic Chocoano accent, which pronounces the *d* something like an *r*—"Merellín," for example—and this is soon dropped in an Antioqueño environment. Equally, Chocoanos in La Iguaná eat *arepas,* corn cakes, the renowned symbol of *paisa* identity. In the dance halls, the apparently simple but rhythmically rather difficult and more intimate salsa step often found in the Chocó tends to lose ground to the more distant and energetic style of the Antioqueños, adopted from *la Costa.* People also remain on the dance floor between numbers, a practice never seen in the Chocó, where everyone returns religiously to their tables, if only to leave again at once. So there are subtle changes, and these are involved in a process of negotiation in which both cultural behavior and the context in which it is practiced enter as factors defining identity. Thus the behavior of the Chocoanos, even if different from that in the Chocó, may continue to be defined as black culture, both by the Chocoanos and by the Antioqueños, chiefly because it is being practiced by Chocoanos in a context in which blackness is, even if only temporarily, the normal state of affairs. Equally, assimilation of urban Antioqueño culture is not simply a matter of altering specific patterns of behavior but of altering the social context of behavior by associating more with Antioqueños and cutting links with the Chocoano ethnic network. In short, it is not only the actual cultural elements that define "black culture" but also the context in which they appear and from which they derive their meaning. This context is essentially formed by the ethnic relations and interactions existing between the Chocoanos and the Antioqueños, relations in this case partly manifested in urban spatial arrangements: the constitution of a black space itself tends to define what happens in it as black culture, for the purposes of Medellín and its people. It has, of course, long been recognized that the maintenance of ethnic difference takes place contextually and on the basis of potentially shifting sets of cultural signs (e.g., Barth 1969). But these signs are not necessarily arbitrary (cf. Eriksen 1991). There is some continuity perceived by both Chocoanos and Antioqueños between black culture in the Chocó and in Medellín —black culture is not created from scratch but reelaborated from previous forms. These reelaborations remain as, or become, "black culture" in the context of establishing black community in the city and as part of continuing distinctions, claimed and ascribed, between Chocoanos and Antioqueños. It is this, rather than the nearness of these reelaborated urban forms to "authentic," chronologically prior forms, which defines "black culture" in Medellín.

The recurrent theme of music appears once more here, binding these ideas together. It was shown previously that music and dance were often involved in the black nuclei, whether as *bailaderos* in invasion settlements and outlying barrios or as city center bars patronized by blacks on the weekends; in a more transient fashion, music and dance create nuclei at parties in the houses of Chocoano families, which are often, though not always, patronized mainly by Chocoanos and where, apparently, they sometimes "won't let whites in." It is frequently around these *bailaderos* and fiestas that ethnic antagonisms arise, and it is clear that they are an important nexus in Antioqueño-Chocoano relations. Historically, in the creation of their own forms of culture, music and celebration, often of a religious nature, have been important cultural foci for the blacks: in Medellín, too, music has been crucial in the establishing of a Chocoano identity. It has been a focus for community for Chocoanos and an important aspect of how they are seen in the city.

To understand the relation between blacks and music in Medellín today, it is necessary to have some background to black music in Colombia in general and to develop some themes about its interaction with the nonblack world.

Black Music in Colombia

My purpose here is not to give a general account of black music in Colombia (see Béhague 1985 and the references cited below for a bibliography; see also Abadía Morales 1973, 1983; Escalante 1964; Velásquez 1961a; List 1980, 1983). However, a basic picture of the range of musical development involved is a necessary framework for

272

the Colombian material. Musically, Colombia can be seen as part of the Caribbean basin. Bilby (1985) traces for this region a process of creolization which gave rise to a musical spectrum, ranging from neo-African styles, through Euro-African hybrids, to mostly European styles. The spectrum is analogous to a linguistic continuum (cf. Drummond's [1980] idea of a cultural continuum) in that individuals can operate with several different styles within it, according to the appropriate context, although Bilby fails to explore the idea of hierarchy which is fundamental to these continua. Frequently the most neo-African styles are associated with African-derived religious complexes, although this is not always the case. The Euro-African hybrids were often descendants of European dances, military band styles (and sometimes religious music) which became creolized in the hands of black and mulatto musicians. But there were also new creations, rooted, of course, in African and European forms but essentially original developments. Finally, there are European forms with little black influence.

Crosscutting this continuum are different musical contexts: religion (African-derived sects, wakes, European-derived sects); diversion (whether everyday dances or those centered on the great carnivals or saints' days); labor (for example, work songs). In all these contexts, blacks made their musical presence felt to a greater or lesser degree.

In Colombia, many of these styles and contexts are to be found, although African-derived religions and their associated music are more or less absent: most black music fits into the Euro-African hybrid segment of the continuum (see, however, Escalante 1954; Friedemann and Patiño Roselli 1983). Nevertheless, the dynamics of the racial order and its hierarchies have operated in this process of hybridization. The syncretic development of music, with individual musicians inventively weaving together elements inherited from an increasingly varied musical milieu, is complex in the extreme, but it is not divorced from its overall context. In effect, I argue that certain processes can be observed in the historical development of black music in Colombia which are paralleled in a transfigured form in the recent history of music in Medellín. Specifically, I develop three themes. One, the blacks establish a musical independence of some kind which is a symbol of their identity as a black group and of their separateness. This corresponds to black community. Two, they may do this using elements that come from a variety of sources and which are already a product of cultural syncretism and do not necessarily come from their own autochthonous tradition. That is, black community is not dependent on Africanisms. Three, the music they create or use, although frequently looked down upon as inferior and crude, noisy and licentious, may also be taken up again by the dominant nonblack society and reincorporated into their world, perhaps because it seems to embody some Dionysian impulse that is particularly attractive. This corresponds to processes of nonblack discrimination against black community and to nonblack fascination with blackness. It also relates to blacks' adaptation to the nonblack world, where they and their culture can be accepted on condition that it adapts and is made acceptable.

Black Musical Traditions. In the past, blacks have established independent traditions using elements that are at hand and which are copied to a large extent from the dominant culture but infused with a specifically black, often African, style or feel. Marulanda (1979, 6) says of Pacific coastal dances, "The choreographic rhythms learned by [the blacks, slave and free] could not be reproduced by them with the soft and well-studied European cadences. . . . The movements were copied by the slaves with the ardor of African rhythm, with the freedom conferred by erotic gestures and the force transmitted by a mode of being and feeling which was very different from the tastes of the Old Continent. Although some schemas [of movement] were conserved . . . the rhythmic content was profoundly altered." Of the *contradanza* of the Chocó, a traditional dance derived originally from the Scottish country dance and taken to the New World by several European powers, Marulanda says, "The apprenticeship of the mining slaves in the fiestas of their masters . . . established a type of black style which took possession of the refined gallantries and coquetries of the courtly style." The blacks substituted for the dance square "a complex circle, whose accelerated rhythm dissolves the traditional waltz-like 6/8 and creates its own syncopation more in tune with the tastes of mulatto-ization" (Marulanda 1979, 13). Equally, the *danza*, a derivation from the *contradanza*, underwent in the Chocó "an acclimatization that allowed it to acquire a different structure . . . the gallant and evocative feel conferred on it by stringed instruments was eliminated, and its content became varnished over with the virility and pagan nuances of the blacks" (Marulanda 1979, 10). Marulanda's use of words such as ardor, freedom, erotic, force, virility, and pagan tells us as much about how nonblacks see black music as about black music itself, but that is, in fact, half my argument. In any event, his commentary serves to establish that, although the *chirimía* bands of the Chocó are derived in instrumentation from the colonial military bands and they play mazurkas, polkas, *jugas* (from fugues), and *contradanzas,* all these are stamped with their own particularly black feel. The *chirimías* of the Andean region not only have a different instrumentation but have a very different style to them as well.

The principal rhythm and dance genre of the Pacific coast south of the San Juan River of the southern Chocó is the *currulao,* which in its various forms is one of the most undiluted and independent black genres. The origin of the word itself is unclear, but it was used to describe a "slave dance" in seventeenth-century Cartagena (Marulanda 1979, 8), and both Cordovez Moure (1957, 484) and Samper (quoted in Ocampo López 1988, 220) in their late nineteenth-century writings use the word to describe the dance of the *bogas,* or black boatmen, of the Magdalena River. Nowadays, the term refers exclusively to the Pacific coast genre, and its Africanness is quite apparent. Marulanda (1979, 8) refers to it as "the rhythm that best synthesizes the survival of Africanness," and Whitten (1974, 111) remarks that it has an African rhythm completely distinct from that of Afro-Caribbean musical styles (see also Whitten 1968; Lomax 1970; Abadía Morales 1983, 212). The *currulao* involves the marimba, a type of xylophone of African origin, two *cununos* or conical drums designated male and female, one or two *bombos* or double-headed drums, *guasás* or bamboo tube rattles, and a lead male singer with several female vocalists who sing in a call-response fashion.

It is harder for the case of *la Costa* to pinpoint an independent black musical tradition due to the advanced cultural and racial mixture that has occurred there, and most Costeño music is clearly of mixed origins. Nevertheless, it is clear that the blacks created their own musical forms and were the main driving force in the creation of the Euro-African hybrids that form the basis of later developments. José Cassiani, a Jesuit commentator on the life of San Pedro Claver of seventeenth-century Cartagena, noted that the blacks were trying to introduce dancing, that drums were publicly on sale, and that one black woman had opened up a "public dance house and tavern" (quoted in Valtierra 1980, 2:217). In 1769, the king requested a report on dances known as *bundes* in Cartagena. *Bunde,* according to Marulanda (1979, 9) was a general term for black dances, although now it refers to funerary songs in the Pacific region (Abadía Morales 1983, 220). The 1770 report stated that the *bundes* were "very old" and widespread and took the form of a circle of men and women in the center of which pairs danced in turn to the sound of drums and singing (quoted in Valtierra 1980, 2:219). In another case, there are reports from Cartagena between 1777 and 1780 of a *cabildo* of Carabalís which was the object of a complaint from another *cabildo* protesting that the noise of the Carabalís in their reunion was too loud—"as if they did not also create their own *guachafita* [hubbub, din]" (Raul Porto del Portillo, quoted in Escalante 1964, 153).

Later, around 1830, Joaquín Posada Gutiérrez (1920, 334–49) describes the great annual festival to venerate the Virgin of La Candelaria in Cartagena which he witnessed as a youth. Each day different guilds had their festivities until the last day, Carnival Sunday, which was for the slaves, African and creole. Each *cabildo* then had a formal procession with a king and queen holding umbrellas as a signal of their rank and with male dancers with faces, legs, and chests painted red, holding wooden swords, and wearing leopard-skin aprons and paper crowns with bright feathers, "imitating the customs and costumes of their native lands"; the women wore jewels lent by their mistresses. They danced along "singing, leaping, and making contortions to the sound of drums and tambourines and beating cymbals and copper mortars [i.e., bells]." They proceeded to La Popa, a church set on a hill overlooking the city, and here they heard a mass before descending back into the town. They were then "completely free to enjoy themselves in their *cabildos*" for three days. During the evenings leading up to this final day, dances were held. These were nominally organized around the women, and there were several recognized classes of women who held separate dances, although the men were free to enter the dances of groups socially inferior to their own. There were three dances *de sala,* in a special hall: a first class of *blancas de Castilla,* whites from Spain, a second class of *pardas,* mixed-blood women, and a third class of free blacks. Only those people who "occupied a certain social position" could enter in these dances *de sala.* They danced to the military bands of racially segregated regiments which played minuets, *contradanzas,* waltzes, and some *bailes de la tierra,* or local dances: these bands were based on brass and percussion instruments (Triana 1987, 84). Another category was the *blancas de la tierra,* locally born whites, such as small merchants and priests, who could not enter the first-class dance and disdained the second. They danced in their own houses to guitar music: men from the first-class dance would abandon their own women to dance with the *blancas de tierra.* A further group was made up of the *cuarterones,* light-skinned mixed-bloods, poorer people, such as cigar makers, tailors, and seamstresses, who also danced in their homes to the sound of "one or two Cartagenean harps"; the women also had as dance partners men who were *blancos de Castilla* and *blancos de tierra,* since these men "furtively deserted" their own women.

Below all these groups, and out in the streets, were the poor people and slaves, blacks for the most part but also mulattoes and other mixed-bloods, who, "to the thundering sound of African drums,"

276

danced in a large circle that rotated around a group of male drummers accompanied by female singers who kept rhythm with handclaps "enough to swell within ten minutes the hands of any other than they." Men and women danced barefoot in pairs, without touching, and the woman held aloft in her hand two or three candles wrapped in a cheap muslin cloth which she threw outside the circle when they had burnt down. The basic circular structure of the dance with the use of candles and the accompaniment of drums, handclapping, and singing is typical of the period, although it receives different names from different observers. Posada calls it a *currulao* and later remarks that by the time of writing in 1865 it was called *mapalé*. The observers of the *bogas* also called it *currulao*. Nowadays, such a dance with only drums, singing, and handclapping might be termed a *bullerengue*.

The current Costeño repertoire of traditional folkloric genres is very diverse and includes a wide variety of forms, which are often somewhat inaccurately grouped under the vague umbrella term of *cumbia*. Principal genres include *cumbia, bullerengue, mapalé, gaita, porro,* and merengue, and these are played by a variety of instrumental lineups such as *cañamilleros, gaiteros,* and *tamboras* which use different types of flutes, drums, rattles, and scrapers. My purpose is not to describe these (see Triana 1987; Abadía Morales 1983; Delia Zapata Olivella 1962; Manuel Zapata Olivella 1960–62, 1967) but rather to highlight how the blacks laid the basis for a series of musical and dance forms that, although they received indian and European influences and became more and more syncretized over time, remained heavily identified with the blacks. Names such as *mapalé, cumbia* (in its folkloric form), and *bullerengue* were and still are seen as essentially black dances. The indian influence, whatever its real impact, is generally taken to be via the *gaita,* a long vertical flute occasionally mistaken for an arabesque import akin to the oboe (Chamorro 1982) but which has no vibrating reed and is of well-documented indigenous origin (Abadía Morales 1983, 234; Triana 1987, 72). The black tradition today retains its purest form in the *tambora* lineup of conical drums, *tablitas* (small wooden spatulas beaten together), and responsorial singing (Triana 1987, 75), a lineup that harks back to the eighteenth- and nineteenth-century descriptions of black Costeño dances. In *la Costa,* then, it is clear that the blacks early on established their own kind of music, based in large part on the drum, and this was influenced by and influenced in its turn white and to a lesser extent indian music to produce a series of syncretic forms.

In the north of the department of Cauca, blacks celebrate various festivals, including the Adoration of the Child. The blacks there say that these are *fiestas de negros,* which date from colonial times and,

277

according to one black informant, have their roots in "pagan ceremonies" from Africa (Atencio Babilonia and Castellanos Córdova 1982, 36). A local historian is quoted as saying that all the fiestas in honor of Saint John, Saint Peter, Saint Paul, the Immaculate Conception, the Child Jesus, the Virgin Mary, and so on "had their syndicates, some from the city, others from the countryside, [which] all included the contracting of a band of musicians which enlivened the evening preceding [the fiesta]." Almost certainly in colonial times these syndicates were the *cabildos*. Again, then, the blacks took an essentially Spanish tradition—this time the fiesta itself as well as the music—and made it into something that expressed their own sense of identity, even imputing to it African origins. Today there are still fundamental black features: "the presence of dance in sacred ceremonies, the rhythmic structure of the music . . . the interaction between soloist and the chorus in the religious songs" (Atencio Babilonia and Castellanos Córdova 1982, 38). The basic musical form is the *fuga*, played by a band that is essentially like a *chirimía* and sung by a female chorus and the general public. The *fuga* is clearly a European derivation, and the lyrics are Catholic in reference, but Atencio and Castellanos emphasize the particularity of the *fuga* in these black fiestas and attribute the call-response pattern to an African past (1982, 118). Another important form in the fiestas, overlapping with the recitations of the *fuga*, is the *copla*, or rhyming verse. This Atencio and Castellanos trace to old Spanish ballad forms and quote an authority on the Colombian ballad tradition to the effect that "the black population represents the most important exponent of traditional Spanish music and oral poetic forms" (1982, 110). In *la Costa*, too, the black presence was important in the development of oral poetic musical forms, manifested in a variety of work songs that became the basis for the more modern *vallenato* forms (see below; Triana 1987, 66).

Persecution, Attraction, and Syncretism. To talk of syncretism in this whole process is insufficient to the extent that it implies a neutral mixing: we look at the end result and see the disparate elements—syncretism is the answer. But the process by which this mixture is created is not neutral at all. Just as *mestizaje* can be in fact the morally loaded process of *blanqueamiento,* so musical syncretism involves the whole relationship between blacks and nonblacks, including whites—and, to complicate matters, indians—as it happens to manifest itself through music. Hierarchy was fundamental to this process, as indeed was the ambivalent fascination of the nonblack world with black music.

The persecution of black music was a direct expression of this hierarchy. San Pedro Claver, the great seventeenth-century healer and evangelist of the Cartagena slaves, who licked clean their ulcerous sores in an apotheosis of self-abnegation, also repressed their dances and confiscated their drums. Cassiani recounts, "He would walk along the public streets where these dances used to take place, and finding one he would disperse the blacks and take away their drum . . . ; at first, the bewildered blacks obeyed him, but later it appeared to them too great a submission, and they resisted him; . . . when he encountered resistance . . . he would take out his scourge, instrument of his penitence, and . . . with lashes disperse that cloud which blinded modesty" (quoted in Valtierra 1980, 2:217). In another instance, the bishop of Popayán decreed in 1763, "Since there have been introduced several dances called *zaraza, el castillar, zamo de cabro, bundes* and others of the same class and type, with actions and movements both dishonest and provocative . . . we order, under pain of excommunication, that under no pretext, neither in public nor in private, should these prejudicial dances be played or sung" (Perdomo Escobar 1963, 54). The bishop of Cartagena prohibited *bundes* and fandangos in the early 1730s, "recognizing the inconveniences and sins which originate in such dishonest diversions" (Perdomo Escobar 1963, 318). Friedemann and Arocha (1986, 418) recount a campaign directed against the "diabolical" marimba dances of the blacks of the southern Pacific coastal region by one Father Manuel Mera in 1908.

A good deal of dancing and celebration was organized through the *cabildos,* and these were subject to constant suspicion and persecution. Roberto Arrázola (1970, 129) reports on the interrogation in Cartagena in 1693 of blacks from *palenques* and *cabildos* who were allegedly plotting a rebellion together. One Francisco Arará (a slave in the Santa Clara convent; Borrego Pla 1973, 102) testified that "the Arará are a people who today have no *cabildo,* that he had been named governor [of the *cabildo*] and that when they have the *fiesta de la Popa* [i.e., of La Candelaria], they collect in the house of Manuel Arará, slave of the Company of Jesus, who is the king [of the *cabildo*], and there they give alms and go to enjoy themselves, and that he only takes care [of the burial] when a relative dies, because since the Provisor removed the drum and took it to his house there is no *lloro*." *Lloro,* literally a crying or wailing, was the name given to the funerary ceremonies and dances of the blacks. Jaramillo Uribe also reports on a 1785 court case against blacks accused of conspiring to form a *palenque* in the Cauca region: they had a *cabildo* with mayors, governors, and viceroys, and those elected to such posts "paid for the necessary refreshments at their dances and celebrations" (1968, 70). The conflict between the Carabalí *cabildo* and its neighbor in Cartagena in 1777 led the governor of the city to try to shut down the *cabildos*—apparently to little effect since they were still there and active in 1830.

This type of repression has parallels in other New World contexts. Aretz (1977) gives many examples of the repression of *cabildos* all over Latin America. For Cuba, Díaz Ayala (1981, 84) reproduces a 1922 resolution that orders the suppression of dances, "especially that known by the name of Bembé" carried out under the auspices of the Societies of Mutual Aid and Recreation, which were nothing less than the old *cabildos* under a new name and which worshiped African deities. These dances allegedly led to the murder of white children as sacrifices to their gods and were "prejudicial to public security and contrary to morals and good customs." Ortiz (1917, 400) also recommends the surveillance of the "African dances" in Cuba which harbored witchcraft practices that led to delinquency, fraud, and even the murder of white children. In a much later work, Ortiz observes that in Cuba "there was a time when the music of the blacks was looked down upon. . . . It was not even music; it was said to be merely 'noise'" (1965, 146). Words of African origin meaning dance or music came to be synonymous with disorderliness or rowdiness (1965, 150), and he states that "the slave owners in their eagerness to justify subjugation by the supposed 'racial inferiority' of the slave, saw in the musical fervor of the blacks not only banal and infantile entertainment . . . but also a blemish characteristic of 'races' classified as deficient and destined always to domination by others" (1965, 153). Not surprisingly, the same repression occurred in the United States. Walton (1972, 20) produces as an example an 1811 decree of Georgia stating: "It is absolutely necessary to the safety of the province that all due care be taken to restrain negroes from using or keeping drums."

Persecution existed, and yet the nonblacks' attitude to black music, or more accurately black musicians, was not so simple. While in Cuba, for example, they might recoil at a "savage" and "rowdy" *merienda de negros* (*merienda* signifies tranquil picnic; when it is *de negros,* it means bedlam), the blacks, parallel or as an alternative to immersing themselves in their *bailes,* also conquered the minuet, the waltz, and the *contradanza* and, "taking over the orchestra, adapted it to their tastes." The black plays "white music in the drawing rooms, the churches, and the theaters; but . . . he infiltrates into this . . . African elements; dance music, above all, would have its African imprint" (Díaz Ayala 1981, 28, 39). Carpentier notes that blacks and mulattoes predominated in musical production in late nineteenth-century Cuba and notes that "certain *contradanzas* were better liked when played by *pardos* [mulattoes]. Blacks and whites played the same popular pieces. But the blacks added an accent, a vitality, an unwritten 'something' which 'picked you up'" (1946, 112). They added, for example, a "simple ligature" to the *contradanza* to create the conga, and "Tu madre es conga" was the rage among "the most aristocratic society" of Santiago in 1856. Díaz Ayala (1981, 39) writes that the Cuban *contradanza* bore the mark of black participation, as did its later derivative, the *danzón,* "the first genuinely Cuban creation" and a principal musical genre from the 1870s until quite recently. African roots also showed in the Cuban *son,* a major genre on the basis of which salsa later emerged (see also Urfé 1977; Bilby 1985). The Euro-African hybrids that arose from the creolization of European forms in the hands of the blacks and mulattoes had an "irrepressible vitality" (Bilby 1985, 195) that was very attractive.

In Colombia, too, whites found black-influenced music attractive. Posada Gutiérrez (1920, 341) observes that in the smart *bailes de salón,* the younger people of all three classes "yawned and dozed" during the minuets but gave shouts of joy when the *contradanza* and the waltz were played, music that, though of European origin, had become "Hispanicized" and "adapted to [Colombia's] fiery climate." The *bailes de la tierra* had their place from midnight onwards and were "happy and vivacious," although not, God forbid, indecent. Since the military bands were of blacks and mulattoes for the third-class dance, it is likely that the *contradanzas,* the waltzes, and even more probably the *bailes de la tierra* had by that time picked up some of that "unwritten something" that the blacks had given the salon dances in Cuba. Interestingly, the men of the higher-class dances deserted their own women to dance in the lower-class ones: perhaps it was not only the women there which they found attractive.

In more recent periods, the process is also obvious. The *cumbia* and associated Costeño genres received much of their creative impulse from black traditions, and although they are still practiced by the traditional *conjuntos* (groups), from the nineteenth century they also began to be played by the brass bands that were playing the minuets, *contradanzas,* waltzes, and so on of the higher social classes; the music played by these *bandas* is generically known as *porro.* In this century, Costeño genres also evolved into more commercial music that, under the generic title *cumbia,* spread across the nation. From the 1930s onwards, people in the interior of the country listened and danced to *cumbias* from *la Costa* alongside Caribbean musical genres from Cuba (see Ulloa Sanmiguel 1988 for data on Cali). Later, in the 1960s, *cumbia* also formed a major element in the repertoire of Costeño bands such as the Corraleros de Majagual, which made use of more brass instrumentation and the accordion and helped popularize Costeño music on a nationwide basis. The *cumbia* has eventually become rather far removed from the traditional folkloric genres or even the music played by the Corraleros—although, confusingly, the term is still applied to all three variants of music since they are basically developments of the same tradition. *Cumbia* in its most modern form is now a highly commercial product, popular not only in the interior of Colombia but also as far afield as Peru and Mexico, where it is subsumed under generic titles such as *música tropical* which include many Caribbean styles. It is a classic instance of a black-inspired tradition that has been steadily "whitened" over time, persecuted in the past when practiced independently by blacks but becoming more and more acceptable as it spreads into the nonblack world, losing both its Africanness and its main association with black people and yet retaining its attractive "hot" quality. It is no coincidence that *música tropical* is also known as *música caliente,* hot music. It may be hard to recognize in the slick pop music that is now commercialized as *cumbia* the "noisy African singing" of Cartagena's nineteenth-century blacks, but the continuity is a real one, and I would argue that its generative force lies partly in the taste of the nonblack world for black rhythms.

This cultural dynamic is a complex one because Colombia cannot be represented as a simple opposition between black and white. Although at an early stage it was a matter of the blacks creating their own tradition with different rhythms and musical forms, in places such as *la Costa* musical and dance genres soon arose which were intermediate between black music and white music, giving rise to the nineteenth-century hierarchy that ranged from a minuet to a "Hispanicized" waltz, to the *bailes de la tierra,* and from there to *cumbias* and other such music that had soon spread beyond the confines of black *cabildos* and became traditional Costeño folk music played and danced to by the very mixed-blood population of *la Costa*—here, too, the indians played a part with their *gaitas.* Díaz and Carpentier refer to the "white" world in Cuba, but this was almost certainly a mixed nonblack world like that of Cartagena, with *blancos de Castilla, blancos de la tierra, cuarterones, pardos,* and even, paradoxically, some *negros libres* of a "certain social position" who were in the process of leaving the black world. The exact mechanisms by which these intermediate forms arose and continued to emerge are far from clear. Several processes could occur under these circumstances. Blacks might enter the nonblack world as musicians and "tropicalize" the music there, primarily derived from white forms, adding an "unwritten something" that became fashionable—this is the process Díaz and Carpentier note for Cuba. Blacks could integrate into an increasingly mixed popular society and take traditions partly elaborated in *cabildos* with them to form a major element in the evolving forms of that society—this is probably the history of *cumbia*. Black music, or indeed intermediate forms strongly associated with the blacks, can be adapted by black and mixed-blood musicians for consumption by other nonblacks who are more estranged from from black traditions—this, I think, is how *cumbia* evolved into commercial, fashionable pop music. Finally, nonblacks can simply appropriate black or black-influenced music and imitate it or alter it to suit their tastes—a process particularly noticeable in the United States (Walton 1972; Levine 1977, 290) but which also occurs in Colombia, with white bands in the interior playing music derived from *cumbia*. Also in Colombia there were and still are constant importations from the Caribbean, particularly Cuba itself, which are the products of these kinds of mixture and which because of their origin are categorized as rather black in the moral hierarchy of music and subjected once more within Colombia to these processes of syncretism. In short, there is a whole series of intermediate forms of mixed origins which because of their ambiguity are subject to potential classification as "white" or "black" depending on the context of ethnic relations in which they exist. In all this, white and black remain as two poles in antagonistic hierarchical tension, by which the intermediate forms are themselves hierarchized and from which they draw their meaning. *Cumbia,* for example, is not an entirely black dance: although its roots are primarily black, it is a Costeño genre, and the Costeños are a mulatto and mestizo population. But in Medellín or Bogotá, the *cumbias* popular in, say, the 1950s were classified as *música tropical* or *música caliente* and, insofar as they were Costeño, were located as black in the Colombian sense of place.

Salsa and Vallenato. Popular music for blacks in Colombia today, especially in towns but also in rural areas, now usually centers around genres other than the traditional Pacific *currulao* or the Costeño folkloric *cumbia*. Even the commercial *cumbia* has been taken over largely by nonblack audiences. Instead, salsa and *vallenato* are the main cultural foci. Salsa made an explosive appearance in New York in the late 1960s. There, Puerto Rican, Cuban, Panamanian, and other Latin American immigrants were creating a "new" sound out of what was essentially Cuban and to a lesser extent Puerto Rican music, a sound that was also an expression of their Latin identity in a North American city. Salsa differed from its antecedents in the use of a wider range of instruments, especially brass, an electric bass, more percussion, and so on (see Díaz Ayala 1981, 335; Roberts 1979; Gerhard and Sheller

283

1989; Duany 1984; Singer 1983). The word *salsa* (literally "sauce"), used to indicate a genre of music, is difficult to date. Ignacio Piñeiro titled a song "Echale Salsita" (Give It Some Sauce) as long ago as 1929, but the word began to suggest a certain style of music when a Venezuelan radio station broadcast a program entitled "La Hora del Sabor, la Salsa y el Bembé" (The Hour of Flavor, Sauce and Bembé, a Cuban dance). By the early seventies, the usage was well established and began to be applied retrospectively to Cuban and other music that had in fact predated it. Salsa quickly became heavily commercialized and promoted by the publicity machines of New York record companies; the two films *Nuestra cosa latina* (ca. 1972) and *Salsa* (ca. 1975) increased its popularity even further.

Salsa grew out of Cuban genres such as the *son,* which emerged from the blacks' role in adapting, and adapting to, earlier European forms. It was created in New York, and as many whites as blacks have been and are its star figures. Nevertheless, the black influence is a historical fact, and it is evident partly in the almost uncanny predominance of blacks and mulattoes in the drumming and percussion sections of the salsa bands (a feature also noticeable in the *vallenato* groups). Moreover, some salsa lyrics—although they may be sung by whites in later cover versions—make explicit reference to this in lines such as: "I'm black because I was born of the rumba, and the *sabor* I inherited from the *guaguancó.*" Rumba and *guaguancó* are both Cuban genres associated principally with blacks (Crook 1982); *sabor* literally means "flavor" and is commonly used to denote the "hot," danceable quality of music. Another song declares, "Sure, I'm black, I'm of the race. . . . Where there are no blacks, there is no salsa." Artists such as Alfredo de la Fe and Monguito, among others, make references to Africa in songs such as "Vamos pa' Dakar" and "Guaguancó."

Vallenato only emerged as a specific genre in the 1940s, and it derived from traditional Costeño genres based not so much on the drum and dance as on sung verses, work songs, picaresque songs, and so on, which also formed part of the Costeño and the black Colombian musical traditions, as the material on the Cauca Valley showed (Atencio Babilonia and Castellanos Córdova 1982; see also Triana 1987, 66, 88; Llerena Villalobos 1985; Quiroz Otero 1982; Araújo Molina 1973). Earlier forms were sung with some guitar accompaniment, and in the 1940s the accordion emerged as the main instrument, with the *caja vallenata* (a small drum) and the *guacharaca* (a scraper) joining it to form the *conjunto vallenato,* centered originally on the town of Valledupar in the eastern region of the Atlantic coast. Like *cumbia* and salsa, *vallenato* has recently become a heavily commercialized genre that enjoys national popularity.

Although black musical traditions were fundamental to both salsa and *vallenato,* these two genres actually have very mixed origins and are not "black music" in an unambiguous sense. Nevertheless, they are strongly associated with blacks, and blacks are seen as the ambassadors of this kind of music in Colombia. Salsa traveled a direct route from New York to places such as Bogotá and Medellín, where it installed itself in clubs and bars that are patronized by whites as well as blacks. But it is only in places such as Quibdó and Cartagena that salsa is pervasive and ubiquitous; it is the blacks of Cali who have the reputation as *the* dancers of salsa, and Ulloa Sanmiguel cites the black cultural heritage of Cali as one reason that salsa became so popular there (1988, 7). Equally, *vallenato* is a nationally commercialized type of pop music, but it only forms an integral part of popular culture in places such as *la Costa,* the Chocó, and in black nuclei in the interior: its identity is essentially Costeño and, to that extent, black. In this way, cultural traits that appear to be simply Colombian (or Latin American) have, on closer examination, become integrated into the black world in specific ways that in the national context can constitute "black culture."

Chocoanos and Music in Medellín

This discussion clears the way for a consideration of Chocoanos and music in Medellín, where what happens with salsa and *vallenato* is a microcosmic version of the cultural dynamics outlined above. In Medellín there is a fairly clear opposition between blacks and nonblacks, and this simplifies the cultural dynamics involved. Music, in the form of salsa and *vallenato,* has been a crucial element in focusing black nuclei in the city. The various residential and more temporary congregations of Chocoanos, and blacks in general, have all been connected with *bailaderos* or bars where music is a central feature. That music, although not unambiguously black in origin or identity, is strongly associated with blacks in Colombia, and especially so in Medellín, where they were its principal ambassadors and audience. Its black association was increased by the very fact that in black communities, transient or residential, that music was played loudly and to the general exclusion of other genres in contexts in which Chocoano and Antioqueño identities were being opposed in a fairly clear and unambiguous fashion. Thus, part of the process by which blacks in Medellín establish a definite presence, temporary or permanent, in specific locales in the city is through music (and sometimes dance), and this plays a role in defining a Chocoano and black identity with respect to the Antioqueños. This musical identity, as in the general argument outlined above, is relatively independent, although not therefore derivatively "pure" or autochthonous. Its persecution by Antioqueños is not, of course, of the same order as the civil and religious persecution of colonial music and dance traditions, but the attacks on the Iguaná and Zafra *bailaderos* and the local media complaints about how "the Chocó has inundated [the] main recreational centers in Medellín" (*El Colombiano*, 16 July 1986, 13A) are both indicative of the disapproval vented on Chocoano nuclei and their associated music. At the same time, however, this black music is seen as "hot," exciting music and, usually in more diluted and controlled forms, has become part of the Antioqueño scene, at least among the younger generation. An outline of the development of Chocoano entertainment and of the impact of salsa and *vallenato* in Medellín illustrates these processes.

In the 1950s, there was no specific place where the Chocoanos would congregate. La Bayadera and the nearby Plaza de Cisneros, where the marketplace was then located, were general areas where the domestic servants and other Chocoanos would go, but in interviews with the older Chocoanos, no single place stood out as *the* Chocoano spot. The Bosque de la Independencia, today converted into the Botanic Gardens, was then a sort of amusement park with dance halls, and it was a popular place among the domestic servants too: there they would dance to *cumbias* and *porros* from *la Costa* and guaracha and mambo from Cuba—already at that time, the danceable music was of Caribbean origin with strong black roots. In the 1960s, Barrio Antioquia became an important focus, due to the location there of the Association of Chocoanos Resident in Medellín. This would have dances on weekends, and it stimulated the opening of other *bailaderos,* one of which was called El Congo (perhaps after the Congo dances of the Barranquilla carnival, perhaps after the famous Cuban *contradanza* of the 1850s entitled "Tu madre es conga," perhaps after the *cabildo* of that name in colonial Cartagena, perhaps simply after the African place name that served as a slave surname in colonial Latin America). Also in the sixties, two city center bars were founded—by Antioqueños—which became meccas for Chocoanos and Costeños. In 1962, Mario Quinceno bought El Atlántico. He was already a lover of music from the Caribbean:

> To me falls the honor of being the first to play *música caliente* in Guayaquil. First I had El Cuba [another bar] when around here you could

only hear *música de carrilera, cuyos,* and tango [types of music associated with Antioqueños]. I started to travel to *la Costa* and bring back the music of Daniel Santos, Celia Cruz, and the Trio Matamoros [all Cuban artists]. Eventually, it began to get popular, until other bar owners would ask me to buy for them too. But El Cuba was knocked down when they widened Bolívar Avenue, and afterwards I bought El Atlántico. By then we were listening to rock and roll, and the music of the bar began to get a bit boring. From that time, the blacks arrived and with them *vallenato.* After a while there were so many *morochos* [brown people] round the tables that I didn't know where to put them all, and they'd have *unas rumbas tan severas* [such boisterous parties] that you couldn't walk around. . . . The bar became the embassy of the Chocoanos here. And not only them, but [blacks] from Cali, Buenaventura, and Puerto Tejada. Teachers, students, even professionals: if they were black, they'd come to El Atlántico. People asked me how I could put up with *esa negramenta* [all those blacks], but not at all: I used to like it when they'd come in dancing; their happiness was so infectious, it made me want to dance too. (From an interview in *El Mundo,* 17 March 1985)

One recalls Perdomo's remark about the black music that fills the highland man with irresponsible happiness! Quinceno was not the first one to play *música caliente* in Medellín: we already know that people, from the Chocó and from Medellín, were dancing *cumbia, porro,* guaracha, and mambo in the 1950s in the Bosque de la Independencia. In the 1960s, too, the music of Costeño bands such as Los Corraleros de Majagual could be heard in Medellín. At the same time, many Costeños would congregate around the baseball diamond in El Estadio, near La Iguaná—baseball being particularly popular among Costeños—where they would listen to Costeño and Caribbean music in the bars nearby.

Nearer to El Atlántico and also at the beginning of the sixties, Jaime and Mario, two Antioqueño brothers, started a bar called El Suizo. At first, Costeños were the main clientele, and the music was mainly *vallenato,* at that time a relatively rare commodity in Medellín. The Costeños crowded in there until the owners desisted entirely from playing *música guasca,* guitar music associated with the Antioqueños, and put on exclusively *vallenato.* Soon they opened another bar nearby to accommodate more people, and the Chocoanos also began to overflow from the nearby Atlántico. The sale of *gaseosa,* soft drinks, was not allowed, except to mix with rum, in order to prevent domestic servants from sitting all Sunday afternoon with the one or two Coca-Colas they could afford. Around 1979, the whole sector surrounding El Suizo was demolished as part of the city center improvement schemes, and the brothers moved to a nearby premises

The interior of El Salón Suizo, on a Sunday afternoon in 1987.

called El Rincón del Vallenato (The Vallenato Corner), at the same
time opening the current Salón Suizo. In 1985, El Atlántico was also
demolished to allow another road widening, and the brothers' bars,
El Rincón and El Suizo, became the main focal points for Chocoanos
and Costeños, although the former heavily predominate. In the same
area, there are a few other bars that catch the overspill from the two
main ones, and next to the site of the old Atlántico, El Príncipe has
been largely taken over by Chocoanos since their "embassy" was
knocked down. All these bars are in an area of town still considered
to be lower class, rough, and dangerous, despite redevelopment of El
Centro, and consequently many Chocoanos and Costeños avoid going
there, sometimes considering them as below their status. Nevertheless,
they are points of Chocoano congregation, and, as in Mario
Quinceno's bar, one finds students and a few professionals alongside
the many domestic servants, construction workers, and the odd Chocoano policeman.

These places are all owned and run by Antioqueños: why do they
allow their places to become stamping grounds for "*esa negramenta*"?
In the case of Mario and the two brothers, there seems to have been
an initial liking for *vallenato* or *música tropical*. The owner of El

Rincón told me that he had always liked *vallenato* and had got hold of records quite easily even early on, since many of the artists recorded in Medellín, where several record companies had their headquarters. He commented, "Well, the blacks have settled in here now, and there's no way to get them out." Of course, changing the music would be an easy tactic, but he did not seem to take the idea very seriously—not surprising, given that these bars are packed to the doors on weekends, while neighboring bars with an Antioqueño clientele do a much lesser trade. There is clearly a move here to corner a certain market that, while it might lead to a few bullet holes in the ceiling (something that would probably happen anyway), is also quite profitable. El Príncipe and El Exquisito (next to El Rincón), according to their owners, both consciously began to put *vallenato* and salsa on their jukeboxes to attract more black trade: and this is a specific option—the owner of El Príncipe remarked that if Antioqueños step inside, "they leave again straight away when they realize it's not their atmosphere."

Salsa is closely linked to this history, but it maintains a separate identity, expressed in its spatial location. It also started in Guayaquil, but its focus was a particular avenue called Palacé. Its arrival in Medellín was quite sudden and postdated the explosive appearance of salsa in the New York scene of the sixties. By the mid-seventies there were about ten bars on Palacé Avenue which played nothing but salsa—and at full volume. These places were also focal points for blacks, but they were never as segregated as the *vallenato* bars: salsa was soon popular with Latin Americans all over the continent, among them some of Medellín's working-class Antioqueño youth. Quite soon, other bars, now more upmarket as well, began to appear in other zones of the city—one appeared on La Setenta, Seventieth Avenue, an area of mainly middle-class entertainment, a couple emerged near the University of Antioquia, others were established in more outlying working-class barrios; later, big salsa stars came and gave concerts in the city. Nowadays there is a salsa-only local radio station, and some salsa and even some *vallenato* are common at most younger-generation Antioqueño parties. Palacé has lost its monopoly: after a fire there and some violent incidents in the late seventies, a decline set in, and by the time Carlos and I used to go there to listen to records that had not changed much for more than fifteen years, there were only three bars left.

A curious phenomenon in this history is that in these salsa and *vallenato* bars there are no dance floors. Other places now exist where dancing takes place, but the whole salsa and *vallenato* fashion started without dancing, its close associate or even raison d'être, and bars such as El Suizo and El Rincón still do not have facilities for dancing.

The reason seems to be basically economic: Mario Quinceno said of El Atlántico, "In 1974, I had the idea of turning it into a *grill* [a euphemism for a dancing place]. But it was a failure: the blacks start dancing and they forget to drink." Equally in one local place, now closed, which did have a dance floor, Los Magnates, the music included a slow ballad for every salsa and *vallenato* number, so that people would sit out and drink more. Basically, dance floors take up space and distract people from spending money on drink. Thus most of the places that do have a dance floor in Medellín charge high prices, and this would be inappropriate for the down-market area of these bars and would exclude most of their clientele. The precise way that salsa and *vallenato* entered Medellín in formal establishments was thus influenced by its class status: only when salsa at least began to attract a clientele that could afford higher prices was dancing included. The *bailaderos* of the Chocoanos form a contrast in this respect, because although they cater to a low-earning, working-class clientele, dancing is an essential feature and has been so from the start. Clearly the Chocoanos have created their own institutions in view of the limited possibilities presented by those established by Antioqueños in El Centro.

In Medellín, salsa and *vallenato* are taken up by the Chocoanos, and by virtue of their particular mode of use in *bailaderos* and black bars, these styles participate in the establishing of a black world around nuclei such as El Suizo or La Playita in La Iguaná. In this process, these genres can constitute part of a black nucleus which implicitly repels nonblacks—that is, when they are played loudly, exclusively, and continuously in places where blacks congregate. In this sense, they participate in the constitution of localized black identity in the city, an identity that becomes opposed to the Antioqueño world and an identity that helps define a space in which blackness is normal and black culture can be lived and reproduced, although this autonomy is subject to attack and interference from Antioqueños, as the Iguaná and Zafra cases illustrate. At the same time, however, these musical genres have become part of the Antioqueño scene in Medellín, usually watered down with selections of ballads and *música tropical*. It is my argument that the nonblack world in Medellín, or more accurately the youth of that world, took up salsa and to a lesser extent *vallenato* partly because, like the *música tropical* of previous decades, they were seen as hot, tropical, exciting, and perhaps erotic, all qualities covertly associated with the blacks who were such public consumers of these genres in the city center. Typically, however, these genres were not adopted unchanged but were adapted into more acceptable forms. In Medellín, the blacks have adapted, to greater or lesser extent, but the Antioqueños have changed too, despite their dominant position. "People have changed," as one Chocoano woman said, "beginning with the fact that they've learned how to dance the rhythms of the blacks. Because here they didn't know how. To watch a full-blooded Antioqueño dancing was enough to make you cry. And now it's a pleasure to watch them—well, those under 30 . . ." It is, of course, difficult to weight the precise contribution that the presence of the Chocoanos in Medellín made to the impact of salsa and *vallenato* on the city, since both genres were nationally growing forces at the time. The history of past relations between the black and the nonblack worlds via their music suggests a crucial catalytic role for them in this respect.

Black Religion: A Parallel Process

The history of black religion is inseparable from that of black music, and although I cannot expand on this here, it is worth making a couple of observations. All over the New World, blacks established religious traditions that were independent of orthodox church traditions and even of the popular religious forms of the nonblack world. These could be as specific and distinct as *santería* or *candomblé,* but in Colombia blacks took on Catholic models and developed them, often in areas where religious authority was weak or corrupt, in what Friedemann (1966–69) calls an "independent religious context," to produce the distinctive "black Catholicism" that Bastide also found in Brazil (1978, 109). In the religious realm, as well as the musical one, practices that look simply Latin American on closer examination turn out to have specific characteristics. As both Bastide (1978) and Marks (1974) note for Brazil, and as Friedemann (1966–69) notes for Colombia, this includes an opposition between "church" and "street" in which black religious activities tend to focus strongly on the "street" context, rather outside the spatial and clerical control of the church.

One feature of black religion was that religion, music, dance, and celebration went hand in hand from an early date. *Cabildos* clearly embodied both and were thus persecuted by the church as well as civil authorities. In Cuban *santería,* as in Brazilian *candomblé* and Haitian Voodoo, music and dance are essential components of ceremonial observance. A recent film, *Cuyagua,* by Henley and Drion (1987) shows graphically the nature of black Catholicism as practiced by Venezuelan coastal blacks, with organizations of dancers, clearly derived from the old *cabildos,* celebrating with rum and endless dancing the festival days of Corpus Christi and Saint John the Baptist.

291

Interestingly, there are said to be two Saint Johns: San Juan *el parrandero,* the fun lover, who goes out on the streets, and San Juan *el evangélico,* the religious one. There are hints here of survivals of the process in which a pantheon of African gods was hidden behind a parallel pantheon of Christian saints, allowing their worship behind the mask of Christian sainthood (Bastide 1971, 157; Friedemann and Arocha 1986, 381). This duality corresponds to the split noted by Friedemann (1966–69) between the official church context and the popular, black street context. In the Chocó and in other black areas of Colombia, celebrations in honor of the saints tend to focus on the people and the street, or the river, rather than the church and the priest. During patron saint celebrations, for example, there is a marked absence of the long confessional queues at the church doors and the open-air masses that one sees in the more piously Catholic interior of the country (see Velásquez 1960b; Villa 1985; Friedemann and Arocha 1986, 402–14). For Chocoano *velorios,* too, Velásquez quotes church observations that characterize these as "ridiculous fiesta" (1961b, 35). The funeral banquet of the last day of the wake seems to the church especially irreverent: "Only in the Chocó could this abomination of the *ninth day* exist in which people of all ages and conditions congregate, festive and gay . . . they play cards, draughts, dominoes; they sing absurd verses, they tell obscene stories which cause laughter, they smoke, they drink *aguardiente* and they eat in abundance . . . as if with cups of liquor they would win indulgences" (Velásquez 1961b, 56).

Black religion was, not surprisingly, hounded by the religious authorities. Apart from being seen as simply dissolute and impious, blacks were often considered heretics and practitioners of magic. Medina (1978) cites many cases of the Inquisition in Cartagena interrogating blacks for witchcraft and heresy, and Arrázola (1970, 205) quotes a letter from the governor of Cartagena to the king in which he reports the sudden death of two of the torturers of the blacks arrested in the 1693 slave conspiracy. The letter says they had been poisoned because "the majority [of the blacks] are witches, herbalists and of perverse customs." Eduardo Lemaitre reports that the leader of a 1692 expedition against the Palenque de San Basilio died suddenly, and witchcraft was again widely suspected (1983, 2:189). Taussig (1980a, 65) and Borrego Pla (1973, 83) also mention reports of *brujos,* sorcerers, being leaders of *palenques.* In Cuba, the existence of *santería* cults that worshiped African gods behind a thin veneer of Catholicism also provoked negative reactions from the church (Ortiz 1917).

However, we find the same two-edged reaction. Taussig reports that "female slaves served as healers to such exalted personages as the bishop of Cartagena and the inquisitors themselves" (1980a, 42). Fernando Ortiz remarks acutely that the priests in Cuba believed implicitly in the power of the black *brujos* because they thought them to be in league with the devil (1917, 257). Moreover, "rich women of elevated lineage" submitted themselves to ceremonies conducted by *brujos* "at the altar of fanatical belief" (1917, 147). In the present, Taussig (1980b) observes that blacks from the Pacific coast are feared and admired as healers and *brujos*. Equally, Bastide (1978) and Hamilton (1970) both give plenty of evidence of how whites have recourse to the services of the priests and priestesses of the Brazilian *candomblés*. In her work on Umbanda in Rio, Brown notes that the sorcery that derived from the city's various Afro-Brazilian syncretic religions is "a lower sector skill catering in part to an upper sector clientele" (1986, 34). She also observes that Umbanda originated partly because the "middle sector does not see itself as powerful enough to solve its own problems, so it turns to the greater vitality of the religions of the poor," using African and indian spirits "whom they considered far more competent in curing" than the highly evolved European Kardecist spirits (1986, 40–41).

Carlos Pino was a good dancer. In the salsa bars on Palacé Avenue, there were no dance floors, but people would get up occasionally and dance between the tables, nearly always single men. Carlos would watch them—and me—critically, pass the odd judgment such as "He's just learning," recall former black friends whose talents were so admired that people would pay to watch them dance, and, when the mood took him, get up and dance himself. His son, Wilmer, was well trained and, although embarrassed when made to dance in front of adults at parties, could outperform most of them once warmed up and was streets ahead of his Antioqueño contemporaries at their parties. Even though he had been brought up in Medellín, dancing was part of his cultural competence in much the same way as it was for children in, for example, the Atlantic or Pacific coastal regions.

Blackness and dancing, especially nowadays to salsa or *vallenato*, are closely connected, and although the connection is partly an imposed stereotype, it is also a real part of black culture and one that some blacks enjoy reiterating to a nonblack audience. On a couple of occasions, we went as a group to rather restrained parties given by friends of Noris, his wife, and here Carlos would be the life and soul, acting like a "typical" Costeño. He would laugh loudly and make raucous remarks, raid the record collection and put on danceable music, grab the mother or even the grandmother of the household and whirl her around the floor, cracking risqué jokes concerning possible amorous encounters between him and her. This, for him, was not serious partying: it was just a way to have some fun at what would otherwise be a rather boring event. For a proper *parranda,* one needed plenty of *aguardiente,* a group of good paisanos, a powerful ghetto blaster to produce hour after hour of *vallenato* and salsa, and women to dance with—although actually female companions were not considered indispensable by some: they could get in the way of serious drinking.

16

Whitening

It is an open question whether a society that sees every addition of white blood as a step towards purification is more, or less, prejudiced than a society that sees any appreciable trace of Negro blood as a mark of degradation.

Barely emerging from slavery and in their eagerness to rise, [*los negritos catedráticos*] took advantage of any occasion to wear a dress coat and top hat, like the powerful whites, and to talk in a refined manner, like eminent people . . . and aspiring to pass for superior people . . . won only ridicule, indifference, and disillusionment.

Both through necessity and choice, blacks in Colombia have in certain contexts grouped together and resisted white-oriented definitions of reality and white domination—sometimes explicitly, sometimes by the simple act of congregating as blacks. They have carved out their own niches or been relegated to them and have created specific forms of culture, identified as black and often persecuted, even when these are reelaborated versions of European models. The alternative has been to escape blackness, if possible, and this maneuver can take different forms. First, of course, there is race mixture as an intergenerational process—one's children can be physically whitened. Race mixture is, however, one of the later steps on the ladder to whitening. A second form of escape thus consists of the earlier steps of moving outside the black nuclei and integrating oneself into nonblack networks, a process

Epigraphs: (1) David Brion Davis (1969); (2) From Fernando Ortiz (1965, 129); *los negritos catedráticos* means the black professors, or at least those who aspired or pretended to be such.

that involves adapting one's behavior and assimilating models identified as nonblack—bearing in mind, of course, that what was nonblack at one point may be reidentified as black at another. This process can be seen as social whitening, part of the general process of *blanqueamiento*. As always, there is a complex interplay between ethnic factors and politico-economic and geographic factors and between personal motives and larger-scale structures. It is never simply a question of "to be or not to be black": the very posing of the option is always situated in a context that predisposes certain answers and makes some alternatives untenable. The very process of leaving the Chocó and going to Medellín, for economic motives, for example, exposes the individual to a series of influences and contacts which may have the effect of "whitening" him or her, without there being a specific and conscious desire to "escape blackness": rather, it may seem simply absurd to try to remain in a black world. One Chocoano mother remarked of her daughters born in Medellín, "They live with whites, so if they fall in love with a white man, what fault is it of theirs?" How, she asked, could she go around the city recruiting black men to come to the house for her daughters to fall in love with? Similarly, a Chocoano woman in Bogotá with a master of arts degree observed that there were simply very few Chocoano men around at her educational level who could be suitable partners. So, geographical and/or upward mobility can draw blacks out of a black environment and make staying black a difficult process. But even if a motive of *blanqueamiento* is absent here—which it may not be, as in the case of the Chocoano mother's daughters, some of whom made remarks such as *"negro no come negro"* (black doesn't eat [i.e., have sex with] black)—it is often inferred by others. The Chocoano mother said, "I've been called a racist [by other blacks] because most of my daughters have had children with white men." And the Chocoano woman in Bogotá, although herself a researcher on black culture and the family and connected to the black consciousness movements that exist in Colombia, had been reproved by a black male friend when seen with a white man: "It looks very bad for a woman in your position." In short, then, *blanqueamiento* is a complex process embedded in the regional and politico-economic structures of the country which has an ambiguous relationship to personal motives. The classic case is the upwardly mobile black who marries a white and adopts behavior characteristic of the middle-class nonblack world, but the reality is more varied. For example, there used to be old settlements of free blacks, some of which took the name of *palenque,* around the rural outskirts of Medellín (Yépez Henao 1984). These disappeared as they were included in the growing urban network, and whatever the personal motives involved, this too was a process of *blanqueamiento* equal to that which affected the whole of Antioquia's highland black and mulatto population. Many working-class Chocoanos in Medellín end up married to or living with Antioqueños—again, their motives are varied. The choice of whether to remain in the black world or move out of it is rarely an isolated one about cultural values, personal identity, and loyalties alone—rather, it takes place within a context that includes many material factors. Nevertheless, at the roots of *blanqueamiento* lies the specter of racism, because whitening, however accomplished and with whatever motives, means leaving the disdained status of blackness. This is particularly evident in the accusations and reprovals often leveled by some blacks at other blacks who whiten themselves in some way: they are deserting the fold.

In comparisons with North America, the existence of *blanqueamiento* has often been taken as indicative of a lack of racial discrimination, but Latin American racial orders need to be understood in their own terms. As the different contexts explored in this book have shown, it is clear that the possibility of whitening admits some flexibility into the system. But first, it is a conditional flexibility that becomes noticeably less yielding when blacks do not adapt or when they challenge the system in larger numbers. And second, it is a flexibility predicated upon the low status of blackness: every maneuver in processes of *blanqueamiento* reiterates this fundament of the system (Banton 1967). Moreover, it may mean that blacks themselves come to adopt disdainful attitudes towards blacks and black culture, while being unable to fully escape categorization as blacks themselves. Hence the accusations of betrayal which infer from the choice of a white or nonblack partner—or simply the choice of a nonblack world as an environment—a public rejection of blackness by a black. In addition, if upwardly mobile blacks marry lighter-skinned people, blackness is inevitably bleached out of the middle strata of society, maintaining the overall correlation between black and poor. And this correlation will remain as long as black upward mobility and its acceptance remain individualistic and conditional. Last, as I discuss in more detail in the next chapter, if at least some blacks are avoiding blackness and having their strategies to this end accepted by nonblack society, the identification of these people, and even more so that of their children, with black people in general is obviously very problematic. To the extent that such identification is needed to create a consciousness and organization capable of articulating protest and attempting to redefine the meaning of blackness, *blanqueamiento* is a mechanism that defuses black solidarity. In all these senses, *blanquea-miento,* far from being indicative of the absence of racial prejudice, is its principal manifestation in Latin American society.

Blanqueamiento needs to be understood in a wider context than that of simple physical race mixture. In this sense, *"blanqueamiento,"* like "black" or "black culture," is not a simple term but refers to a complex process of competing claims and ascriptions about identity. *Blanqueamiento* is part of the forces that act so as to dilute and disperse blackness and black culture—forces that do indeed generally culminate in actual race mixture but which include geographical mobility out of black regions into nonblack ones and, in general, estrangement from the black nuclei that exist in different forms and from aspects of behavior and culture identified as black. These forces very often, but not always, work in tandem with the specific motives of some blacks to escape the stigmatized status of black.

The argument pursued here recalls in some respects Degler's (1971) concept of the "mulatto escape hatch" but also goes considerably beyond it, and it is important to specify the differences between his and my ideas on this matter, especially in view of recent attacks on the notion of "the mulatto escape hatch" by Nelson do Valle Silva (1985). Degler (1971) argues for Brazil that various historical circumstances created not only miscegenation but also the social recognition of the offspring, the mulattoes, who were accorded a "special place" (1971, 107). He also implies at various points, without really giving any evidence (except from contemporary marital acceptability studies), that mulattoes were more favorably treated than blacks and thus able to advance—he does show that mulattoes have in particular instances enjoyed more social mobility than blacks (1971, 108), but that, of course, is not the same thing, unless one falsely assumes that upward mobility is determined uniquely by discrimination. Silva (1985) uses data from the Brazilian 1976 National Household Survey to contest this implication, affirming that mulattoes are discriminated against equally with, or indeed more than, blacks.

There are initial difficulties with Silva's critique which stem from the use of self-assigned census categories of color and their adequacy for statistically analyzing processes of discrimination which rely on ascribed categories. The data that Silva uses clearly show that mulattoes and blacks are both lower than whites on various socioeconomic scales and that "discrimination" (calculated according to statistical formulae) explains more of the white-mulatto income differential than the black-white differential (Silva 1985, 53). However, his categories of *preto* (black), *pardo* (brown), and *branco* (white) are self-assigned identifications, whereas "discrimination" is a social process in which some people identify others. In the case of discrimination as a factor in explaining income differentials, it is presumably a matter of some people ("whites") who control strategic resources classifying others ("blacks" and "mulattoes") and on this basis denying them certain opportunities. But we have no indication of to what extent *preto* and *pardo* capture a socially significant aspect of physical and cultural variation with respect to discrimination. Silva shows that people who classify themselves as *pardo* suffer more "discrimination" (in terms of his calculations) than those who classify themselves as *preto*. But it is quite possible that those who classify themselves as *branco,* who are presumably practicing the discrimination being measured, would ascribe the term *preto* to many who claim to be *pardo*.

Even if we grant that there is sufficient overlap between claimed and ascribed categories to make Silva's calculations meaningful, there are other factors that need to be taken into account. *Pardos* may suffer greater discrimination in some respects, but as Silva himself shows, mulattoes are still consistently above blacks on a variety of socioeconomic scales. Hasenbalg (1985) reiterates this point. Degler may be wrong in asserting that this is because mulattoes suffer less discrimination, but this hardly clarifies the overall relation between upward mobility and race mixture, which is really the heart of the issue. We need to address the fact that mulattoes may be intermediate between blacks and whites because their white parent gave them a material start in life, or because a black parent was upwardly mobile, adapted culturally, and married a lighter-skinned person, giving birth to mulattoes who thus also had a head start. Silva does not address these issues and confines himself to attempting to refute Degler's particular point. Degler himself, whose argument could be recast by these considerations, does not really bring them into play.

My argument looks at the general relation between upward mobility and race mixture. These are not inevitably linked in a simple fashion. Friedemann (1977a), for example, shows that in colonial Cartagena destitute white men married black women. Equally, in Unguía and Medellín poor Chocoanos and Antioqueños marry each other. But there is a strong structural link between upward mobility and race mixture. Blacks are subject to pressures, stemming from the high value attributed to lightness and the negative value attributed to blackness, which can induce them to adapt culturally to the mores of the nonblack world and which may involve finding a lighter-skinned partner. Very often those who adapt culturally and seek such a partner are those who have attained some upward mobility—and this has be understood in a broad sense. Destitute white men in colonial Cartagena were, in effect, downwardly mobile into the lower, darker-skinned classes, and blacks moving into Unguía or Medellín *are* experiencing a form of upward mobility in the sense of leaving a poor black region and entering economically more dynamic areas where there is more wealth and infrastructure. This inevitably creates a structural link between economic improvement and possibilities of race mixture. Or alternatively, a black may achieve upward mobility by marrying a white with a superior material position that is passed on to offspring. Either case shows that it is misguided to assume, as Degler tends to, that mobility is dependent on discrimination alone and that it generally follows miscegenation. Mobility equally or more often precedes race mixture. Mulattoes may then suffer more discrimination (if Silva's calculations are meaningful), but they have already achieved some upward mobility. They can also claim greater social status in the color hierarchy, something that Silva's statistical manipulations cannot capture. On the other side of the coin, when I talk of nonblack conditional acceptance of blacks, this does not imply that mulattoes are necessarily less discriminated against but simply means that discrimination against blacks (and mulattoes for that matter) is not thoroughgoing and systematic. Some blacks and mulattoes are accepted as marriage partners, as social equals, as employees in jobs usually occupied by nonblacks, as friends, and so on. In short, Silva's point, even if it is true, is not an obstacle for my argument. Moreover, outside the limitations of his statistical analysis, there remains the fundamental idea that a hierarchy of race and color exists in which lighter is better than darker. Even from my perspective, then, there comes a point at which someone who is far enough away from the stereotype of *negro* can avoid the discrimination aimed at that type. This, I think, is unquestionable.

With respect to the relation between upward mobility and *blanqueamiento,* one of the interesting things about Medellín is that these processes of adaptation take place among working-class blacks. The typical format found in much of the Brazilian literature on race relations (e.g., Fernandes 1969) is that of the upwardly mobile black adapting him- or herself to a middle-class white world (see Solaún and Kronus 1973 for a Colombian example). Medellín indicates that this type of upward mobility is not a necessary condition: the simple act of moving into the nonblack world of Antioquia can be envisaged as a move upwards in the hierarchy of wealth and region in Colombia. Moving into Medellín represents a cultural step as great as, or greater than, rising from the working class into the middle class.

Blanqueamiento in Unguía

What is happening in both Unguía and Medellín forms part of processes of the dispersal, dilution, and adaptation of blackness and black culture to the nonblack world, that is, of *blanqueamiento* in the widest sense. The area of Urabá has been for centuries a point of interaction between Chocoanos and Costeños, and the Chocoanos have, so to speak, used the area as an outlet from the blackness of the Chocó, physically and culturally. Race mixture was an active force in Unguía, and most of it was between Chocoanos and Costeños: many of the offspring of the unions, past and present, represented a significant lightening of color from their Chocoano parent. Equally, the area has always been culturally distinct from the rest of the Chocó, due to its proximity to the Caribbean coast, and with the advent of the Antioqueños, it has changed dramatically. The Chocoano migrants to the region, now an overall minority, do not have cultural dominion, and they, and especially their children, progressively adopt ways that are heavily influenced by Costeños in accent, food, music, *velorios*. I have yet to hear a Chocoano in Unguía adopt an Antioqueño accent, but only among the older, more rustic migrants does one hear the strong, typical Chocoano turn of phrase. Interestingly, it was commented by blacks in Unguía that those Chocoanos who moved over the gulf and lived in the Antioqueño town of Turbo would begin to consider themselves superior to their cousins over in the Chocó.

In Unguía, there is also an important relation between race mixture and upward mobility. In chapter 9, I referred to three families who accounted for most of the reasonably well-off Chocoanos. One family was the product of an Antioqueño man's marriage to a Chocoano woman: the children were mulattoes, and with the exception of the eldest son, who married a mulatto woman, the other children all married people substantially whiter than themselves. Another family was parented by a Chocoano man and a Costeño woman: almost all of their seven children had university educations in Bogotá, and the two sons who have married have done so with women lighter skinned than themselves. The third family, or more accurately kindred, is rather different in that they are not themselves the products of mixed unions. The kindred consists of several interlinked Chocoano families with farming and some political and mining interests. Only two men of that group—who are not its richest members—have married white women. Clearly, then, once race mixture is under way, it tends to continue, especially if combined with upward social mobility: mulatto offspring will often marry up racially if they can. In addition, it is not only upward mobility but also the coincidence of this with moving out of a mainly black world which form the most impelling conditions for *blanqueamiento*. Naturally, such coincidences are not random but are highly structured: upward mobility leads to emigration from the Chocó for education in Bogotá; equally, the possibility of the initial Antioqueño-Chocoano union that produced the second family was contingent on the migration into the area of Antioqueños, who also gave a boost to the local economy. The structured coincidence of upward mobility and increased social contact with the nonblack world goes beyond actual marriages and unions. In Unguía, for example, the richest member of the Chocoano farming kindred, like two of his half brothers, had cattle *a utilidades* (split-profit cattle-sharing deals) with Antioqueños: naturally, the number of Chocoanos who owned sufficient capital to participate in these deals with them—that is, to buy cattle and have them raised on their farms—was practically zero. It was the Antioqueños who had the capital, and the Chocoanos who were running relatively successful farms had to rely on Antioqueños for this kind of arrangement. This man was accused by some other blacks of "sticking with the Antioqueños," because he rented premises to an Antioqueño and lived in an Antioqueño boarding house in the center of town, instead of in another house of his nearer the rest of the group. There was, however, very little evidence that he was trying to "escape blackness," since he had a black wife and was heavily involved in Chocoano political networks, but the mere fact of being relatively wealthy put him into more contact with Antioqueños, albeit on a mainly commercial basis. This was enough to provoke some resentment from other Chocoanos, who expected greater solidarity from him. In short, the possibility of increasing wealth depends on increased contact with the nonblack world: whether this leads to social or physical whitening is, of course, another matter, but the preconditions exist.

Blanqueamiento in Medellín

In Medellín, the forces that disperse blackness and are conducive to both social and physical whitening are even stronger than in the Urabá region. On the Chocoano side of the Urabá, at least, the Antioqueños are still regarded as intruders even if they now effectively dominate the area, and the Costeños are a strong intermediary element—indeed, several of the female partners of the mixed unions in the families noted above were Costeños. More generally, moves away from the black world of the Chocó can be made in the direction of *la Costa*, which, while its national image is generally construed in terms of blackness, is not seen as totally black and primitive as the Pacific coastal region and which also has some cultural similarities to the Chocó in terms of family structure, music, and dance. In contrast, in Medellín the Chocoanos come face to face with a nonblack—indeed, effectively white—world on its own territory, a world that is not only white and condemns blackness but which is also urban and scorns rough rural ways and which is relatively economically developed and looks down on poor, underdeveloped regions. What is more, there are very few Costeños there to act as potential intermediaries. The creation of black nuclei such as La Iguaná or getting together in El Suizo may be a measure of defense against this world, but in real terms it is a minority of Chocoanos who participate in this. As I showed in chapter 12, most Chocoanos live in a fairly dispersed fashion; they do not have the intensive relation to the Chocoano network implied by active participation in these nuclei. In addition, analysis of the citywide survey showed that about half the Chocoanos in common-law or legal marriages had a non-Chocoano, usually Antioqueño, partner (see below). Last, a great many of the Chocoano families I interviewed in ordinary working-class barrios said that they had as many Antioqueño friends as Chocoano ones, or even more. In some cases that I knew personally, this was a misrepresentation insofar as the close circle of friends was clearly mostly Chocoano: it seemed that some people were eager to portray themselves as nonpartisan in their friendships, as if admitting to having mostly black friends would imply that one was socially inept, unacceptable, or perhaps *acomplejado*. A couple of comments in the written statements by Chocoano students recognized this process of adaptation. One said, "My relations with Chocoanos are few, not because I don't want them, but because living in this environment, one adapts oneself to the 'whites.'" Another wrote that Medellín at first seemed to her another world but that she "gradually adapted to the environment, the customs and even the speech."

The ethnic network is a highly varied patchwork. Although few Chocoanos are totally estranged from the network, there are certain areas of it, some permanent, some temporary, where the density and interconnectedness of linkages is high, the links themselves are intensive and frequent, and their content is multistranded, embracing neighborliness, kinship, friendship, and a whole range of utilitarian and symbolic exchanges. Outside these dense areas, the network becomes more rarified, and the urban Antioqueño networks, with which the Chocoano network always interpenetrates to a greater or lesser extent, intrude more. The links with Chocoanos are less intense and frequent, and their content is limited to, say, friendship. In the dense parts of the network, linkages back into the Chocó are important and fairly durable; in the rarified parts, these begin to lose importance and may virtually disappear. There are many possible positions on a continuum between the highest and the lowest density of the network. The highest would be typified by, say, Marleny, one of my principal informants in La Playita. Although born herself in Medellín, she lived with a Chocoano common-law husband in an environment in which the vast majority of her contacts were with Chocoanos. Through her husband and her parents, she entered into the tight kinship network of La Playita; she spent time in the Chocó with her husband, who retained rights to land there, and from time to time she could be heard slipping into something approaching a Chocoano accent. She played cards with the Chocoanos in the afternoons and went to the Chocoano *bailaderos* in the evenings. On Sundays, I might run into her in El Suizo in the center of town. Her husband worked in construction excavating foundations with a Chocoano team, and she would occasionally leave town with a group of Chocoanos destined for some provincial town's annual festivals, where they would sell cooked food on the streets. Later she got a job as a domestic servant.

The opposite end of the scale could be exemplified by the mother of Rosario, my research assistant and friend. She arrived in Medellín in 1941 and worked for nine years as a domestic servant until she married a Chocoano who worked first selling *paletas*, flavored ices, on the streets and then found employment as a manual worker in the city council's public services division, where he stayed until he was killed in a traffic accident in 1975. Initially, they rented a house in the city center, near La Bayadera in Guayaquil. Later, the city council helped them buy a house in an outlying barrio and gave them further loans to improve it. The council was to some extent instrumental in the location of the house: Luz, the mother, found a house in Barrio Antioquia, then a nucleus of Chocoano activity, but the council vetoed this choice, saying that, because of prostitution and so forth, it was not a suitable barrio. Luz is now quite old and rarely sees any of her Chocoano friends; there are a couple of other Chocoano families in the barrio, but no real links are maintained with them. Her daughters, eight of them, likewise have little to do with the Chocoano network, except Rosario, who had done a year's secondary schooling in Quibdó and had some contact with the network through her university, where several Chocoanos studied—even then, however, it was largely through her association with me that she became more integrated into the ethnic network, as she revitalized her mother's old links for interview purposes and got to know the Chocoano nuclei. Four of the daughters have had children with Antioqueños; three of them work

304

as kindergarten assistants in the Antioqueño atmosphere of the Colombian Institute for Family Welfare.

An intermediate level in the network might be illustrated by my friend Carlos Pino, with whom I shared a house. He is not entirely typical in that he is a Costeño from Turbo, but his father was Chocoano and he has family in Quibdó, and his relationship to the two somewhat overlapping networks of Turbeños and Chocoanos, which is what I want to illustrate, is of the intermediate kind to which I am referring, although it tends towards the denser end of the spectrum. He has many friends and acquaintances who are Antioqueños: after fourteen years living in the city, studying, teaching in a school, and participating in sport nationally and internationally it would be surprising if he did not. His wife, Noris, is also from Turbo and in 1987 started work in a factory, studying at night school in the evenings: the friends she makes and brings home are Antioqueños. We lived, and he has lived previously, in ordinary working-class barrios and never in a black nucleus. However, Carlos's intimate circle of friends and drinking companions is almost entirely made up of Turbeños, mostly blacks like himself, and Chocoanos. Virtually all his compadres, men who have asked him to be godfather to their child, are Turbeños and Chocoanos. The people who are invited to his home on weekends to *parrandear,* party, are mostly from this group, although Noris's Antioqueño friends and the Antioqueño spouses of a couple of his friends are also included from time to time. When Carlos needs favors, loans, and assistance, he goes to his richer Turbeño friends for help, and equally other blacks come to him. Cousins and friends from the Chocó come and stay at the house en route elsewhere or just for a visit: occasionally he goes to Quibdó for the yearly patron saint festivals, the Fiestas de San Pacho. If we went to El Suizo or across the road to El Rincón del Vallenato, he would almost inevitably run into some Costeño or Chocoano he knew, since throughout his years in the city he had taken care to maintain his own personal network within the ethnic one.

These sketches give some idea of the variety of possible relations to the ethnic network: the question is what determines these relations. A major factor is the nature of racism in the city and generally in Colombia: the contempt in which black culture is generally held can lead blacks to create niches for their own defense; equally, given that contempt plus the possibility of acceptance through adaptation on an individualistic basis, blacks may distance themselves from the dense focal points of the network and even estrange themselves from the whole network, attempting to integrate into urban Antioqueño networks as much as possible. But this alone is an insufficient explanation, because it does not account for why some blacks take one path and some another: there are obviously some determining variables, and these are connected with the economic and residential structures of the city, as I showed in chapter 12. In theoretical terms, ethnic choices and processes are structured by the economic, residential, and spatial relations of the city which they themselves partly orchestrate. The basic economic and class structure of the city is the framework within which ethnic choices and processes operate, whether the city is Medellín, Chicago, or London—ethnicity and race do not determine that structure, although they are part of its organization and create their own patterns within it.

In chapter 12, I argued that economic position and the nature of the housing market were the principal factors affecting Chocoanos' relationship to the ethnic network, along with familiarity with the city and the family cycle. As a general rule, those who have a higher economic status live rather isolated from other Chocoanos and will tend to be more estranged from the ethnic network as a whole. But choice plays a crucial role here, because if people *choose*, they can still participate actively in the network. What is at issue here is that older residents who live in a dispersed fashion and have a reasonably firm working-class status are most open to pressures from the Antioqueño milieu to dissociate themselves from Chocoano culture, seen as primitive, rowdy, aggressive, immoral, and even lower down the hierarchy than working class. These people, apart from being in one sense physically estranged from the network, may also want to distance themselves from it and may even grow to disdain it. On the other hand, they may still find it of material use and may value or relish their participation in it because of the way they feel about being black, about black culture, and about being with paisanos: this was clearly the case with Carlos, whose mentality of *parrandero* could only really find expression among his paisanos and others who enjoyed listening to *vallenato* at full volume for hours on end.

For example, I went once with Carlos to the house of Fernando, my Costeño friend who worked in Desarrollo Comunitario and used to take me to visit Chocoano families in Moravia. He shared a house with some friends in a middle-class area of town, and as Carlos and I leaned over the balcony and surveyed the quiet streets—a far cry from the streets below our own balcony in Aranjuez, in which a virtually permanent football game was in progress, with associated shouts and exclamations, and where people congregated in their doorways and on street corners—he reflected, not without some scorn, on the "dead" atmosphere of middle-class barrios, where none of the noise and liveliness of working-class areas could erupt. More particularly, it was impossible to *parrandear*, party, in any serious fashion in such a barrio. He recounted the stories of a few friends who had felt their position in society such as to warrant residence in a middle-class area but who had not left behind their Costeño predilection for the *parrandas*, loud, long, and regular, which frequently formed the basis of Carlos's stories. Their white middle-class neighbors lost no time in bringing the law down on their necks with a regularity that made the choice clear—either move out or shut up. On the contrary, in Aranjuez the general noise level was higher, and, although our house was probably the noisiest in terms of music and *parrandas*, neighborly tolerance was high.

The physical dispersal of black people in Medellín, then, is structured by certain economic and spatial processes, but these constantly interact with factors related specifically to ethnicity. Blacks are not only physically dispersed but are also laid open to forces of cultural adaptation which individuals may choose to ignore, give some leeway to, or take on board wholeheartedly. Certain circumstances are conducive to nucleation—recent arrival, poverty, invasion settlements, and tenement blocks—but the business of forming a residential ethnic niche or participating in the temporary weekend black congregations is also a choice and a statement about blackness and black culture. Such nuclei can create their own atmosphere, drawing in people such as Marleny, who has plenty of city experience but who participates more in the Chocoano network than either of her parents.

The Second Generation. The second generation of blacks born of Chocoano parents in Medellín tend to become even more separated from the ethnic network. Examples such as Marleny are, frankly, atypical, although undoubtedly black children brought up in La Iguaná have a more intensive relationship to the ethnic network than others. Generally, the second generation is quite young, so it is difficult to draw firm conclusions, but among those who are in their teens and older, it is clear that adaptation to the Antioqueño milieu advances even further than among their parents. The Antioqueño accent is adopted, the individuals consider themselves Antioqueños by birth, they go to school among Antioqueños, where any other regional accent, especially Costeño or Chocoano, is quickly noted and made the butt of jokes and so forth. Their relationship to the ethnic network is liable to be more tenuous and have little utilitarian value for them, while the Chocó is now a foreign land and Chocoano culture something experienced at second hand via their parents and visiting relatives from the Chocó. However, as children of Chocoanos, they are black, and whatever their cultural loyalties and their claims to Antioqueño identity, they may find these claims accepted only with suspicion or ridicule by other Antioqueños: the very term *paisa negro* is an oxymoron that produces laughter among Antioqueños and Chocoanos alike. People are surprised to hear an Antioqueño accent coming from an obviously black person, and the question always arises: "Where are you from?"—to which the answer has to be, "I'm from here, but my parents are Chocoanos." One young black woman commented, "Sometimes it's useful to be Antioqueño when you're black. In social relations, for example, the accent doesn't seem so strange to them; rather, they find it really amusing and make fun of it. When I was working in a lawyer's office, the first thing he noticed was the accent: but what am I supposed to do if I'm an Antioqueño like any other? To him, it seemed like he was hearing things that were Chocoano. It was as if I was demeaning myself with everything I did or said." Rosario, who always declared herself to be "*paisa* to the death," might have this claim accepted but might also be met with this comment, delivered among guffaws from office workers at her university: "Oh really, and what happened then: did you get a good suntan or what?" One black student born in Medellín wrote that problems for the *paisas negros* were "the same problems that confront other blacks" in Antioquia.

To speak of blacks of the second generation as "torn between two cultures" is inappropriate insofar as it tends to imply two rather homogeneous and static cultures, whereas in Medellín both Chocoano and Antioqueño culture are differentiated and dynamic. Rather, the Medellín-born blacks continue to cope, through their personal strategies, with the same basic racial order that their parents live in. Adaptation proceeds further, largely through the schooling process, and acceptance is widespread because of their Antioqueño accents and experience. But they are still blacks, and the conditional nature of their acceptability is occasionally made manifest to them. The acid test is, of course, whether they form unions with Antioqueños. I personally knew of twenty-nine Medellín-born blacks who were or had been in some kind of union, and of these, seventeen (or 58%) had unions with Antioqueños—sometimes only temporary ones leading to single motherhood. This, however, is unlikely to be a representative sample.

Mixed Unions and Upward Mobility in Medellín. Marriage patterns are, in many senses, a crucial element in structural and cultural integration, and in a racially stratified society they are even more crucial since they can lead in the next generation to an escape from the social category of black. The citywide survey revealed that 266 Chocoanos over the age of 12 declared themselves to be either married or in *unión libre* (common-law marriage). For technical reasons, of these I was able to isolate only those Chocoanos who were heads of household, or were spouses (legal and common law) of heads of household, and were actually living with their spouse at the time. These came to 216 individuals. Of these, 104, or 48 percent, were living with or married to a non-Chocoano. The other 112 were paired with one another. However, intermarriage rates are generally calculated in terms of the ratio of mixed to unmixed pairs (Rodman 1965). In these terms, there were a total of 160 unions (104 plus half of 112), of which 104, or 65 percent, were mixed. This compares with the Chocoano intermarriage rate in Unguía, which for pairs was 58 percent (see table 5 in appendix A). As in that case, however, the relevant figure is the ratio of the observed to the expected intermarriage rate, the latter calculated assuming a pattern of random unions (Besanceney 1965). Since the Chocoanos are such a tiny percentage of the city's population, the expected intermarriage rate is around 99 percent (calculated using people over 12 years old who are the married heads of household and their spouses, legal or common law). This gives an observed/expected ratio of 66 percent, compared with the same ratio of 77 percent for Chocoanos in Unguía. In Unguía, much of the Chocoano intermarriage was with Costeños; in Medellín, with mostly Antioqueños to choose from, the real intermarriage rate goes down. Nevertheless, 66 percent represents quite a high ratio and indicates that *blanqueamiento* as a process of race mixture is active in Medellín.

There was also a relation between people who had unions with non-Chocoanos and upward mobility. It was obvious that in a very general sense, those Chocoanos who lived with or were married to non-Chocoanos were not people upwardly mobile into the middle class: many were construction workers or ran small food-selling operations; most lived in working-class barrios. However, when compared with other Chocoanos in general, it was clear that the Chocoanos in the mixed-union group were older, better educated, and better off in terms of occupation.

More pertinent, however, is a comparison between Chocoanos who have unions with each other and those who have unions with non-Chocoanos. Analysis of the city-wide survey looked at Chocoanos over 12 years old who were heads of household or the spouse (common-law or legal) of a head of household. Despite the fact that Chocoano women outnumber men by 60 to 40 in the city, as many Chocoano men as women form unions with non-Chocoanos. This may indicate that Chocoano men have more opportunities for forming mixed unions, but it is more probably due to the large number of young female Chocoanos who are single domestic servants. If female domestics under twenty-five years old are taken out of the Chocoano sample in the census, the male/female ratio is balanced. Chocoanos in mixed unions are legally married in 85 percent of cases compared with 65 percent for unmixed Chocoano couples. They are better educated than Chocoano couples, with 23 percent having complete secondary education or more, versus 9 percent for Chocoano couples, and 53 percent having primary or less, compared with 71 percent for the others. They are also slightly older, with 58 percent being over 35, versus 54 percent for Chocoano couples. They tend to have smaller families, 65 percent having six children or less, compared with 57 percent for the others. Further analysis of these subsamples looked at only those Chocoanos currently working in the paid labor force. When comparing occupations, a shift into higher-level occupations is noticeable among the mixed-union Chocoanos: whereas 7% of the Chocoanos in nonmixed unions ($n = 70$) work in the occupational categories of professional-technical, teacher, and white-collar administrative, this figure is 21 percent for the Chocoanos in mixed unions ($n = 63$). Work in domestic service, hotels, and restaurants is also less important for mixed-union Chocoanos than for Chocoano couples, with 16 percent of the latter working in these occupations, compared with only 3 percent of the former. Construction remains important for both categories, although slightly more common for the nonmixed unions, and participation in those occupational classes that include selling food in public places is also equally important for both categories of Chocoanos. In terms of housing, these differences are reflected in the fact that, while roughly 46 percent of both categories live in stratum three, more of the mixed union Chocoanos live in higher strata (18% vs. 11%) and less in lower strata (35% vs. 43%). In general, then, there emerged a clear relationship between a higher economic position and *blanqueamiento:* blacks who lived in mixed unions were more likely to have a slightly better economic profile. Apparently, the more visible phenomenon of the black who moves into the middle classes and marries a white person is just the more eye-catching aspect of a larger, more subtle process.

The Meaning of Mixed Unions

Race mixture is never a neutral process, and it is logical that the moral loading of *blanqueamiento* should enter to a greater or lesser extent into the actual interpersonal relationships between black and nonblack partners or, failing that, into other people's attitudes towards them. In Bastide's florid phrase, "It is not so much that love breaks down barriers and unites human beings as that racial ideologies extend their conflicts even into love's embraces" (1961, 18). Indeed, Bastide found that in Brazil "the question 'race' always provoked the answer 'sex,'" while Hernton (1965) claims that for the United States race relations are fundamentally sexual relations (see also Wallace 1979 and Hooks 1981 for analyses of the construction of sexual meanings around race in the United States). I found that in Colombia the question "race" did not always provoke the answer "sex," even though in certain circumstances ideas expressed about the sexuality of blacks would show there to be a strong connection in people's minds—especially when white men talked about black women. Here I am more concerned with how marriage and sexual liaison provide a social arena in which ideologies of *blanqueamiento* are reiterated.

In Unguía, I found examples of women who openly admitted to wanting to find a lighter-colored mate: "Well, of course, it's better for my children." Another woman said that she knew that some members of her family were in favor of *blanqueamiento*, although she refused to name the people involved: she herself remarked that it was like "grinding [one's] own face into the dirt," since it was a frank admission of the worthlessness of being black and a desire to escape blackness. In Medellín, too, I came across black women who openly rejected the idea of having a black boyfriend, and in Cartagena a black woman remarked on how her family would comment unfavorably on the dark color of a prospective suitor. Even when there is no such open motive, it is generally inferred by others, whatever protests may be made by the couple involved about a love match. In Unguía, a Chocoano man described as "racist" a Chocoano woman, saying he had noticed the light color of her young child: he deduced that she preferred white men. When it was revealed that she had in fact lived with an Antioqueño for several years, he said conclusively, "See what I mean?" In Medellín, I have already quoted the mother accused of racism because several of her daughters had had children by Antioqueños, and there is also the case of the Chocoano woman in Bogotá reproved by Chocoano friends for going out with a white man.

The union of black men with white women involves a different set of meanings. In Unguía, during a discussion with Chocoanos about the fact that Diego Luis Córdoba, the founder of Cordobism and the political hero of the Chocó, had married a white Antioqueño woman, one opinion held that this was a betrayal of what he had stood for; another replied that it was in fact a demonstration that blacks could have the power to marry white women: one in the eye for the whites. Bastide (1961) also notes an underlying motive of revenge in black male/white female unions, and I would say that the black male is much less likely to be criticized for a racially hypergamous union than a black female: this is seen as much as a victory and a demonstration of prowess and social status as it is a betrayal. In contrast, the woman tends to be subject to much more criticism. This is partly due to historical patterns that have established the idea that white male/ black female unions express exploitation and dominance. It also stems from gender ideologies of male domination which dictate that men can have the freedom to be sexually adventurous, while the women should submit to their men: to the extent that racial divisions and hierarchy impinge, black women are required to submit to black men, and submitting to whites is seen as a betrayal of black men as well as a betrayal of blackness per se (Hooks 1981; Wallace 1979).

Meanings are also attached to the behavior of whites and other nonblacks in their unions with blacks, and these can be quite complex. A white man, for example, may be thought to be simply exploiting a black woman sexually, being particularly attracted to her because of widespread ideas about black female sexuality. A Chocoano student observed that in his experience Antioqueño men tended to think of Chocoano women primarily as sex objects, making remarks to him such as "Let's go to the Chocó and screw some black women" (*vamos al Chocó a comer negra*). When it comes to marriage, however, the white man finds a partner of his own color. Virginia Gutiérrez de Pineda (1975, 282) notes a common arrangement in *la Costa* in which a high-status man has a wife at his own social level plus a lower-status, darker-skinned mistress. Underlying this is the rather muted idea that these white men are getting out of their relationships with black women an emotional, not to mention sexual, intimacy and satisfaction that they fail to get with their white wives—the black woman is seen as the repository of some intangible value that white society is alienated from. There is also, however, the realization that white men may be exploiting their color to gain sexual access to darker-skinned women; often, of course, the lighter men are also wealthier, and this gives them a further advantage. This can give rise to resentment from black men, who feel white men have a greater access to women for both sex and marriage than they do. White men who actually marry black women can, of course, escape criticisms of sexual exploitation.

On white women who get involved with black men I have very few data. One Chocoano student in Unguía wrote that Antioqueños would criticize such a woman: "They say 'Look, she's got tied up with that black man, isn't she ashamed of herself.' They no longer consider her a *paisa*, but take her for a Chocoano." One or two Chocoano men also told me tales of white women approaching them for sex, presumably with ideas about the sexual virility of black men

312

in mind, but this pattern does not seem to have the force it has in other areas (see Bastide 1961 on Africans in France).

"In these bodies finding each other, fusing, there are two races at each other's throats" (Bastide 1961, 10). For Colombia, and I would guess for Brazil as well, Bastide's rhetoric is overloaded. It is certainly the case that sexual and marital relations form an arena in which meanings about blackness and whiteness—especially their relative statuses—are rehearsed and acted out, but I failed to find the strong antagonism that Bastide talks of. The data from Medellín are interesting because they show that the classic pattern of white men having informal unions with black or mulatto women is not always the case: there are also a good many formal marriages, and, given the sex ratio among Chocoanos in the city, proportionally more Chocoano men marry Antioqueño women than Antioqueño men marry Chocoano women. This again shows that the classic patterns of race mixture noted in the literature (richer white men with poorer black women, or richer black men with poorer white women) may be the most obvious, but they are not the only ones. Despite this, hierarchy still pervades the realm of race mixture, and whatever the particular configurations involved, motives stemming from *blanqueamiento,* conscious or inferred, are pervasive, and this is especially the case for black women whose unions move them up the racial hierarchy.

17

Prestige and Equality,

Egotism and Envy

Notions of human equality are dominant in a sub-group to the extent that it is denied social equality by the wider society or its dominant class.

Universal *envy* setting itself up as a power is only a camouflaged form of *cupidity* which re-establishes itself and satisfies itself in a *different* way.

Some Chocoanos in Medellín observed that Antioqueños thought that blacks were all the same—all domestic servants, all construction workers, all *montañeros*, rural peasants. In a different way, I found very widespread among the blacks themselves the idea that they were "all the same." The sameness involved was, however, much more complex. The Antioqueños assumed an actual equality of social condition—or at least, so it seemed to some Chocoanos. The Chocoanos tended to assume what Jayawardena (1968) calls "human equality," or equality of essential worth as human beings. An underlying notion existed that because someone was Chocoano, or more widely, black, a basic sameness of human condition existed, an essential solidarity, and that although a person might be richer or better educated, he or she should not assume airs of superiority or refuse claims on his or her time, energy, and resources. To do either was to risk being called *creído,* stuck up, self-important, pretentious, thinking oneself above one's neighbors. Naturally, real differences in social condition exist within the Chocoano world, transient and permanent, minor and major, and people recognize that these create real gulfs between, say, an

Epigraphs: (1) Jayawardena (1968, 414); (2) Karl Marx, from *Karl Marx, Early Writings,* edited by T. Bottomore (New York, 1964), p. 154.

educated Chocoano from Quibdó and a peasant from Bebará: what creates the accusation of *creído* is when the higher-status person shows some kind of disdain or lack of respect for his or her lower-status paisano or when requests for aid and assistance are brushed off like the solicitations of an importunate beggar.

A powerful contradiction emerges between ideas of equality and the attempts of people to gain prestige and social status. Predictably, status and prestige are linked fundamentally to the central regions and their hierarchies and the processes of blacks adapting to the nonblack world. Equality, on the other hand, is an ideal embedded in the black community, whose locus is the region. There are internal processes of upward mobility characteristic of rural Chocoano society, indigenous scales by which prestige is accorded to older people, to healers, hunters, sexually active men, experienced travelers, central female figures, and so on; but parallel to these and particularly pronounced in the urban centers are prestige hierarchies defined and controlled by the central regions, which deal in the currency of wealth, education, material possessions, a smart house, fashionable clothes, occupation in the local bureaucracy, and office in the political institutions. These national hierarchies are an integral part of Chocoano society and have been since colonial times: they live in a permanent state of tension with the ethic of essential equality, part of the overall tension between Chocoano society as a black nucleus with its own culture and the dominant white-mestizo culture, which despises blackness. In this way, equality and prestige are implicated in the basic opposition between black community and the dispersal of blackness into, and its adaptation to, the nonblack world. The feeling of essential equality is in part a reaction to having been located together first as slaves and then simply as blacks at the lower end of the national scales of race, region, wealth, and culture; it is also an expression of ethnic solidarity, a solidarity that is constantly under threat from people's attempts to achieve social status according to nationally defined hierarchies and from the invidious resentments and reprisals directed at them.

What emerges, then, in this Chocoano world is an intense concern with social status and social equality and their outward symbols. People are sensitive to the behavior of others in terms of what this is taken to imply about their respective statuses. This concern is a coin with two faces. On one side, people try to police the ethic of equality. Accusations of *creído* can easily lead to bad relations, a falling off of clientele for a small shopkeeper, for example, and ultimately to *brujería,* witchcraft, which threatens the accused with becoming *salado,* salted, a state in which bad luck, illness, failing fortunes, and even death loom over them. To avoid accusations of *creído,* a person has

315

to act *sencillo* and *formal,* straightforward and reliable (i.e., can be relied upon to act "correctly" and fulfill obligations), and he or she has to be *servicial,* helpful and cooperative. The other face of the coin is to compete for the prestige and status defined within national hierarchies and to keep up with those neighbors who are being superior and not let them get ahead. Rather than bringing them down, people may try to keep level—thus, of course, risking the bad feeling of yet others who think they are *creído* too. From this perspective, the accusations and resentments of neighbors who think certain persons are getting above themselves are put down simply to *envidia,* envy, and as such are petty, vicious, and interfering—after all, it might be said, these persons are just making the most of their own lives, and it's nobody's business but their own. Those who, in one way or another, acquire the symbols of higher status can put down the carping of their erstwhile equals to small-mindedness or *envidia* and defend their right to progress as a normal feature of the national society that defines the overall hierarchies of status in which they are competing. But it is very hard for them to free themselves entirely from this social matrix of expectations, and even if they move up and out of a particular social level—say, out of Quibdó society and into middle-class Medellín society—not only will they continue to be judged within their new milieu, but other poorer paisanos will still expect assistance and favors from someone with access to certain resources.

This kind of contradiction between an ethic of equality and the prestige hierarchies associated with a wider society exists in other contexts. Willmott (1966, 64) finds the same type of ethic of loyalty and equality among working-class adolescents in London, as does Gans (1962, 219–23) for Italian Americans in Boston. Jayawardena (1968) gives many examples from all over the world. His idea is that low status and powerlessness, plus in some cases the absence of a formal organization to represent group interests, lead to a strong ethic of human equality and that this is opposed to national hierarchies of social status. Among the Chocoanos, and indeed the blacks in general, color and race become entangled in ideas about equality, status, and hierarchy, for the simple reason that they are themselves symbols of status and hierarchy. Thus going out with or marriage to a lighter-skinned person may be interpreted not just as demeaning one's own blackness but as putting on airs of superiority. Likewise, adopting the ways and customs of Antioquia or other regions may be seen as *creído* because region is closely intertwined with color, race, and social status. In this sense, particular acts related to *blanqueamiento* and blackness feed into the mutually empowering tension between prestige and equality, which in turn feeds into an overarching tension between

316

the nucleation and reaffirmation of blackness and its dispersal and whitening, as seen in a historical perspective.

The Practice of Prestige and Equality

These issues of equality and prestige actually manifest themselves in different ways. Let us look first at the policing of the ethic of equality. In chapter 11, I mentioned Carlos and his group of drinking companions and friends, mostly Chocoanos and Turbeños, many of them teachers like himself, who would meet in the town center to socialize and to discuss whether that month's salary was coming through. In the interaction between these men, the precariousness of their economic situation was evident: there was constant attention to who was spending what, who would disappear for a day or two after payday to avoid spending on *aguardiente* for the group, who would reappear shortly after, *pelado y pidiendo pasajes,* broke and asking for the bus fare home, who had been seen with money earlier on in the day and might be cajoled into spending it now on a round of *aguardiente,* who would attach himself to someone with a bit of money in order to get a few drinks, who owed whom a favor. Clearly, however, not all this was simply economic. Also involved were strong ethics of equality, expressed in expectations of generosity, reciprocity, and loyalty to one's friends. Much of this was manifested in patterns of drinking within this loose group of friends. The more one could be seen to be displaying these qualities, the better one's reputation, but economic hardship meant that one had to be tactical about when and to whom to offer a drink or when and from whom reciprocity could be demanded.

Norman Whitten (1968) noted similar patterns of behavior among males drinking together in secular contexts among blacks on the Pacific littoral, and it is tempting to see it as characteristic of black culture. My impression is that it is characteristic of any cultural complex in which an ethic of human equality is present and reciprocity is an important feature of economic and political strategies. What is characteristically "black" in the Colombian context is the loudness with which favors are given and demanded, the constant ribbing of people considered to be *amarrado,* tight-fisted, the jocular assertions that so-and-so has got money in his pocket; this contrasts neatly with the silent disappearances that occasionally occur when a creditor comes into sight along the sidewalk.

The pressure to make others spend if they had money, the vigilance over the to-and-fro of favors and reciprocations, the gestures of generosity—these are all part of an ethic of social equality which is constantly reaffirmed in acts of reciprocity, constantly policed by cajoling and mockery, and constantly belied by quiet, self-interested strategies. Through his association with me, Carlos ran several risks. Shortly after meeting me, he went out one day with a friend to learn that rumors were already flying about how Carlos was going around with an "American" who had lots of money to spend and how he was getting above himself and forgetting his friends. My presence was initially a threat to his position among his companions in that he could be accused of monopolizing the potential material benefits of friendship with me: correctly handled, however, those benefits could also be used to reinforce his position within the group, both by channeling resources (mostly in the form of *aguardiente*) towards his friends and by integrating me into the group as an individual with my own obligations and rights. Carlos trod an astute line between making the resources of his network available to me and making my resources available to his network.

Successful Chocoanos are also subject to the ethic of equality, expressed in demands for material assistance from other Chocoanos. An ex-governor of the Chocó with a dentist's practice in Medellín said, "My paisanos are very bad clients, because sometimes they come to me for free treatment or else for me to deal with a toothache, after which they never come back." Here the idea is that as a successful person he should help out his fellow Chocoanos—he, of course, sees it as simply taking advantage. Other middle-class Chocoanos in Medellín told me that when they returned to Quibdó, they would be besieged by requests for money from relatives. Success, however, can also bring *envidia* if people think someone is *creído* and not reciprocating properly. A Chocoano woman who lived in Barrio Antioquia told me how she started up a small business selling food outside her house. Things went well, but her paisanos were very *envidiosos*, envious, and she suspected *brujería*. Not long before, she had found in her house what she described as *moscas de cementerio*, or cemetery flies, big sleepy flies reputedly made magically from the earth of a graveyard. Around that time, her clients failed her, problems arose with the neighbors, and her houseplants started to die—"Of course," she said, "I don't believe in all that stuff."

Another facet of this ethic of equality is the idea that blacks who attain a certain level of social status start to look down on other blacks: the attempt by the successful to differentiate themselves from the less fortunate is seen as contradicting the ethic of equality. Whether or not the successful actually do this is, of course, of less importance than whether they are thought to be doing it: the essence of the accusation lies in the categorization of a certain person's activity and attitudes by others. In Unguía, the richer Chocoano farmer who was said by some others to be "sticking with the *paisas*" was accused on occasion of being *creído*, despite his numerous connections with the Chocoano group in Unguía and elsewhere: to me, there was little evidence that he looked down on other blacks, but the accusations of *creído* were fueled by other blacks' perceptions of him, not by some objective index of his behavior. The most common expression of this set of ideas, indeed very widespread among Chocoanos, was that blacks discriminate against blacks: *nosotros mismos nos discriminamos*, we ourselves discriminate against each other (see also appendix C, cases 5, 6, and 8). This type of comment is provoked simply by those who are thought to feel themselves superior to other blacks, but it is often connected to color. Rosario, for example, went to stay with her cousins in Quibdó. She started going out on dates with an Antioqueño there and soon found herself the object of derisory comments and cutting remarks from black friends and relatives, who, apart from discouraging her from associating with this man, made observations such as, "Oh well, she thinks a lot of herself, being from Medellín, so the blacks aren't good enough for her." A similar idea lies behind the epithet of "racist" applied to the Chocoano mother of the previous chapter whose daughters had Antioqueño partners. On one occasion in Medellín, I went to visit the Chocoano cousin of an acquaintance of mine from Unguía; later, I met up with Carlos and mentioned the visit. It turned out he knew her, and he commented rather scathingly, "She had children by a white guy just because of a racial complex." In this comment, it is unclear whether he thought the woman thought herself inferior because she was black or considered herself superior and therefore above forming a union with other blacks: the implication is one and the same—blackness is bad. The act of having a white partner, from which is easily inferred an admission of the low value of blackness, can also be interpreted as a statement of superiority: "Blackness is bad, but *I'm* alright because I've got a white partner and lighter-colored children."

Another example again shows the expectation of equality challenged by color differences. I was talking to a young woman outside a house where a Chocoano gathering was under way. Her mother was a black Costeño woman and her father, by then deceased, a *turco*, a Lebanese immigrant: she was an olive-skinned mulatto with wavy hair, and her sisters ran the gamut from her own appearance to dark mulatto with *pelo pegado* or *pelo quieto*, stuck-together or still hair (i.e., unmoved by the wind). As we talked, with her sisters standing nearby, a well-dressed black man emerged from the house and obviously tried to introduce himself into our conversation, offering her his hand. She rather pointedly ignored him (it turned out later that she had been trying to escape his attentions beforehand), and although his approach seemed to me to lack a certain tact, I felt uncomfortable at her bland avoidance of him, and I was not surprised by his umbrage: "Don't think I'm any less than your friend here [indicating me]. *Yo soy un personal* [I'm a person, i.e., of worth], so how can you turn your nose up at me like that?" Hovering between his lines were the unspoken words "just because I'm black" and their automatic, but even more subliminal counterparts, "and he's white, and you're almost white." His remarks, which at first sight concern the pique of an offended suitor, were also packed with meanings concerning ideas about race and color. He implied his recognition that some people might rank white above black, but he challenged that ranking by asserting his own worth relative to me. Underlying this was a tacit rebuke of her for daring to imply that he was not her equal when she herself was partly black. The scene was redolent with racial overtones that remained masked.

After the man left, however, the mask was lifted for a second by a sister, clearly mulatto, who remarked in contempt, "There's no need to take any notice of that *negrito idiota* [stupid little black guy]." The other sisters half-laughed at, half-censured her outspokenness, but their response was very muted—for it to have been otherwise, it would have been necessary to unmask further the racial meanings of the encounter, momentarily revealed in that remark. Nevertheless, I, and I'm sure the others, were thinking, "*Y tu mamá dónde está?*" ("And your mother, where is she?"—an adage used in Colombia to refer to someone's racial origins), not to mention the whereabouts of the blackest sister, who was standing right next to her. The remark *negrito idiota* not only made explicit reference to masked issues of color, but it also reiterated precisely the hierarchies the man was challenging. It implied the right of the more mixed, the lighter skinned, to look down on the "*negritos*." The irony of the implication was forced into the situation by the presence of the blackest sister.

Color is only one symbol of superiority: the *creído* syndrome can fuel itself on any index of status. In one interview with a Chocoano woman, we were discussing a salsa club in a middle-class area of town which was patronized by blacks who could afford the prices charged there. She remarked that blacks who had made a bit of money looked down on other, poorer blacks. I asked her if this was not normal—after all, whites discriminate against one another all the time on this basis. She replied that among the blacks it was "*más notorio: se les nota más,*" it's more flagrant, it shows more. She went on: "It's something we blacks have, you could say it's almost instinctive." Here emerges very clearly the expectation of equality among *blacks,* even when real social differences exist. Richer whites looking down on poorer whites is seen as a more normal state of affairs.

In an attempt to police the ethic of equality, *envidia* can be directed at someone who does reasonably well in material terms. But the status competition can also be a matter of keeping up with others, rather than bringing them down to your level. One Chocoano family told me that *envidia* was a common phenomenon in Quibdó: "People go without food to keep up appearances." They recounted a story about a family they knew in Quibdó who skimped on food in order to honor an agreement with the neighbors to paint their houses freshly each year. José Domingo, a Chocoano friend of mine, used to talk to me quite a bit about social status in the Chocó, and his observations illustrate nicely the issues involved. He comments on how the search for prestige creates divisiveness in the Chocó, especially in Quibdó, an arena where national hierarchies are most prevalent and obvious.

> It's a subproduct, it's more than just economic, it's a child of segregation. The Chocoano has got to the point where he considers himself of so little value that psychologically in order to rise he attacks his fellow. . . . Let's say, a school teacher in the Chocó is very black: he's achieved a certain level which he didn't have before—he's originally from the countryside—and he says, "I'm a tough guy in my subject: whoever doesn't study will fail the year." In the schoolroom there may be kids who are the sons of the mayor, the doctor, another teacher; and another who's the son of a farmer—and he's blacker as well. So the poorer, blacker one fails the year.
>
> It's almost economic, but really it's an influence so marked that you can't reason with sentiments in a normal human way: let's say in the relationship father, mother, son. For example, a boy comes from a low economic level and his parents have lived a basic life, their bodies are physically damaged, they dress simply, they don't give the appearance of being well off. So the boy is here with you and his Dad goes past and he's not capable of saying hello to him, because he doesn't want you to realize that that person is his father.
>
> One black wants to be more than the other and he tries to rise by treading on the other's back. It's something in the atmosphere. It's all against all. Quibdó is a heavy place to live, it sucks you in, it's like a sharp tool which cuts you every which way. (Edited extracts from a taped interview, August 1985, Unguía)

This commentary touches on a number of themes. Very strong is the idea of an overwhelming concern with status: the boy who ignores his father and the "normal human sentiments." To achieve status people are prepared to "tread on each other's back." This is perhaps simply a product of economic relations, but really it is more than that: there is something specific to the Chocó, which is the product of "segregation" and of the blacks' lack of self-esteem. And color is tied into questions of status and prestige, so that the black teacher discriminates against the blackest, poorest student. In sum, there is a feel of intense competition for status in which ascent is achieved at the expense of others, thus provoking envy, and in which color can become involved as itself a symbol of status.

José Domingo said his family had been *salado*, ensorcelled with *brujería*, in Quibdó, so perhaps he had particular reason to feel the sharpness of the atmosphere there. Once when I was at his house near Unguía, they found under a bed a bottle roughly stitched up in black cloth and filled with needles—a sorcery packet intended to *salar* the house and bring it bad luck. Whether or not a person believes in such "superstitions," as José Domingo sometimes called them, the fact that someone, probably among that person's neighbors, clearly wishes him or her ill is a disturbing feeling. In Unguía, his family was not a particularly well-off one at that time, although they had known more prosperous times in the past, but it is not necessary to be rich to attract *envidia*. All the children had finished secondary schooling, while José had spent some time in Bogotá: all of them had experience and horizons beyond the Chocó itself; a daughter who was light skinned and considered by many in town to be *creída* had married an Antioqueño; the family tried ventures in cattle farming and commerce, starting a restaurant in town, selling gasoline to the miners for their *motobombas*, and buying gold—José and his brothers even tried at one point to corner the local gold market, an attempt that provoked menaces from local Antioqueño merchant-landowners more concrete than sorcery packets found under beds. For all these reasons, the family could attract accusations of being *creído* and the corresponding attempts to police the ethic of equality which they were supposedly transgressing. This highlights the problem of human equality as opposed to social equality. The latter can be assessed in concrete material terms of relative wealth, but the former is judged by perceptions of personal interaction. A person's behavior may be perceived by others to be *creído*, even if he or she thinks it is not. And marks of ascent in social condition may themselves be taken as signs of a rupture with the ethic of human equality, so that material success may easily lead to assumptions that someone "feels superior."

Treading your black fellows underfoot in an attempt to rise or dragging them down to your own level are both aspects of the same basic opposition between prestige and equality, or more distantly, between black participation in national society (which often includes upward mobility) and black community. Both processes give rise to invidious comparisons and resentments, both make inroads into ethnic solidarity. When people rise, they may look down on their lower-status fellows; or they may simply become estranged from their social sphere. In either case, because of the ethic of essential equality, it is easily assumed that people who rise *do* feel superior, and this is felt to be unjustified and even a betrayal. One may consider it perfectly "normal" for higher-status people to feel superior, in that it is probably a very common reaction, but it inevitably conflicts with the idea that there is an essential human equality among Chocoanos, and more generally, blacks. For Colombian blacks, higher status very often means more contact with or integration into the nonblack world and its hierarchies, whether these are manifest in the nonblack world itself or in places such as Quibdó. The roots of the conflict thus run even deeper into issues of race and color and cut even closer to the quick. This is all the more evident for mobile blacks who cannot simply disappear into their new milieu: their color remains as a symbol of their origins.

Fernandes observed that Brazilian blacks were aware that "success will bring the loss of their companion, that he will end up being ashamed of his relatives and—and this is what seems intolerable to them—that he will put on white airs" (1969, 317). Fernandes is simplifying by depicting the extreme case of black upward mobility. In fact, the hierarchical relation of the black and nonblack worlds is so pervasive that these processes can be based on much smaller kinds of cues and occur *within* the black world itself—that is, in a context in which there is no apparent and direct "loss" of a black person into a nonblack world. Indeed, the greatest tangle of *envidiosos* and *creídos* seems to be in Quibdó itself, where national hierarchies of prestige have always intruded forcefully into black community. Quibdó is "a sharp tool which cuts you every which way."

Prestige and Politics

Some middle-class blacks see in all this a major obstacle to the progress of the Chocó. Marco Tobias Cuesta, a lawyer and Quibdó city councillor, states in his book, *El Chocó, ayer, hoy y mañana,*

> A complete social structure does not exist. . . . The absence of a bourgeoisie, an oligarchy, or an aristocracy can be observed. . . . There is only a lower class, a middle class, and a rising middle class. . . . The majority of Chocoanos today . . . are descendants of African slaves who obtained their liberty about a century ago; a fact that, together with a false sense of equality which characterizes Chocoano social be-

havior, has prevented the formation of a truly representative leadership. . . . Egotism and envy have enthroned themselves in the Chocó to such an extent that no one's value is recognized, no one is respected, and, on the basis of a false feeling of equality, people are denied their worth, their merits, and their works (1986, 82, 85).

In interview (March 1987) he was more down to earth: "If you've got a Mercedes here, they'll scratch the paintwork and puncture the tires." Political organization is hampered, he said, because no one will accept that another can be boss and tell others what to do. Felix Arenas, ex-mayor of Quibdó, agrees. He says about in the Chocó:

> [There is] a lack of social stratification, and this creates one basic level. Obedience comes from subordination and the recognition of greater capacity and a higher level in the hierarchy. When there is no hierarchy, subordination is lost: there's no chain of command, and people won't recognize one. And you can see that the highest posts here are occupied by imported people [from outside the Chocó] who try and create this because those who come from outside haven't been pawed and handled, so no one knows their defects. But in small towns [such as Quibdó], everyone has been pawed, and there are no strata. It's not that the Chocoano is a bad administrator, it's the social structure of our milieu. In the Chocó everyone aspires to be everything: in Quibdó everyone wants to be governor, mayor, and so on—and it's possible for them to be so, and they are because of political situations. So that creates a distortion in the society.
>
> When I was mayor, I found in Third Avenue that some people had their sewers running straight out into the street. So I said, "Either you organize this properly, or I'll close down your shop." And that created a bad impression of me among many people. That's a lack of structure, lack of direction. The garbage collection which I tried to do was also a problem and still is: no one wanted to pay the taxes, saying the truck didn't reach them because there were no roads. But I'd say, "You benefit from the cleanliness of other parts of the city to which you also have access." And they'd damage the garbage containers and all that. (Unedited extracts from a taped interview, February 1987, Medellín)

In both these accounts, there is some rhetorical exaggeration—"no one is respected," "everyone wants to be governor"—but the basic idea of a sense of equality which finds it hard to brook hierarchy is quite plain. In both cases, the triumph of national hierarchies of prestige and power over community values of essential equality is seen as the proper way forward in order to break out of a situation in which competition for status conflicts with ethics of equality and creates a "distortion in society."

Both these men have held political positions in Quibdó, and we are now on frankly political terrain: but this is no coincidence. In the

Chocó, and especially in Quibdó, politics is one of the main forms of achieving social status and upward mobility. It is also closely linked to education in that most of the political elite nowadays have at least a degree. It is therefore perfectly logical that all of the contradictions between prestige and equality should manifest themselves most sharply in the political sphere, which is in any case of a nature that entrenches competition and factionalism. When I discussed Chocoano identity in Unguía, I noted that politics was a resource on which claims could be made by Chocoanos and that this reinforced Chocoano identity. This is true in the sense that it opposes Chocoanos to non-Chocoanos in a minimal fashion, but as a basic focus for solidarity in their relationships with one another, politics tends instead to create divisive factions and mutual recriminations. In chapter 7, I gave some taste of departmental politics under the black and mulatto elite that succeeded the white ruling class of the first half of the century. There we saw many people fighting over a small political pie through the Colombian medium of clientelistic political machinations. Now we can also see a further harmony played on this chord: those who rise to power enter into a jungle where they are accused of egotism and despotism, of trying to line their own pockets at the expense of their paisanos, and of lording it over them—another variation on the accusation of *creído*—while those below them, the accusers, are seen as envious and small-mindedly obstructive of progress. The same behavior and ideologies that characterize concerns with status in general are played out in the political arena. To make matters worse, the very vagaries of departmental politics mean that last year's power holders can be next year's unemployed, so despotism and nepotistic power wielding bring a swift backlash, while any conceited airs affected on the basis of a good salary and an important office can be doubly ridiculed when sudden shifts in the power balance divest officeholders of their responsibilities and political status. The fact that many of the Chocó's political elite are mulattoes and that almost all leave the Chocó temporarily or permanently to pursue an education or to practice as lawyers or doctors strikes the constant and ever-reverberating chord of color, race, and region as the political elite is accused of deserting the Chocó and betraying its race: some see in even Diego Luis Córdoba's marriage to a white woman a betrayal of his outspoken principles.

Solidarity and Black Organization in Medellín

Solidarity for blacks in Colombia is inherently a hard goal to achieve: the very structure of the black category and its relationship to the nonblack world is an obstacle. The boundaries of the category at a national level, whatever their relative clarity in the Chocó or in Medellín, are fuzzy and shifting; opportunities for escape from blackness exist and are made the most of by some blacks, and whatever the personal motives involved, these strategies are frequently understood as a rejection of blackness by some other blacks. Under these conditions, solidarity is hard to achieve. In comparison, in the United States the category "black" includes even people of highly mixed parentage, the black-white boundary is relatively clear-cut, and although some blacks might despise their own blackness, it is much harder to escape the category of black except in rather occasional cases of passing. Solidarity therefore has a better starting point, and the very overt nature of discrimination and segregation there, until recently legally enforced, clearly drew blacks together for defense and mutual support in a much more decisive way than in Colombia. This is not to say that blacks in the United States have no internecine divisions and hatreds, but there have been notable instances of solidarity based on a struggle for civil rights and on an attempt to redefine the value and meaning of blackness—"black is beautiful"—both movements that are only nascent in Colombia and have received little support from blacks there (see Degler 1971, Fernandes 1969, and Fontaine 1985 for comments on the situation in Brazil). Even in a region such as the Chocó, which is virtually entirely black, political, as opposed to kin-based, solidarity is a distant goal, whether this be in order to protest about the Chocó as a region or about the position of blacks in Colombia in general. The structural conditions that undermine solidarity on a national scale penetrate the Chocó as well, creating infighting and jealousies about prestige, equality, and color.

Solidarity in Medellín is perhaps even harder to achieve, given the powerful influence of Antioqueño culture. Although the ethnic network is important to many people and especially to the black nuclei within it, there is no overall solidarity of the Chocoanos which might raise a collective voice in protest about racial discrimination, the situation of the Chocó, or the negative stereotypes and images surrounding black culture. Nevertheless, attempts have been made to create Chocoano organizations in Medellín, and in this section I look at some of these in order to illustrate how internecine divisions, often formed around power and status, frustrate attempts at solidarity and organization.

The first organization was the Association for Chocoanos Resident in Antioquia, founded around 1962. It was created by Chocoano professionals as a mutual aid society for Chocoano immigrants in general. There was a headquarters in the city center where the needy could go for help and advice, and a couple of Chocoano doctors and a lawyer also offered some services. Soon it was moved to Barrio Antioquia with the aim of creating closer contact with the poorer Chocoanos, especially the domestic servants, who were meant as the main beneficiaries of the organization's legal aid and its courses on sewing, first aid, and so forth. Finance came from personal contributions paid by members and from the Sunday dances that were organized. My enquiries into the rather hazy past of this association led to different versions of its fate, a fact in itself indicative of a lack of coordination and collective purpose. Some say it collapsed after six months, others assured me it continued until at least 1968: apparently it meant more to some people than others. At any rate, people began to default on subscriptions; it was also alleged by some I talked to that the better-off men took advantage of their position to make advances towards the young women; and generally, there was what one woman euphemistically called "ungratefulness," that is, lack of cooperation and collaboration.

La Corporación de Negritudes. Another organization of this kind appeared in 1983, founded by a Chocoano named Ramón Cossio, also a founding member of the previous one. He had been involved in the political campaign of a man named Pablo Escobar, better known in the international press as a principal member of the Medellín cocaine cartel but who at that time was running as a candidate for the House of Representatives—such are the vagaries of Colombian politics. Escobar—also a contributor to La Iguaná's church and the financier behind a football pitch and a housing project for Moravia—helped Cossio found the Corporación de Negritudes, which was set up with the express purposes of

> a) promoting the integration of the black man . . . with the aim of finding the path to improvement and identification as an ethnic group and thus contributing to the development of [the] country; b) stimulating . . . investigation into the historical evolution, the cultural manifestations, and the contributions of the black man in America and Colombia; c) promoting sociocultural activities which tend towards the promotion, education, and the cultural and economic training of the domestic workers of Medellín with no distinction of race, political creed, or religion. (From the statutes of the Corporación)

The Corporación ran classes for domestic servants—in fact almost entirely blacks—teaching literacy and also up to fourth-year secondary schooling in selected subjects. It was also a general gathering place for many Chocoanos, especially on Sunday nights, when the desks

327

and chairs gave way to salsa, *vallenato,* and dancing. Although most were working class, students and a few professionals would also assist.

The Corporación played out in miniature many of the contradictions inherent in the blacks' situation both in Medellín and in Colombia. Ironically, it depended almost entirely on whites for financial support, partly Escobar and partly the regional administration, from which Cossio obtained some grants via his political contacts there (no mean feat, considering they were for a black organization in Antioquia): the Corporación's own fund-raising activities added minimal amounts. Its ideological stance was ambiguous. The statutes proclaimed identification as an ethnic group, but Cossio's main aim was to teach the blacks to adapt to Antioqueño society. In interview, he told me he was directing his efforts at the "black who is uncultured, he who lacks the *compostura* [good sense, modesty] needed to be in society." He deplored the domestics' "uncultured" manners, their "exaggerated" style of applying cosmetics, their "loud" voices, the fights they had in El Suizo over men. Whatever one thinks of these aims—and when he expressed his views in a newspaper interview, some domestics took understandable exception to them—there was little here about black consciousness or "identification as an ethnic group." Cossio's idea was that first things came first. On my initial visit to the Corporación, I was somewhat surprised to see posters exhorting discretion in the application of makeup in which only white women figured. Yet some months later, I saw posters with pictures of black personalities—African heads of state, Martin Luther King—with the caption "You too will find your place in the world." The contrast could hardly have been more striking, hovering between timid affirmations of black identity and ingenuous approbations of whiteness.

But it was the relationship of the Corporación to Chocoanos in Medellín as a whole that was particularly interesting. In one sense, it was a black nucleus: although an overall minority of Chocoanos went there, the majority had heard of it, and it was a meeting place for Chocoanos from different social strata—once again, music and dance were a central feature of the reunions. In another sense, however, the Corporación was at the center of jealousies and resentments, factions and infighting. There was a feeling among many that Cossio was a despot. When he moved his office from the ground to the first floor, some interpreted this as a symbolic distancing of himself from the "riffraff." Cossio employed a white secretary and a white worker, because, as he stated quite openly to me, he felt he could not trust his paisanos to work hard and honestly for him. More seriously, a group of Chocoanos who were involved as teaching staff clearly did not trust him: in July 1986, they resigned in force from the Corporación and later sent a letter to the Quibdó newspaper *El Presente*—with the editor of which Cossio maintained a running battle in the correspondence columns over alleged improprieties with their respective treasuries—accusing him of unconstitutional and despotic behavior, hiring and firing people at will, fraud and embezzlement, and so forth (*El Presente*, October/November 1986). He, on the other hand, complained constantly of the ingratitude of his paisanos, of their petty carpings and lack of cooperation, of their jealousies and backstabbing. Financial support from Escobar had become intermittent since the 1984 assassination of the minister of justice, Lara Bonilla, which had forced the drug cartel to adopt a low profile in the face of a government crackdown. Tired of scraping around for support and of the accusations of fraud, Cossio finally decided to withdraw and hold elections for a new committee to run the Corporación. Elections were duly held in December 1986, and the group who had authored the letter to *El Presente* won an easy—some say fraudulent—victory.

The circumstances of the election itself give some insight into the divisive politics of the organization. Having been interviewing in an outlying barrio, I missed the election and turned up when it was all over bar the celebrations. I ran into the victorious group emerging from the headquarters, and they invited me for a celebratory drink. Several bottles of *aguardiente* later, they decided to return to headquarters for a spontaneous meeting. There was much talk about how to arrange things with the outgoing director, Cossio, and how to obtain more financial support. The feeling was that victimization of Cossio should be avoided. At this point, he himself appeared, clearly having been softening the blows of defeat as others had been toasting the fruits of victory: he made no fuss, however, and shut himself firmly in his office (no longer officially his). On his heels followed another man, also a failed presidential candidate and a good deal sorer about his misfortunes: he had been initially unable to gain access to the premises and was incensed at having been "shut out." Things rapidly disintegrated as he roundly accused the new committee of perpetrating an electoral fraud—and of having mothers engaged in licentious soliciting. People dispersed in disarray. Some time later, hanging around on a city center street corner with Carlos, a few cronies, and a bottle of *aguardiente*, I came across the man who had so effectively broken up that first meeting. He lost no time in filling me in on the faults of the new director, even going so far as to show me a copy of a letter from the owner of a hotel where the latter had purportedly stayed and left without paying the bill—this was the kind of man we were dealing with, he said. Where or how he obtained such a letter I cannot say; but the familiar cycle of accusations and recriminations was clearly under way again.

The Chocoano Action Committee. The Chocoano Action Committee of Medellín was a rather different sort of organization. With a middle-class Chocoano membership, it centered around a small pharmacy in the city center run by a man named Victor Hugo Lozano, a Chocoano from Quibdó. Here a group of well-educated and relatively well-off Chocoanos would congregate in the evenings and on weekends to play dominoes, drink some *aguardiente,* and exchange political gossip. The group participated in the clientelistic machine of Colombian politics. Their aim was to drum up support in the barrios of Medellín and within their personal networks: with the voting power they then represented they could offer support to established or up-and-coming politicians who, hopefully, would favor them with jobs, educational grants for their dependents, community services for the people whose votes they had guaranteed, and so forth. In this, they did not make particular use of the ethnic network: if there was a willing and politically active Chocoano in a certain barrio, so much the better, but they also had non-Chocoano contacts in the local Liberal barrio committees. Equally, their contacts with politicians led them outside the Chocoano network: although they maintained contact with Chocoano senators and representatives through the votes they could still muster in the Chocó itself, their main sphere of action was Medellín, and they had to woo Antioqueño politicians. At first sight, then, the group acted as a dispersing influence within the ethnic network. Nevertheless, the group represented a ready-made political vehicle to which other Chocoanos with political interests and ambitions could easily attach themselves and begin to participate in local political currents; it was also as much a method of keeping abreast of political ups and downs in the Chocó as of advancing political interests in Medellín. For both reasons, it reinforced that small nucleus of Chocoano activity: as in Unguía, political interests were a positive reason for identifying as a Chocoano.

As with the Corporación, however, there was little indication of overall unity. To start with, the group was seen by most other Chocoanos who were not involved in it as a rather self-serving politicking enterprise that had no real links with the Chocoano community as such. Certainly there was no explicit plan for speaking out on behalf of the community or of voicing an interest in black consciousness. At one point in the past, attempts had been made to organize the domestics in some fashion, but the details I managed to collect were rather hazy. Within the group, too, there were the usual kinds of problems. Victor Hugo:

> Since I arrived here fifteen years ago, I have tried to organize the Chocoanos at all levels and it has been a failure. The Chocoano who earns a living doing manual work has no interest in politics. . . . [On the other hand], there is the problem I was telling you about: that I could never organize this group because of egotism. It was thought that I had certain economic and political interests, despite the fact that I was the one who gave the little I had to help them. The Chocoanos are very egotistic with each other. It's ancestral. Our ancestors were slaves, so with respect to each other we're egotistic. We don't like our friends, our paisanos to prosper. (Edited extracts from a taped interview, April 1986, Medellín)

This was a comment about relations between Chocoanos in general from my first interview with him. On a more concrete level, he complained about the lack of cooperation and collaboration: he supplied the premises for their meetings, but would his paisanos help with a small contribution towards the costs of water and electricity? No. He supplied the glasses for *aguardiente:* when they got broken, would people replace them? No. The committee was for the good of all its participants, but who did all the bureaucratic legwork to get legal status for it? He did. He organized a *homenaje,* or homage, a dinner for two senators the committee had links with. Everyone who went had to pay two thousand pesos for a dinner ticket, but who ended up owing fourteen thousand pesos to the hotel? He did. "Despite being professionals, this is how they think." This was the general substance of his complaints. Everyone looked out for themselves (egotism), and would not help their fellow (lack of cooperation) because this might result in the other prospering at their expense (envy). As with the Corporación, others thought Victor Hugo Lozano was lining his own nest, while he thought they were taking advantage of him and obstructing the progress of the group.

Other Black Movements in Colombia

If in Medellín the Chocoano associations do not adopt a position in which the reaffirmation of blackness is elevated from the everyday, lived discourse of Colombia's or Medellín's black nuclei to a more confrontational ideology with a discourse of *negritud* and *reivindicación* (the reclamation of black identity), this does not mean that such an ideology does not exist in Colombia. It does indicate that *negritud* is a minority movement, adopted by certain rather more radical intellectuals among the black population. *Negritud* as a movement appeared in Colombia in the 1970s, based on the ideas of authors such as Aimé Césaire and Frantz Fanon. Gutiérrez Azopardo (1980, 88) gives a brief history of its progress in Colombia and notes as one of its first achievements the proposal in 1975 of a black as a presidential candidate. The man involved was Juan Zapata Olivella, the brother of Manuel, the celebrated folklorist and writer. Some of the contradictions inherent in the ideological position of blacks in Colombia can be seen in his statement to the press: "We do not agree with racial discrimination and we are certain that in Colombia it does not exist" (*El Tiempo*, 16 November 1975, 6A). It is hard to believe that *negritud* was a main preoccupation there. On the contrary, such an assertion seems designed to avoid alienating potential voters who might see protest about racial discrimination as an irrelevance or even "racism in reverse." During the seventies, a number of black groups sprang up including two that are still active: Cimarrón (subtitled the National Movement for the Human Rights of Black Communities in Colombia), headed by Juan de Dios Mosquera, and the Center for the Investigation of Black Culture, headed by Amir Smith-Córdoba. Both these organizations frankly adopt an ideology of *negritud*. Mosquera, for example, writes, "It is necessary to create a community conscience and construct our own forms of organization which, with national and collective mobilization, can conquer respect for human rights and rescue the historical personality and the ethnic and cultural identity [of blacks] as an historical component of national culture and identity" (1985, 25). He states that black consciousness has two aspects, the first an awareness of "economic exploitation and historical oppression" of blacks by capitalist society and the second a consciousness of "national ethnic identity" understood as the reaffirmation of the positive value of blackness against the dominant ideology of its inferiority to whiteness: "To assume the consciousness of ethnic identity is to recognize and appreciate our brothers everywhere, with no regard for what white friends may say. . . . When a black person avoids the gaze or the presence of a brother because of humble appearance or inferior intellectual condition, he is renouncing his communitarian ethnic identity; the solidarity and cohesion of the group must always be above external aspects of such insignificance" (1985, 146). Here there is a direct contrast with the more conservative ideologies of Felix Arenas and Marco Tobias Cuesta, who envisage the benefits of an increasingly stratified Chocoano society with an effective chain of command built on recognized hierarchy. Whereas they see a future in which the hierarchies of national society penetrate fully and completely into the Chocó, Mosquera is in effect appealing precisely to the ethic of essential human equality which Cuesta calls "false."

332

Amir Smith-Córdoba takes a similiar stance. His center produced a journal, *Negritud,* which only ran to about three numbers due to lack of finance, and also a paper, *Presencia Negra,* which is still running. In *Negritud* (1978, vol. 3) he says, "We are not Africa, but we are backed in terms of pigment and geography by a quantity of black inhabitants which makes it possible to think of the concept of *Negritud* as the initial ethnic flag for the achievement of our objectives. From there stems the importance of creating in the first instance appropriate conditions, not so the blacks can dance, since it is well known that the blacks can dance, and very well at that; what we want in the best case is to do more than just dance" (quoted in Gutiérrez Azopardo 1980, 88). In *Presencia Negra* (1982, no. 22) he writes, "The fundamental objective of the Center is to investigate and disseminate the significance of the true black contribution to the construction of national identity. Thus, everything which leads the blacks to an encounter with their own cultural values, apart from being invigorating, is dignifying within the just purpose of *reivindicación.* . . . We work as an ethnic group . . . contributing to the cultural enrichment of the country and the strengthening of national unity." (See also Smith-Córdoba 1980.) Both Mosquera and Smith-Córdoba talk of their task within the framework of national identity partly because they want blacks and black culture to be fully accepted in Colombia, where currently national ideologies of identity negate either their existence or their worth. But it is also a tactic to avoid charges of "racism in reverse" which nonblacks tend to make against *negritud* movements: these writers do not speak of separatism but rather of integration as blacks.

The two themes explored in this chapter—equality and prestige, and solidarity and organization—are both rooted in the basic racial order of Colombia. The ethic of equality among the Chocoanos derives from the nature of black community, its low status, and also its spatial characteristic of regional concentration. The fight for prestige has its foundations in the possibility of climbing the national hierarchies of status which are open in a conditional manner to black people; this struggle is connected to processes of physical *blanqueamiento* which give it a particular intensity, but it can occur also without actual processes of race mixture. The gaining of status in hierarchies of wealth and power at the local level may occur without mixed marriage, but such achievement is still linked into the nonblack world because it is this world that defines the basic hierarchy, and the acceptance of such hierarchies is also a move away from—some would say a betrayal of—the black community ethic of essential equality.

333

The lack of solidarity of the black category in Colombia, or even of the blacks in Medellín, is based fundamentally on the possibility of black assimilation into the nonblack world and nonblack acceptance, both conditional in nature. This undermines the structural conditions for potential solidarity. And in everyday practice, this is manifest in the type of internecine struggles over equality and prestige which I have documented in this chapter. The point is to see behind these struggles, often petty in themselves, the larger structures of Colombia's racial order.

Conclusion

My purpose in this book has been to examine in detail one "black" region and its people in a variety of contexts and in different domains of social practice. In the process, I aimed to provide an approach that can capture the Colombian racial order—and by extension the racial orders characteristic of other Latin American societies with a similar history of slavery. The problem has been to look both at the Chocó as a black region and at its location in Colombia as a mixed nation, at blacks and at miscegenation. It is tempting when concentrating on blacks and racial discrimination to begin to overlook processes of miscegenation. Indeed, the radical black organizations in Colombia consciously label mulattoes as *negros* in an attempt to invent a solidarity that does not really exist. On the other hand, an emphasis simply on miscegenation tends to neglect the real and vital presence of blackness in Colombia. The volume *Discrimination without Violence* by Solaún and Kronus (1973) is a case in point here.

The approach I adopt in examining the Chocó attempts to encompass both these aspects and to see them as interrelated parts of one overall order. The precise nature of their relationship has been historically and is currently structured by material forces of wealth and power. These also constitute themselves in space, giving a spatial dimension to both blackness and miscegenation. My aim has been to demonstrate how the same basic racial order underlies apparently different contexts and practices: Unguía and Medellín, regional politics and music, residential patterns and personal identity, the regional histories of areas as apparently different as the Chocó, Antioquia, and *la Costa*. In each context, black nucleation and community have interwoven with *mestizaje*, understood as perceptions of culture as well as "physical appearance" and "ancestry"—and also often understood as *blanqueamiento*, the hierarchical version of *mestizaje*. In each context, the way these two sets of processes work themselves out is structured by the local political economy, but there is a recursive relationship in that racial identity forms a relatively autonomous dimension of action which can also structure people's economic opportunities.

By focusing on the Chocó, my aim has been to build up a multidimensional picture of "blackness" in Colombia, considering a variety of contexts. Blackness is not only one ingredient in a set of criteria for assigning social status; nor is it only a reason for discrimination. It is an integral, although heterogeneous, part of Colombian cultural topography. It is constitutive of Colombian nationhood, in the sense that this differentiated whole is based on relational contrasts that include "black," "white," "mestizo," and "indian" as terms. The constant possibility for nonblacks of both including blacks (as citizens, or potential mestizos) and excluding them (as inferior, refractory to progress), or for blacks of including themselves or setting themselves apart—both slippages that are markedly more frictional for "indians"—maintains a dynamic tension among positional images of Colombia which at once suggest the unity and the hierarchical differentiation of the nation. In contexts such as Quibdó, Unguía, or Medellín, these tensions are particularly dynamic, open, and occasionally antagonistic as people in their embodied experience of migration and colonization, of movement across the cultural topography of the country, constitute themselves intersubjectively in a welter of claims and attributions of identities, made, of course, in the context of differentials of power and wealth which may separate "black" from "black" as well as from "mestizo" or "white." These differentials structure such claims and ascriptions, privileging, for example, a relation between "*blanqueamiento*" and upward mobility, or between poor recent migrant status in Medellín and black community there, or between Antioqueño economic dominance in Unguía or Quibdó and the prominence of ethnic difference in those places. And claims and ascriptions structure differentials of power and wealth, helping to reproduce them, although they also have the power to change them. In all this, "blackness" is far from homogeneous, being established relationally and contextually within the shifting framework of the Colombian nation, but neither is it completely heterogeneous, since powerful hierarchies tend to structure these relations and contexts in analogous directions.

It is not my aim here, however, to summarize the principal themes and arguments of the book. Rather, I want to refer to some broader concerns of relevance not only to Colombia and Latin America but also to issues of "race" in general.

Race and Class

The example of the Chocó illustrates that blacks have a particular place in Latin American racial orders. They are at once included and excluded. Indigenous populations are often seen from the perspective of mainstream society as a specific cultural and legal category, a status that may prejudice as well as privilege them. In contrast, blacks tend to be seen as just so many more citizens, linguistically and culturally less distinctive, historically less segregated from the bosom of colonial and republican society, fulfilling, for example, the role of servant. At the same time, blackness is considered inferior and, in Colombia, black regions seen as primitive and backward. Discrimination may be directed against blacks but not systematically, and the cause and effect of this is the uncertainty of the boundaries of categories such as ";black" and "black culture." The ambiguity of this boundary is part of the coexistence of inclusion and exclusion, of *mestizaje* and discrimination.

One aspect of this is the commonly held idea that the position of blacks in Colombia and in Latin America generally should be characterized in terms of "class" rather than "race" (see Wade 1985; Pierson 1942; Harris 1952; Solaún and Kronus 1973). This position admits that most blacks are poor due to historical factors but that nowadays a poor black person is in the same position as a poor person of any color and that racial identity and racial discrimination have virtually no role to play in maintaining the low status of blacks. I hope to have shown that racial identities and discriminations are important issues in Colombia for both blacks and nonblacks and that, whatever the ambiguities, categories such as "black," "black culture," and "*blanqueamiento*" have real meaning and force for some people in a variety of contexts. I have been able to show this partly because both in Unguía and in Medellín racial identity and class position could be differentiated quite easily: although most blacks were poor, most poor people were not black. Therefore the difference between poor blacks and poor nonblacks was easier to assess than in Brazilian contexts reported in the literature, where "race" and "class" tended to overlap quite heavily (e.g., Harris 1952; Degler 1971).

More generally, however, slogans such as "class rather than race" need to be analyzed theoretically. The main difficulty here is that "race" and "class" are seen as two determinants of "status" which both occupy theoretically equal status. In my view, this obscures the real differences between race and class, which is that the latter refers to the control of material forces and power, whereas the former is essentially a signifier, built primarily around historically constituted aspects of "physical appearance," which has usually been made to signify, among other things, some difference of wealth and power. In this sense, it is a question of seeing how racial identities and racialized relations orchestrate relations in the class system and thus create their own patterns within it, rather than of balancing race and class as determinants of status. Part of the problem in Latin America is that very often an implicit or explicit comparison is being made with the United States. This used to be characterized as a rigid "caste" society in which "race" was the dominant factor for blacks, although later literature by scholars such as Sowell (1975) or Wilson (1978) argues for the growing importance of "class" factors in determining life chances. The point is, however, that comparisons between Latin America (frequently Brazil) and the United States, while of course valid in principle, can, by opposing the two in a polar fashion, obscure their common basis. Thus there is no radical division between the United States and Latin America—racial meanings have simply been constructed in rather different ways. Of course, racial identities generally speaking are a more potent force in the United States than in Latin America, but simple dichotomies may lose sight of their real role in the latter region.

It is from this point of view, for example, that the well-known phrase "money whitens" needs to be examined. In the Latin American context, this has been taken to show the power of "class" in defining status and, correspondingly, the relative insignificance of race. Racial identity can even be recast, since in experiments some people use a lighter color term for a photo of a person who looks well off and a darker classification for the same person looking poor (see Solaún and Kronus 1973). This, in my experience, is very context specific, since a typically black person is always classified as such, no matter how wealthy he or she is. This kind of reclassification is open to people of already mixed blood and more ambiguous identity. More to the point, the trope really means that rich black or mulatto people are treated *as if* they were white (or nearly white). They generally have access to the things to which white people have access—although this is, in fact, *conditional*. Blacks have difficulty gaining entry to Cartagena's elite clubs (Solaún and Kronus 1973), and in a well-known case, Katherine Dunham, a black North American dancer and evidently not a member of the Brazilian working class, was refused entry to the prestigious Hotel Esplanada in São Paulo in 1950 (Fernandes 1969, 406;

see also Wright 1990, 97, for a similar incident in Caracas). However, the trope is not "wrong": it simply needs to be understood in context. The fact that money can "whiten" does not mean that "race" is insignificant in Latin American societies. Rather, it testifies to the possibility of nonblack acceptance of blacks and the possibility of black mobility into the nonblack world. It does indeed testify to the greater determining power of material factors. But in the long run, the same holds for the United States. The acquisition by some blacks of some degree of wealth and power has spelled the gradual demise of the rigid "caste" system. There, too, money "whitens," albeit in a different way.

The Autonomy of Race

The foregoing discussion raises a series of issues about how to grasp theoretically the exact relation between "race" and "class." Attempts to simply reduce one to the other—that is, account directly for changing patterns of racial identities and relations in terms of relations between, say, capital and labor—have generally become outmoded, due primarily to the difficulty of accounting for the complexities of race using purely economic categories (Rex 1977, Parkin 1979, Omi and Winant 1986). More subtle revisionist Marxist accounts attribute "relative autonomy" to ideological and political levels, and hence to racial ideologies. In an example of this kind of approach, class relations "function as race relations [and] race is the modality in which class is 'lived'" (Hall 1980, 340; see also Rex and Mason 1986; Gilroy 1982). As Hall (1980, 314) notes, there is a theoretical convergence between such a position and a Weberian approach as used by John Rex, who sees political factors, particularly coercion of labor, and especially in a colonial situation, as having the power to create different groups in society, which may be more or less open or closed and which may compete for, say, jobs or housing (Rex 1977, 1980, 1986a, Rex and Tomlinson 1979; Rex and Moore 1967).

I retreat from a position that simply gives complete and radical autonomy to racial dynamics (Omi and Winant 1986) because I think this runs the danger of obscuring the real analytical differences between the concepts of race and class. I prefer an approach that starts from the kind of theoretical convergence which Hall mentioned, because I think that the material basis of class gives it in the long run more power to construct and alter racial meanings than vice versa. That the United States and Latin America came, at a broad level, to attach very different meanings to the category "black" was fundamentally due, in my view, to economic, political, and demographic factors.

However, once certain racial meanings exist in a specific situation—meanings that in any case are not constituted from scratch—they clearly have an autonomous impact, creating a recursive relation between race and material factors. The nature of this relation is partly seen in the fact that "material factors" never appear in some neutral, technical, asocial form but are always socialized to the core, as Marx himself recognized (Ulin 1991; cf. Sahlins 1976). People are social beings by their very nature, so nothing—environment, biology, economic "facts"—can present itself to them in a pre- or asocial form (Haraway 1989). The point remains, however, that the way people organize themselves with respect to subsistence, accumulation of wealth, and the mobilization of power has greater power in the long run to recast racial dynamics than the other way around; and this is because power and wealth can be inherent in the mobilization of people and resources, whereas nothing can inhere in "race" except certain aspects of human phenotypical variation themselves selected through a colonial history. Logically, then, meanings must become attached to, and become apparently inherent in, perceptions of physical difference—perceptions that are not, in practice, presocial. A given set of meanings constituted in practice—and they are generally meanings closely interwoven with concerns of power, wealth, and status—has an autonomous role.

The material presented on the Chocoanos supports this position. In chapter 1, I argued that the overall racial order of Colombia of which the Chocó is a part was formed by the economic, political, and demographic nature of the Spanish colonial enterprise. But purely economic explanations are insufficient to explain the dynamics of specific contexts of social relations or cultural dynamics—for example, racism in Medellín or in Unguía. For instance, I think it is inadequate to explain the attacks on La Iguaná's or Zafra's *bailaderos* purely in terms of competition for jobs and housing. There is a real sense in which the Antioqueños were also defending a cultural space and a moral authority against threat by a perceived alien intrusion and a sense in which they were fighting to retain the right to define "normal" and "proper" behavior. Complaints about the Chocoanos' "invasions" of the Parque Berrío are attempts to defend the racial and cultural purity of the symbolic center of *paisa* identity. In Unguía, too, the Antioqueños were culturally invading the territory and "civilizing" it after their own image. They are defending or re-creating Antioqueño identity not just as an economic resource but as a way of life that is also, in Bourdieu's (1977) phrase, "symbolic capital" in the national hierarchy of color and civilization. Equally, the Chocoanos' establishment of black community does not occur simply because of certain configurations of residential differentiation and economic wherewithal. It is also a process of establishing a moral ground in which blackness and black culture can locally and/or temporarily be right and proper. In this sense, while the occurrence of racism is structured by other factors that combine to put Chocoanos and Antioqueños together in large numbers in low-income invasion settlements, pirate urbanizations, and tenement districts, there is also an autonomous dynamic to racism which is about cultural and moral power, the authority to define proper and improper, good and bad, or normal and abnormal within a certain community or territory.

Equally, *blanqueamiento* is a process structured by economic factors, so that it occurs and is accepted more easily under some circumstances than others. But while there are material interests at play here, there is also a dynamic that involves culture, identity, and values and which cannot be explained away as an epiphenomenon of economic relations. Adaptation is also involved in a series of meanings about the relative value of whiteness and blackness: adopting the culture of the nonblack world means, or can be taken to mean, an admission of the superiority of culture associated with whiteness and of the inferiority of culture associated with blackness. This is not a mere idiom that clothes economic realities but is a discourse in its own right. Of course, the hierarchies inherent in that discourse are not accidental but themselves derive from the political economic realities of the colonial era which located "white" at the top and "black" and "indian" at the bottom. The point is that the cultural hierarchy can act as a relatively autonomous realm that, although structured, and in the long term fashioned, by the regionalized political economy, remains a nonreducible dimension of action and thought.

The Heterogeneity of Race and Racism

Theoretical debates about the autonomy of race have important connections with how "race" is lived and perceived. Seeing race as more than a precipitate of economic determinants means it can be addressed in its own right; seeing it as nevertheless intimately linked to material factors means that it cannot be addressed in isolation.

This balance is important in other ways, too. Emphasis on race as a discourse *sui generis* does not mean that issues about race and racism can be undifferentiated; but neither does it mean that different contexts are unrelated. There are deeply rooted ideas about the nature of blackness and whiteness which underlie many different situations, but racial dynamics and forms of racism are also specific to particular historically given contexts. Eriksen (1991) argues that the study of ethnicity should not be only a formal Barthian study of boundary maintenance in which the cultural context of ethnic symbols is seen as of little consequence. Instead, the historically specific context may make a difference to ethnic relations at a variety of levels, systemic and personal. Equally, while racism clearly is a process of oppression, racisms need to be located in their spatial and temporal context. Thus, to account for racial inequality as it affects Chocoanos, one has to make recourse to explanations based on a particular experience of slavery which left them in a peripheral region, the exploitation of labor which uses stereotypes of blacks as a justification, the social closure of an ethnic group which denies "outsiders," and especially blacks, access to certain opportunities, the colonization of a frontier territory which is legitimated in terms of the backwardness of blacks, and conflicts over the symbolic capital of color and prestige which use ideas about the primitiveness and ugliness of blackness. All these explanations have a common thread of ideas about the inferiority of blackness, but they also have different implications for the way racism is experienced and the way racial identities interact in a given situation. In short, there is an important element of heterogeneity in racial dynamics and in racism itself. This implies that to tackle racial inequality and racism, it is necessary but not sufficient to attack a notion of "racism" as an undifferentiated set of ideas about the inferiority of blackness. Racisms are woven into specific sets of unequal social relations, and these must be addressed too.

Thus, for example, combating racial inequality for the Chocoanos might take the form of both attempting to reconstruct people's ideas about blackness and addressing specific sets of economic problems. This would take different forms in different contexts. Within the Chocó, negative images center on blacks as lazy and untrustworthy, while in Medellín the images focus more on blacks as fit only for menial work. The two foci of images are clearly connected, but they are slightly different. Similarly, in the Chocó economic projects would have to be designed specifically to target black communities, since development aimed at "opening up" the Chocó often benefits outsiders. In Medellín, on the other hand, measures aimed at low-income settlements and certain informal economic activities in general would be a possible strategy, since blacks participate in these activities in a relatively equal fashion. In both contexts, improvements in education and training would be necessary.

This is perhaps to say no more than that blacks in the Chocó are largely peasants, while in Medellín they are mostly low-income dwellers and workers, and that policies addressed to racial inequality, were they to be formulated, would have to take that into account. At a more general level, it implies that while "anti-racism" is a valid perspective, differences in structures of racial inequality and in forms of racism between, say, the United States, Europe, South Africa, and Latin America need to be addressed as well.

The Constructedness of "Race"

Throughout the Chocoano material I have emphasized the difficult and uncertain nature of categories such as "black" and "black culture." I have shown that the ambiguity surrounding these categories does not mean that blackness vanishes as an issue or that racial discrimination disappears, and that the cause and result of this ambiguity, that is, *mestizaje,* is intimately linked with discrimination. At the same time, however, it becomes very obvious that "black" is not a self-evident category but is negotiable and manipulable. This, in a sense, is not surprising, since work on ethnicity has long emphasized the processual nature of ethnic identifications (Barth 1969; Epstein 1978; Wallman 1979). But race, perhaps because its ideologies seem to "discover what other ideologies have to construct," that is, physical difference (Gilroy 1982, 281), is often seen as less negotiable in this way. Clearly physical markers play a role in "fixing" identity (Wade 1985), but it is vital to recognize that these physical markers are themselves historically constructed. Racial ideologies do not "discover" the unmediated fact of physical difference but have constituted certain very specific physical traits as powerful signifiers, as Gilroy himself later recognizes (1987, 39).

The Colombian material can help us reflect on how radical is the social constitution of racial categories in two ways. First, the very "physical differences" that racial ideologies supposedly discover are less than obvious: how "black" does a "black" have to be? Or more generally, what is it physically which acts as a cue for racial identification: "color"? "hair type"? "facial features"? This encourages reflection on how the notion of physical difference is itself socially constituted, that is, on how certain physical differences between Africans, Amerindians, and Europeans in the New World have been worked into "racial" difference. And this makes more problematic the assertion that racial categories are "naturally" more socially durable because they refer to physical difference: durability in this sense is a social effect. Second, Latin American racial categories are frequently opposed to those of other areas such as the United States, in terms of ambiguity versus clarity, and social insignificance versus social sa-

343

lience. This contrast in social forms can become transposed into arguments about biological bases of classification which then themselves seem to generate the contrast.

Let me expand on these two points, because beneath both lies a common problem: an unacknowledged aspect of the enduring nature/culture binarism which in its different guises has proved so powerful in Western thought and social science (MacCormack and Strathern 1980; Haraway 1989). In what Haraway identifies as a "productionist logic," nature is a raw material for appropriation by culture, and in the social sciences culture indeed is seen to build "races" from a "natural" basis. This basis is, of course, no longer held to have any determinative impact of its own, and "race" is held to be a purely social construct, but "nature" is not in fact consigned to irrelevance. Its continuing presence lies not simply in the recognition that a racializing discourse is also a naturalizing one but also in the very analytic definition of race itself. Many analysts state or imply that the social construction of race appropriates the "natural fact" of phenotypical variation, as if certain aspects of this (e.g., skin color) were intrinsically more liable to be attributed with meanings than others (e.g., height). Treating phenotypical difference as a self-evident biological category (e.g., Banton 1983; 1986b) fails to highlight what Gilroy (1987, 39) calls the "ideological work" that has to be done on physical difference to turn it into "racial" signifiers in the first place. Using phenotypical variation as a taken-for-granted category reveals the presence of a nature/culture binarism that invokes a culture building meaning onto an elemental nature instead of recognizing the mutually constitutive relationship between them. This tends to reproduce "race" as a naturally obdurate category, when its unyielding qualities are really socially determined. Racial discourse does have a naturalizing tendency, but this is not through the unmediated appropriation of natural facts to social ends; it is an effect of the social constitution of the realm of nature itself. People do not naturally find phenotypical difference a problem that has to be explained; the problem must arise within a certain social context that mediates the very perception of that difference and the ideas that it provokes.

In comparisons between Latin America and, say, the United States, the nature/culture binarism reappears once more, and the shift from culture to nature is repeated in a different way. In Latin America (usually Brazil) "racial" classifications are often said to be made on the basis of "appearance" (even though all "race" is supposed to be about "appearance"); in contrast, in the United States they are said to turn on ideas about "ancestry" (Banton 1983, chap. 2; Degler 1971, 103; Harris 1974, 55–59). I would argue that in most places "racial" identifications use a socially constituted appearance as a primary, although not an exhaustive nor an exclusive, cue for classification: in the United States this is also the case, although what appearance is taken to signify (e.g., about ancestry and its significance) is of course different from in Latin America. But in the opposition Brazil/appearance versus United States/ancestry I detect a subtle reference to an undeconstructed vision of the nature/culture binarism. "Ancestry" is about descent, reproduction, genetics, an underlying code or essence. It is deeper, more "natural," more ingrained, less easy to shake off, manipulate, mask, or equivocate with. In contrast, "appearance" is more transient, changeable, superficial, supplementary, derivative—the icing, as it were, on the cake of nature. Its superficiality and changeability is often highlighted in the Latin American context by a further maneuver in which "physical" appearance is only one element of the appearance that overall defines status: clothes, for example, are also important (Harris 1974, 59; cf. Banton 1983, 29), whereas in the United States a black is a black whatever he or she wears.

A powerful metaphor is thus set up contrasting essence with surface, inner with outer realities, in which the inner essence is accorded more power than the surface. When "nature" is appropriated by "culture," the inner essence of the former leaves its mark on the latter more strongly than do its superficial manifestations, themselves subject to the cultural manipulations of extrasomatic accouterments. Thus socially "significant" racial classifications are based on ideas about essential "biology," while "insignificant" ones are based on merely superficial "biology." Although everyone "knows" that racial classifications are purely social, underneath this apparent common sense lies a real and important contrast in the way culture is said to appropriate different levels of nature. If, however, we consider "nature," we find that phenotype is as biological as genotype and that both alter in intergenerational recombinations. In a typical deconstruction, it is not the original "natural" genotype/phenotype distinction from which derives the supplementary "cultural" significance/insignificance-of-race distinction but precisely the latter that makes possible the former.

This is not to deny differences between the United States and Latin America regarding the classification and treatment of "blacks." The ambiguities surrounding blackness in Colombia are important, as I have tried to show throughout this book, but the contrasts and the similarities have to be understood, with careful attention to the meanings subtly given to "race" in the process. To move in the Latin American case from the "maximization of ambiguity" (Harris 1970) to the insignificance of race glosses over the fact that ambiguity undermines the *politicization* of race in the public arena. Race may then be a "personal" issue, but as feminists have convincingly argued, the personal is political: the racial identifications made in the personal space of everyday life reproduce the larger structures of inequality which are the context, or as Giddens (1984, 27) has it, the "unacknowledged conditions of action," for those identifications. Equally, the politicization of race in the United States should not be simply equated with unambiguous and unproblematic "racial identities." Not only is the politicization of race internally heterogeneous and conflictive (Omi and Winant 1986), but, as feminist and postmodernist critiques have argued, subjectivity itself is also multiply constituted, so that blackness in the United States is by no means a simple category (cf. Toplin 1981).

In sum then, it is all too easy to reify racial categories by reference to "phenotype," just as it is tempting to oppose Latin American ambiguity to the apparently unequivocal nature of racial categories in the United States, Britain, or South Africa. Ultimately, however, they are all constructions. Even in apparently unambiguous contexts, this becomes evident on close examination. Benson (1981) uncovers ambiguity in a British context, and this challenge to easy boundaries and taken-for-granted categories has long existed in ports such as Liverpool, Cardiff, or Bristol, where long-established "black" communities have significant mixed-blood populations. Toplin (1981) also challenges the apparent clarity of the black-white distinction in the United States. And perhaps the clearest case of the ultimate constructedness of racial categories is South Africa, where until recently tribunals could alter a person's "race" from one category to another, and members of the same family could be in different categories (Dudgard 1978, Watson 1970). In this sense, then, Colombia is different in degree not kind.

The Future

For the Chocó and indeed for Colombia as a whole, the question remains of what the future will bring: of whether miscegenation will eventually produce racial indistinction and thus equality (within the confines of the class system) or whether blackness will persist in its subordinate position. As the Pacific coast and its people are increasingly incorporated into national society through colonization of the area and migration of blacks into the interior, the evidence indicates that more miscegenation will occur. But if more competition means more discrimination, this process will be hindered. In Unguía we saw that competition between Chocoanos and Antioqueños was now quite low, since each group occupied rather different economic niches. Nevertheless, the Antioqueños were an intrusive, monopolistic element, and ethnic antagonism was more marked at an earlier date when the Antioqueños were competing more actively for the control of the area: amelioration followed their victory in this respect. In Medellín, a critical factor is the very small percentage of Chocoanos in the city: they represent the vast majority of blacks there and yet form less than 1 percent of the total population. There is some competition and therefore some antagonism, but this remains low due to the small number of blacks present. When they become a more intrusive element—whatever their real competition on the labor market—they experience rejection, and this is followed generally by amelioration based on either de facto segregation or black adaptation to Antioqueño mores. In the barrios, blacks retreat into more peripheral locations—in La Iguaná they have even managed to establish a small sector that is more or less theirs; or they adapt—they stop the parties, they have less rowdy *velorios;* or they disperse around the city, and again their lifestyles adapt to a form more acceptable to urban Antioqueños. So Chocoanos are largely accommodated, but, as always, on the condition that they adapt culturally at least to some degree and do not constitute a threat. Some higher-status Chocoanos are accepted (although occasionally taken for lower-status people) because they are a tiny group and are accommodated on an individualistic basis. Equally, as we saw in chapter 16, mixed marriages, legal and common law, occur quite widely.

The logical conclusion of this argument is that if the Chocoanos migrated in greater numbers, and especially if they tried to be socially mobile and claim higher status on a large scale, there would be greater ethnic and racial antagonism directed at them from both working-class and bourgeois Antioqueños, a conclusion echoed for Brazil by Harris (in an early essay, 1952), Van den Berghe (1967, 74), Degler (1972, 284), Toplin (1981, 115), Fernandes (1969, 337), and Silva (1985). For the moment, however, this has not come to pass in Medellín, although the incidents of racial antagonism which have appeared are indicative warnings.

The ultimate balance of these two forces of *mestizaje* and discrimination remains speculative precisely because it is structured by the regionally varied development of the country's political economy, and the future of this is far from clear. If opportunities are abundant, then the autonomous dynamic of the racial order will dictate that blacks will tend to assimilate into the nonblack world, and miscegenation will be the major trend. If, however, opportunities are scarce, then competition will remain a powerful force, and the majority of blacks will continue to suffer discrimination, perhaps at an even greater level.

Uncertainty in the future, however, does not rule out the possibility of action in the present; the problem is, of what kind? If blacks continue to suffer disadvantage, one option, already partly under way, would be to organize politically and lobby government for specific action directed at "blacks" or at regions and activities where they are present in large numbers. This option leads straight into a philosophical debate about the ethics of positive discrimination or affirmative action (see Lustgarten 1980; Banton 1983, chap. 14). In its simplest terms, the question centers on whether one should aim for "fair shares for groups," which means specifying and drawing attention to group boundaries and, in this case, racial differences and then allocating benefits to certain groups, or their individual members, who have been discriminated against in the past in such a way as to deserve collective compensation for the accrued disadvantage they suffer in the competition for material goods, power, and status. In Colombia, this would imply trying to make the category "black" less ambiguous, more solidary, and politically self-aware, initially to pressure for such action but also to define more clearly who might be its beneficiaries. The alternative would be to aim for "fair shares for individuals," which means guaranteeing equal opportunities and letting competition take care of the rest, such that group boundaries dissolve as individuals compete on the basis of their own skills, with no reference to their ascribed characteristics. In Colombia, this would effectively mean leaving the situation as it is, in the hope that the category "black" would eventually cease to have any real meaning—a state of affairs which some would say already exists. It is clear, of course, that "equal opportunities" is something of a mirage, not to mention a handy political catchphrase, and that the difficulty lies in making sure not only that opportunities are equal—which they obviously are not for the blacks in Colombia—but also that people first take them up equally and then follow them through. It also assumes that certain categories of people will not act so as to exclude certain other categories from opportunities perceived as scarce. On the other hand, the politicization of race might threaten to emphasize boundaries and difference, to increase conflict and even violence: the threat of "racism in reverse." In addition, instead of destabilizing meanings about race, this strategy might reinforce them in attempting to construct a homogeneous "black" interest, implying that blacks are the same: identification is stressed rather than difference.

In the case of the Colombian blacks, the accumulated precipitate of the historical discriminations of which they have been the object

348

puts them at a material disadvantage in any competition. Whether or not they currently suffer discrimination—and the evidence indicates that they do suffer some—they began the race behind the majority of the field. There is therefore a logical case for directing funds and resources towards blacks as a category—assuming that the notion of collective national responsibility for social equality is admitted. In practice, however, given the ambiguity of this category, a more realistic alternative would be to direct action at the regions (or activities) where they are present in large numbers. To the extent that such material support has to be lobbied for in the national arena, movements formed on a regional basis—which would perforce be mostly black—are a justifiable development. Of course, locating demands at a regional level, while more practical and probably easier to justify publicly, does little to address the devaluation of blackness as such. Indeed, it would contribute to the fragmentation of an already highly ambiguous black category.

Going one step further, then, and onto trickier terrain, one can argue that in order to take proper advantage of material opportunities, black people need a solid sense of their own value and legitimacy as blacks; or, going further still and leaving the domain of material equality, one could argue that the accumulated weight of disdain which bears down on black culture—either ignored, despised, or accepted only as exotic or exciting but also as primitive—can only be shrugged off by the concentrated efforts of blacks to reaffirm its value. This last position would assume the legitimacy of a culturally plural society, something that is officially "recognized and protected" in Article Seven of the 1991 Constitution. Such cultural *reivindicación* (reclaiming) is more inherently problematic, since it envisages an end goal of continuing cultural difference, while claims for material equality anticipate eventual economic indistinction (at least within the confines of the class system).

My own view is that protest for material equality is a more easily justifiable strategy since it invokes ideals of democratic social justice. Such protest would be easiest on a regional and local level, since it would not *need* to make reference to blacks as such and because such protests already have some history in Colombia. But such localized demands could not hope to redefine the meanings surrounding blackness, except perhaps implicitly or by means of the long-term effects of improving the economic position of blacks (an effect that is by no means straightforward, as the debate on the position of blackness in post-Revolutionary Cuba shows; see, for example, Casal 1979; Taylor 1988). Redefinition of blackness so that it can be a "normal state of affairs" in cultural terms is difficult to envisage in Colombia, since in a situation in which at least some blacks are escaping the category of black, protest on a collective scale is unlikely to evolve very far without a conscious attempt to organize on the part of a minority of blacks who are prepared to push for a more coherent black identity. In this sense, attempts to create black solidarity directed both at reevaluating blackness and at protesting about racial inequality and lobbying for positive measures can be seen as a legitimate initial and short- to medium-term strategy. There are, of course, real dangers in attempting to construct a new category of "black," in emphasizing identification rather than difference, in perhaps implying that blacks all have the same interests or even that they are all in some sense "the same." The danger is not an automatic one, however. The crucial point is not to ground that identification in specious natural categories but to justify it in terms of a contingent identification of political interests; this can exist alongside a deconstruction of the apparent naturalness of racial categories and a challenge to the standard meanings attached to blackness. In any case, to push black solidarity or positive discrimination too far or too blindly risks engendering antagonism, and although a certain amount of antagonism may be inevitable, and even necessary, in a struggle for racial equality, it cannot be seen as an end in itself. As the Chocoano singer Jairo Varela says in his song "Cicatrices" (Scars), "I do not want this to end in hate."

Epilogue

The research for this book was done in Colombia between 1982 and 1983, and between 1986 and 1987. In the summer of 1992, courtesy of a grant from the British Academy, I completed six weeks' fieldwork, mostly in the Pacific coast region, and found that important changes were taking place that I thought should not go without notice in this book.

I did not go to Unguía, but in Quibdó I met many friends from Unguía who had since moved. In the last decade, the Urabá region has become a virtual battleground between guerrilla forces and the state, with paramilitary groups and drug traffickers adding to the violence.[1] The Antioqueño side of the Gulf is the worst hit, but the violence has spread to the Chocoano side and many people I knew in Unguía are now dead, many of them murdered by guerrilla or paramilitary forces. Some of the big Antioqueño merchant-farmers had been killed, but one of the main effects of the violence on the area has been to accelerate the exodus of Chocoanos that I identified in 1982–83. Specifically, three of the more successful Chocoano families had suffered threats and even, in one case, an assassination attempt. In short, the area is now more completely Antioqueño than before.

Medellín has not changed much. It is just as violent and as trapped in the ups and downs of the drug war. The Chocoano presence is very much as I found it in 1986–87, although the Corporación de Negritudes and the Chocoano Action Committee (see chapter 17) have both collapsed. La Playita in La Iguaná (see chapter 12) has also undergone many changes after a flood swept away most of the settlement in 1988 (see notes to figure 4 in appendix B).

More substantial changes have taken place in the political sphere.

351

I argued in chapter 17 that black political organization was weak and incipient, plagued by fragmentation and divisiveness. Problems included the difficulty of knowing who was and who was not "black," the tendency of mulattoes not to identify with blacks, and the tendency of some successful blacks—potential leaders—to engage in one way or another in processes of *blanqueamiento*. None of this has been radically altered, but there are signs of significant changes.

On 5 July 1991, a new constitution was approved in Colombia. This recognized the "pluricultural and multiethnic" character of the Colombian nation and gave certain rights to indigenous minorities. It included a Transitory Article 55 requiring the promulgation of a law, subject to study by a government-created special commission, that "in accordance with their traditional production practices, and in areas to be demarcated by the same law, recognizes collective property rights for black communities which have been occupying *tierras baldías* [public or state lands] in the rural riverine zones of the rivers of the Pacific Basin." The law must also establish "mechanisms for the protection of the cultural identity and rights of these communities, and for the promotion of their economic and social development." The article may be applied to other communities that "present similar conditions." The transitory nature of the article means that Congress must pass the law by 5 July 1993, or the power to draft it defaults to the President himself, who could, of course, let the article lapse if he chose.

The background to the inclusion of this article is very revealing of the nature of black political organization. The scene in the late 1980s included three important elements. First, there already existed a certain level of black politicization. On the one hand there was the type noted in chapter 17: basically urban movements formed by a minority of black intellectuals with barely any funding, inspired by such events on the international scene as the civil rights and black power movements in the United States, black resistance in South Africa, and the independence of other African states.[2] On the other hand were grass-roots organizations, mainly in the Chocó, for example, the Integrated Peasant Association of the Atrato, which was formed in 1984 at the instigation of the church's Afro-American Pastoral program. Also formed in 1984 in Quibdó, the Organization of Popular Barrios was an autonomous movement that pushed for better urban services and organized productive small-scale projects. Thus some community organization existed, albeit often impelled by the church.

Second, the Pacific region had become an area of increasing interest for the state. The whole Pacific basin was seen as a focus of immense future geopolitical potential, and the government was eager to exploit

Colombia's position. Hence the presidency's grandiose plan for a "New Pacific Dimension for Colombia" (see chapter 8), based on huge infrastructural developments. Hence also a more recent international forum on "Colombia in the Pacific Era" attended by a plethora of government top brass and foreign ambassadors (Cali, July 1992). This attention has translated practically into more roads, more colonization, and more development of precisely the distorted, inegalitarian, and destructive kind documented in chapter 8. One consequence was that blacks, in search of timber and new mining lands, began to encroach on indian lands. Conflicts had emerged already as the government demarcated indian reserves that often included established black settlements. Now the conflict has worsened. However, indian organizations such as the Chocó's Regional Organization of Waunamas and Emberás, an entity originally created by the church in 1986, attempted to defuse the situation by creating black-indian alliances to fight for land rights and against environmental degradation (even though, of course, blacks themselves, as miners and loggers, did some of the degrading). One such alliance was the Chocó's Peasant Association of the San Juan, formed in 1990 during the Second Meeting for the Unity and Defense of Indian and Black Communities. The point is that indian organization in Colombia is older, is better financed, and has better advisory back-up than do black movements. This unstable marriage of convenience thus gave Pacific coast blacks, more accurately Chocoanos, a further point of leverage.

Third, during the governments of Belisario Betancur (1982–86) and Virgilio Barco (1986–90), state peace plans for demobilizing guerrilla movements had long been at odds with informal, but vicious and efficient, repression of all leftist elements and social movements effected (often surreptitiously) by the armed forces and by paramilitary forces, sometimes financed by drug money. Part of the attempt to create a more open political system was the idea of reforming the country's rigid constitution. Although the intent of this initiative was not the benefit of ethnic minorities, the initiative opened a forum in which they were able to debate. In sum, then, a particular conjuncture came about in which black people, among whom there were already some elements of organization, and of whom some had a few unstable alliances with more powerful indian movements, might gain a political space.

The Constituent Assembly to draft the new constitution was voted in on 9 December 1990, but prior to this a series of preparatory discussions took place. Existing black organizations participated, as did individual blacks and academics such as Nina de Friedemann and Jaime Arocha. A new black organization was formed, based in

Buenaventura and called the Coordinator of Black Communities. A proposal was signed by a variety of black and indian groups that referred to blacks as an "ethnic group" with equal rights to the indian communities. Meanwhile a variety of black individuals came forward as candidates for the Constituent Assembly elections. Some were essentially politicians whose connection with any kind of community participation was dubious. One was Carlos Rosero, a representative of the Coordinator, which did have more solid community links.

In any event, no black candidate gained a seat. However, two indian representatives were elected, Francisco Rojas Birry and Lorenzo Muelas, and this is where the indian-black alliance of the Chocó had an impact. The former, an Emberá from the Chocó, had campaigned as a representative of both black and indian communities in the Pacific region and, enjoying greater financial and advisory backing than the black candidates, had convinced many blacks to vote for him. The greater success of the indians in conquering a political space (they also elected three indigenous senators to Congress in the 1991 elections) derives in part from their particular position in the racial order and the differences between blacks and indians discussed in chapter 2.

During the Constituent Assembly, the proposal agreed to in the preparatory sessions was thrown out: some indian delegates even denied all knowledge of it, underlining the unstable nature of the indian-black alliance.[3] Instead, Lorenzo Muelas, along with Orlando Fals Borda, an academic and representative of the party Acción Democrática-M19, formed by the M19 guerrilla movement when it demobilized in March 1990, launched a proposal on ethnic minorities that barely even mentioned blacks, and focused almost entirely on indian groups. Finally, however, after town hall occupations in Quibdó and lobbying of the delegates, Transitory Article 55 was passed.

This event has intensified the process of black organization, mostly in the Pacific region. Peasant associations have begun to emerge all over the coast. Many of them have been initiated by the church, but this is not a straightforward process. In some cases, for example, the clergyman involved has been a local black and a member of the Cimarrón movement. Cimarrón is the National Movement for the Human Rights of Black Communities in Colombia, formed in 1982 and for many years an urban intellectual movement of the familiar kind. Recently it has begun to engage in grass-roots community organization and has been an inspiration for many individual blacks (see chapter 17). In other cases, the Coordinator was involved in advising community organizations. All of these peasant associations are essentially concerned with land rights, but in the discussions and seminars that form much of their early activities, black history, culture, and identity are always subjects, even when the church is a main initiator of the process.

One of the main spurs for organization was the need to influence the special commission called for by Transitory Article 55. The government dragged its heels on this, and only officially inaugurated the commission on 14 July 1992, effectively wasting half the time permitted for the drafting of the requisite law. However, the black communities did achieve representation: four consultative commissions were established by the government for the Pacific coast departments. They are composed of local black community organizations and each has three delegates on the special commission. The latter, which also includes representatives from government agencies and a group of politicians and academics, has so far met twice.

This is not the place to enter into details of the discussions of the special commission.[4] The government's motives appear to be clear. The Pacific region, like the Amazon region, is to be opened up for colonization and development. Transitory Article 55 and the rights given to indian communities are concessions to the local people. In the case of the blacks, the only concrete result of the special commission is liable to be the granting of collective land title to some communities: the rest of the provisions concerning cultural identity, rights, and the promotion of development are so vague and so hard to put into juridical practice, especially in the time available, that the black delegates will be fighting a losing battle in trying to achieve something effective in this area.

But, like it or not, the government has provided a significant political space for black communities. Although much of the recent organization has been promoted by the church and is in direct response to a state concession granted partly through the offices of indian representatives, important precedents have been established that may well feed into a wider movement.

Reflecting on these developments in the context of the problems facing black organization and politicization in general in Colombia (see chapter 17), it is clear that the present politicization relies heavily on a regional focus, even though, for example, some of the black delegates on the special commission are from the north of Cauca, or from Palenque de San Basilio. In this way, the problem of who is to be classed as black does not arise so obviously, since the Pacific coast is the black region *par excellence*. Even so, most of the black representatives that I spoke to did not conceive of the ambiguity of black identity as a problem in itself, although they admitted that there were "black" people who refused to admit it and mulattoes who wanted to reject their black heritage. In other words, for them the problem was not of structural ambiguity, but of personal identification, and recent events show that there are plenty of people willing to identify as black and participate in political or social movements that overtly address a black audience.

In this sense, focusing on the fragmented racial loyalties of blacks or on the structural ambiguity of blackness as the main problems facing black organization may bias the analysis by isolating blacks and mulattoes from their political context to concentrate on their internal characteristics. Political context—international as well as national—is also a crucial factor, and change in that arena can cause people to alter their loyalties and identifications (as it has done in Colombia and in Brazil). Black organization in Colombia has its problems, but it is not paralyzed. In this respect, Amir Smith-Córdoba, leader of the Center for the Investigation and Development of Black Culture in Bogotá (see chapter 17), who is notorious for his habit of approaching people in the street whom he considers black and saying "¡Hola, negro!" recounts that his victims (classified by him with more North than Latin American definitions of black tend to react with less surprise or hostility today than they would have ten or fifteen years ago.

What we are witnessing, then, is the emergence of a more solid ethnic identity than previously existed. Whereas before, if a black identity could be said to exist, then it was based on very general ideas of a shared history, a shared notion of being "black" (itself an ambiguous status), and the shared suffering of discrimination (which was not even agreed on by all "blacks"). Now, there is a definite element claiming that blacks are an ethnic group, and does so in privileged encounters with the state (i.e., in the Constituent Assembly and in the special commission). Thus, an "imagined community" of blacks is emerging (Anderson 1983), not just of its own accord but in a complex and dialectic relation between the state (in the form of various specific agencies), the church, the black communities, and the black organizations that claim to represent them. The state is playing an equivocal game: the Constitution has several articles that refer to "ethnic groups," but the term is never defined and essentially refers to indians and perhaps the English-speaking blacks of Colombia's Caribbean island possessions. The general tenor of the Constituent Assembly was to deny ethnic group status to blacks. Transitory Article 55 itself confirms this, being directed at the blacks of a specific geographical area rather than at an ethnic group as such. The article has fed a movement which does claim an ethnic identity for blacks, however, and the church and state development agencies include sessions on black history and culture in their social development programs that help to make such a claim more likely to attract adherents.

The potential problems of antagonism noted in the concluding chapter are muted insofar as the discourse of ethnicity used by most of these organizations is not exclusivist. This is true, in part, because an exclusive definition of black people is not necessary to mobilize self-identifying blacks. Black peasant associations often invite indians to their meetings, and even the more radical black groups such as Cimarrón or the Coordinator (the personnel of which sometimes use African names) tend to have a double-stranded discourse that addresses both blacks and people with black heritage, inviting the latter to look at the presence and value of blackness within themselves and the nation. It remains to be seen whether this delicate balance between openness and exclusiveness can be maintained, whether it is possible to make progress without pushing toward an ever more exclusive ethnicity. The results achieved so far, although modest, are encouraging.

Postscript for the Paperback Edition

In Quibdó on August 27th 1993, President Gaviria announced Law 70 on "black communities," the outcome of the special commission's negotiations.[5] The law recognizes land rights for the Pacific region black communities identified in Transitory Article 55. It also establishes certain mechanisms for the protection of the cultural identity of black communities "as an ethnic group" (Art. 1): it outlaws discrimination against them, promotes educational curricula adapted to their cultural background, includes black representatives in some state agencies, and creates a special electoral constituency to vote two blacks into the Chamber of Representatives.[6]

In my view and that of many black leaders, the law brings blackness into the national frame in an unprecedented, positive way; it is a testament to blacks' resilience; it raises the possibility of seeing the Pacific region as a political, ecological and cultural space. Drawbacks include a pragmatic focusing of the "black issue" on the Pacific region, despite the scope of the broader measures; the use of a (state) model of indian identity—based on small, "traditional," rooted communities—to understand black identity; and the lack of environmental safeguards on the activities of non-blacks in the region, while black communities must use sustainable practices. The law is without doubt an important foot in the door of state; it is also, in my opinion, a cooptative strategy by a state bent on opening up the Pacific region for "development".[7] As such, it will have to be fought over.

Black political organization continues to have the problems of many minority movements: fragmentation, cooptation, internal disputes, and lack of both finance and financial autonomy.[8] Nevertheless, the movement—in which women play an important role—has stronger grass-roots links than ever before. In this respect, research into the impact of new articulations of black identity at community level is a priority.

Notes

1. See Jenny Pearce, *Colombia: Inside the Labyrinth* (London: Latin American Bureau, 1990); J. Arocha, "Violencia contra minorías étnicas en Colombia." In *Colombia: violencia y democracia,* edited by Comisión de Estudios sobre la Violencia en Colombia, pp. 105–33 (Bogotá: Universidad Nacional, 1986).

2. See Pierre-Michel Fontaine, "Transnational Relations and Racial Mobilization: Emerging Black Movements in Brazil." *In Ethnic Identities in a Transnational World,* edited by John F. Stack (Westport, Conn.: Greenwood Press, 1981).

3. See Jaime Arocha, "Los Negros y la Nueva Constitución Colombiana de 1991," *América Negra* 3 (1992): 39–54.

4. See P. Wade, "El movimiento negro en Colombia," *América Negra* 5 (1993): 173–91.

5. See J. Arocha, "Entorno y derechos territoriales." In *Colombia: país de regiones,* edited by CINEP, pp. 497-512 (Bogotá: CINEP, *El Colombiano,* 1994); A. Cifuentes, M. Adarve and J. Veláquez, *La nueva constitución y la territorialidad en el Pacífico colombiano.* (Cali: Viva la Ciudadanía, Corporación SOS-Colombia, 1993); E. Sánchez, R. Roldán and M. F. Sánchez, *Derechos e identidad: los pueblos indígenas y negros en la constitución política de Colombia de 1991* (Bogotá: Disloque, 1993); P. Wade. "The Cultural Politics of Blackness in Colombia," *American Ethnologist* 22(2): 342–58.

6. Elected were Zulia Mena, Leader of the Organization of Popular Barrios (see p. 352) and Agustín Valencia, connected to Piedad de Córdoba, a Liberal senator for Antioquia of Chocoano descent.

7. The director of Proyecto BioPacífico, which investigates the conservation of biological diversity in the region, estimates that 40 percent of the region's 12 million hectares of rainforest has already been destroyed (*The Colombian Post,* 31 August 1994, p. 1). See J. Barnes, "Driving Roads Through Land Rights: The Colombian Plan Pacífico, "*The Ecologist* 23(4) (1993): 135–140. A. Escobar, "Cultural Politics and Biological Diversity: State, Capital and Social Movements in the Pacific coast of Colombia," in *Cultures of Protest: Dissent and Direct Action in the Late Twentieth Century* edited by R. Fox and O. Stam (forthcoming).

8. In June 1994, the High Level Consultative Commission charged with overseeing Law 70 was installed. In meetings to select a representative from Antioquia, some 20 different black organizations participated, of which over half appeared to be allied to traditional Liberal politicians.

Appendix A

Tables

Table 1. The Population of Four Regions and Santa Fe, Various Years (%)

	Chocó		Atlantic Coast		Antioquia		Popayán		Santa Fe	
	1778	1808	1778	1825	1778	1808	1778	1825	1778	1825
Whites	2.3	1.6	11.3	—	16.7	25.6	20.5	—	25.3	—
Indians	36.9	17.8	17.7	—	4.4	4.5	27.7	—	18.9	—
Libres	21.5	60.7	62.4	—	59.4	57.7	32.6	—	49.2	—
Slaves	39.2	19.8	8.0	3.9	19.3	12.2	18.6	14.2	5.4	3.8
Total N	14,662	25,000	158,232	166,058	46,366	106,856	100,290	87,519	742,750	1,229,259

Note: In colonial times, Colombia as such did not exist. Instead, what now roughly corresponds to Panama, Colombia, and Ecuador were combined in 1718 into the Virreinato de Santa Fe de Bogotá, composed of the Audiencia of Quito and the Audiencia of Santa Fe de Bogotá. The latter consisted of Panama, together with Colombia minus the present-day departments of Nariño, Cauca, and Valle del Cauca. These three were part of the province of Popayán, which was in the Audiencia of Quito (see Silvestre 1950). The figures for the Atlantic coast are the combined figures from the provinces of Cartagena and Santa Marta. By 1825, the picture had changed somewhat, and the viceroyalty as such no longer existed: Popayán was a much smaller area (hence its lower total population figure) and was included within the new republic.

Sources: For the Chocó: Sharp (1976, 199), who uses regional archival material for 1778 and regional archival plus secondary sources for 1808. For the Atlantic coast and Popayán: Pérez Ayala (1951) for 1778 and Fernando Gómez (1970) for 1825; as yet, I have not been able to locate 1808 data for these regions. The 1825 figures do not break down the free population into socioracial groups. For Antioquia: Pérez Ayala (1951) for 1778 and Parsons

359

(1968, 4, quoting Pérez 1863) for 1808. Ann Twinam (pers. com., Feb. 1985), who kindly made the statistics from Pérez Ayala and from the Anuario Estadístico del Departamento de Antioquia (1888) available to me, observes that the latter gives accurate data for 1808. However, it only breaks down the population into slaves and others: therefore I have used Parsons' figures, despite discrepancies between the two reckonings (e.g., the Anuario gives 9.1% slaves). For Santa Fe: Pérez Ayala (1951) for 1778 and Fernando Gómez (1970) for 1825. An alternative source for the 1778 figures is Silvestre 1950 [1789]: there are some discrepancies between his reckonings and those of Antonio Caballero y Góngora presented in Pérez Ayala (1951)—total population figures vary by about 80,000, and the percentages vary by 5 to 8 percent—but the basic patterns are similar.

Table 2. Distribution of Cattle by Origin of Farmer, Unguía, 1982

Size of Herd	Chocoano		Antioqueño		Costeño		Total	
	Farms	Cattle	Farms	Cattle	Farms	Cattle	Farms	Cattle
<10	2	15	10	52	19	118	31	185
10–20	3	37	17	243	5	60	25	340
20–50	4	128	24	796	21	664	49	1,588
50–100	4	301	9	648	13	939	26	1,888
100–200	3	399	6	671	5	665	14	1,735
200–500	—	—	9	2,795	1	220	10	3,015
500–1000	—	—	1	879	—	—	1	879
>1000	—	—	3	4,529	—	—	3	4,529
Total	16	880	79	10,613	64	2,666	159	14,159

Note: These data were collected from the records of the Instituto Colombiano Agropecuario, the Colombian Agricultural and Stock-Raising Institute, in October 1982. The ethnic origin of the farmers was ascertained from interviews with the institute's employees, who toured the farms counting cattle and knew each farmer personally. The number of cattle on a farm is not necessarily the number actually owned by the farmer: he or she may rent pasture to other cattle owners and may also have cattle a utilidades, an arrangement whereby one person buys young cattle and puts them on another's farm to fatten, the farm owner paying for the costs incurred meanwhile; when the cattle is sold, the profits are split. Furthermore, a farmer may have cattle bought on credit. Thus, for example, of the 880 head of cattle on the land of Chocoano farmers, about a third were not actually owned by them. These patterns mean that the actual dominance of the larger cattle owners is underestimated in the table, since some of their cattle is on the farms of poorer farmers. Even taking the table as it stands, it is clear that the Antioqueños own the great majority (75%) of the cattle. The Costeños are on a roughly equal footing with them up to a ceiling of 200 cattle, but thereafter they fall behind. The Chocoanos own only 6 percent of the cattle.

A recount made in July 1985 showed the same basic patterns. There was an overall increase of about 2,300 animals on roughly the same number of farms. The Antioqueños accounted for 76 percent of this increase, but interestingly the Chocoanos had registered the greatest percentage increase over the 1982 level, rising from 880 to 1,543 head of cattle. As before, much of this belonged to other farmers, Antioqueños and some Costeños: the colonization of this part of the Chocó by outsiders clearly offered economic opportunities to this handful of Chocoano farmers, even while it made them dependent on outside capital.

Table 3.   Registered Landholdings by Area and Origin of Owner, Unguía, 1986

Area (ha)	Origin of Owner			Total
	Costeño	Antioqueño	Chocoano	
<5	6	4	2	12
5–10	7	6	8	21
10–50	55	45	30	130
50–100	18	24	6	48
>100	4	19	1	24
Total	90	98	47	235

Note: These data were collected from the local land registry records in Unguía in April 1986. They must be considered incomplete, since in a frontier zone such as this farmers do not necessarily register their holdings, partly because doing so makes them liable to taxation. The data on the origin of the owners are not entirely reliable either: land registry records do not have the place of birth of the owner but only the place of issue of his or her *cédula,* or identity card. This is usually the same as place of birth or, more probably, place of upbringing, but in some cases people get their *cédulas* late in life when they have already moved away from their place of birth or upbringing. Furthermore, I have excluded from the table 17 people with *cédulas* issued in the Urabá Antioqueño—for example, in places such as Turbo: these people should be classed as Antioqueños, and in many cases they may be individuals, Antioqueño by upbringing, who migrated to the area and had their *cédulas* issued there, but they are more likely to be people of Costeño origin. (For the record, 12 of these 17 cases have farms between 10 and 50 hectares, with another 4 owning farms between 50 and 100 hectares.) Therefore, this table can only be considered a rough guide. Nevertheless, it indicates that the Antioqueños dominate in the large-farm category and are also overrepresented in the 50–100 hectare bracket compared with the average for all farmers, while they are relatively underrepresented in the 10–50 hectare bracket. Conversely, the Costeños, and even more the Chocoanos, are relatively overrepresented in the 10–50 hectare bracket, with the Chocoanos also over the average in the 5–10 hectare group. It is worth noting that in the Chocoano group, 35 of the 47 cases represent people with *cédulas* issued in the Unguía area itself: they are as liable to be people of Costeño origin, either born and raised in Unguía or having migrated and obtained their *cédulas* there, as they are to be of Chocoano origin.

Table 4. Marriage and Consensual Union by Place of Birth, Unguía, 1982

Place of Birth of Women	Place of Birth of Men					
	Coast	Interior	Total Chocó	Urabá Chocoano	Rest of Chocó	Total Women
Coast	**35**	**2**	11	*8*	*3*	**48**
Interior	**3**	**38**	3	*1*	*2*	**44**
Total Chocó	24	8	**33**	*11*	*22*	**65**
Urabá Chocoano	*18*	*6*	*21*	(9)	(12)	*45*
Rest of Chocó	*6*	*2*	*12*	(2)	(10)	*20*
Total Men	**62**	**48**	**47**	*20*	*27*	**157**

Note: These data are taken from a random sample of 200 households to which a questionnaire was administered, eliciting data from the respondent and his or her spouse in the 157 cases in which a couple was cohabiting or married. The category Total Chocó is broken down into those born in the Urabá Chocoano and those born elsewhere in the Chocó in order to show more clearly the patterns of intermarriage. Rows and column totals in bold type are the sum of their respective rows and column figures in bold. Row and column totals in italic type are the sum of their respective row and column figures in italics, excepting figures in parentheses. Enquiry into the genealogies of the longest-resident families of the town indicated that these people are often the children of an earlier Chocoano-Costeño mix. It can be seen that, in the sample, there are many more women than men born in the Urabá Chocoano: the men tend to emigrate more, and the women form a pool of available partners for incoming Chocoanos and Costeños and for a few men from the interior (mostly Antioqueños). Direct unions between Costeños and Chocoanos from the rest of the Chocoano are not all that frequent, and most of the mixture between these two categories occurs via the people born in the Urabá Chocoano (see Wade 1984, 86, for more detail).

Intermarriage rates can be calculated from the data in table 4 by computing the proportion of mixed couples in the total number of couples in each ethnic category (Besanceney 1965). An expected intermarriage rate (E), based on a random union hypothesis, can be compared with an observed intermarriage rate (O) and a ratio (O/E) calculated (see Besanceney 1965 and Rodman 1965 for details). This gives the following results for the three basic ethnic categories.

Table 5. Intermarriage rates, Unguía, 1982

	Percentages		
	E	O	O/E
Chocoanos	75	58	77
Costeños	75	53	71
Antioqueños	75	29	39

Appendix B

Figures

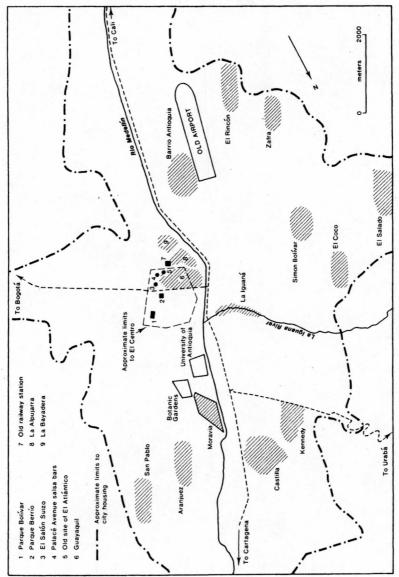

1 Parque Bolívar
2 Parque Berrío
3 El Salón Suizo
4 Palacé Avenue salsa bars
5 Old site of El Atlántico
6 Guayaquil
7 Old railway station
8 La Alpujarra
9 La Bayadera

— · — · — Approximate limits to city housing

Approximate limits to El Centro

University of Antioquia

Botanic Gardens

Moravia

San Pablo

Aranjuez

Castilla

Kennedy

La Iguaná

La Iguaná River

Simón Bolívar

El Coco

El Salado

Barrio Antioquia

OLD AIRPORT

El Rincón

Zafra

Río Medellín

To Cali

To Bogotá

To Cartagena

To Urabá

N

2000

meters

0

Figure 1. Medellín

366

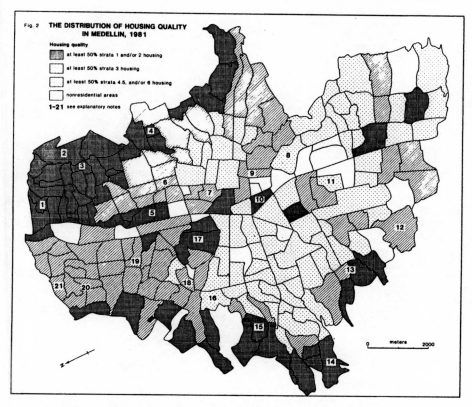

Figure 2.   The Distribution of Housing Quality in Medellín, 1981

Notes to Figures 2 and 3.   Figure 2 gives a general indication of the spatial distribution of housing according to quality in the census tracts of Medellín, which correspond roughly to barrios. It is based on the 1981 Estudio de Población carried out by DANE and which used DANE's six-level hierarchy of housing quality in which each city block is assigned to a quality level, one being low and six being high. Although only three categories are used in this map, this gives a general idea of the city's class-space patterns, since barrios in which two or more strata are represented with anything approaching equal frequency are uncommon (about 15 in a total of 210). These are often barrios in which more middle-class, stratum-four residential units intrude into working-class, stratum-three areas, or where rather unconsolidated, stratum-two housing coexists with older, more consolidated, stratum-three housing.

Figure 3 shows the distribution of the Chocoanos picked up by the same study. The map shows barrios in which Chocoanos, other than live-in domestics, were censused. One qualification needs to be made. The numbers of Chocoanos in each barrio are small and can therefore be rather arbitrary: the chance sampling of one big family can push up the apparent density of Chocoanos in that barrio by an unrealistic amount.

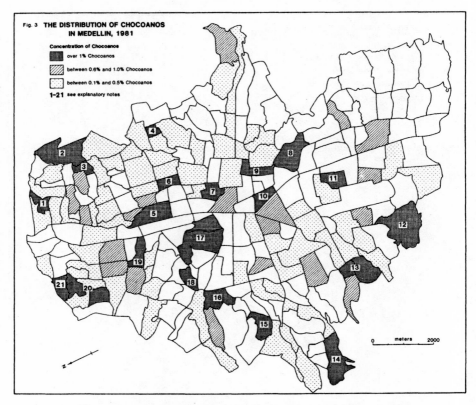

Figure 3. The Distribution of Chocoanos in Medellín, 1981

Bearing in mind these problems, we can still get a rough picture of the distribution of Chocoanos in the city. It is clear, for example, that places such as La Iguaná, Zafra, and Moravia show up as having relatively high concentrations and/or large numbers of Chocoanos. Below I look at each of the numbered neighborhoods in turn, in each of which Chocoanos form at least 1 percent of the population. I make comments about each one, sometimes on the basis of information collected in the field, sometimes on the basis of the citywide sample data that I use to give specific information about selected households in order to give a detailed feel for the kind of families to which I am referring. For each barrio the first figure in parentheses indicates the map key number, the second gives the number of individuals born in the Chocó who appeared in the barrio sample, and the third is the percentage they form of that barrio's sampled population. Theoretically, the second number is about 10 percent of the total Chocoano population of that barrio.

• Popular Dos (1, 12, 1.3%). This and the nearby barrio of La Esperanza (2, 8, 1.6%) are both part of the urban periphery, formed around what are now more consolidated working-class barrios that grew up in the northeastern quarter of the city in the thirties, forties, and fifties. Both Popular and La Esperanza are quite recent settlements that began in the sixties as invasions and/or pirate urbanization of a basic kind in which plots of land are sold to individuals for their housing needs without the necessary legal permits (CEHAP 1986). The Chocoano households sampled here are three female-headed households, two with an attached kinswoman, and one nuclear family. Three working people are employed as domestic servants and two as industrial workers (food and textile production), although the size of the enterprises they work in is not revealed. There is also a Chocoano man, who farms or raises stock, married to an Antioqueño woman, a textile worker; and a Chocoano housewife living with a non-Chocoano man who does *ventas ambulantes*. Neighboring San Pablo (3, 7, 1.0%) also forms part of this general pattern, as does Versalles (4, 9, 1.2%), farther south. In Versalles there is apparently a more affluent family that, despite living in stratum-two housing, has an industrial worker as male head of household, a daughter who is a commercial secretary, and two relatives who are a teacher and a small merchant (quite probably doing *ventas ambulantes*). There is also a Chocoano man engaged in *ventas ambulantes* living in stratum-one housing with an Antioqueño woman and their three children.

• Moravia (5, 14, 1.6%). On the river and south of Popular, this is the site that appears in the main text (see chapters 11 and 12). Used until the sixties as agricultural land and a gravel pit despite its proximity to the city center, it became the municipal garbage dump in the seventies. Invasions were sporadic in the fifties and sixties and multiplied in the seventies. Chocoano settlement is generally quite recent.

• San Pedro (6, 11, 2.0%). This is a well-consolidated and quite old area that bounds to the north what used to be an area, comprising Prado and Brasilia, occupied by the middle class and elite before it was abandoned in favor of quieter suburbs in the southeastern quarter of the city. Prado and Brasilia are now largely multiroom dwellings and institutional buildings; San Pedro has also been affected to some extent by these changes. According to the sample data, the eleven Chocoanos are in three households, one of which is an extended family of twelve people (including one nonrelative) headed by a 62-year-old Chocoano woman who lives with her grown-up children, one of whom has married a Chocoano man and has four children herself. The workers in this family are two teachers, a cleaner, a security man, and a domestic servant. This family lives in its own house. The other two are small female-headed households that rent their housing; one mother is a cleaner, the other a "service worker" in a government institution (e.g., a kindergarten assistant).

Close to San Pedro is Jesus Nazareno (7, 4, 1.1%), where three young Chocoano male students rent accommodations and a 52-year-old Chocoano mother lives in her own house with four daughters and a son, who are employed as a telephone switchboard operator, an agricultural worker, a public administration employee, and an industrial worker and one of whom is a schoolgirl.

- San Diego (8, 1, 1.2%). This tract sample only includes eighty-five people, hence the high percentage. This Chocoano woman is a professional married to a non-Chocoano sales representative.
- Colón (9, 22, 4.7%). This is a survival of the tenement zone that used to include Guayaquil and La Bayadera. There are ten households here consisting of thirty-two people, including children born outside the Chocó, and all but nine of them live in a single building. There are four young couples with small children, two single mothers, two single people, and two female-headed households with additional kin attached, also mostly female. There is also a Chocoano woman living with an Antioqueño man. The workers are nearly all involved in the street sale of food, with one washerwoman and a restaurant cook.
- La Alpujarra (10, 5, 5.4%). This was an invasion settlement in 1981, since eradicated in 1982 as part of the restructuring of the city center (see chapter 12). There are three families in the sample, two female headed. Both of these include several young children, and one has some relatives and nonrelatives attached. Out of a total of twelve people, only two work: a domestic servant and a washerwoman. The third family is a Chocoano couple living together, the man being employed in the construction industry.
- San Pablo (11, 8, 1.2%). This is a slightly more upmarket area. Here one Chocoano middle-aged married couple lives with six children: none of the family works, and apparently they live on income from rent; seven of the children study.
- El Rincón (12, 19, 1.9%). A rural settlement in the eighteenth and nineteenth centuries, El Rincón began to link into expanding urban networks in the 1930s. Chocoano settlement began after about 1965, when several men who lived in Barrio Antioquia and worked in the same soft-drinks factory bought plots in the barrio. One of them had run a small *bailadero* in Barrio Antioquia, and he continued this enterprise in his new home; another, Ildefonso Perea, rented rooms to paisanos in a house that came to act as an arrival point for many Chocoano from his home town. Today, this man has kin links with a dozen Chocoano families in the barrio, and his present house still has about sixteen rooms that he rents and lends to paisanos: his stated motive for building such a house, apart from the income, was "as a Chocoano and as a black." Interestingly, one of the few cases of Chocoano-owned industry is located here, in the form of a small clothing factory, built up by Marino Perea, nephew of Ildefonso. Several Chocoanos here work as cooks in the Intercontinental Hotel, and here, as in the soft-drinks factory, the role of the ethnic network in finding employment was important.
- Zafra (13, 15, 5.2%). See chapter 12 for details of this barrio, here shown as one of the densest concentrations of Chocoanos in the city. In fact, the sample only shows two families. One is a construction worker living with a cook and their three young children plus a relative working in construction and his common-law wife and two small children. The other is a huge household of twenty-five people, headed by a 60-year-old woman with her six children, three of whom have spouses and four of whom have children. Occupations range from a worker in a printing house, to domestic servant, to

construction workers. By chance, it appears that this family is the one to which my principal informants in the barrio belonged. The printing worker and one of the daughters both graduated from university with degrees in history and philosophy during the time I knew them. The man was by then unemployed, and the woman expected to find a job as a secondary school teacher, probably in a provincial town.

- El Corazón/Corazones (14, 11, 1.5%). This area includes recent invasions such as Nuevas Conquistadores and Independencia which have overtaken neighboring settlements such as El Salado (see fig. 1) which were old rural villages, quite probably originally populated by freed blacks and mulattoes. Invasion began around 1979 and was initially unusual in Medellín for being organized and large scale rather than slow and accretive, although illegal subdivision of invaded land and accretive invasion continued thereafter (Sierra et al. 1985). Five of these eleven individuals live in stratum-one housing (shacks constructed out of planks, plastic, odds and ends): these include a Chocoano construction worker living with an Antioqueño woman.

- La Pradera/Juan XXIII (15, 11, 1.2%). This is an area made up of invasions and pirate urbanizations that emerged between 1957 and 1960. The census data show three families: one with old, non-Chocoano parents and two children nearly 20 years old born in the Chocó, and two nuclear families of four and eight people with workers employed as a driver, a construction worker, and a service worker in the oil/gas industry. There is also a mixed union between a Chocoano construction worker and an Antioqueño woman.

- La Soledad/Ferrini (16, 14, 3.6%). This is one of the overlap cases with strata-one to -four housing in the same barrio. This is due to the fact, which does not emerge clearly from the map, that the area immediately to the west of the barrio is unurbanized land, clearly inviting invasion, while the area to the southeast is an upmarket, middle-class area. There are two Chocoano families: one, a nuclear family in stratum-two housing, with a male head of household working as a security man or nightwatchman, and the other an extended family in stratum-four housing, with the grandmother or an old aunt present, the head of which is a driver, with one son working in white-collar administration.

- La Iguaná (17, 24, 4.3%). The number of Chocoanos seems to be a rather low count in my estimation, even for 1981. See the main text for more details, especially chapter 12. The shaded area does not correspond to the actual territory occupied by La Iguaná but to the census tracts that include it: much of the rest of these tracts is taken up with nonresidential areas.

- Facultades de la Universidad Nacional (18, 1, 2.1%). This largely nonresidential tract, belonging mostly to the National University, has only one Chocoano in it, a woman who has a part-time job in a dental surgery or a chemist's shop. She is married to an Antioqueño teacher, and they have five children.

- Alfonso López (19, 13, 1.1%). The data show three nuclear families: one with two old parents and five children, two of whom are teachers; another whose head and offspring are unemployed; and a third whose head works in construction. There is also an old Chocoano man married to an Antioqueño woman living with their two sons, who are industrial workers, and a daughter, who is an administrative employee in the construction industry.

• Doce de Octubre (20, 7, 1.1%) and Doce de Octubre Sur (20, 9, 1.4%). Doce de Octubre is an area divided into four census tracts, two of which figure here. It is a neighborhood formed through pirate subdivision and invasion. The Doce de Octubre tract has two families, both female headed: occupations include domestic servant, cook, washerwoman, construction worker, cleaner, and commercial secretary. The Doce de Octubre Sur tract has three families: a Chocoano policeman or security man married to a Chocoano woman with four children; a Chocoano postman married to a Chocoano woman with six children; and a Chocoano self-employed driver married to an Antioqueño woman with three children.

• Santander/Efe Gómez (21, 13, 1.1%). Santander and Efe Gómez were partly constructed by government agencies, beginning in 1957 and 1968, respectively. The housing was distributed to relocated shantytown dwellers, including some early La Iguaná settlers (Corvide 1986). Of course, both barrios have since been swelled by invaders and purchasers of plots illegally subdivided for urban construction. The sample data show three families for Santander-Efe Gómez, two nuclear and one female headed with some attached kin and nonkin: occupations range from hairdresser through shoe mender and cook to agricultural worker. There is also a Chocoano woman married to an Antioqueño man who works as a security guard in a hotel or restaurant.

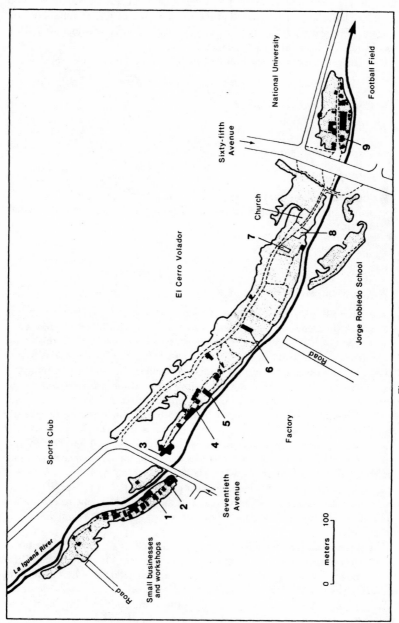

Figure 4. La Iguaná, 1985

373

Notes to Figure 4. This map shows La Iguaná in 1985, when the local authorities had the barrio mapped and censused for a projected rehabilitation program. The areas of housing are lightly shaded, and, within these, Chocoano households are shown in black.

The numbers represent the following features:

1. a Chocoano open house and part-time *bailadero*

2. Chocoano weekend *bailadero*

3. Chocoano *bailadero*

4. former Chocoano *bailadero*

5. former Chocoano *bailadero*

6. the house of the first Chocoano resident of the barrio, who also used it initially as a *bailadero* (I rented a room here during my time in the barrio)

7. Antioqueño discotheque

8. school

9. Chocoano *bailadero*

The barrio has a clear three-part structure. The sector between Seventieth and Sixty-fifth avenues is the oldest, and here there are relatively few Chocoanos. The black families tend to concentrate in one small area of this sector where there were or still are several *bailaderos*. The two former *bailaderos* (4 and 5) were involved in the ethnic antagonism referred to in the text. Number 3 is still functioning, but it is in a peripheral location with respect to the barrio as a whole. The other Chocoano *bailaderos* are either in the sector west of Seventieth or east of Sixty-fifth, both of which are more recently formed sectors where Chocoano concentration is greater. The part west of Seventieth Avenue is La Playita. The westernmost part of La Playita was settled first, being on higher ground and safer from the river's periodic flooding. The more easterly half is lower, less favorable terrain, and it is here that the Chocoanos concentrate. The area east of Sixty-fifth has no specific name; it is again a more recently formed area, and the houses near the riverbank are also quite susceptible to flooding. Chocoanos also concentrate quite heavily in this sector.

The surroundings of the barrio are also indicated on the map. To the north of the central sector lies El Cerro Volador (literally "the Flying Hill"), a green area fenced off and reserved for trees and vegetation. There is a fence separating the barrio from the hill, and any invasion on the other side of the fence is immediately eradicated by the authorities. South of the barrio, the small businesses and workshops shown give way to middle-class residential areas, served in part by the Jorge Robledo school. Just south of the football field shown is a middle-class residential unit, Carlos E. Restrepo.

Today the barrio has changed somewhat from its 1985 layout. The river changed course during a flood on 15 September 1988 and wiped out the lower part of La Playita. Many of these people were relocated into "temporary" shelter in Moravia, the other city center invasion area. In addition, a road has been built going west from Seventieth, parallel to the river. Some of the people from La Playita have reinvaded between the road and the river, on higher, more secure ground. As of 1991, however, the proposed upgrading plan had not materialized, having been grounded by political conflicts between barrio leaders and the city housing authorities.

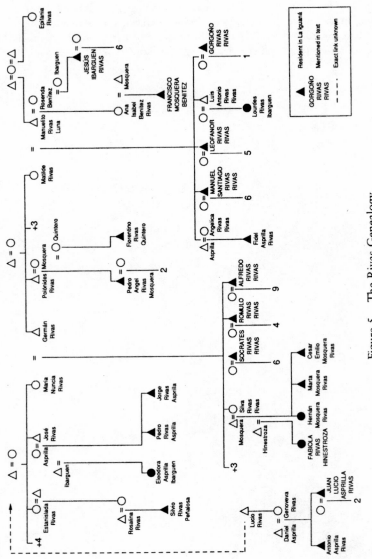

Figure 5. The Rivas Genealogy

376

Appendix C

Transcripts of Responses
by Chocoanos to Questions
about Medellín

In February 1987, nineteen Chocoano students, plus three students of Chocoano parentage, wrote answers to the following prompt, as part of a questionnaire, completed in their own time.

> In this section, write something about your life as a black person in Medellín. You may do this from any point of view: you can recount some anecdotes, write about your feelings, your experiences in the neighborhood where you live, in the street, in school or university. Feel free to write about anything you want.
>
> The following themes might serve as points for reflection: racial discrimination; what Chocoanos are at a general level in Medellín; the impression you have of the Antioqueños; the impression the Antioqueños have of the Chocoanos and black people in general; the importance to you of social relations with other Chocoanos or people descended from Chocoanos, and the relations you have with Antioqueños; the position of some young people, children of Chocoano parents, but born and raised in Antioquia—perhaps this could cause them some problems or contradictions.

I have selected eight responses here, four each from men and women, which give some idea of the variety of reaction. I have included all three of the blacks born in Medellín partly because their responses do not differ notably from those of blacks born in the Chocó and also because they make a couple of comments about the process of adaptation to the city environment.

Case 1. A 17-year-old woman from Quibdó, studying public accountancy. She plays down discrimination, attributing it to ignorance. She also reveals the images people from the interior have of the Chocó. And she highlights the importance of the Chocoano network.

> My life as a black person in Medellín up until now, I can't complain, since I've been treated very well. Every now and then, ignorant people in the street call one *mono* [i.e., blondie], but I couldn't care less about

that because one takes things according to whom they come from. With my fellow university students, I feel fine, the same as the people that I live with; I clear up a lot of the uncertainties they have about the Chocó, since the majority think that it's all jungle, and that in order to walk around you have to go out with a machete to open up paths and kill snakes.

On the Chocoanos who live in Medellín, I see a lot of those that I know in the sense that they all look out for you and they explain how life is here, they give you advice, and do everything possible so that you feel at home.

Case 2. A 21-year-old man from Vigía del Fuerte, studying civil engineering. He is uncompromising about the existence of racism and produces some evidence often adduced by blacks: the negative connotations of blackness, being called names, comments about hair. Like others, he notes that many Antioqueños seem to think blacks are all the same.

The situation is always a little complex. First of all, [here] they don't make distinctions between black people, as we do with *gente amarilla* [yellow people, i.e. mestizos]. To people here all blacks are the same, above all when some black *la caga* [literally "shits," i.e., screws up]. People think that black is the worst, so the sewage waters are black [in Colombia, sewage is termed "black waters"], black is a synonym for evil. Another thing: you have a friend and if you did something bad, he doesn't correct you, but says, "You just had to be a black." If a black does something good, he says, he doesn't seem like a black. Of course, in many cases this is characteristic of ignorant people.

One of the things in which there is no discrimination is in begging, [that is] if we give something. If we have no money, then they say, nothing from this black.

There are some anecdotes such as what happened one day in the university. The janitors always let all the students in, but when we used to go in, they used to ask us for our cards, until one day we got annoyed and we wouldn't show them and the first thing they said to me was *negro marica* [*marica* is an insulting term for homosexual]. In the university, the truth is that the most far advanced in this respect are the teachers; many of them even understand the situation and up until now I haven't had any problem with them.

Another problem which we have to put up with is the economic problem, because nearly all the blacks in Medellín have few economic resources. Another thing is that all the women are considered to be cooks [i.e., domestic servants], and people don't understand that each peasant from each region has his own customs and way of talking. Generally, the domestic servants are from the countryside, and since the situation there [in the Chocó] is difficult, they come here. To us, the Antioqueño peasant also speaks strangely and we can't understand him. And the worst thing is that when someone from here goes to the Chocó, he is well treated.

In sum, racial discrimination exists and I am aware of it. Another thing: a student said to me in the middle of the university, if I had hair like yours, I wouldn't comb it. Just listen to that! That hair like ours can't be combed!

I have the impression that the Antioqueños are regionalist and racist, and avaricious—they want to get everything any way they can. I should make clear that they are not all like that, there are some Antioqueños who are good people, and free from racial prejudice. In any case, it is possible to live here.

Case 3. A 27-year-old female from Condoto, studying to be a teacher. She sees discrimination as a minor problem but also notes that there appears to be a deeply rooted exclusiveness among Antioqueños.

In my experience as a Chocoano in Antioquia, I have in some cases met with some obstacles which I have dealt with quite easily. In addition, I have some brothers and sisters who are Antioqueños [i.e., presumably, born in Antioquia].

In the student field, it is a little difficult, since one's fellows often look down on one simply for being Chocoano, but when you show them that you have the same capabilities as them, they accept you a little more, although with suspicion.

In Antioquia, people are very regionalist, and so black people encounter obstacles to getting along. Also, Antioqueños have the idea that by the simple fact of being black, you have to come from the Chocó, knowing there are blacks in all parts of Colombia, although obviously the biggest black population in Colombia is in the Chocó.

Case 4. A 32-year-old female, born in Medellín of Chocoano parents, studying to finish secondary education. Here, any problems are put down to the Chocoanos themselves, and they are implicitly urged to adapt.

My life as a black person has been marvelous, since I am a person who will share with anybody, and I am not timid. In college, my fellow students appreciate me and I have never felt offended because of my color. My neighbors like me, and I don't have any problems with anyone.

In my opinion, I think that the Chocoanos sometimes feel bad here in Medellín or in any different department from their own, because of their sour character; and because some are quite quarrelsome and bad-mouthed.

In general, I think that each person can win people's affection with the way they are.

Case 5. An 18-year-old male, born in Medellín of Chocoano parents, studying sanitary engineering. He thinks discrimination is a problem and also observes that well-educated blacks tend to dissociate themselves from poorer blacks (see chapter 17). At the end, he comments briefly on the process of adaptation to the "whites."

Black people in Medellín, in my opinion, are not well treated. As a child, one was always taken for an object of fun, given nicknames and generally bothered. In the particular case of my brothers, they were rejected [socially]; there were few people who accepted them.

As time goes by, the people who we know, accept us more, but in our case it's because we have studied. Black people in general are assumed to be unclean, and often thieves. People always concentrate on the bad things that a few blacks do (like stealing), emphasizing it by saying, "Just had to be a black." Most people think that blacks work, in the case of women, as domestic servants, and in the case of the men, as construction workers. They always find them the hardest jobs, as if they had been born for that. Unfortunately, many blacks who have studied or who have good economic possibilities forget or ignore their race, as if it didn't matter to them.

In my opinion, the Antioqueños are gradually accepting blacks more and more into their society. This is because blacks are showing their abilities and people recognize that, in addition to which blacks excel in various areas.

My relations with Chocoanos are few, not because I don't want them, but because by living in this environment, one adapts more to the "whites."

Case 6.   A 20-year-old female, born in Medellín of Chocoano parents, studying educational administration. Perhaps the most uncompromising view comes from this woman, who consciously tries to find a "black" identity for herself and distrusts Antioqueños, despite the fact that she was born and raised in Medellín. Interestingly, she comments on the idea that blacks raised in Antioquia, and thus "whitened" by the influence of Antioqueño culture, discriminate against (i.e., consider themselves superior to) blacks from the Chocó, an issue discussed in more detail in chapter 17.

On racial discrimination in Medellín, I can say that it is very obvious, since blacks are always taken to be someone who can only work in the kitchen or in construction. If someone asks for a different job, it is difficult for them to be accepted unless they have money or powerful influence.

In educational establishments, one is also discriminated against, not only by the teaching staff but by fellow students who in the majority of cases isolate one and believe one to be incapable, unless you excel enough to be able to help them and virtually work for them.

We can say that the Chocoanos in Medellín form a group apart and almost always communicate with each other, and generally they are called eccentric because they don't act the same as the Antioqueños (something these people don't understand, because each people has its own culture).

The Antioqueños think they are a unique race and so tend to look down on other regions, above all on the Chocoanos. To them, the Chocoano is stupid and inept at anything other than domestic jobs;

they are considered to be noisy, uncultured, and immoral, and when someone comes from there to study or to practice a sport, one can often hear phrases like, "It's going to be difficult for him to leave behind his loincloth and come down from the trees." For me it is very important to communicate with Chocoanos or with their descendants, because that way I believe I can find an identity, because I am the descendant of Chocoanos and that way I can find out more about a culture, and a people which has always been forgotten and looked down on.

The relations I have with Antioqueños are normal, but I never trust them completely, since although they accept me because they are accustomed to living with me, in general they look down on other blacks, because although with words (of pity) they say that they like the blacks, there is a latent racism there.

Some blacks born in the Chocó think that the blacks who are born and raised in Medellín discriminate against them, but that is not true; it is just that it is clear that we are a bit different because of the influence of paisa culture; but how could we discriminate if we too suffer discrimination from the "white" Antioqueños?

For me as a black, what I have to do in this society is take an impartial position and try to do well for my own well-being and the well-being of *los míos* [my own family, or people].

Case 7. A 21-year-old male from Quibdó, studying economics.

My life as a black and a Chocoano in Medellín so far has been good. I have not felt the racial discrimination that I was expecting to encounter, bearing in mind that there are people who want to make you feel inferior to themselves.

In my opinion, the majority of Antioqueños are friendly and hospitable.

With respect to the impression that the Antioqueños have of blacks and Chocoanos, I think they are the best situated to give you an answer.

Case 8. A 25-year-old male from Quibdó, studying administration and law. This man has obviously thought a lot about the issues in question, and some of the ambiguity surrounding them is apparent in his writing. At first he more or less denies that racism exists or says that its occurrence does not deserve consideration. Then he says that it does exist, and he finally makes the acute point that social, regional, and racial discrimination all work together against the Chocoano in Medellín. He makes a great deal of the supposed separation of the well-educated black from his or her poorer compatriots and in doing so implies an adherence to values of black community, a position usually associated with a clear awareness of racism (see chapter 17).

In general, my life in Medellín from a racial point of view can be considered normal. This opinion derives from the fact that in the social environment where I have had the opportunity to be, the treatment I have received from nonblacks has been the same as among the blacks themselves, or as among the whites. Clearly, there are situations in which blacks are not well looked upon, but I think these are isolated situations which do not deserve consideration. The black is generally looked down upon or discriminated against by white people who are far from having a sufficient academic education, or are ignorant people. I personally admire the Antioqueños' open mind which can think up ways of working to get their daily bread. In this field, I consider them unequaled and frankly I have learned a lot from them, and still have a lot to learn. In general terms, I think that Chocoanos are seen in Antioquia in the image represented by our [female] companions who work in domestic service, and this is perhaps due largely to the fact that us professional and better-educated Chocoanos have ignored that these girls who so humbly obtain their livelihood are also part of our race. Personally, I think, without denying that discrimination exists in Antioquia, that the greatest problem that confronts a person as a black Chocoano is the discrimination of one's fellow black Chocoano who has had the fortune to have graduated from university, be there, or have a good job. I think that in Antioquia, rather than racial discrimination, there is regionalism and social discrimination; these latter two are certainly quite clear: what happens is that for the Chocoano, the three almost always work together.

I have always proposed to my fellow Chocoano university students that we should not distance ourselves from the girls who do domestic service, because they are really our flag, our image here in Antioquia. Therefore, it is them and only them who we should encourage to better themselves, to study (one thing that is certainly true is that there are many women who have finished secondary education who are working as domestic servants), to take courses, etc. In this respect, all us Chocoanos who are in a position to work for the integration of the black into all the social areas of Antioquia have failed.

References

Abad, J. et al. 1982. *Una economía familiar de reproducción simple: La pequeña minería chocoana*. Medellín: Centro de Investigación, Universidad de Antioquia.

Abadía Morales, Guillermo. 1973. *La música folklórica colombiana*. Bogotá: Dirección de Divulgación Cultural, Universidad Nacional.

————. 1977. *Festival folklórico de la Costa: La música y la danza del litoral pacífico: Valle del Cauca, Chocó, Cauca y Nariño*. Cali: Instituto Colombiano de Cultura.

————. 1983. *Compendio general del folklore colombiano*. Bogotá: Fondo de Promoción de la Cultura del Banco Popular.

Alvarez, Victor. 1985. La significación del negro en la vida de Antioquia. Paper presented at the Forty-fifth International Congress of Americanists, Bogotá.

Anderson, Benedict. 1983. *Imagined communities: Reflections on the origin and spread of nationalism*. London: Verso.

Arango Jaramillo, Mario. 1988. *Impacto del narcotráfico en Antioquia*. Medellín: Editorial J. M. Arango.

Araújo Molina, Consuelo. 1973. *Vallenatología: Orígenes y fundamentos de la música vallenata*. Bogotá: Ediciones Tercer Mundo.

Arboleda Llorente, José Rafael. 1950. The ethnohistory of Colombian negroes. Master's thesis. Northwestern University.

————. 1952. Nuevas investigaciones afro-colombianas. *Revista Javeriana* 34:197–206.

Ardila, Rubén. 1986. *Psicología del hombre colombiano: Cultura y comportamiento social*. Bogotá: Planeta.

Aretz, Isabel. 1977. Música y danza en América Latina continental (excepto Brazil). In *Africa en América Latina*, edited by Manuel Moreno Fraginals. Mexico and Paris: Siglo XXI and UNESCO.

Aronson, Dan. 1976. Ethnicity as a cultural system. In *Ethnicity in the Americas*, edited by Frances Henry. The Hague: Mouton.

Arrázola, Roberto. 1970. *Palenque, primer pueblo libre de América*. Cartagena: Ediciones Hernández.

Arroyo, Miguel Antonio. 1953. *El Cauca es así*. Popayán: Editorial Universidad.

Ashton, Guido. 1970. Barrio Piloto: Variables económicos y culturales de una erradicación de tugurios en Cali, Colombia. *Revista Colombiana de Antropología* 15:216–48.

Atencio Babilonia, Jaime. 1973. Hacia un marco histórico-cultural en las relaciones de negros e indios. *Revista de Humanidades de la Universidad del Valle* 7:83–91.

Atencio Babilonia, Jaime and Isabel Castellanos Córdova. 1982. *Fiestas del negro en el norte del Cauca: Las adoraciones del Niño Dios*. Cali: Universidad del Valle.

Banton, Michael. 1967. *Race relations*. London: Tavistock.

———. 1983. *Racial and ethnic competition*. Cambridge: At the University Press.

Baracaldo Aldana, Rafael. 1977. *Tenencia de la tierra en el litoral pacífico*. Bogotá: Instituto Colombiano de Reforma Agraria (Incora).

Barretto Reyes, Amanda. 1971. *Familia y economía en Andagoya y Condoto*. Graduate thesis, Universidad Nacional, Bogotá.

Barth, Frederick. 1969. *Ethnic groups and boundaries*. London: George Allen and Unwin.

Bastide, Roger. 1957. Race relations in Brazil. *International Social Science Bulletin* 9:495–512.

———. 1961. Dusky Venus, black Apollo. *Race* 3:10–19.

———. 1965. The development of race relations in Brazil. In *Industrialisation and Race Relations,* edited by Guy Hunter. London: Institute of Race Relations.

———. 1967. Color, racism and Christianity. *Daedalus* 96(2): 312–28.

———. 1971. *African civilizations in the New World*. London: C. Hurst.

———. 1978. *African religions of Brazil: Towards a sociology of the interpenetration of civilizations*. Baltimore: Johns Hopkins University Press.

Bauer, Arnold. 1979. Rural workers in Spanish America: Problems of peonage and oppression. *Hispanic American Historical Review* 59(1): 34–63.

———. 1984. Rural Spanish America, 1870–1930. In *The Cambridge history of Latin America*, Vol. 4, edited by Leslie Bethell.

Beavon, K. and C. Rogerson. 1986. The changing role of women in the urban informal sector of Johannesburg. In *Urbanisation in the developing world,* edited by David Drakakis-Smith. London: Croom Helm.

Béhague, Gerard. 1985. Popular music. In *Handbook of Latin American popular culture,* edited by Harold Hinds and Charles Tatum. Westport, Conn.: Greenwood Press.

Bell, P. L. 1921. *Colombia: A commercial and industrial handbook*. Washington, D.C.: Chamber of Commerce.

Benítez Rojo, Antonio. 1984. La cultura caribeña en Cuba: Continuidad *versus* ruptura. *Cuban Studies* 14(1): 1–15.

Benson, Sue. 1981. *Ambiguous ethnicity: Interracial families in London.* Cambridge: At the University Press.

Bernal, Segundo. 1977. *Las regiones colombianas y sus estructuras espaciales.* Bogotá: Departamento de Geografía, Universidad Nacional.

Besanceney, P. H. 1965. On reporting rates of intermarriage. *American Journal of Sociology* 70:717–21.

Bilby, Kenneth. 1985. The Caribbean as a musical region. In *Caribbean contours,* edited by Sidney Mintz and Sally Price. Baltimore: Johns Hopkins University Press.

Blauner, Robert. 1972. *Racial oppression in America.* New York: Harper and Row.

Bohman, Kristina. 1984. *Women of the barrio: Class and gender in a Colombian city.* Stockholm: At the University Press.

Bolívar, Astolfo. N.d. *Apuntes de diez años en Urabá.* Medellín: Editorial Granamerica.

Borrego Pla, María del Carmen. 1973. *Palenques de negros en Cartagena de Índias a fines del siglo diecisiete.* Sevilla: Escuela de Estudios Hispanoamericanos.

Boserup, Ester. 1974. *Women's role in economic development.* London: George Allen and Unwin.

Botero, Fabio. 1966. *Salamina: Aspectos sociales.* Manizales: Biblioteca de Autores Caldenses.

Botero Restrepo, Juan. 1978. *Sonsón en el siglo veinte.* Medellín: Editorial Difusión.

Bourdieu, Pierre. 1977. *Outline of a theory of practice.* Cambridge: At the University Press.

Bowser, Frederick. 1972. Colonial Spanish America. In *Neither slave nor free: Freedmen of African descent in the slave societies of the New World,* edited by David Cohen and Jack Greene. Baltimore: Johns Hopkins University Press.

Brading, David. 1988. Manuel Gamio and official *indigenismo. Bulletin of Latin American Research* 7(1): 75–90.

Brew, Roger. 1977. *El desarrollo económico de Antioquia desde la Independencia hasta 1920.* Bogotá: Publicaciones del Banco de la República.

Brisson, Jorge. 1895. *Exploración en el Alto Chocó.* Bogotá: Imprenta Nacional.

Bromley, Ray. 1979. Organization, regulation and exploitation of the so-called urban informal sector: The street traders of Cali, Colombia. In *The urban informal sector,* edited by Ray Bromley. London: Pergamon.

Brown, Diana. 1986. *Umbanda: Religion and politics in Brazil.* Ann Arbor, Mich.: UMI Research Press.

Bunster, Ximena and Elsa Chaney, eds. 1985. *Sellers and servants: Working women in Lima, Peru.* New York: Praeger.

Burgess, Rod. 1979. Petty commodity housing or dweller control: A critique of John Turner's views on housing policy. In *The urban informal sector,* edited by Ray Bromley. London: Pergamon.

Burton, Clare. 1985. *Subordination: Feminism and social theory.* London: George Allen and Unwin.

Bushnell, David. 1954. *The Santander regime in Gran Colombia.* Newark, Del.: University of Delaware Press.

Caicedo, Miguel A. 1973. *Del sentimiento de la poesía popular chocoana.* Medellín: Tipografía Italiana.

———. 1977. *Verdad, leyenda y locura.* Quibdó: Gráficas Universitarias.

Caicedo Licona, Carlos Arturo. 1980. *El Chocó por dentro.* Medellín: Editorial Lealón.

Camacho Perea, Miguel. 1962. *El Valle del Cauca: Constante socioeconómico de Colombia.* Cali: Imprenta Departamental.

Camacol. 1986. Estudio metropolitano de vivienda y otras edificaciones. Report prepared by the Cámara de Construcción Colombiana (Camacol) and the Servicio Nacional de Aprendizaje (SENA), Medellín.

Cardoso, Fernando Enrique. 1962. *Capitalismo e escravidão no Brasil meridional: O negro no sociedade escravocrata do Rio Grande do Sul.* São Paulo: Difusão Européia do Livro.

Carpentier, Alejo. 1946. *La música en Cuba.* Mexico: Fondo de Cultura Económica.

Carrasquilla, Tomás. 1964. *Obras completas.* Medellín: Editorial Bedout.

Carrera Damas, Germán. 1977. Huida y enfrentamiento. In *Africa en América Latina,* edited by Manuel Moreno Fraginals. Mexico and Paris: Siglo XXI and UNESCO.

Casal, Lourdes. 1979. Race relations in contemporary Cuba. In *The position of blacks in Brazilian and Cuban society,* by A. Dzidzienyo and Lourdes Casal. London: Minority Rights Group.

Castillo, Fabio. 1987. *Los jinetes de la cocaína.* Bogotá: Editorial Documentos Periodísticos.

Cedetrabajo. 1984. El oro: Una historia sin brillo que oscurece el desarrollo nacional. Report prepared by the Centro de Estudios de Trabajo (Cedetrabajo), Medellín.

CEHAP (Centro de Estudios del Habitat Popular).1986. *La calidad espacial urbana de los barrios para sectores de bajos ingresos en Medellín.* Medellín: CEHAP, Universidad Nacional.

Chamorro, Arturo. 1982. Chirimías, sondeo histórico de un modelo islámico en América Latina. *Latin American Music Review* 3(2): 165–87.

Chaney, Elsa and Mary García Castro, eds. 1989. *Muchachas no more: Household workers in Latin America and the Caribbean.* Philadelphia: Temple University Press.

Christie, Keith. 1978. Antioqueño colonisation in western Colombia: A reappraisal. *Hispanic American Historical Review* 58(2): 260–83.

CIDA (Comité Interamericano para el Desarrollo Agrícola). 1966. *Tenencia de la tierra y el desarrollo socioeconómico del sector agrícola: Colombia.* Washington, D.C.: Panamerican Union, OAS.

Cifuentes, Alexander. 1986. Introducción. In *La participación del negro en la formación de las sociedades latinoamericanas,* edited by Alexander Cifuentes. Bogotá: Instituto Colombiano de Cultura and Instituto Colombiano de Antropología.

Cochrane, Charles Stuart. 1825. *Journal of a residence and travels in Colombia, 1823–1824.* 2 vols. London: H. Colburn.

Cock, Jacklyn. 1980. *Maids and madams: A study in the politics of exploitation.* Johannesburg: Raven Press.

Codechocó (Corporación para el Desarrollo del Chocó). 1970. *Codechocó.* Quibdó, Chocó: Codechocó and the Ministry of Agriculture.

Cohen, D. and J. Greene, eds. 1972. *Neither slave nor free: Freedmen of African descent in the slave societies of the New World.* Baltimore: Johns Hopkins University Press.

Colmenares, Germán. 1979. *Historia económica y social de Colombia.* Vol. 2, *Popayán: Una sociedad esclavista, 1680–1800.* Bogotá: La Carreta Ineditos.

Comisión Corográfica. 1958. *Jeografía física i política de la Nueva Granada.* Bogotá: Banco de la República.

Contraloría General de la República. 1943. *Geografía económica de Colombia.* Vol. 6, *El Chocó.* Bogotá.

Córdoba, Juan Tulio. 1983. *Etnicidad y estructura social en el Chocó.* Medellín: Editorial Lealón.

Cordovez Moure, José María. 1957 [1893]. *Reminiscencias de Santa Fe y Bogotá.* Madrid: Aguilar.

Corvide (Corporación de Vivienda y Desarrollo Social). 1986. *Treinta años entregando vivienda popular, 1956–1986.* Medellín: Municipio de Medellín.

Crook, Larry. 1982. A musical analysis of the Cuban rumba. *Latin American Music Review* 3(1): 92–123.

Cruz, Juan Evangelista. 1921. *Visita al Chocó, 1920.* Cali: Tipografía Moderna.

Cuesta, Marco Tobias. 1986. *El Chocó, ayer, hoy y mañana.* Bogotá: Fundación Publicaciones Consigna.

DANE (Departamento Administrativo Nacional de Estadística). 1985a. *Chocó estadístico, 1974–1983.* Bogotá: DANE.

———. 1985b. *Colombia estadística, 1985.* Bogotá: DANE.

———. 1986a. *Colombia estadística, 1986.* Bogotá: DANE.

———. 1986b. *Metodología de los estudios de población.* Bogotá: DANE.

———. 1989. *La pobreza en Colombia.* Vol. 1. Bogotá: DANE.

Davis, David Brion. 1969. A comparison of British America and Latin America. In *Slavery in the New World,* edited by Laura Foner and Eugene Genovese. Englewood Cliffs, N.J.: Prentice-Hall.

———. 1970. *The problem of slavery in Western culture.* Harmondsworth, Middlesex: Penguin.

Dean, Warren. 1989. Economy. In *Brazil: Empire and Republic, 1822–1930,* edited by Leslie Bethell. Cambridge: At the University Press.

Degler, Carl. 1971. *Neither black nor white: Slavery and race relations in Brazil and the United States.* New York: Macmillan.

De Soto, Hernando. 1989. *The other path: The invisible revolution in the Third World.* New York: Harper and Row.

Díaz Ayala, Cristobal. 1981. *Música cubana: Del Areyto a la nueva trova.* San Juan, Puerto Rico: Ediciones Cubanacan.

Díez, Jorge A. 1944. *Itinerarios del trópico.* Quito: Editorial Industria.

DNP (Departamento Nacional de Planeación). 1961. *Chocó: un plan de fomento regional, 1959.* Cali: Editorial Norma.

DNP-CVC. 1983. *Plan de desarrollo integral para la Costa Pacífica.* 2 vols. Cali: Departamento Nacional de Planeación and Corporación para el Desarrollo del Valle del Cauca.

Dobyns, Henry and Mario González. 1977. Proyecto Darién, Colombia-Organización de Estados Americanos: Aspectos sociológicos. Report for the Organization of American States and the National Department of Planning, Bogotá.

Dodson, Jualynne. 1981. Conceptualizations of black families. In *Black families,* edited by Harriet Pipes McAdoo. Beverly Hills, Calif.: Sage Publications.

Drummond, Lee. 1980. The cultural continuum: The theory of intersystems. *Man* 15:352–74.

Duany, Jorge. 1984. Popular music in Puerto Rico: Toward an anthropology of *salsa. Latin American Music Review* 5(2): 186–216.

Dudgard, John. 1978. *Human rights and the South African legal order.* Princeton, N.J.: At the University Press.

Dussán de Reichel, Alicia. 1958. La estructura de la familia en la costa caribe de Colombia. In *Minutes of Thirty-third International Congress of Americanists.* Vol. 2. Mexico: Universidad Nacional Autónoma de México.

Dzidzienyo, Anani. 1979. The position of blacks in Brazilian society. In *The position of blacks in Brazilian and Cuban society,* by A. Dzidzienyo and Lourdes Casal. London: Minority Rights Group.

Eder, Phanor J. 1913. *Colombia.* London: Fisher Unwin.

Elkins, Stanley. 1969. Slavery in capitalist and non-capitalist countries. In *Slavery in the New World: A reader in comparative history,* edited by Laura Foner and Eugene Genovese. Englewood Cliffs, N.J.: Prentice-Hall.

Engram, Eleanor. 1982. *Science, myth and reality: The black family in one-half century of research.* Westport, Conn.: Greenwood Press.

Epstein, A. L. 1978. *Ethos and identity.* London: Tavistock.

Eriksen, Thomas Hylland. 1991. The cultural contexts of ethnic differences. *Man* 26(1): 127–44.

Escalante, Aquiles. 1954. Notas sobre el Palenque de San Basilio, una comunidad negra de Colombia. *Divulgaciones Etnológicas* 3(5): 207–358.

———. 1964. *El negro en Colombia.* Monografías Sociológicas, no. 18. Bogotá: Facultad de Sociología, Universidad Nacional.

Fajardo, Luis. 1966. *The Protestant ethic of the Antioqueños.* Cali: Universidad del Valle.

Fals Borda, Orlando. 1976. *Capitalismo, hacienda y poblamiento en la Costa Atlántica.* Bogotá: Punta de Lanza.

―――. 1979. *Historia doble de la Costa*. Vol. 1, *Mompox y Loba*. Bogotá: Carlos Valencia Editores.

―――. 1981. *Historia doble de la Costa*. Vol. 2, *El presidente Nieto*. Bogotá: Carlos Valencia Editores.

―――. 1984. *Historia doble de la Costa*. Vol. 3, *Resistencia en el San Jorge*. Bogotá: Carlos Valencia Editores.

―――. 1986. *Historia doble de la Costa*. Vol. 4, *Retorno a la tierra*. Bogotá: Carlos Valencia Editores.

FCIF (Fundación Colombiana de Investigaciones Folclóricas) 1988. *El primer congreso de la cultura negra de las Américas*. Bogotá: FCIF, UNESCO.

Fernandes, Florestan. 1969. *The Negro in Brazilian society*. Translated from the Portuguese by J. D. Skiles, A. Brunel, and A. Rothwell and edited by Phyllis Eveleth. New York: Colombia University Press.

Fernández Gómez, Alcides. 1976. *Alas sobre la selva*. Medellín: Ediciones Mysterium.

Foner, Laura and Eugene Genovese, eds. 1969. *Slavery in the New World: A reader in comparative history*. Englewood Cliffs, N.J.: Prentice-Hall.

Fontaine, Pierre-Michel. 1980. The political economy of Afro-Latin America. *Latin American Research Review* 15(2): 111–41.

―――, ed. 1985. *Race, class and power in Brazil*. Los Angeles: Center for Afro-American Studies, University of California.

Foucault, Michel. 1980. *Power/knowledge: Selected interviews and other writings*. Brighton: Harvester Press.

Foweraker, Joseph. 1981. *The struggle for land: A political economy of the pioneer frontier in Brazil, from 1930 to the present day*. Cambridge: At the University Press.

Friede, Juan and Benjamin Keen. 1971. *Bartolomé de las Casas in history*. De Kalb: Northern Illinois University Press.

Friedemann, Nina S. de. 1966–69. Contextos religiosos en un área negra de Barbacoas (Nariño). *Revista Colombiana de Folclor* 4(10): 63–83.

―――. 1974. Minería del oro y descendencia: Güelmambí, Nariño. *Revista Colombiana de Antropología* 16:9–86.

―――. 1975. Niveles contemporáneos de indigenismo en Colombia. In *Indigenismo y aniquilamiento de indígenas en Colombia,* by Juan Friede, Nina de Friedemann, and Darío Fajardo. Bogotá: Universidad Nacional.

―――. 1976. Negros, monopolio de la tierra, agricultores y desarrollo de plantaciones de azúcar en el valle del río Cauca. In *Tierra, tradición y poder en Colombia: Enfoques antropológicos,* edited by Nina de Friedemann. Bogotá: Colcultura.

―――. 1977a. La chapetonada y el fundamento de castas en Cartagena de Indias. *Negritud* (Bogotá) 1:13–14.

―――. 1977b. La fiesta del indio en Quibdó: un caso de relaciones interétnicas en Colombia. *Revista Colombiana de Antropología* 19(2): 65–78.

―――. 1978. *The study of culture on the Caribbean coasts of Colombia*. Paris: UNESCO.

―――. 1980. *Ma ngombe: guerreros y ganaderos en Palenque*. Bogotá: Carlos Valencia Editores.

————. 1984a. Estudios de negros en la antropología colombiana. In *Un siglo de investigación social: Antropología en Colombia,* edited by Jaime Arocha and Nina de Friedemann. Bogotá: Etno.

————. 1984b. Perfiles sociales del carnaval en Barranquilla, Colombia. *Revista Montalban* 15:127–52.

————. 1985a. *Carnaval en Barranquilla.* Bogotá: Editorial La Rosa.

————. 1985b. "Troncos" among black miners in Colombia. In *Miners and mining in the Americas,* edited by T. Greaves and W. Culver. Manchester: At the University Press.

Friedemann, Nina de and Jaime Arocha. 1979. *Bibliografía anotada y directorio de antropólogos colombianos.* Bogotá: Sociedad Antropológica de Colombia.

————. 1986. *De sol a sol: Génesis, transformación y presencia de los negros en Colombia.* Bogotá: Planeta.

Friedemann, Nina de and Carlos Patiño Rosselli. 1983. *Lengua y sociedad en el Palenque de San Basilio.* Bogotá: Instituto de Caro y Cuervo.

Gaitskell, Deborah et al. 1983. Class, race and gender: Domestic workers in South Africa. *Review of African Political Economy* 27/28:86–109.

Gans, Herbert. 1962. *Urban villagers.* New York: Free Press.

García, Antonio. 1978. Legislación indígena y la política del estado. In *Indigenismo.* Enfoques Colombianos, Temas Latinoamericanos, Monograph no. 11. Bogotá: Fundación Freidrich Neumann.

García Castro, Mary. 1982. ¿Qué se compra y qué se paga en el servicio doméstico? El caso de Bogotá. In *Debate sobre la mujer en América Latina y el Caribe.* Vol. 1, *La realidad colombiana,* edited by Magdalena León. Bogotá: Asociación Colombiana para el Estudio de la Población.

————. 1989. What is bought and what is sold in domestic service? The case of Bogotá: A critical review. In *Muchachas no more: Household workers in Latin America and the Caribbean,* edited by Elsa Chaney and Mary García Castro. Philadelphia: Temple University Press.

García Márquez, Gabriel. 1982. *Crónicas y reportajes.* Bogotá: Oveja Negra.

Gaviria, Luis M. 1930. *Urabá y la carretera al mar.* Medellín: Tipografía Industrial.

Gerhard, Charley and Marty Sheller. 1989. *Salsa! The rhythm of Latin music.* Crown Point, Ind.: White Cliffs Media Co.

Giddens, Anthony. 1984. *The constitution of society: Outline of a theory of structuration.* Cambridge, England: Polity Press.

Gilbert, Alan. 1986. Self-help housing and state intervention: Illustrated reflections on the petty commodity production debate. In *Urbanisation in the developing world,* edited by David Drakakis-Smith. London: Croom Helm.

Gilbert, Alan and Josef Gugler. 1981. *Cities, poverty and development: Urbanization in the Third World.* Oxford: At the University Press.

Gilbert, Alan and Peter Ward. 1982. Residential movement among the poor: Constraints on housing choice in Latin American cities. *Transactions of the Institute of British Geographers,* n.s. 7:129–49.

Gilmore, Robert Louis and John Parker Harrison. 1948. Juan Bernardo Elbers and the introduction of steam navigation on the Magdalena River. *Hispanic American Historical Review* 28(3): 335–59.

Gilroy, Paul. 1982. Steppin' out of Babylon: Race, class and autonomy. In *The empire strikes back,* edited by the Centre for Contemporary Cultural Studies, Birmingham University. London: Hutchinson and CCCS.

———. 1987. *There ain't no black in the Union Jack: The cultural politics of race and nation.* London: Hutchinson.

Goez, Ramón Carlos. 1947. *Geografía de Colombia.* Mexico: Fondo de Cultura Económica.

Gómez, Fernando. 1970. Los censos en Colombia antes de 1905. In *Compendio de estadísticas históricas de Colombia,* edited by Miguel Urrutia and M. Arrubla. Bogotá: Universidad Nacional.

Gómez, Francisco. 1980. *El Chocó: 500 años de espera.* Medellín: Editorial Lealón.

Gómez, Laureano. 1970. *Interrogantes sobre el progreso de Colombia.* Bogotá: Colección Populibro.

González, Antonio. 1982. *Agenda de Antioquia.* Medellín: Publicaciones Agon.

González Casanova, Pablo. 1971. *La sociología de la explotación.* Mexico: Siglo XXI.

González Ochoa, Gustavo. 1942. La raza antioqueña. In *El pueblo antioqueño,* edited by the Universidad de Antioquia. Medellín: Universidad de Antioquia.

Graff, Gary. 1973. *Cofradías in the New Kingdom of Granada: Lay fraternities in a Spanish American frontier society, 1600–1755.* Ann Arbor, Mich.: University Microfilms.

Graham, Richard. 1970. Brazilian slavery: A review. *Journal of Social History* 3:431–53.

———, ed. 1990. *The idea of race in Latin America, 1870–1940.* Austin: University of Texas Press.

Granda, Germán de. 1977. *Estudios sobre un área dialectal hispanoamericana de población negra: Las tierras bajas occidentales de Colombia.* Bogotá: Publicaciones del Instituto de Caro y Cuervo.

Gregory, Derek. 1978. *Ideology, science and human geography.* London: Hutchinson.

———. 1989. Areal differentiation and post-modern human geography. In *Horizons in human geography,* edited by Derek Gregory and Rex Walford. London: Macmillan.

Gregory, Derek and John Urry, eds. 1985. *Social relations and spatial structures.* London: Macmillan.

Groot, José Manuel. 1953 [1869]. *Historia eclesiástica y civil de Nueva Granada.* 5 vols. Bogotá: Ministerio de Educación Nacional.

Gros, Christian. 1988. Colombie: Nouvelle politique indigeniste et organisations indiennes. Working paper no. 41. Equipe de Recherches sur les Sociétés Indiennes Paysannes d'Amérique Latine, Centre Nacional de la Recherche Scientifique, Ivry, France.

Gudiño Keifer, Eduardo. N.d. Graffiti. Graduate thesis, Department of Spanish, Universidad de Antioquia, Medellín.

Gutiérrez, Francisco. 1929. *Informe de la prefectura apostólica del Chocó.* Quibdó: Imprenta Claretiana.

Gutiérrez Azopardo, Ildefonso. 1980. *La historia del negro en Colombia.* Bogotá: Editorial Nueva América.

Gutiérrez de Pineda, Virginia. 1975. *Familia y cultura en Colombia.* Bogotá: Colcultura.

Hall, Stuart. 1977. Pluralism, race and class in Caribbean society. In *Race and class in post-colonial society,* edited by UNESCO. Paris: UNESCO.

———. 1980. Race, articulation and societies structured in dominance. In *Sociological theories: Race and colonialism,* edited by UNESCO. Paris: UNESCO.

Hall, Stuart et al. 1978. *Policing the crisis.* New York: Macmillan.

Halperín Donghi, Tulio. 1987. Economy and society. In *Spanish America after Independence, c.1820–c.1870,* edited by Leslie Bethell. Cambridge: At the University Press.

Hamilton, John Potter. 1827. *Travels through the interior provinces of Colombia.* London: John Murray.

Hamilton, Russell G. 1970. The present state of African cults in Bahía. *Journal of Social History* 3:357–73.

Hanke, Lewis. 1959. *Aristotle and the American indians: A study in race prejudice in the modern world.* Bloomington: Indiana University Press.

———. 1969. Indians and Spaniards in the New World: A personal view. In *The attitudes of colonial powers towards American indians,* edited by Howard Peckham and Charles Gibson. Salt Lake City: University of Utah Press.

Hansen, Karen Tranberg. 1986. Domestic service in Zambia. *Journal of African Studies* 13(1): 57–81.

Haraway, Donna. 1989. *Primate visions: Gender, race and nature in the world of modern science.* New York: Routledge.

Harris, Marvin. 1952. Race and class in Minas Velhas. In *Race and class in rural Brazil,* edited by Charles Wagley. Paris: UNESCO.

———. 1968. Race. In *The International Encyclopaedia of the Social Sciences.* New York: Macmillan.

———. 1970. Referential ambiguity in the calculus of Brazilian racial terms. *Southwestern Journal of Anthropology* 27:1–14.

———. 1974. *Patterns of race in the Americas.* New York: Norton Library.

Harvey, David. 1982. *The limits to capital.* Oxford: Basil Blackwell.

Hasenbalg, Carlos. 1979. *Discriminação e desigualdades racais no Brazil.* Translated from English Ph.D. thesis by Patrick Burglin. Rio de Janeiro: Graal.

———. 1985. Race and socio-economic inequalities in Brazil. In *Race, class and power in Brazil,* edited by P-M. Fontaine. Los Angeles: Center for Afro-American Studies, University of California.

Havens, Eugene and W. L. Flinn. 1970. *Internal colonialism and structural change in Colombia.* Praeger Special Studies in Internal Economics and Development. New York: Praeger.

Hechter, Michael. 1975. *Internal colonialism: The Celtic fringe in British national development, 1536–1966.* London: Routledge and Kegan Paul.

Helg, Aline. 1990. Race in Argentina and Cuba, 1880–1930. In *The idea of race in Latin America, 1870–1940,* edited by Richard Graham. Austin: University of Texas Press.

Hemming, John. 1987. Indians and the frontier. In *Colonial Brazil,* edited by Leslie Bethell. Cambridge: At the University Press.

Henley, Paul and George Drion. 1987. *Cuyagua* (A film). The National Film and Television School and the Royal Anthropological Institute, London.

Hernton, Calvin. 1965. *Sex and racism.* London: Paladin.

Herskovits, Melville. 1966. *The New World negro.* Edited by Frances Herskovits. London: Indiana University Press.

Hewitt de Alcántara, Cynthia. 1984. *Anthropological perspectives on rural Mexico.* London: Routledge and Kegan Paul.

Hoetink, Harry. 1969. Race relations in Curaçao and Surinam. In *Slavery in the New World: A reader in comparative history,* edited by Laura Foner and Eugene Genovese. Englewood Cliffs, N.J.: Prentice-Hall.

———. 1973. *Slavery and race relations.* New York: Harper Torchbooks.

Holford, Ingrid. 1977. *Guinness book of weather facts and figures.* London: Guinness Superlatives.

Hooks, Bell. 1981. *Ain't I a woman? Black women and feminism.* London: Pluto Press.

Humphreys, Robert Arthur, ed. 1940. *British consular reports on the trade and politics of Latin America.* London: The Royal Historical Society.

Ianni, Octavio. 1966. *Raças e clases socais no Brazil.* Rio de Janeiro: Civilizacão Brasileira.

Jackson, Richard. 1976. *The black image in Latin American literature.* Albuquerque: University of New Mexico Press.

Jaramillo Uribe, Jaime. 1964. *El pensamiento social colombiana en el siglo diecinueve.* Bogotá: Editorial Temis.

———. 1968. *Ensayos sobre historia social colombiana.* Vol. 1, *La sociedad neogranadina.* Bogotá: Universidad Nacional.

———. 1989. *Ensayos sobre la historia social colombiana.* Vol. 2, *Temas americanos y otros ensayos.* Bogotá: Tercer Mundo.

Jayawardena, Chandra. 1968. Ideology and conflict in lower class communities. *Comparative Studies in Society and History* 10:413–46.

Jiménez López, Miguel et al. 1920. *Los problemas de la raza en Colombia.* Bogotá: Biblioteca Cultura.

Jordan, Winthrop. 1969. American chiaroscuro: The status and definition of mulattoes in the British colonies. In *Slavery in the New World: A reader in comparative history,* edited by Laura Foner and Eugene Genovese. Englewood Cliffs, N.J.: Prentice-Hall.

Juan, Jorge and Antonio de Ulloa. 1772 [1758]. *A voyage to South America.* Translated from the Spanish by John Adams. 3d ed. London.

Kalmanovitz, Salomon. 1984. El régimen agrario durante el siglo diecinueve en Colombia. In *Manual de historia de Colombia*, Vol. 2. Bogotá: Procultura.

King, James Ferguson. 1945. Negro slavery in New Granada. In *Greater America: Essays in honor of H. E. Bolton*, edited by A. Ogden and E. Sluiter. Berkeley: University of California Press.

Klein, Herbert. 1967. *Slavery in the Americas: A comparative study of Virginia and Cuba*. Chicago: At the University Press.

———. 1969. Anglicanism, Catholicism and the negro slave. In *Slavery in the New World: A reader in comparative history*, edited by Laura Foner and Eugene Genovese. Englewood Cliffs, N.J.: Prentice-Hall.

———. 1984. Bolivia: From the war of the Pacific to the Chaco war, 1880–1932. In *The Cambridge history of Latin America*, Vol. 5, edited by Leslie Bethell. Cambridge: At the University Press.

Knight, Alan. 1990. Racism, revolution and *indigenismo*: 1910–1940. In *The idea of race in Latin America, 1870–1940*, edited by Richard Graham. Austin: University of Texas Press.

Lakoff, George. 1987. *Women, fire and dangerous things*. Chicago: At the University Press.

LeGrand, Catherine. 1986. *Frontier expansion and peasant protest in Colombia, 1830–1936*. Albuquerque: University of New Mexico Press.

Lemaitre, Eduardo. 1983. *Historia general de Colombia*. 4 vols. Bogotá: Banco de la República.

León, Magdalena. 1989. Domestic labor and domestic service in Colombia. In *Muchachas no more: Household workers in Latin America and the Caribbean*, edited by Elsa Chaney and Mary García Castro. Philadelphia: Temple University Press.

Levine, Lawrence. 1977. *Black culture and black consciousness: Afro-American folk thought from slavery to freedom*. New York: Oxford University Press.

Lipsitz, George. 1981. *Class and culture in cold-war America*. New York: Praeger.

List, George. 1980. Colombia: Folk music. In *New Grove dictionary of music and musicians*, Vol. 4, edited by Stanley Sadie. London: Macmillan.

———. 1983. *Music and poetry in a Colombian village*. Bloomington: Indiana University Press.

Llerena Villalobos, Rito. 1985. *Memoria cultural en el vallenato*. Medellín: Centro de Investigaciones, Universidad de Antioquia.

Lockhart, James and Stuart Schwartz. 1983. *Early Latin America: A history of colonial Spanish America and Brazil*. Cambridge: At the University Press.

Lomax, Alan. 1970. The homogeneity of African-Afro-American musical style. In *Afro-American anthropology*, edited by Norman Whitten and John Szwed. New York: Free Press.

Londoño, María Eugenia. 1985. Introducción al vallenato como fenómeno musical. In *Memoria cultural en el vallenato*, edited by Rito Llerena. Medellín: Centro de Investigaciones, Universidad de Antioquia.

López de Mesa, Luis. 1970. *De cómo se ha formado la nación colombiana*. Medellín: Editorial Bedout.

López Lozano, Clemente. 1967. *Rionegro: narraciones de su historia*. Medellín: Editorial Granamerica.

Lustgarten, Laurence. 1980. *The legal control of racial discrimination*. London: Macmillan.

McAdoo, Harriet Pipes. 1981. Introduction. In *Black families*, edited by Harriet Pipes McAdoo. Beverly Hills, Calif.: Sage Publications.

MacCormack, Carol and Marilyn Strathern, eds. 1980. *Nature, culture and gender*. Cambridge: At the University Press.

MacDonald, John and Leatrice MacDonald. 1978. The black family in the Americas: A review of the literature. *Sage Race Relations Abstracts* 3(1): 1–42.

McFarlane, Anthony. 1977. Economics and politics in the vice-royalty of New Granada, 1739–1810. Ph.D. thesis, London School of Economics.

———. 1985. *Cimarrones* and *palenques:* Runaways and resistance in colonial Colombia. *Slavery and Abolition, A Journal of Comparative Studies* 6(3): 131–51.

McGreevey, William. 1971. *An economic history of Colombia, 1845–1930*. Cambridge: At the University Press.

Marks, Morton. 1974. Uncovering ritual structures in Afro-American music. In *Religious movements in contemporary America*, edited by Irving Zaretsky and Mark Leone. Princeton, N.J.: At the University Press.

Martin, Elmer and Joanne Martin. 1978. *The black extended family*. Chicago: At the University Press.

Martínez-Alier, Verena. 1974. *Marriage, colour and class in nineteenth-century Cuba*. Cambridge: At the University Press.

Martínez de Varela, Teresa. 1983. *Mi Cristo negro*. Bogotá: Imprenta del Fondo Rotatorio de la Policia Nacional.

Marulanda, Octavio. 1979. *Colección música folclórica*. Vol. 1, *Costa pacífica de Colombia*. (Sleeve notes.) Bogotá: Instituto Colombiano de Cultura.

Marzahl, Peter. 1978. *Town in the empire: Politics and society in seventeenth-century Popayán*. Austin: University of Texas Press.

Massey, Doreen. 1984. *Spatial divisions of labour: Social structures and the geography of production*. London: Macmillan.

Maya, Luz Mercedes. 1987. Familia, parentesco y explotación minera desde el fin de la esclavitud hasta hoy. Field report. Ecole des Hautes Etudes en Science Sociales, Paris.

Medina, José Toribio. 1978 [1889]. *La Inquisición en Cartagena de Indias*. Bogotá: Carlos Valencia Editores.

Meisel Roca, Adolfo. 1988. Esclavitud, mestizaje y haciendas en la Provincia de Cartagena, 1533–1851. In *El Caribe colombiano*. Edited by Gustavo Bell Lemus. Barranquilla: Editorial Uninorte.

Melo, Hector. 1975. *La maniobra del oro en Colombia*. Medellín: Ediciones La Pulga.

Mena, María. 1975. Estudio sociológico sobre la marginalidad de las trabajadoras chocoanas en Medellín. Graduate thesis, Universidad Pontificia Bolivariana, Medellín.

Mina, Mateo. 1975. *Esclavitud y libertad en el valle del río Cauca*. Bogotá: Publicaciones de la Rosca.

Mintz, Sidney. 1969. Slavery and emergent capitalism. In *Slavery in the New World: A reader in comparative history,* edited by Laura Foner and Eugene Genovese. Englewood Cliffs, N.J.: Prentice-Hall.

Mintz, Sidney and Richard Price. 1976. *An anthropological approach to the Afro-American past: A Caribbean perspective.* Philadelphia: Institute for the Study of Human Issues.

Mollien, Gaspar. 1824. *Travels in the Republic of Colombia, 1822–1823.* London: C. Knight.

Moncada Roa, Olga. 1979. *Chocó: Explotación de minas y mineros.* Bogotá: Editorial Latina America.

Montes, José Joaquin. 1975. El español hablado en Antioquia, Cauca y el Chocó. *Noticias Culturales del Instituto Caro y Cuervo* 178:1–21.

Morales, Otto. 1984. *Memorias del mestizaje.* Bogotá: Plaza y Janes.

Mörner, Magnus. 1967. *Race mixture in the history of Latin America.* Boston: Little, Brown.

Moser, Caroline. 1979. Informal sector or petty commodity production: Dualism or dependence in urban development. In *The urban informal sector,* edited by Ray Bromley. London: Pergamon.

Mosquera, Gilma. 1976. Diagnóstico general sobre el problema de la vivienda en Medellín. Report of the Departamento Administrativo de Planeación, Medellín.

Mosquera, Juan de Dios. 1985. *Las comunidades negras de Colombia.* Medellín: Editorial Lealón.

Mullen, Edward. 1988. The emergence of Afro-Hispanic poetry: Some notes on canon formation. *Hispanic Review* 56:435–53.

Netherlands Ministry for Development Cooperation. 1984. Colombia: Netherlands' Bilateral Aid. Report, The Hague.

Ocampo López, Javier. 1988. *Las fiestas y el folclor en Colombia.* Bogotá: El Ancora Editores.

Oddone, Juan. 1986. Regionalismo y nacionalismo. In *América Latina en sus ideas,* edited by Leopoldo Zea. Mexico: Siglo XXI and UNESCO.

Office of the President. 1988. *A new Pacific dimension for Colombia.* Bogotá: Office of the President.

Olano, Ricardo. 1939. Historia y crónicas de la Plaza de Berrío. *Revista Progreso,* 3d ser., 1:267–83.

Omi, Michael and Howard Winant. 1986. *Racial formation in the United States from the 1960s to the 1980s.* New York: Routledge.

Ortega Ricuarte, Enrique. 1954. *Historia documental del Chocó.* Bogotá: Editorial Kelly.

Ortiz, Fernando. 1916. Los negros esclavos. *Revista Bimestre Cubana* 11. Extract reprinted in *La órbita de Fernando Ortiz,* 1973, pp. 81–98, edited by Julio Le Riverend. Havana: Colección Orbita.

————. 1917 [1906]. *Hampa afro-cubana: Los negros brujos*. Madrid: Editorial America.

————. 1920. La fiesta afro-cubana del Día de Reyes. *Revista Bimestre Cubana* 15. Reprinted in Ortiz 1984, pp. 41–78.

————. 1921. Los cabildos afro-cubanos. *Revista Bimestre Cubana* 16(1). Reprinted in Ortiz 1984, pp. 11–40.

————. 1926–28. Los negros curros. *Archivos del Folklore Cubano* 2(3,4), 3(1–4). Reprinted in Ortiz 1984, pp. 79–161.

————. 1951. *Los bailes y el teatro de los negros en el folklore de Cuba*. Havana: Editorial Cardenas.

————. 1952. *Los instrumentos de la música afro-cubana*. 5 vols. Havana: Publicaciones de la Dirección de Cultura del Ministerio de Educación.

————. 1965 [1950]. *La africanía de la música folklórica cubana*. Havana: Editorial Universitaria.

————. 1984. *Ensayos etnográficos*. Edited by Miguel Barnet and Angel Fernández. Havana: Editorial de Ciencias Sociales.

Pagden, Anthony. 1982. *The fall of natural man: The American indian and the origins of comparative ethnology*. Cambridge: At the University Press.

Palacios de la Vega, José. 1955 [1789]. *Diario de viaje entre los indios de la Provincia de Cartagena en el Nuevo Reino de Granada, 1787–1788*. Edited by Gerardo Reichel-Dolmatoff. Bogotá: Editorial ABC.

Pareja, Antonio. 1981. Características de la familia en las áreas mineras del Chocó. Graduate thesis, Universidad Pontificia Bolivariana, Medellín.

Park, James William. 1985. *Rafael Núñez and the politics of Colombian regionalism, 1863–1886*. Baton Rouge: Louisiana State University Press.

Parkin, Frank. 1979. *Marxism and class theory: A bourgeois critique*. London: Tavistock.

Parry, Jonathan. 1979. *The discovery of South America*. London: Paul Elek.

Parsons, James. 1952. Settlement of the Sinú Valley. *Geographical Review* 42:67–86.

————. 1967. *Antioquia's corridor to the sea: An historical geography of the settlement of Urabá*. Ibero-Americano Monograph Series, no. 49. Berkeley: University of California Press.

————. 1968 [1949]. *Antioqueño colonization in western Colombia*. Rev. ed. Berkeley: University of California Press.

Partridge, William. 1974. *Exchange relations in a north Colombian coastal community*. Ann Arbor, Mich.: University Microfilms.

Patiño, Beatriz. 1985. Población negra y trabajo minero en la provincia de Antioquia durante el siglo dieciocho. Manuscript, Departamento de Historia, Universidad de Antioquia, Medellín.

Peach, Ceri and Susan Smith. 1981. Introduction. In *Ethnic segregation in cities*, edited by Ceri Peach, Vaughan Robinson, and Susan Smith. London: Croom Helm.

Peattie, Lisa. 1979. Housing policy in developing countries. *World Development* 7:1017–22.

Peñas Galindo, David. 1988. *Los bogas de Mompox: Historia del zambaje*. Bogotá: Tercer Mundo Editores.

References

Perdomo Escobar, José Ignacio. 1963. *La historia de la música en Colombia.* 3d ed. Bogotá: Editorial ABC.

Perea Díaz, Berta Inés. 1986. La familia minera afrocolombiana del Pacífico. Report for the Ford Foundation, Bogotá.

Pérez, F. 1863. *Jeografía física y política del Estado de Antioquia.* Bogotá: Imprenta Nacional.

Pérez Ayala, J. M. 1951. *Antonio Caballero y Góngora, virrey y arzobispo de Santa Fe, 1723–1796.* Bogotá: Imprenta Municipal.

Pérez Ramírez, Gustavo. 1961. *La iglesia en Colombia: Estructuras eclesiásticas.* Fribourg, Switzerland: FERES.

Pierson, Donald. 1942. *Negroes in Brazil: A study of race contact at Bahía.* Chicago: At the University Press.

Pineda Camacho, Roberto. 1984. La reivindicación del indio en el pensamiento social colombiano, 1850–1950. In *Un siglo de investigación social: La antropología colombiana,* edited by Jaime Arocha and Nina de Friedemann. Bogotá: Etno.

Pineda Giraldo, Roberto. 1987. A manera de prólogo. In *Introducción a la Colombia amerindia,* edited by Roberto Pineda Giraldo. Bogotá: Instituto Colombiano de Antropología.

Planeación Metropolitana. 1985. Inventario de barrios subnormales. Report, Medellín.

Planeación Municipal. 1980. La Alpujarra. Report, Medellín.

Plazas, Clemencia and Ana-María Falchetti. 1981. *Asentamientos prehispánicos en el Bajo San Jorge.* Bogotá: Banco de la República.

Pollak-Eltz, Angelina. 1974. *The black family in Venezuela.* Horn, Austria: Wein, Berger.

Portes, Alejandro, Manuel Castells and Lauren Benton, eds. 1989. *The informal economy: Studies in advanced and less developed countries.* Baltimore: Johns Hopkins University Press.

Posada, Eduardo. 1983. An introduction to a modern history of the Caribbean coast of Colombia, 1904–1926. Master's thesis, Oxford University.

Posada Gutiérrez, Joaquín. 1920. *Ultimos días de la Gran Colombia y del libertador.* Madrid: Editorial America.

Prescott, Laurence. 1985. Negras, morenas, zambas y mulatas: Presencia de la mujer afroamericana en la poesía colombiana. Paper presented at the Forty-fifth International Congress of Americanists, Bogotá.

Presidency of the Republic of Colombia. 1989. *The Pacific: A new dimension for Colombia.* Vol. 4, *Annexes.* Bogotá: Presidency of the Republic of Colombia.

Price, Richard, ed. 1973. Introduction. In *Maroon societies: Rebel slave communities in the Americas.* Garden City, N.Y.: Anchor Books.

Price, Thomas J. 1954. Estado y necesidades actuales de las investigaciones afrocolombianas. *Revista Colombiana de Antropología* 3(2): 13–62.

———. 1955. *Saints and spirits: A study of differential acculturation in Colombian Negro communities.* Ann Arbor, Mich.: University Microfilms.

Quiroz Otero, Ciro. 1982. *Vallenato: Hombre y canto.* Bogotá: Editorial Icaro.

Radcliffe, Sarah. 1990. Ethnicity, patriarchy and incorporation into the nation: Female migrants as domestic servants in southern Peru. *Environment and Planning D: Society and Space* 8:379–93.

Restrepo, José Manuel. 1952. *Historia de la Nueva Granada, 1832–1854.* 2 vols. Bogotá: Editorial Cromos.

Restrepo, Olga. 1984. La Comisión Corográfica y las ciencias sociales. In *Un siglo de investigación social: La antropología en Colombia,* edited by Jaime Arocha and Nina de Friedemann. Bogotá: Etno.

Restrepo, Vicente. 1952 [1888]. *Estudio sobre las minas de plata y oro de Colombia.* Bogotá: Publicaciones del Banco de la República.

Rex, John. 1970. *Race relations in sociological theory.* London: Weidenfeld and Nicolas.

———. 1977. New nations and ethnic minorities: Comparative and theoretical questions. In *Race and class in post-colonial society,* edited by UNESCO. Paris: UNESCO.

———. 1980. The theory of race relations: A Weberian approach. In *Sociological theories: Race and colonialism,* edited by UNESCO. Paris: UNESCO.

———. 1986a. Class analysis: A Weberian approach. In *Theories of race and ethnic relations,* edited by John Rex and David Mason. Cambridge: At the University Press.

———. 1986b. *Race and ethnicity.* Milton Keynes, England: Open University Press.

Rex, John and David Mason, eds. 1986. *Theories of race and ethnic relations.* Cambridge: At the University Press.

Rex, John and R. Moore. 1967. *Race, community and conflict.* London: Oxford University Press.

Rex, John and Sally Tomlinson. 1979. *Colonial immigrants in a British city: A class analysis.* London: Routledge and Kegan Paul.

Rivas Lara, Cesar. 1986. *Perfiles de Diego Luis Córdoba.* Medellín: Editorial Lealón.

Roberts, Bryan. 1978. *Cities of peasants: The political economy of urbanization in the Third World.* London: Edward Arnold.

Roberts, John Storm. 1979. *The Latin tinge: The impact of Latin American music on the United States.* New York: Oxford University Press.

Rodman, Hyman. 1965. Technical notes on two rates of intermarriage. *American Sociological Review* 30:776.

Rout, Leslie. 1976. *The African experience in Spanish America: 1502 to the present day.* Cambridge: At the University Press.

Ruiz, Jorge Eliécer. 1977. *Cultural policy in Colombia.* Paris: UNESCO.

Russell-Wood, A. J. R. 1974. Black and mulatto brotherhoods in colonial Brazil. *Hispanic-American Historical Review* 54(4): 567–602.

———. 1982. *The black man in slavery and freedom in colonial Brazil.* London: St. Anthony's College and Macmillan.

Saffioti, Heleieth. 1978. *Emprego doméstico e capitalismo.* Petrópolis, Brazil: Editorial Vozes.

Safford, Frank. 1987. Politics, ideology and society. In *Spanish America after*

Independence, c.1820–c.1870, edited by Leslie Bethell. Cambridge: At the University Press.

Sahlins, Marshall. 1976. *Culture and practical reason.* Chicago: At the University Press.

Sanders, Thomas G. 1970. Economy, education and emigration in the Chocó. American Universities Field Staff Report, West Coast South America Series, 17(9).

Sanjek, R. 1971. Brazilian racial terms: Some aspects of meaning and learning. *American Anthropologist* 73:1126–44.

Saunders, A. C. de C. M. 1982. *A social history of black slaves and freedmen in Portugal, 1441–1555.* Cambridge: At the University Press.

Saunders, Peter. 1986. *Social theory and the urban question.* London: Hutchinson.

Scarano, J. 1979. Black brotherhoods: Integration or contradiction? *Luso-Brazilian Review* 16(1): 1–17.

Schubert, Grace. 1981. To be black is offensive: Racist attitudes in San Lorenzo. In *Cultural transformations and ethnicity in modern Ecuador,* edited by Norman E. Whitten. Urbana: Illinois University Press.

Severino de Santa Teresa, P. 1957. *Historia documental del la iglesia en Urabá y el Darién.* 5 vols. Bogotá: Biblioteca de la Presidencia de la República.

Sharp, William. 1974. Manumission, *libres* and black resistance: The Chocó 1680–1810. In *Slavery and race relations in Latin America,* edited by Robert Toplin. Westport, Conn.: Greenwood Press.

———. 1976. *Slavery on the Spanish frontier: The Colombian Chocó, 1680–1810.* Norman: University of Oklahoma Press.

Sierra, Carlos Mario et al. 1985. Hacia un modelo de mejoramiento de los barrios Nuevos Conquistadores e Independencia. Report, Faculty of Sociology, Universidad Pontificia Bolivariana, Medellín.

Silva, Nelson do Valle. 1985. Updating the cost of not being white in Brazil. In *Race, class and power in Brazil,* edited by P-M. Fontaine. Los Angeles: Center for Afro-American Studies, University of California.

Silvestre, Francisco. 1950 [1789]. *Descripción del Reino de Santa Fe de Bogotá, 1789.* Bogotá: Biblioteca Popular de Cultura Colombiana.

Singer, Roberta. 1983. Tradition and innovation in contemporary Latin music in New York City. *Latin American Music Review* 4(2): 183–202.

Skidmore, Thomas. 1974. *Black into white: Race and nationality in Brazilian thought.* New York: Oxford University Press.

———. 1990. Racial ideas and social policy in Brazil, 1870–1940. In *The idea of race in Latin America, 1870–1940,* edited by Richard Graham. Austin: University of Texas Press.

Smith, Margo. 1973. Domestic service as a channel of upward mobility. In *Male and female in Latin America,* edited by Ann Pescatello. Pittsburgh: At the University Press.

———. 1989. Where is María now? Former domestic workers in Peru. In *Muchachas no more: Household workers in Latin America and the Caribbean,* edited by Elsa Chaney and Mary García Castro. Philadelphia: Temple University Press.

Smith, Paul. 1978. Domestic labour and Marx's theory of value. In *Feminism and materialism*, edited by Annette Kuhn and Ann Marie Wolpe. London: Routledge and Kegan Paul.

Smith, T. Lynn. 1966. The racial composition of Colombia. *Journal of Inter-American Studies* 8:213–35.

Smith-Córdoba, Amir. 1980. *Cultura negra y avasallamiento cultural*. Bogotá: MAP Publicaciones.

Soja, Edward. 1985. The spatiality of social life: Towards a transformative theorisation. In *Social relations and spatial structures*, edited by Derek Gregory and John Urry. London: Macmillan.

Solaún, Mauricio and Sidney Kronus. 1973. *Discrimination without violence: Miscegenation and racial conflict in Latin America*. New York: John Wiley and Sons.

Solomos, John. 1986. Varieties of Marxist conceptions of "race," class and the state: A critical analysis. In *Theories of race and ethnic relations*, edited by John Rex and David Mason. Cambridge: At the University Press.

Sowell, Thomas. 1975. *Race and economics*. New York: Longman.

Spencer, Jonathan. 1989. Anthropology as a kind of writing. *Man* 24(1): 145–64.

Stipeck, George. 1976. Sociocultural responses to modernization among the Colombian Emberá. Thesis, State University of New York at Binghamton.

Stone, John. 1979. Introduction: Internal colonialism in comparative perspective. *Ethnic and Racial Studies* 2(3): 253–59.

Stutzman, Ronald. 1981. El mestizaje: An all-inclusive ideology of exclusion. In *Cultural transformations and ethnicity in modern Ecuador*, edited by Norman E. Whitten. Urbana: University of Illinois Press.

Suárez, Marco Fidel. 1958. *Obras*. Vol. 1. Bogotá: Instituto Caro y Cuervo.

Tannenbaum, Frank. 1948. *Slave and citizen*. New York: Vintage Books.

Taussig, Michael. 1978. *Destrucción y resistencia campesina: El caso del litoral pacífico*. Bogotá: Punta de Lanza.

———. 1980a. *The devil and commodity fetishism in South America*. Chapel Hill: University of North Carolina Press.

———. 1980b. Folk healing and the structure of conquest in South-West Colombia. *Journal of Latin American Folklore* 6(2): 217–78.

———. 1987. *Shamanism, colonialism and the wild man: A study in terror and healing*. Chicago: At the University Press.

Taylor, Frank. 1988. Revolution, race and some aspects of foreign relations in Cuba since 1959. *Cuban Studies* 18:19–44.

Tirado Mejía, Alvaro. 1984. El estado y política en el siglo diecinueve. In *Manual de historia*, Vol. 2, edited by Procultura. Bogotá: Instituto Colombiano de Cultura.

Toplin, Robert. 1981. *Freedom and prejudice: The legacy of slavery in the United States and Brazil*. Westport, Conn.: Greenwood Press.

Tovar Pinzón, Hermes. 1987. Problemas de la estructura rural antioqueña en la segunda mitad del siglo dieciocho. *Ibero-Americanishes Archiv* 13: 363–441.

Triana, Gloria. 1987. *Música tradicional y popular colombiana*. Vols. 5–7, *El Litoral Caribe*. Bogotá: Procultura.

Twinam, Ann. 1980. From Jew to Basque: Ethnic myths and Antioqueño entrepreneurship. *Journal of Inter-American Studies* 22:81–107.

———. 1982. *Miners, merchants and farmers in colonial Colombia*. Austin: University of Texas Press.

Ulin, Robert. 1991. Critical anthropology twenty years later: Modernism and post-modernism in anthropology. *Critique of anthropology* 11(1): 63–90.

Ulloa Sanmiguel, Alejandro. 1988. La música afro-antillana—"salsa"—y su relación con la cultura urbana y popular en Cali, Colombia. Paper presented at the Forty-sixth International Congress of Americanists, Amsterdam.

Upeguí Benítez, Alberto. 1957. *Guayaquil: Síntesis del poderío de una raza*. Medellín: Carpel.

Urfé, Odilio. 1977. La música y la danza en Cuba. In *Africa en América Latina*, edited by Manuel Moreno Fraginals. Mexico and Paris: Siglo XXI and UNESCO.

Uribe, G. and C. Uribe. 1975. Baru. Graduate thesis, University of the Andes, Bogotá.

Urry, John. 1981. Localities, regions and social class. *International Journal of Urban and Regional Research* 5:455–74.

———. 1985. Social relations, space and time. In *Social relations and spatial structures*, edited by Derek Gregory and John Urry. London: Macmillan.

Valencia Chávez, Emperatriz. 1982. *La colonización en el Urabá chocoano*. Graduate thesis, Universidad Nacional, Bogotá.

———. 1984. Informe parcial del sector de Murrí. Field report for the Corporación para el Desarrollo del Chocó, Quibdó.

———. 1985. Informe parcial del sector de Tagachí. Field report for the Corporación para el Desarrollo del Chocó, Quibdó.

Valencia y Valencia, Jaime. 1972. Consideraciones generales sobre la política indigenista de Colombia. *América Indígena* 32(4): 1285–93.

Valtierra, Angel. 1980. *Pedro Claver: El santo redentor de los negros*. 2 vols. Bogotá: Banco de la República.

Van den Berghe, Pierre. 1967. *Race and racism*. New York: John Wiley and Sons.

Varela, Jairo. 1983. Soy Atrateño. On the LP *Directo desde Nueva York*. Codiscos, Medellín. Catalogue number 222 00430.

Varela, Jairo. 1985. Cicatrices. On the LP *Triunfo*. Codiscos, Medellín. Catalogue number 222 00490.

Velásquez, Rogerio. 1953. *Memorias del odio*. Bogotá: Alianza de Escritores Colombianos.

———. 1959. La canoa chocoana en el folclor. *Revista Colombiana de Folclor* 3:107–26.

———. 1960a. Cantares de los tres ríos. *Revista Colombiana de Folclor* 2(5): 9–100.

———. 1960b. Fiestas de San Francisco. *Revista Colombiana de Folclor* 2(4): 15–37.

————. 1961a. Instrumentos musicales del alto y bajo Chocó. *Revista Colombiana de Folclor* 2(6): 77–114.

————. 1961b. Ritos de la muerte. *Revista Colombiana de Folclor* 2(6): 9–74.

————. 1983. Breve historia del Chocó. *Revista de la Corporación para el Desarrollo del Chocó* 1:51–97 and 2:47–77.

Venture Young, Ann. 1977. The black woman in Afro-Caribbean poetry. In *The black in Hispanic literature: Critical essays,* edited by Miriam De-Costa. Port Washington, N.Y.: National University Publications.

Villa, William. 1985. Carnaval, política y religión: Fiestas en el Chocó. Fieldwork report, Departamento de Antropología, Universidad Nacional, Bogotá.

Viviescas, Fernando. 1983. Medellín: El centro de la ciudad y el ciudadano. *Revista de Extensión Cultural de la Universidad Nacional de Colombia* 15:46–56.

Vogel, Lise. 1983. *Marxism and the oppression of women.* London: Pluto Press.

Wade, Peter. 1984. Blacks in Colombia: Identity and racial discrimination. Ph.D. dissertation, Department of Social Anthropology, Cambridge University.

————. 1985. Race and class: The case of South American blacks. *Ethnic and Racial Studies* 8(2): 233–49.

————. 1986. Patterns of race in Colombia. *Bulletin of Latin American Research* 5(2): 1–19.

————. 1992. Sex and masculinity in fieldwork among Colombian blacks. In *Gendered Fields,* edited by Wazir Karim, Diane Bell, and Pat Caplan. London: Routledge.

Wallace, Michèle. 1979. *Black macho and the myth of the superwoman.* London: John Calder.

Wallman, Sandra, ed. 1979. *Ethnicity at work.* London: Macmillan and SSRC (Social Science Research Council).

Walton, Ortiz. 1972. *Music, black, white and blue: A sociological survey of the use and misuse of Afro-American music.* New York: Morrow and Co.

Watson, Graham. 1970. *Passing for white: A study of assimilation in a South African school.* London: Tavistock.

Wernstedt, Frederick. 1972. *World climatic data.* Lemont, Pa.: Climatic Data Press.

West, Robert C. 1952. *Alluvial placer mining in Colombia during the colonial period.* Baton Rouge: Louisiana State University Press.

————. 1957. *The Pacific lowlands of Colombia.* Baton Rouge: Louisiana State University Press.

Whitten, Norman. 1965. *Class, kinship and power in an Ecuadorian town.* Stanford: At the University Press.

————. 1968. Personal networks and musical contexts in the Pacific lowlands of Colombia and Ecuador. *Man* 3(1): 50–63.

————. 1969. Strategies of adaptive mobility. *American Anthropologist* 71: 228–42.

————. 1974. *Black frontiersmen: A South American case.* New York: John Wiley and Sons.

————. 1985. *Sicuanga Runa: The other side of development in Amazonian Ecuador.* Urbana: University of Illinois Press.

Whitten, Norman and Nina de Friedemann. 1974. La cultura negra del litoral ecuatoriano y colombiano: Un modelo de adaptación étnica. *Revista Colombiana de Antropología* 17:75–115.

Whitten, Norman and John Szwed. 1970. *Afro-American anthropology.* New York: Free Press.

Willmott, Peter. 1966. *Adolescent boys of East London.* London: Routledge and Kegan Paul.

Wilson, William J. 1978. *The declining significance of race.* Chicago: At the University Press.

Wolpe, Harold. 1972. Capitalism and cheap labour power in South Africa. *Economy and Society* 1:425–56.

————. 1975. The theory of internal colonialism. In *Beyond the sociology of development,* edited by I. Oxaal, T. Barnett, and D. Booth. London: Routledge and Kegan Paul.

Wright, Winthrop. 1990. *Café con leche: Race, class and national image in Venezuela.* Austin: University of Texas Press.

Yépez Henao, Jorge Enrique. 1984. Aspectos históricos y socio-culturales de un palenque urbano. Fieldwork report. Departmento de Antropología, Universidad de Antioquia, Medellín.

————. 1985. Diagnóstico social-organizativo del alto bajo Atrato. Field report for the Corporación para el Desarrollo del Chocó, Quibdó.

————. 1986. Brazo de Montaño. Field report for the Corporación para el Desarrollo del Chocó, Quibdó.

Yinger, J. Milton. 1986. Intersecting strands in the theorisation of race and ethnic relations. In *Theories of race and ethnic relations,* edited by John Rex and David Mason. Cambridge: At the University Press.

Zapata Olivella, Delia. 1962. La cumbia: Síntesis musical de la nación colombiana; reseña histórica y coreográfica. *Revista Colombiana de Folclor* 3(7): 189–204.

Zapata Olivella, Manuel. 1960–62. Los pasos del folklore colombiano. *Boletín Cultural de la Biblioteca Luis Angel Arango* 3(8), 4(3,4,7,8), 5(1,5,11).

————. 1967. Aportes materiales y sicoafectivos del negro en el folklore colombiano. *Boletín Cultural de la Biblioteca Luis Angel Arango* 10(6).

Zea, Leopoldo. 1963. *The Latin American mind.* Norman: University of Oklahoma Press.

Zuluaga, Francisco Uriel. 1986. Patía: Un caso de producción de una cultura. In *La participación del negro en la formación de las sociedades latinoamericanas,* edited by Alexander Cifuentes. Bogotá: Instituto Colombiano de Cultura and Instituto Colombiano de Antropología.

Index

Acceptance, conditional, of blacks, 7–8; on frontier, 61; in Medellín, 218–19, 244, 256; in Quibdó, 107; in Unguía, 174–75, 177–78
ACEP. *See* Colombian Association of Population Studies
Africa, European views of, 31
African heritage: in Atlantic region, 88–90; in Brazilian identity, 34; in Colombian black culture, 267–68; in Colombian black music, 274, 275; in Colombian identity, 35, 268; in Cuban identity, 35; in Cuban music, 281; whites' view of, 248
Amazon region, 54
Ancestry, and racial identity, 3, 9, 345–46
Anderson, Benedict, on nationalism, 10
Anthropology: black studies in Colombian, 35–36; early Colombian, 33–34; and Other, 36; and space, 52
Antioqueños: acceptance of blacks by, 242–44, 379, 380; arrival of, in Unguía, 166; Catholicism of, 69; on Chocoanos, 240–45; colonization of Colombia by, 71–72; compared to Chocoanos, in Medellín, 186, 189–90, 195; as defenders of regional identity, 340; and drug trafficking, 70; economic history of, 70–72; entrepreneurial spirit of, 69–72; ethnic identity as resource for, 169–71; exclusiveness of, in Unguía, 169–70; images of, in Quibdó, 112, 121–22, 124, 127;—in Unguía, 167, 254; as monopolizers of wealth in Unguía, 156, 169; notion of Jewish origins of,

72, 74; as owners of black bars in Medellín, 288–89; as progressive, 171; racial identity of, 73–78; racism of, 127, 176, 254–55, 379; regional identity of, 67–70, 72–73, 92, 250–51; traditional garb of, 69, 250–51; in Unguía economy, 155–59, 169–70
Antioquia: black community in, 269; blacks in, 74–77; compared to Atlantic region, 82–85, 92; compared with Chocó, 102; indians in, 70, 76; population of, 70, 74, 82; slavery in, 70–71, 74; slaves in, 55, 56, 103; as whitened region, 5, 7–8, 56, 73–78
Aranjuez, as field site, 184
Arboleda, José Rafael, 33, 40
Argentina, race in, 12
Arocha, Jaime, and constitutional reform, 353, 357
Association for Chocoanos Resident in Antioquia, 210, 326–27
Atlantic coast region, 54; as ambiguous region, 82, 92; black community in, 269; as black region, 5, 58, 82, 92; British consul on, 12–13; compared to Antioquia, 82–85, 92; compared with Chocó, 101–2, 174; compared to Pacific region, 82; economic history of, 83; family structure in, 91; indian-black mixture in, 56; internal variety of, 92; *mestizaje* in, 82–85; music in, 89–91, 275–77, 281–82; music of, in Medellín, 286, 287; opposed to interior, 81–82, 92; population of, 82–83; slaves in, 55, 56, 83, 103

405

Varela, Jairo, songs of, 128–30, 263–65, 350
Velásquez, Rogerio: on Manuel Saturio Valencia, 107; as seminal, 33, 41
Velorio, Chocoano, as source of conflict, 229
Venezuela: black Catholicism in, 291–92; race in, 12, 35
Voodoo, 89, 291

West, Robert Cooper: on mining, 99; on Pacific region, 62
Whiteness: certificate of, 9; cult of, 240; status of, 9, 10, 20. *See also* Hierarchy of race
Whitening. *See Blanqueamiento*
Whites: in Antioquia, 75; in Atlantic region, 83, 84; in Chocó, 98–99, 102–3, 105, 133; colonial population

of, 55–56; and intermarriage, 31; in Quibdó, 108, 112–13, 116. *See also* Antioqueños
Whitten, Norman: on blacks' kinship networks, 160; on Ecuadorian racial order, 20, 36; influence on author, 41–42; on polygyny, 190; on social demography of Pacific region, 60–61; on wet littoral, 41–42, 134
Witchcraft, and ethic of equality, 315, 318, 322
Wright, Winthrop, on Venezuela, 12, 35

Zafra, as Chocoano nucleus, 222, 228–30, 370–71
Zambos: in Atlantic region, 84–85; in Chocó, 101; in racial order, 22
Zapata Olivella, Juan, 332
Zapata Olivella, Manuel, 40–41, 267